Confederate Veterans
in Northern California

# Confederate Veterans
# in Northern California

## 101 Biographies

JEFF ERZIN

McFarland & Company, Inc., Publishers
*Jefferson, North Carolina*

ISBN (print) 978-1-4766-8103-0
ISBN (ebook) 978-1-4766-3956-7

Library of Congress and British Library
Cataloguing data are available

Library of Congress Control Number 2020020596

Front cover: *top to bottom* Edward Derrell Beard (photograph courtesy of Nancy Wilson),
Edwin Augustus Garrison (courtesy of David M. Pierce),
Lieutenant Colonel John Gotea Pressley (courtesy of Bruce Tognazzini),
James Fowler Pressley (courtesy of Bruce Tognazzini)

Printed in the United States of America

*McFarland & Company, Inc., Publishers
Box 611, Jefferson, North Carolina 28640
www.mcfarlandpub.com*

For my wife, Tracy

# Table of Contents

# *Preface*

The Civil War destroyed lives, families, fortunes and the desire to stay within the war-torn areas of the East Coast and its western fringes. With the onset of Reconstruction, the South continued to be at war with the government and to deal with unsavory elements of the northern population who headed south to take advantage of that now weakened section of the country. California offered new hope for these families, not only to start a new life far from the horrors but also to build families that would become prominent members of California society.

I was fascinated by the Civil War from an early age, growing up in Pennsylvania and spending many summers in Gettysburg. Many years later, living in the San Francisco Bay Area, I came across a story involving ex–Confederate soldiers who were buried in Santa Rosa in Sonoma County. This intrigued me, for I wondered just how many Southerners had moved to northern California after the war. After taking the Gettysburg Battlefield Guide test in 2012 just for fun and to test my knowledge of the battle, I started work on collecting information on these ex–Confederate Californians at the National Archives center just south of San Francisco. I decided to write about their lives in the war, since my expertise was in the military aspect of the War Between the States. I then proceeded to locate these individuals in their regiments using the National Archives, which houses all the muster sheets from American servicemen (only deceased), starting with the American Revolution and going through the present day. As I worked deeper and deeper into the lives of these men, I realized that some of the biographies written many years later were embellished with deeds that really didn't occur. Great-grandfather supposedly fought heroically in many a battle, but I would discover he had deserted two months after enlisting. On the other hand, many of these men led very quiet lives in California after the war but had seen much bloodshed in their four years of service, witnessing many very famous and historic events.

The most difficult part of writing this book was keeping the stories manageable, since I had come across over six hundred individuals. I decided to make a line from Fresno to Monterey my division between northern and southern California. I have been told that it is a stretch calling that area northern California, since it is known as Central California. Those areas, especially Fresno County, included a large proportion of Confederate veterans, hence I consider it the cutoff point. The book covers a cross section of the over six hundred veterans I have researched. I am very grateful to all the individuals who have generously allowed me to use their ancestors' photographs in the book. Special thanks go to Sal Manna, Calaveras County historian and author, and John Morton, Colusa County historical researcher, for supplying me with many photographs; Millie Starr and

Janet Lancaster of Stanislaus County, both researchers extraordinaire; my mother-in-law, Maureen Fischl, who helped me translate many letters in unintelligible handwriting; and finally my wife Tracy, who helped me with much of the individual research and has not complained about my very early morning wakeups to write on the weekends. In closing, I hope the reader is as excited as I have been to learn the untold stories of these Californians.

Jeff Erzin
*Spring 2020*

# *Introduction*

After the war, the Confederate veterans returned to a land devastated by battles and bloodshed. Farms had been destroyed, plantations burned and families torn apart by the death of loved ones. The decision to leave a home that may have been in the family for generations must have been very difficult.

Just after the war, some wealthier families booked passage on ships bound for San Francisco, where they settled or moved out to locations known and already settled by members of their community back East. Many of the farmer class joined wagon trains headed west, arriving in the central valley of California, where they settled in groups.

The Alabama Colony, near the present town of Madera, was just such a community. Started in 1868 by families from Alabama, Georgia and Mississippi, they farmed until around 1874, when drought caused them to abandon the community. The settlers in the Central Valley were able to farm different crops from their plantings in the South. Many of the families planted vineyards and orchards or crops such as wheat and alfalfa. Seeing the wide-open areas, many of the veterans decided that raising livestock would benefit them financially. Another "colony" of Missouri Southerners settled in Yolo County. The wealthier families settled in cities such as Sacramento, Stockton, San Francisco and Oakland. Lawyers, doctors and professionals settled in San Francisco, where they could service the elite of the city. Near Hollister, San Benito County, a small community of Southern families were nicknamed "Confederate Corners." In Santa Rosa, Sonoma County, the prestigious families of Pressley and Robert Press Smith settled. Members of the plantation class in South Carolina, the families became pillars of the Santa Rosa community. The Dozier family, also of South Carolina, settled in the area of Rio Vista, Solano County, where they too became prestigious pioneers of the community. The wealthy Vaughn family moved from Missouri with their slaves to Benicia, Solano County. California being a free state, their slaves were freed. The oldest son, Joseph, went back East to fight for the Confederacy and was killed in battle. The family were rich enough to have the body brought back to Benicia. This may be the only Confederate soldier killed in battle to be buried in California. Joe's story is profiled in this book. The veterans tried to live quietly and start their lives anew.

But what of their time in the war? Little if anything has been written, and what has been is in memoirs and newspapers or handed down through the family. When the war started, many of these individuals were students or already working in the professions they had chosen. Most felt the war would be short and an adventure they could not pass up. Some felt they needed to protect their homes from the invading North, and others wanted to protect a way of life from financial destruction that would be caused by freeing their slaves. Some would fight for the next four years; some would desert. The following stories follow the battles, the hardships of army life, and for some, their changing view of what war really meant and their new understanding of the immorality of slavery.

The most logical way for the families to divest themselves of this horrid past was to move to a land untouched by the devastation of war and where they could rebuild their lives: California.

# The Veterans

## James Seale Austin

Lieutenant and captain, Company F (Davis Guards), Hampton's Legion Infantry
Commandant and captain, Company A, Georgia Military Institute, 1864–65
Born August 14, 1838; died October 26, 1917.

James came from one of the South's prestigious families. He graduated from Charleston's Citadel military institute in 1861.[1] He and his fellow cadets were instrumental in driving off the federal ship *Star of the West,* which was trying to resupply Fort Sumter, on January 9, 1861. Their artillery shots are considered by many to have been the first shots of the war.[2] James, his brothers William and Wiley, and his father, Dr. William Lawrence Manning Austin, enlisted in Wade Hampton's Infantry Legion on June 13, 1861, in Columbia, South Carolina, for 12 months. His father became the company captain at age 57 but resigned on July 1, 1861. James was elected to replace him.[3]

William returned to Virginia and worked as a volunteer doctor in the Richmond hospital, dying of typhoid fever on December 13, 1861. James commanded the company at First and Second Manassas, the Peninsular campaign, the Seven Days Battles and Sharpsburg. Sharpsburg was James's last battle with the legion. When the positions of major and lieutenant colonel opened up in the regiment, James was passed by for both positions despite being the senior captain in the regiment. He resigned from the company on March 24, 1863. By late summer, James decided he wanted another line officer position and enlisted a friend, Major White, to send a recommendation to Secretary of War James Seddon. We next find James as professor of English literature and commandant of cadets at the Georgia Military Institute at Marietta. In May 1864, the cadets were called into active service in the Georgia Militia. James was captain of Company A of the two companies that made up the Cadet Battalion. They were noted many times for their outstanding service. General Henry C. Wayne, commanding the Georgia troops, reported:

> I would conspicuously mention Majors Hartridge and Capers, and Captains Talbot, Pruden, Austin, and Warthen. The gallantry of these gentlemen cannot be surpassed. To Major Capers I am under the greatest obligations. His qualifications for military command are of the highest order, and entitle him to a prominent position. They have been brilliantly illustrated by the corps of cadets, whose gallantry, discipline, and skill equal anything I have ever seen in any military service. I cannot speak too highly of these youths, who go into a fight as cheerfully as they would enter a ball-room, and with the cadence and steadiness of veterans.[4]

After the war ended, they were ordered to Augusta to do provost duty as ex–Confederate soldiers and citizens rioted. Finally, enough Union soldiers arrived to relieve them, and they were eventually paroled and sent home. James was commandant of cadets from May 10, 1864 to May 20, 1865, when the battalion was disbanded.

In 1868, James and his wife moved to Maryland after his election as professor at the Maryland Military Institute. They then moved on to Kentucky in 1869, where James was elected professor of mathematics at the Kentucky Military Institute until 1876 when he became president of the Franklin Female College at Franklin, Kentucky. He was twice appointed aide-de-camp to governors of Kentucky with the rank of colonel.[5]

## California

In 1880 he moved to Georgia to serve as president of a female college, and in 1885 he was elected president of the Pacific Methodist College in Santa Rosa, California. James's wife was Essie Earle, whom he had married soon after his graduation from the Citadel. She was a native of South Carolina. The couple had four daughters and a son. James died on October 26, 1917, and was buried in Santa Rosa Rural Cemetery, Santa Rosa, Sonoma County.[6]

## Further Reading

Cisco, Walter B. *Wade Hampton: Confederate Warrior, Conservative Statesman.*
Confederate States of America, Army, Hampton Legion. *Company F Muster Roll of Co. F or Davis Guards, Hampton Legion, in Late War Between the U.S. and Southern Confederacy.*
Scaife, William Robert, and William Harris Bragg. *Joe Brown's Pets: The Georgia Militia, 1861–1865.*
Thomas, John Peyre. *The History of the South Carolina Military Academy: With Appendixes.*

# Alvis Early Averett

Private, Company A (Cantery Rifles), 15th Alabama Infantry
Born November 13, 1846; died March 27, 1894.

Alvis Early Averett was one of twelve children born to the farm family of John Averett and his wife May Ledbetter in Putnam, Georgia. John moved the family to Reeltown in Tallapoosa County, Alabama, sometime during 1850–1860 and continued to farm. In 1861, Alvis's brother David enlisted in the Cantery Rifles of the 15th Alabama Infantry. Alvis, too young to enlist, read the newspaper articles about the exploits of his brother and the hometown boys in such battles as Antietam, Fredericksburg and Gettysburg. By age 17, Alvis felt ready to march and fight alongside his brother, who had become 1st sergeant of Company A. On February 5, 1864, he enlisted in his brother's company of the 15th Alabama Infantry for the war.[7] He was now in a unit that gained fame in later years as one of the regiments that attacked Gettysburg's Little Round Top and the section of the line held by Colonel Joshua Chamberlain and the 20th Maine Infantry. Colonel William C. Oates, who was still in command at the time of Alvis's enlistment, commanded the 15th.[8]

The regiment had just returned from winter quarters in east Tennessee with Longstreet's Corps and were now back with Lee's Army of Northern Virginia. Alvis first experienced combat at the Wilderness in Virginia on May 5 to 7, 1864. Colonel W.F. Perry, commanding the brigade, wrote:

> On returning to the line I first struck the Forty-fourth Alabama, the second regiment in size in the brigade. Colonel Jones had been wounded and the command had devolved upon its youthful Major, George W Carey. The line was well closed up. The gallantry of Major Carey was very conspicuous, as was usual. His commanding form was in front of the center of his line, his countenance ablaze, the flag in his left hand, and his long sword waving in his right. Moving to the left I found the Forty-eighth giving evident signs of faltering. Many of the men were leaving the ranks and taking shelter behind the trees. The fire was severe, but the enemy, being a little back of the crest of the hill, sent most of their balls over our heads. At this critical moment the gallant Fifteenth appeared upon the left. Colonel Oates, finding no enemy in his immediate front, swung his regiment round to the right, and delivered a single volley up the line which confronted us, and the work was done. The enemy instantly disappeared, and the heights were carried.[9]

David received a severe head wound during the battle but eventually returned to the unit after spending some time in a hospital. Alvis continued fighting the next day with the regiment.

It was nonstop fighting for Alvis for the next few months, with the regiment fighting the Battle of Spotsylvania Court House, Cold Harbor and the Siege of Petersburg from June 18 to 26 and July 19 to 25, 1864. At the Battle of Fussell's Mill on August 14, 1864, Alvis received his first wound and was admitted to the Howard's Grove Hospital on August 27, 1864. On October 7, 1864, at the Battle of Darbytown and New Market Roads, Alvis again was wounded. Though he received only a slight hand wound, he was given a 35-day furlough on October 22, 1864. On December 10, 1864, by General Order No. 87, Alvis was awarded the Southern Cross of Honor for his performance at the Battle of Darbytown and New Market Roads. He continued with the regiment until Lee's surrender at Appomattox on April 9, 1865.

## California

In 1869 or 1870, Alvis moved to California and was living with Alexander and Mary Lewis in Watsonville, Santa Cruz County, working as a store clerk in Mr. Lewis's general store.[10]

From 1871 to 1875 he is listed as living in Soledad, Monterey County. On February 26, 1871, Alvis married Emma Luella Pratt. The couple would have 4 children. During this time, he was working as a general merchant; by 1888, the family moved to San Jose.[11] They eventually moved to Watsonville, where on May 27, 1894, Alvis passed away at the young age of 48 and was buried in the Pioneer Cemetery, Watsonville, Santa Cruz County.[12]

## Further Reading

Bertram, Peter. *The Southern Cross of Honor: Historical Notes and Trial List of Varieties.*
LaFantasie, Glenn W. *Gettysburg Requiem: The Life and Lost Causes of Confederate Colonel William C. Oates.*
Tucker, Phillip Thomas. *Storming Little Round Top: The 15th Alabama and Their Fight for the High Ground, July 2, 1863.*

# John Randolph Avis

Private, Captain Avis's Company, Virginia Provost Guard
Born May 23, 1847; died June 9, 1914.

John Randolph Avis was born to John Avis, Jr., and Imogene D. Little in Charles Town, Jefferson County, Virginia (West Virginia). His mother passed away when he was just six. John Jr. had been a lieutenant in the Mexican–American War and later a justice of the peace in Jefferson County. He was also deputy sheriff of the county and, along with 20 picked men plus Colonel Robert E. Lee's federal troops, participated in the capture of John Brown at Harpers Ferry. Brown was sent to Charles Town, where he was jailed under the supervision of John Avis, Jr. John Randolph Avis's older brother, James Little Avis, was assigned as a guard to John Brown during his incarceration. In his will, John Brown wished, as a return for John Jr.'s kindness, to give him a Sharp's rifle he owned and a pistol.[13]

When the war came, John Jr. was commissioned as a lieutenant in the Floyd Guards, 1st Virginia Infantry, in April 1861 at the age of 42. Within a month, he was allowed to form his own company and was commissioned captain. The company became Company A, 5th Virginia Infantry. John Randolph's brother James Little was appointed 1st lieutenant in the company. In November 1861, James Little was detailed as apothecary in a Winchester, Virginia, hospital.[14]

On June 22, 1862, John Jr. was given authorization to form a provost guard company, and on July 12, 1862, the company formed in Staunton, Virginia, under the orders of General Robert E. Lee. John Randolph had enlisted in the company two days earlier along with brother James Little.[15] Their youngest brother, Braxton Davenport Avis, who was only 12, became a member of the company in September 1862 and was made a musician. On May 1, 1863, John Randolph was detailed as an orderly to Colonel H.B. Davidson, military commander of Staunton, Virginia. He remained on this detail through December 1864, at which time he was part of the provost guard, which became mounted and received pay as cavalrymen. The provost company was officially paroled on April 27, 1865.

## CALIFORNIA

In 1872, John Randolph Avis worked for the Wheeler and Wilson Sewing Machine Company, relocating to Savannah, Missouri. He married Isabelle "Belle" Phillips on May 29, 1877, in Savannah. They would have 4 children. That same year, John moved the family to San Antonio, Texas, after he became a manager with the Singer Sewing Machine Company. Except for a brief four years in 1880 in Kansas City, Missouri, working for the American Sewing Machine company, John continued to work as a manager with the Singer company, finally moving the family to Sacramento.[16] By 1900, the family was in San Francisco, where John acquired a job with McCall Patterns.[17] He passed away in 1914 and was buried in Woodlawn Cemetery, Colma, San Mateo County.

## FURTHER READING

Radley, Kenneth J. *Rebel Watchdog: The Confederate States Army Provost Guard.*
Villard, Oswald Garrison. *John Brown 1800–1859 A Biography Fifty Years After.* 1910.

# Almareane Wellborn Baker

Private, Company E, 2nd Kentucky Mounted Infantry
Corporal, Capt. R. Cobb's Company, 1st Kentucky Light Artillery
Born July 7, 1843; died August 17, 1905.

Born in Louisville, Jefferson County, Kentucky, Almareane enlisted with his brother William Hamilton at Camp Boone, Tennessee, on July 13, 1861, for the duration of the war. They had traveled 175 miles to reach the unit. By November of 1861, Almareane was on detached service to the artillery (Byrne's Company, Kentucky Horse Artillery) and the unit fought at the battle of Shiloh.[18] Al was officially transferred to Cobb's company, Kentucky Light Artillery (also part of the famous Orphan Brigade), on July 7, 1862. Lieutenant Colonel Archer Anderson, in his official report, mentions Cobb's unit in the Battle of Chickamauga:

> On the morning of the 19th Slocomb, with four guns, Cobb, with two, and the remainder of Helm s brigade, were moved across Glass's Ford to ascertain the position of the enemy, while the two rifled pieces of Slocomb's Battery, under Lieut. Vaught, took position on a bluff upon the east side of the stream. An artillery engagement ensued much to our advantage, until the enemy, who occupied the better position, brought forward a number of heavy guns, and showed the greater weight of metal.[19]

Lieutenant Colonel Anderson continued:

> At the request of Brig.-Gen. Forrest, I sent him a section of Cobb's Battery, under the command of Lieut. Gracey, who assisted handsomely in repulsing the enemy. At the request of the brigade commanders, the artillery of the division had been ordered to report to the brigades with which they were accustomed to serve. Cobb's Battery, from the nature of the ground, could not participate to its accustomed extent, yet, as opportunity offered, it displayed its usual gallantry.[20]

Al and his unit went on to fight with the Orphan Brigade and the Army of Tennessee until the battle of Pine Mountain, Georgia, on June 15, 1864, where he was captured. The day before, federal artillery had killed Confederate general Leonidas Polk on Pine Mountain. As prisoners of war, Al and many of his unit were sent on to Louisville, Kentucky, on June 21 and then on to Rock Island, Illinois, where they were transferred to Camp Chase, Ohio, on August 10, 1864. Al spent the next six months in captivity, where he wrote a letter to President Abraham Lincoln asking for his freedom and promising to swear allegiance to the Union:

> Prisoner 3 Barrack 15 Camp Case Ohio
> Jan 15 65

Mr. President,

> For weeks & months, I have expected a release from prison. I have just learned that the petition was never presented for your approval or dis-approval. Mr. Jos. Davis a Christian and perfect gentleman started with the paper for Washington. He arrived at Baltimore where he took sick and died at a Mr. Nadel, a Minister of that place. Mr. N wrote to my relatives at Louisville that the paper was at his house only he would not present to you as it was out of his line of [illegible]. As I have no other way to state my case to you but by writing, I take that chance, hoping you will peruse the few lines. It was in July 1861 when quite a youth and inexperienced in the ways & wiles of the wicked that I was persuaded to join the rebel army by Col. Hunt & Capt. S. Chipley. They sent me to camp Boone in Tenn. & their I soon came to my right mind. I went to Capt. Chipley before the invasion of KY by that army informing him that he & Col Thos. Hunt presented false

means to get me to join them and that I wanted a discharge. He told me I could not get it, more over if I left without it & was caught he would have me shot as I was sworn and had to abide by it. I there & there made my mind up that I never would fire a gun at the U.S. forces and the only way I found to get out of it was by getting detailed in the Commissary department. I succeeded at last & their I stayed till they forced me in the ranks at the [illegible] from the retreat at Dalton. I then came to the conclusion that the only way to keep from fighting against my own country was by giving myself up. The long looked for chance soon arrived. It was at the retreat from Pine Ridge that I stayed behind & was captured—was not released as I expected but sent to this prison. Mr. President my reason for writing & stating my case to you is to ask you to release me from prison upon my taking the oath of which I can only assure you that I will respect & abide by its laws.

Respectfully Almareane W. Baker
1st KY Battery—Prison 3 Barrack 15[21]

On February 1, 1865, Almareane was released from prison. It was the same day President Lincoln signed the amendment outlawing slavery, although this was not ratified by the states until later. The war would drag on for two more months. There is no written proof Al's letter had any bearing on his release, but it is an intriguing prospect that the letter may have guided Lincoln's hand in signing it.

## California

In Ono, California, Almareane was a school teacher, construction superintendent of a mining canal and proprietor of a general store. In 1902, he was appointed superintendent of the Shasta County Hospital. He took the family to live in Sisson (Mount Shasta), where he ran a livery stable and served as a guide for mountain climbers. He died on August 17, 1905, and is buried in the Ono Cemetery, Ono, Shasta County.[22]

## Further Reading

Lincoln, Abraham. *The Papers of Abraham Lincoln*: Doc 283272 Almareane W. Baker to Abraham Lincoln 1865-01-15, Images from the National Archives and Library of Congress.
Thompson, Edwin Porter. *History of the First Kentucky Brigade*.
_____. *History of the Orphan Brigade*.

# Peter Vernon Batte

Private, Company E (Petersburg Riflemen), 12th Virginia Infantry
Private, 1st sergeant, and 2nd lieutenant, Branch's Virginia Artillery (later called Pegram's Co.)
Major, 44th Battalion, Virginia Infantry (Petersburg City Battalion)
Born 1841; died November 21, 1893.

Peter Batte was born in Petersburg, Virginia, to Peter Poythress Batte and Elizabeth West Poindexter. The Batte family had been in Virginia since the early 1700s. Peter had two sisters, Mary and Agnes Atkinson, and an older brother, Cary Dupuy, who died at the Battle of Chancellorsville, Virginia, on May 3, 1863.[23] Peter and Cary enlisted in the 12th Virginia Infantry on April 19, 1861, in Petersburg, Virginia, for one year and mustered into the regiment on May 1, 1861, at the marine hospital in Norfolk.[24] Peter did not see any battle action with the regiment, since all of its time was spent in camp. On April 24, 1862, he was transferred to Branch's Virginia Artillery by Order No. 91 just in time for the Seven Days Battles, around Richmond. He was promoted and listed as 1st sergeant on the July-August 1862 roll. The unit went on to fight at Second Manassas, Antietam and Fredericksburg. The promotions came fast, and next Peter was promoted to 1st sergeant in September-October of 1862. The company was later sent to North Carolina in the early part of 1863. Peter was promoted to junior 2nd lieutenant on May 27, 1863, and senior 2nd lieutenant in June of 1863.[25] He was becoming a valuable asset to the Confederate service, so much so that he was asked to raise a battalion to serve as the Petersburg city guard. He wrote the adjutant in Richmond about the creation of the unit:

> Petersburg Aug 10th 1863
> Major Samuel W. Melton AAG
> Richmond
>
> Maj:
>
> I have yours of the 4th inst: authorizing me to raise Battalion for local service of non-conscript and exempts. The only difficulty that now exists to prevent a prompt and effective organization of the battalion is my inability to assure those proposing to join that are under 18 years of age that they will not be ordered from my command on reaching conscript age. You say "that it is not probable that those now under 18 years will hereafter be withdrawn" and yet your attention is respectfully called to General Order No 98 July 20 1863. [Illegible] persons of such organizations of conscript age to be discharged and returned for enrollment to the bureau of conscription in view of the fact that this battalion will be not only for home defense, but will be regularly on duty as Provost Guard for the city of Petersburg, thus relieving Confederate troops who are now performing this duty here: and moreover that it will not be enlisted for a short period, but mustered into service for the war. I will be greatly obliged if you can give me the assurance asked, if not whether G.O. No 98 referred to would apply in this case and by virtue of it the enrolling officer of the district would be authorized to demand the men as they reach eighteen years of age, all of which is respectfully submitted your obedient Lieutenant
>
> Peter V. Batte Leut. Branch's Artillery[26]

In November, Peter formed the Petersburg City Battalion, also known as the 44th Battalion, Virginia Infantry, which was mainly composed of boys age sixteen and seventeen and men over forty-five. Pete sent a letter requesting his commission as major of the battalion, as he was doing that duty as a lieutenant:

> Head Qtrs. Batte's Battalion
> Petersburg Nov 3 1863
> Gen. S Cooper, Richmond
>
> Gen.
>
> I have the honor to advise you that under your authority granted me August 4, 1863, I have mustered into the Confederate service for the war three companies of Infantry for special service and guard duty in the city of Petersburg, the muster rolls of which are on file in your office. I therefore respectfully ask that I be Commissioned. I have a good prospect of organizing two additional companies at an early day and my Commission will greatly facilitate my efforts and success. I am Sir very respectfully your obedient servant.
>
> Peter V. Batte Lt
> Acting Major Batte's Battalion[27]

Peter's battalion went on to serve in the Department of North Carolina and Southern Virginia. Company B was assigned as provost guard and companies A, C, D, and F to

General Archer's Brigade, Army of Northern Virginia. The battalion was involved in various conflicts south of the James River. On June 15, 1864, the battalion was in the entrenchments near Petersburg when they were attacked by overwhelming numbers of the enemy. Peter and many others were captured, and so began the story of the Immortal 600. In short, 600 imprisoned Confederate officers had been used as "cannon fodder" in an attempt to stop a bombardment on Morris Island, South Carolina. In his book on the Immortal 600, J. Ogden Murray states in his dedication:

> To the dead and living comrades of the Immortal Six Hundred,—Confederate officers, prisoners of war,—who were confined in the stockade on Morris Island, South Carolina, under fire of our own guns shelling that island; and who were subsequently starved on rations of rotten corn meal and onion pickle at Fort Pulaski, Georgia, and Hilton Head, South Carolina, 1864-65, by order of Edwin M. Stanton, United States Secretary of War—to all who remained true unto the end, under the terrible ordeal of fire and starvation, this history is affectionately inscribed with a comrade's love.[28]

Only seventeen of the 600 took the oath of allegiance at the end of the war.[29] Peter did eventually take the oath of allegiance at Fort Delaware on June 20, 1865, and was released, ending four years that he would never forget.

## CALIFORNIA

Peter settled in Stockton after the war. He divorced his first wife, Mary V. Peyton, and later married Katherine Stuart. He had no children from either marriage. He was a bookkeeper by trade and for many years, he worked for Frank Stewart of the Stewart and Smith grain business, and was owner of the Eureka Warehouse. He died in the Stockton Asylum and was buried in an unmarked grave in the Stockton Rural Cemetery, Stockton, San Joaquin County, until its discovery on September 12, 1992.[30]

## FURTHER READING

Greene, A. Wilson. *Civil War Petersburg: Confederate City in the Crucible of War.*
Henderson, William D. *12th Virginia Infantry.*
Joslyn, Mauriel. *The Biographical Roster of the Immortal 600.*
Murray, John Ogden. *The Immortal Six Hundred: A Story of Cruelty to Confederate Prisoners of War.*
Weaver, Jeffrey C. *Branch, Harrington and Staunton Hill Artillery.*

# Edward Derrel Beard

Private, Company D, 1st Special Battalion (Rightor's) Louisiana Infantry
Private, Company D, 11th Louisiana Battalion Infantry
Private and 1st lieutenant, Company B, Consolidated Crescent Regiment, Louisiana Infantry
Born September 30, 1844; died June 14, 1927.

Edward Beard was the son of Edward D. Beard and Caroline Videau Rembert, a native of Lowndes County, Alabama. His parents died soon after Edward was born in an outbreak of typhoid fever. Up to eight years of age Edward lived in Alabama; he then headed to Louisiana, where he completed his private school education. He then continued his education at Emory and Henry College in Virginia. Once his schooling ended, he partnered with his brother in business in Shreveport, Louisiana. They were there when the war broke out.[31] Ned (as family and friends knew him) enlisted in Company D of the 1st Special Battalion (Rightor's), Louisiana Infantry, on April 20, 1861, at Camp Edwards, near Delhi, Louisiana.[32] The captain of the company was his brother, James H. (who was one of the company organizers). The unit was also known as the Shreveport Grays. Ned's brother was promoted to major in August 1861, and Ned became his orderly soon afterward. The regiment then received orders to go to Virginia and left on May 30. They went into camp at Spralley's Farm along the James River, just six miles from Williamsburg.[33] Ned was discharged from service for a disability in May 1862.

Edward Derrel Beard (courtesy Nancy Wilson).

This was not going to stop Ned; he headed home and enlisted as a private in Company D of the 11th Louisiana Battalion Infantry on September 20, 1862, at Mansfield, Desoto Parish, Louisiana.[34] He was soon assigned to service as orderly to the major (again as an aide to his brother, Major James H. Beard, who had been transferred out west and who was on the regimental staff). The 11th Louisiana Battalion Infantry was consolidated on November 3, 1863, along with the Crescent Regiment Louisiana Infantry and 16th Battalion Louisiana Infantry, to form the Louisiana Crescent Infantry.[35] Ned was first assigned to Company B as a private and was later promoted to 1st lieutenant in Company D of the same regiment. His brother James was promoted to colonel of the Consolidated Crescent regiment. On April 8, 1864, Ned and his brother fought in the Battle of Mansfield under the divisional command of General Mouton. In the official report of Major General R. Taylor, he speaks of the gallent charge of the division:

> I ordered Mouton to open the attack from the left. The charge made by Mouton across the open was magnificent. With his little division, consisting of his own and Polignac's brigades, the field was crossed under a murderous fire of artillery and musketry, the wood was reached, and our little line sprang with a yell on the foe. In this charge General Mouton, commanding division, fell. Colonel Armant, of the Eighteenth Louisiana: Colonel Beard, of the Crescent Regiment; Lieutenant-Colonel Walker, commanding Twentyeighth Louisiana; Lieutenant-Colonel Noble, Seventeenth Texas; Major Canfield, of the Crescent Regiment, were killed, and Lieutenant-Colonel Clack, Crescent Regiment, dangerously wounded. Seven standard-bearers fell one after another with the flag of the Crescent Regiment.[36]

As stated, Ned's brother James was killed in the battle. Ned retrieved the body of his brother and brought him back to his wife and children.[37] He continued with the regiment and signed the oath of allegiance at Shreveport, Louisiana, on June 12, 1865, without his brother.

## CALIFORNIA

On January 30, 1867, Ned married Rebecca Inez Coggin of Keatchie, DeSoto parish, Louisiana. They became the parents of two sons and two daughters. Ned and his family arrived in California in 1868, and he took a job in Peter Van Bever's mercantile store. In 1870, Ned bought into the the business with a partner and later became president of the company after the controlling interest was bought out from him. He remained in the position until his death. Ned is buried in Tulocay Cemetery, Napa, Napa County.[38]

## FURTHER READING

Bergeron, Arthur W. *The Civil War in Louisiana: Military Activity.*
Joiner, Gary D., ed. *Little to Eat and Thin Mud to Drink: Letters, Diaries, and Memoirs from the Red River Campaigns, 1863–1864.*
Savas, Theodore P. *A Death at Mansfield: Colonel James H. Beard and the Consolidated Crescent Regiment.*

# Isaac Bell and Tyree Bell (Father and Son)

## Isaac Thomas Bell

Private, Company H, 7th Tennessee Cavalry
Lieutenant and captain, Company A, 12th Tennessee Infantry
Aide-de-camp to Brigadier General Tyree Bell
Born July 17, 1844; died June 3, 1914.

## Tyree Harris Bell

Captain, lieutenant colonel, and colonel, Company G (later A), Newbern Blues, 12th Tennessee
Volunteer Infantry Regiment
Brigadier general (CSA)
Born September 19, 1815; died September 1, 1902.

Tyree Harris Bell was born in Cincinnati, Ohio, and moved to Tennessee with his father in 1817, settling near Camp Creek Station, in Sumner County, where he grew to manhood and was educated. He studied under Seth Thomas, a well-known teacher in the county. Tyree became a farmer and raised stock animals for trade. He married Mary Ann Walton in 1841. In 1857, the family moved to Dyer County and settled near Newbern.[39]

When the war began, Tyree formed an infantry company, which became part of the 12th Tennessee Volunteer Infantry Regiment. On June 4, 1861, he was elected captain of the company and soon became the regiment's lieutenant colonel, leading it in the Battle of Belmont and Shiloh. At Shiloh he was wounded in the leg by the fall of his horse. He lost two horses in the fight.[40]

Tyree's sons, James and Isaac, enlisted, with James eventually becoming his father's aide-de-camp and being killed at the Battle of Belmont, Missouri, in late 1861. Isaac enlisted as a private in the 7th Tennessee Cavalry, but on June 1, 1862, he mustered out of the regiment and enlisted as a private in his father's regiment on September 6, 1862.[41]

*Left:* Isaac Thomas Bell (*Confederate Veteran* magazine, vol. 22, 1914). *Right:* Tyree Harris Bell (*Life of Lieutenant General Nathan Bedford Forrest,* by John Allan Wyeth, 1908).

Tyree was eventually promoted to colonel of the regiment in May 1862, leading the unit in the movement into Kentucky.[42]

By 1864 Tyree was promoted to brigadier general and was placed under the command of Nathan Bedford Forest, where he was to lead a brigade.[43] This promotion allowed Tyree to appoint his son Isaac as his aide-de-camp with the rank of lieutenant.[44]

Tyree led the brigade for the rest of the war, receiving consistent praise. He and his brigade fought in the Battle of Fort Pillow, the Battle of Brice's Crossroads, the Battle of Tupelo and against the federal force of Brigadier General Andrew J. Smith in Mississippi in August 1864. At the battle of Brice's Crossroads on June 10–11, 1864, Isaac was wounded severely in the left arm and side.[45] He would recover and continue as his father's ADC. General Forrest in his account of the battle of Fort Pillow says:

> I cannot compliment too highly the conduct of Colonels Bell and McCulloch and the officers and men of their brigades which composed the forces of Brigadier-General Chalmers. They fought with courage and intrepidity, and without bayonets assaulted and carried one of the strongest fortifications in the country.[46]

In his report of victory at Tishomingo Creek, Forrest stated that General Buford "had abundant reason to be proud of his brigade commanders, Colonels Lyon and Bell, who displayed great gallantry during the day."[47]

At war's end, Tyree and Isaac were paroled at Gainesville, Alabama, on May 10, 1865.

Below is General Tyree Harris Bell's farewell address to his soldiers, as published in *Confederate Veteran Magazine* in 1893:

Headquarters Bell's Brigade, May, 1865

Soldiers: We must part. The relations heretofore existing between us must now terminate. Although we have failed to accomplish the great object for which you took up arms, still you will return to your homes and loved ones with the consciousness of duty performed. The story of your long and gallant struggle for liberty and independence will fill the brightest pages of your country's history.

Soldiers, I am proud to be your commander; proud of the reputation you have won on so many bloody fields of battle, and proud of the firmness, consistency and devotion you have displayed in the closing scene of this dark and fearful drama. In future ages and in other lands, your names will be the synonym of all that is chivalrous, noble, and true. Historians will recount with pleasure your deeds of noble daring, and poets will sing in lofty strains the prowess of your arms. In the camp, on the march and on the field of battle you have ever done your duty, and your danger, toils and privations will never be forgotten by your grateful and admiring commander.

Soldiers, you will return to your homes and the bosoms of your families. Preserve untarnished the brilliant reputation you have so nobly won. Discharge as faithfully the duties of citizens as you have those of soldiers, and all may yet be well. In your future prosperity and welfare I will ever feel and deep and abiding interest. For your many acts of kindness and devotion to me personally I will ever cherish the liveliest sentiments of gratitude.

And now, farewell, May He "who tempers the wind to the shorn lamb" ever have you in His holy keeping and guide and protect you through future years.

T.H. Bell, Brigadier-General[48]

## CALIFORNIA

Following the war, Isaac served as Henderson County, Tennessee, county court clerk for eight years and later moved to McKenzie. In 1868, in Lexington, Tennessee, he married Seraphine Elizabeth Smith. They had four children.[49]

Ten years after the end of the war, Tyree and his wife moved to Fresno County, California. Tyree died in New Orleans, Louisiana, August 30, 1902.[50] He is buried in Bethel Cemetery, near Sanger, Fresno County, California. Isaac died twelve years later and was buried in the Visalia cemetery, Visalia, Tulare County.[51]

## FURTHER READING

Allardice, Bruce S., and Lawrence Lee Hewitt, eds. *Kentuckians in Gray: Confederate Generals and Field Officers of the Blue Grass State.*
Boatner, Mark Mayo. *The Civil War Dictionary.*
Eicher, John H., and David J. Eicher. *Civil War High Commands.*

# Calhoun C. Benham

Captain, aide-de-camp to General Albert Sidney Johnston
Major, assistant inspector general to General John C. Breckinridge
Major, assistant adjutant general to Major General Patrick Ronayne Cleburne
Born 1824; died June 12, 1884.

Although a Northerner by his birth in Ohio, Calhoun Benham spent much of his time in the South and associated with those whose politics leaned towards state's rights and the slavery issue. His father was one of the most eminent criminal lawyers in the Ohio Valley.[52] When the war with Mexico began, Calhoun joined Company F of the 4th Ohio Infantry and was elected 2nd lieutenant.[53] After the war, he studied law and in 1849 moved west to San Francisco, where he practiced law and became district attorney of San Francisco.

He became acquainted with, and then close friends to, Southern sympathizers in California such as Senator William Gwin and Judge David Terry. On April 27, 1855, he married Elizabeth D. Marbury. The couple would have no children. In 1856, Calhoun served as captain of the "Benham Guard," Second Division, Second Brigade, California Volunteers. The unit was organized to police San Francisco, deemed to be in a "State of Insurection" by the governor. The governor used Calhoun and his unit mainly to guard the property of the State. Once the city was secure and order restored, the governor disbanded the troops on September 11, 1856.[54]

By 1859, the state became a political hotbed for those who were for state's rights and advocates of secession, and those for the Union. Being close friends with David Terry, Calhoun was the

*Standing, left to right*: **Major Calhoun Benham, Major Harry Innes Thornton.** *Seated, left to right*: **Major Horace A. Higley and Major Samuel B. Flowers of General Bragg's staff, CSA (Alabama Department of Archives and History Q4295).**

principal second for the chief justice in the duel that killed U.S. Senator David C. Broderick on September 13, 1859.[55] Terry was acquitted. When the war came, Calhoun, along with ex-senator William Gwin and J.L. Brent, left California for New York via Panama. They arrived and were arrested just before docking. In New York, they were told not to leave the city, as they were on parole. Calhoun was arrested by New York City police and confined in the city until November 18, when he was sent to Governor's Island, New York Harbor, and imprisoned.[56] The reason is that information was obtained that he was disloyal to the country and was heading South to join the rebel army. On December 2, 1861, Calhoun was released and ordered to Washington, where he met with the president on December 7, 1861:

Memorandum.
December 7, 1861.

In an interview between President Lincoln and Mr. Calhoun Benham at the White House on the night of the 7th of December, 1861, at which I assisted, Mr. Lincoln stated to Mr. Benham that he (Mr. Benham), Doctor Gwin and Mr. Joseph L. Brent might go their separate ways, they to ask no questions nor any questions to be asked of them, and the pending affair between them and the Government growing out of their arrest and parole to be thus entirely disposed of and ended.

> Geo. D. Prentice.
> Calhoun Benham.
> The above statement is correct.[57]

Calhoun headed south and by April of 1862 volunteered as a civilian aide-de-camp to General Albert Sidney Johnston. The two may have known each other in San Francisco, since Johnston had been stationed there before the war as commander of the Department of the Pacific, and it was where his family still lived. During the battle of Shiloh on April 6–7, 1862, Johnston was killed, which left Calhoun out of a job. On October 28, 1862, Calhoun was made assistant inspector general with the rank of major under Major General John C. Breckinridge, commander of the army of middle Tennessee. Within two months, he was made assistant adjutant general on the staff of Major General Patrick Cleburne. Under Cleburne, Calhoun was of valuable service during the Battle of Stones River, December 31, 1862, to January 2, 1863.[58]

In mid–July 1863, Cleburne suggested to General Bragg that a manual be made for soldiering and marksmanship. Calhoun was recommended to produce the drill manual, which he titled "A System for Conducting Musketry Instruction." The manual was published in September 1863. General Patrick Cleburne had written a plan in December 1863 that required slaves to be enlisted and armed in the Confederate Army. He presented it to his officers first, but Calhoun was totally against it. The idea was dropped by the Confederacy's highest ranking officers.[59]

Calhoun followed Cleburne into Georgia and fought against Sherman at Pickett's Mill on May 27, 1864, and at the battle of Atlanta on July 22, 1864. On September 1, 1864, Calhoun was wounded at the Battle of Jonesboro, Georgia. He was given a 20-day leave but asked that it be extended another 20 days because he had business to attend to and needed more time. What his business dealings were is not known. During this time, General Cleburne recommended Calhoun be made brigadier general of Mercer's Georgia Brigade; the recommendation was declined.[60] General Patrick Cleburne was killed on November 30, 1864, at the Battle of Franklin, Tennessee. Calhoun, still on leave, heard of his commander's death, and not wanting to serve under another, resigned on December 1, 1864, from further Confederate service.[61]

## CALIFORNIA

Calhoun and his wife first went to Mexico and then on to Europe, where they lived until the war ended. On returning to the United States, the couple moved back to San Francisco, where Calhoun returned to the practice of law. On September 3, 1879, he was elected associate justice of the California Supreme Court.[62] Calhoun died four years before his wife in 1884 and was buried at Laurel Hill Cemetery, which was shut down in 1900; most of the burials were moved to Cypress Lawn Cemetery, Colma, in the Laurel Hill Mound Section (a mass grave). Calhoun was either interred in this mass grave or cremated after the Laurel Hill shutdown.[63]

## FURTHER READING

Barrow, Charles Kelly, and J.H. Segars. *Black Southerners in Confederate Armies: A Collection of Historical Accounts.*

Benham, Calhoun, Major. *A System for Conducting Musketry Instruction.*
Haughton, Andrew R.B. *Training, Tactics and Leadership in the Confederate Army of Tennessee.*
Joslyn, Mauriel, ed. *A Meteor Shining Brightly: Essays on the Life and Career of Major General Patrick R. Cleburne.*
Roland, Charles P. *Albert Sidney Johnston: Soldier of Three Republics.*

# Walter Walke Blow

Private, Company H, 16th Virginia Infantry
Private, Grandy's Company, Norfolk Light Artillery Blues
2nd lieutenant, 2nd Texas Field Battery
2nd lieutenant and 1st lieutenant, Company B, Christmas's Light Artillery Battery
Captain, General James Kemper's Staff, Richmond Home Guard
Major, Battery Dantzler

Born April 13, 1842; died February 1896.

Walter Blow was born into a prominent family that had roots in Virginia from the earliest settlers. The Blow family owned plantations in Sussex and Southampton counties of southeast Virginia.[64] His cousin, Peter Blow, was the master of the famous slave Dred Scott. Walter's parents, Robert Blow and Susan McClanahan Walke Blow, moved to Brooklyn, New York—where Walter, one of six children, was born—and lived there until the start of the war. The family moved back to Virginia, where Robert died in 1866. Walter enlisted on July 18, 1861, at Sewells Point Battery in Norfolk, for 12 months. He became a member of the short-lived Company H, 16th Virginia Infantry.[65] In March of 1862, the company officially became Grandy's Company, Norfolk Light Artillery Blues.[66] The Blues were at the battle of Hampton Roads, where the *Monitor* and the *Merrimac* faced off. A flagstaff near the division to which Walter was attached was cut in half in the battle, the upper half falling with the colors to the surface. Walter caught the flag and replaced the colors at the top by scaling the broken pole.[67]

Walter's next fight occurred at the Seven Days Battle, June 25 to July 1, 1862, where he again showed his courage in battle. On August 12, 1862, Walter was sent to the hospital in Petersburg, Virginia, with "Camp Fever," otherwise known as Typhoid Fever, and was transferred to a better hospital in Liberty, Virginia, where he recovered. General John B. Magruder, who had commanded in Virginia in 1862 and was now head of the Department of Texas, heard of Walter's valor and his hard fighting and

**Walter Walke Blow (*San Francisco Call*, 1896).**

requested the young man into his own division in the west. On October 14, 1862, by Special Order No. 240, Walter was sent west and assigned to the 2nd Texas Field Battery with a promotion to 2nd lieutenant.[68] He served with the battery until March 31, 1863, when he was assigned to H.H. Christmas's Texas Light Artillery. On November 25, 1863, Walter was promoted to 1st lieutenant. In early August 1864, Christmas's unit and that of Captain O.G. Jones's battery of heavy artillery were combined, and this displaced Walter. General Magruder sent a letter to Richmond to reassign Walter:

> Head Quarters, District of Texas, New Mexico & Arizona
> Houston August 16, 1864
>
> Hon James A Seddon
> Secretary of War Richmond Va.
>
> Sir.
>
>    This will be handed you by Lieut Walter W Blow, who has served in the light artillery of this district for nearly two years. In consolidating the batteries of the department, he has been deprived of his position. He has manifested zeal and acclivity in the discharge of his duties and I recommend him to your special consideration as an efficient artillery officer for promotion. I am Very respectfully your obedient servant
>
> > Jno Magruder
> > Major Gen Comd[69]

In late August, Walter was back East, promoted to captain and assigned to General James Kemper's staff of the Home Guards in Richmond, Virginia. By November, he was promoted to major and assigned to Battery Dantzler, just south of the city. On April 2, 1865, Walter and the garrison abandoned Battery Dantzler because of Grant's breakthrough on the lines around the naval garrison. The unit surrendered with Lee's Army of Northern Virginia at Appomattox Court House on April 9, 1865.

## CALIFORNIA

In 1867, Walter moved to California and spent many years with the law firm of Haggin and Tevis. He was also engaged in a brokerage company with his brother Alfred after leaving Haggin and Tevis. Walter moved to Oakland in 1870, marrying Mary A. Glascock. He dabbled in real estate until July of 1895, when he gave the company to his son. He and Mary had two children, Alfred Harper Blow and Mary Virginia.[70]

Walter organized the Oakland Canoe Club. The family moved to Berkeley a month before Walter's death due to heart disease at age 54. He was buried in Mountain View Cemetery, Oakland, Alameda County.[71]

## FURTHER READING

Burton, Harrison W. *The History of Norfolk, Virginia.*
Crew, Roger Thomas, and Benjamin H. Trask. *Grimes' Battery, Grandy's Battery and Huger's Battery, Virginia Artillery.*
Wiley, Kenneth, ed. *Norfolk Blues: The Civil War Diary of the Norfolk Light Artillery Blues.*

# Edgar Daniel Boone

Private, Company F (Orleans Light Guards), 1st Louisiana Infantry
Private and 1st lieutenant, Captain Miller's Independent Company, Mounted Rifles, Louisiana
Captain, Company A (Independent Wild Cats), Louisiana Cavalry Battalion
Born April 2, 1836; died October 12, 1903.

E. Daniel Boone led a life of adventure, though he was not related to the great frontiersman. Born near Paducah, Kentucky, he became a circus performer at an early age and traveled the world. In a newspaper article he talks about Paducah and his early life: "We lived there for a while and then moved to a farm where I am informed the village of Woodville now stands. When I was nine years old the family moved to Louisiana and I have never been back into West Kentucky."[72] Edgar grew to manhood in New Orleans. When war came, he enlisted the Orleans Light Guards on April 28, 1862.[73] He experienced his first battle a month later at Seven Pines, May 31 and June 1, 1862. Just before the regiment's next fight during the Seven Day's battle, Edgar deserted on June 21, 1862. By the fall, he was missing the adventure of a soldier and so traveled to Lynchburg, Virginia, to join Captain Miller's Independent Company of Louisiana Mounted Rifles on September 1, 1862, the date of its organization.[74] Edgar was made 1st lieutenant in early 1863. The company was later assigned to Robertson's Virginia Horse Artillery. In mid–June, Edgar was captured, and not wanting to spend any time as a prisoner of war, signed the oath of allegiance and was released on June 21, 1863. Believing that the oath meant nothing,
he returned to his unit and within a few weeks and was made captain of Company A. Edgar tired of war and deserted, going into the federal lines at Strasburg, Virginia, on October 27, 1863. He was sent to Baltimore on November 3 and released on oath of allegiance from Fort Monroe, Virginia, on November 5, 1863.[75] Edgar did not return to war.

## CALIFORNIA

It was written that after leaving the Confederate army, Edgar went to Mexico and offered his services to Maximilian, who was fighting for control of Mexico. He was made a colonel and continued until 1866, when Maximilian was captured and executed by the legitimate leader of Mexico, Benito Juarez. Edgar fled to France, where he led a regiment of Zouaves during the Soudan Campaign and was awarded the French Cross for daring in battle. He then went to Turkey, where he taught cavalry tactics.[76] Wanting to

**Edgar Daniel Boone (*The Guthrie Daily Leader*, Guthrie, Oklahoma, October 9, 1901).**

do something different, Edgar decided he would train lions and tigers and form a traveling show. In 1894, he took the show to San Francisco, where a horrific accident happened. One of his trainers was torn to bits by the lions. Edgar was able to calm the animals down.[77] In 1895, he was back in New Orleans, where he married Ellen Kelly. She became his assistant in the show under the stage name of "Millie Carlotta." The act became part of the Adam Forepaugh Circus, and Edgar and his wife appeared with the lions in all the leading cities of Europe. Edgar retired to San Francisco, where he became the manager of the zoo at the Chutes Amusement Park.[78] He passed away at the California General Hospital in 1903 and was buried at Laurel Hill Cemetery. In 1892, the cemetery closed, and the thirty-five thousand buried were moved to Cypress Lawn in Colma, San Mateo County.[79]

## FURTHER READING

Bergeron, Arthur W., Jr. *Guide to Louisiana Confederate Military Units, 1861–1865.*

## James Otey Bradford

2nd lieutenant, Marine Corps, Virginia Navy
Born November 4, 1841; died February 2, 1919.

James Otey Bradford was born in Virginia. His father was John O. Bradford, a United States Navy Purser. Otey, as he was known, was commissioned a second lieutenant in the Confederate Marine Corps on June 11, 1861. On September 6, 1861, he was appointed a master in the Confederate States Navy.[80]

**James Otey Bradford (courtesy John Bell).**

In early 1862, Otey was assigned to the Charleston Naval Station in South Carolina. He remained there until August, when he was told to report to the CSS *Florida*. He reported on August 7, and the ship departed Nassau the next day.

On November 1, 1862, Otey was listed as an acting master at the Charleston Naval Station in South Carolina. He resigned his commission and on May 4, 1863, reported as a private in Captain Grandy's Company of Virginia Light Artillery on the Nansemond River, near Suffolk Virginia.[81] Otey was discharged on September 21, 1863, after appearing before a naval board to reinstate him as a lieutenant in the navy. He was then assigned as a member of the Johnson Island expedition at Wilmington, North Carolina. It was formed to rescue

Confederate prisoners at Johnson's Island, Ohio. In the end, it failed. Otey was able to depart Halifax, Nova Scotia, onboard the British mail steamer *Alpha* and arrived December 17, 1863, at the harbor of St. George, Bermuda.[82] On January 25, 1864, Otey was assigned to the ironclad CSS *Savannah* at Savannah, Georgia.[83]

On May 4, 1864, Otey was transferred to Howlett's Battery. They were used for monitoring and harassing federal traffic on the James River. We have some of Lt. Bradford's reports while he was stationed with the battery:

Howlett's, June 7—a. m.

Sir: The position of the fleet remains unchanged at 6 a. m. this morning. The following vessels are here: Four monitors, 3 side [wheel] steamers, 3 tugs. The steamer I reported as round the point yesterday is still hid there, and I think she is a gunboat, as she was exchanging signals with the double-turret monitor. Whether a monitor or not, it is impossible to tell. About 5 p.m. last evening, after sending my p. in. dispatch, a side-wheel river steamer, accompanied by a small boat (the same as in the morning), came above the obstructions, and was engaged in sounding river. Sharpshooters drove her off in about one hour. About 8:30 p.m. I walked to Howlett's house and found a strong picket guard of our men there. After being there about fifteen minutes, a steamer was heard moving, and presently the same steamer came in sight and took up the same position as during the day. She remained all night, and at daylight this morning had six or eight boats around her. About half an hour after, she retired and took up her old position below obstructions, near the shore. What can be her object no [one] here can tell, and whether she was sounding or engaged in putting something in the river last night I do not know. She did not remain stationary, but appeared to turn her engines over two or three times, and then stopping ten or fifteen minutes, possibly longer; I had no means of telling exactly. I have also discovered a signal station this side of the river, and abreast of the monitors. It is in a high tree, and is probably for observing our movements. I also observed that they had their torpedoes on their poles this morning. It is my impression they ship them every night. There is no army news. I think, however, from what I can hear that they intend abandoning this line and going back to Drewry's Bluff, as the baggage has all been sent to Petersburg and the men are still under marching orders. I think the next line will be along the railroad from Drewry's Bluff to Petersburg. My three days ended last night. I hope I may be relieved today.

I am, respectfully, your obedient servant,
Otey Bradford[84]

We have a report by Lieutenant Bradford regarding exchange of fire with the enemy:

Howlett's Battery

Sir: The fleet occupies the same position as this morning. The heavy firing today was from one of the wooden gunboats, from a heavy Parrott gun, shelling our lines to annoy a battery playing on the enemy. The other firing was in response to the Yankees, who opened fire from central fort on our center. As soon as the Yankees commenced, five batteries along the line responded. No damage; and as I write this, all quiet. Heard frequent firing in the direction of the Appomattox, and understand it is the Yankees shelling Fort Clifton. I learned from one of the pickets that the Yankees were engaged in putting something in the river last night. I have, since writing the above, learned that two batteries of artillery have been ordered to Petersburg, and that there is quite [a] fight going on there. I also learned that a spy was captured in rear of our lines today.

Otey Bradford, Lieutenant for the War.[85]

On July 27, 1864, Otey was listed as first lieutenant on the CSS *Richmond* and absent on sick leave. He was absent through the October 1, 1864. On October 5, 1864, he was reported as unfit for further military service by a medical board.

CALIFORNIA

After the war, he worked for various English shipping lines. He began his employ with Wells Fargo in New York City. He left Wells Fargo and moved to San Francisco. He shortly returned to the employ of Wells Fargo and remained with them until retirement.[86] In his later years, he served as the director of the Wells Fargo historical exhibit at the Columbian Exhibition of 1893. Later he was placed in charge of all Wells Fargo historical exhibits. He retired after forty years' service with the company. Otey died in 1919 and was buried in the Holy Cross Catholic Cemetery, Colma, San Mateo County.[87]

FURTHER READING

Bell, John. *Rebels on the Great Lakes: Confederate Naval Commando Operations Launched from Canada 1863–1864.*

Donnelly, Ralph W., and David M. Sullivan. *Biographical Sketches of the Commissioned Officers of the Confederate States Marine Corps.*

# Samuel Houston Brooks

Captain, major, and volunteer aide-de-camp to Major General B.F. Cheatham
Lieutenant colonel, Col. David Smith Terry's Texas Cavalry
Born January 1, 1829; died September 16, 1910.

So much has been written on Samuel that we will only give a brief biography. He was born to Samuel Clifford Brooks and Virginia's Elizabeth C. Hailey on a plantation in Fayette, Tennessee. Samuel's father fought in the war of 1812 under Andrew Jackson. As a lieutenant and assistant to General Twiggs, Samuel fought in the Mexican War. He moved to California in the early 1850s after the war, attracted by the gold rush, and served as the treasurer of San Joaquin County from 1853 to 1854. Around 1860, he resided in San Francisco and was elected as California State Treasurer and Controller in 1858. On May 21, 1861, in Marysville, Yuba County, he married Lucy C. Thornton Judge of San Francisco.[88]

Samuel resigned his position after losing re-election in California and returned to Tennessee to serve as a Confederate officer. On November 11, 1861, Volney E. Howard, who was a past adjutant general of California, sent a letter of recommendation to Confederate president Jefferson Davis. R. Augustus Thompson, a public land commissioner of California, also sent a letter.[89] On November 20, 1861, a final letter of recommendation for appointment as an officer from David Terry, whom Samuel had known for 10 years in California and was an advocate of the extension of slavery into California, was sent to President Jefferson Davis. Samuel was appointed captain, and his term of service started in November of 1862 as volunteer aide-de-camp to Major General Benjamin F. Cheatham.[90] He was soon promoted to major. His military service lasted from November of 1862 through 1865. On December 31, 1862, Samuel was wounded at Murfreesboro. He later became the aide-de-camp of General Cheatham until after Chickamauga, September 19–20, 1863. He was then transferred to the Trans-Mississippi Department. Samuel was made lieutenant colonel of David Smith Terry's Texas Cavalry on November 11, 1864. He surrendered with the unit near Houston.[91]

## CALIFORNIA

Samuel and his family lived in Texas for three years, raising cattle. In 1880, the family returned to California, where he became a stockbroker in San Francisco. He served as city treasurer in San Francisco in 1884. Samuel had also been counselor and witness in the Terry-Broderick duel before the war.[92] Upon the death of his wife in 1900, he lived in the city with relatives. He died at his home in Oakland, Alameda County, in 1910.[93]

## FURTHER READING

Bailey, Anne J. *Texans in the Confederate Cavalry.* Civil War Campaigns and Commanders Series.
Losson, Christopher. *Tennessee's Forgotten Warriors: Frank Cheatham and His Confederate Division.*
Moore, Frank, ed. *The Rebellion Record: A Diary of American Events, with Documents,* vol. 10.
Oates, Stephen B. *Confederate Cavalry West of the River.*

Samuel Houston Brooks (courtesy, Thomas Adkins, 3rd great-nephew, from the family genealogy).

# Telemachus Cambridge Brown

Lieutenant and captain, Company F, 12th Battalion Mississippi Cavalry
Lieutenant and captain, Company B, 17th Battalion (Sander's), Tennessee Cavalry
Captain, Company E (Chickasaw Mounted Guards), 9th Mississippi Cavalry
Born September 17, 1824; died April 8, 1910.

Known as Mac because of his long name, Telemachus was born in Giles, Tennessee, to Nathan Brown and Ezella Buchanan. He moved to Mississippi and was living in Okolona, Chickasaw County, Mississippi, as early as 1844, when he married Adaline Westmoreland. A year later his son Elbridge was born.[94] Mac enlisted March 20, 1862, in Okolona, Mississippi, in Company B—known as the Chickasaw Mounted Guards—in the 17th Battalion, Tennessee Cavalry, for the duration of the war. He was elected 2nd lieutenant of the company.[95] The company was then transferred to the 12th Battalion, Mississippi Cavalry, as Company F.

On August 31, 1863, the company went back to the 17th Battalion (Sander's), Tennessee Cavalry.[96] A few months before the transfer, on March 6, 1863, Mac was promoted to captain of the company. On September 19–20, 1863, Mac's company participated in the Battle of Chickamauga as the escort of Major General Patrick R. Cleburne. He was on sick furlough from November 6, 1863, to March 1864 because of the ongoing back problems.

The battalion was consolidated on December 24, 1863, to form the 9th Regiment, Mississippi Cavalry. The company became company E and Mac remained as their captain.[97] Mac was reduced in rank back to 2nd lieutenant due to his chronic back problems, and he tendered a letter of resignation:

> Camp at Antioch Church Miss.
> January 10th, 1865
> Capt. Somerville A.A. Gen.
>
> Sir,
>
> Owing to the very bad state of my health, I am compelled to respectfully tender my resignation as 2nd lieutenant. My health has been bad for the last fifteen years, but feeling it was the duty of everyone to lend their efforts to the great cause for which we are conducting, induced me to join army. Remorseful that I am no longer a benefit to the cause and therefore wish to resign. I append a surgeon's certificate.
>
> Respectfully yr. Obt. Servt.
> T.C. Brown
> 2nd Lieut. Co. E
> Sander's Batt. Cav.[98]

The reports seem to indicate that his resignation was approved, but he continues to be present on the rosters; he may have rescinded his resignation. He appears again in the rosters as captain.[99] Mac was paroled on May 15, 1865.

## California

Mac moved to California in 1869 with his family and settled in Grayson, Stanislaus County. He served on the supervisory board, deputy county assessor, and bridge tender. Mac died April 8, 1910, and was buried in the Modesto Citizens Cemetery.[100]

## Further Reading

Arnold, James. *Chickamauga 1863: The River of Death.*

Cozzens, Peter. *The Darkest Days of the War: The Battles of Iuka and Corinth.*

Hancock, R.R. *Hancock's Diary, 1887: or a History of the Second Tennessee Confederate Cavalry.*

Tenessee Civil War Centennial Commission. *Tennesseans in the Civil War: A Military History of Confederate and Union Units with Available Rosters of Personnel.*

Telemachus Cambridge Brown (courtesy Michael P. Brown).

# Louis Von Buchholtz

Captain, Brigade Ordnance, Wise's Legion
Captain, Ordnance Department, Richmond, Virginia
Born 1807; died January 9, 1889.

Louis von Buchholtz had an illustrious career before ever stepping foot on American soil in 1850. Born in the kingdom of Württemberg, Germany, Louis was part of a military family. When he was of age, he became an officer in the royal service of the kingdom, gaining over twenty years of service in the cavalry and artillery.[101] Around 1830 he married Marie Anna Frederike Von Kettler. They would have five children. In 1850, the family moved to the United States, first settling in Washington, D.C. Within a year, the family found themselves in Richmond, Virginia. Louis wanted to continue some form of military service and so enlisted in Company K, 1st Virginia. Company K, called the Richmond German Rifles, was composed of the German immigrants of Richmond. Louis was appointed captain.[102] Louis, coming from a well-to-do family, was also able to associate himself with the elite of Richmond. He became acquainted with the then-governor of the state, Henry A. Wise, who saw value in Louis as a surveyor and cartographer, a side career he had garnered. Louis was given a commission by the governor in 1855 to survey the state and develop new maps of Virginia.[103]

On October 16, 1859, John Brown and his band raided Harpers Ferry with the intent of obtaining guns and ammunition from the federal arsenal; the guns would be used to emancipate the slaves of Maryland and Virginia. Brown and many of his men were captured and jailed. The next day, Governor Wise, accompanied by Louis, now a member of the governor's staff, headed to Harpers Ferry to assess the situation.[104]

On his return to Richmond, Louis continued his mapping of the state. Seeing the gathering storm of secession in the South, Louis wrote to then-ex-governor and friend Henry Wise asking his favor in gaining a military position in the expected war between the North and South.

**Louis Von Buchholtz (courtesy the Ballard and Gail families).**

Richmond Virginia
November 15, 1860

Hon. H. Wise
Ex-Governor of VA
Dear Sir,

The arrangements being made in the Southern States may offer some chance to be of service. But being without connections and friends, I take myself the liberty to request you, if you deem it proper, to recommend my services to one of the Southern States.

The experience in my former services (having been 10 years officer in regiments, ten and a half years an officer in flying and foot artillery) might, under certain circumstances be of some value. Whatever might be desired in military affairs, I may be fully prepared to perform the duties confided upon me, to complete satisfaction. I have written some short instruction for field service, for fortifications and coast defense for militia and volunteers but I had nobody to recommend it and therefore may fail entirely with my good purpose to render the troops more complete for field service and besides this I may have to pay the printing expenses myself.

In spite of this failure, I have written tactics for officers of Infantry, Cavalry and Artillery, containing all required for campaign instructions. I consider it a valuable instruction, but it is doubtful whether I can have it published.

The correction of the Maps of Virginia had not been continued as contemplated and proposed by you, the legislature did not consider this matter and therefore nothing has been done.

Col. Smith from Lexington proposes to have this work for his cadets, and will get it without doubt in not long a time. Up to the present time, I am still in the position I was honored by you, but I may be dismissed any time and have to run about, anew like a dull boy for some work—such is life.

I am Hon. Sir
Very respectfully
Your most obt. Servant
L.V. Buchholtz[105]

Ex-governor Wise wrote to the governor of South Carolina on November 19, 1860, introducing Louis and his willingness to serve. Nothing seems to have come of this introduction. At the breaking out of war, Henry Wise was commissioned as a brigadier general and ordered to form a brigade. The brigade became known as Wise's Legion. General Wise did not forget about Louis and in June 1861 commissioned him to form the artillery for the brigade and perform as ordnance officer.[106] Louis had been working as a captain in the provisional army in the Richmond Ordnance Department since April 18, 1861.[107] He was still considered a captain in the provisional army (PAC officers were not commissioned in the regular army and therefore did not get official captain's pay) though he officially signed orders as captain of ordnance in Wise's Brigade in late 1861. That same year he was able to get his military tactics book published. On January 20, 1862, General Wise wrote Richmond asking that Louis be officially commissioned as captain of ordnance with pay dated back to his start in the position, being that he had been doing the job for almost a year. The next day, the Confederate secretary of war approved the rank and pay with one stipulation, that Louis was to report to Richmond immediately and be made commander of the Richmond Gas and Water Works. General Wise was angry at this decision and wrote a scathing letter to Richmond demanding an immediate replacement for Louis.[108] Louis commanded the Richmond Gas and Water Works only for a short time. He later became captain in charge of the ordnance department in the city.

## CALIFORNIA

After the war, there were no funds for Louis to continue his cartography of Virginia. He accepted a position in San Francisco as superintendent of a factory for the manufacture of explosives.[109] Louis passed away in 1889 and was buried in Holy Cross Catholic Cemetery, Colma, San Mateo County.[110]

## FURTHER READING

Lonn, Ella. *Foreigners in the Confederacy.*
Mehrländer, Andrea. *The Germans of Charleston, Richmond and New Orleans During the Civil War Period, 1850–1870.*
Schuricht, Herrmann. *History of the German Element in Virginia*, vol. 2.

# John Wesley Clanton

1st corporal, Hamilton County Minute Detachment of Mounted Texas Rangers
Private, Company B, 12th Regiment Texas Cavalry
Private, Company C, 30th Regiment Texas Cavalry (Gurley's 1st Partisan Rangers)
Born July 18, 1841; died April 19, 1916.

John was the eldest son of Newman Clanton, patriarch of the Clanton family of O.K. Corral gunfight fame. He was born in Callaway County, Missouri, and spent his teenage years in Hamilton County, Texas, where at the outbreak of war he enlisted with his father on June 15, 1861, in the Hamilton County Minute Detachment of Mounted Texas Rangers.[111] John was voted in as 1st corporal. For one reason or another, John deserted after serving a little over a month. Newman was discharged because of age and would enlist in a Texas heavy artillery unit; he again was discharged because of age.

On July 1, 1861, John enlisted in Ellis County as a private in company B, 12th Regiment of the Texas Cavalry for three years, listing his occupation as farmer.[112] After serving four months in this regiment, known as Parson's Regiment, John deserted on December 11, 1861, and left for home in Hamilton County. He was soon caught. A court martial was held for him in February 1862, and he offered no defense.[113]

John was found guilty of desertion, but due to his youth and the fact that he had not read the Articles of War, and so was not aware of the seriousness of his crime, his sentence was a stoppage of pay from the time of his desertion to the expiration of his term of enlistment and then to be dishonorably discharged.[114] John and his father again decided to join the Confederate service. Father and son enlisted in company C of the First Texas Partisan Rangers (30th Texas Cavalry) in March of 1862. On July 6, 1862, Newman was discharged a third time because of age.[115] After a year, John deserted on March 2, 1863, having had enough of drilling and protecting supply lines and not ever engaging in a battle with the federal troops.

## CALIFORNIA

After the war, John left for California with his brother Phineas and married seventeen-year-old Nancy Rose Kelsey in Inyo County on January 14, 1869. The three were listed as living in Lone Pine, California. John worked as a farmer and died in Santa Rosa on April 19, 1916, after a brief illness of four or five days. The causes were old age (75) and over-exertion. He was buried in Santa Rosa Rural Cemetery, Santa Rosa, Sonoma County, and Nancy was buried in Mountain View Cemetery, Fresno, Fresno County. Why she was not buried with her husband is unknown to this author.[116]

## FURTHER READING

Aros, Joyce. *The Cochise County Cowboys: Who Were These Men?*
Ivey, Darren L. *The Texas Rangers: A Registry and History.*
Marks, Paula Mitchell. *And Die in the West: The Story of the O.K. Corral Gunfight.*
Oates, Stephen B. *Confederate Cavalry West of the River.*
Parsons' Texas Cavalry Brigade Association. *A Brief and Condensed History of Parson's Texas Cavalry Brigade, Composed of 12th, 19th, 21st Morgan's Battalion, and Pratt's Battery of Artillery of the Confederate States.*

# Charles Clement Clay

Captain and major, Company F (The Forked Deer Rangers), 7th Tennessee Cavalry
Born January 28, 1835; died August 6, 1905.

Charles Clay's ancestors had been in the United States since the 1600s. He was born in Amelia, Virginia, to Joseph Clay and Margaret Bowen and moved with his family to Tennessee in 1850. When the war came, Charles decided to form a company to fight for the confederacy. They became known as the Forked Deer Rangers, named after a river near Haywood. The company was mustered into service on November 4, 1861.[117] They joined the 7th Tennessee Cavalry on April 1, 1862. That same day the partially formed regiment was attacked by a small group of federals and retreated. Charles and his company then covered the retreating Confederate forces of Fort Pillow on June 3, 1862, and fell back to Abbeville.[118]

On August 31 and September 1, 1862, the regiment fought skirmishes at Medon and Britton's Lane.[119] Charles and his unit then fought at the Battle of Corinth on October 3–4, 1862. The regiment spent the winter near Grenada, Mississippi. They did not see serious action again until late spring. In early October, Charles was promoted to major of the regiment.[120] In November, the regiment was assigned to General Nathan Bedford Forrest's command. They were with Forrest in his defeat of Major General W.S. Smith's forces (part of Grierson's federal raiding party) near

**Charles Clement Clay (*The Seventh Tennessee Cavalry*, by J.P. Young, 1890).**

Okolona, Mississippi, on February 24, 1864. Charles was wounded slightly when a bullet grazed the top of his head.[121]

In March, Forrest led a raid into West Kentucky, and at Union City, Charles and the 7th captured about 300 horses and arms and supplies.[122] Charles was appointed colonel April 6, 1864. He declined the promotion for reasons that are lost. The regiment was not with Forrest during the attack on Fort Pillow on April 12, 1864, but was used to stop other federal forces from entering the fight. The unit was left in west Tennessee to conscript for the army after Forrest and his other regiments left the state.[123]

On July 14, Charles and the 7th fought with Forrest in the Battle of Harrisburg. Charles was more severely wounded in this battle, but there are no records on how severe the wound was or how long he was away from his unit.[124]

The regiment went back into Tennessee on a raid with Forrest beginning September 24, 1864, with the capture of Athens, Alabama, and concluded October 6, 1864, when Forrest re-crossed the Tennessee River. The 7th Tennessee remained with Forrest and took part in the Battle of Franklin in Chalmers's Division. On December 15, 1864, Charles and the regiment fought at the Battle of Nashville.[125]

The final actions the unit experienced were near Tuscaloosa, Alabama, on March 31, 1865, and again on April 1 at Scottsville, Alabama. This resulted in the final surrender of Forrest's forces on May 11, 1865, at Gainesville, Alabama, where Charles and the regiment were paroled.[126]

## CALIFORNIA

After the war, Charles settled in Memphis, Tennessee, where ran Farguson and Clay, selling wholesale groceries to stores. In 1875, Charles left the company and moved to California, where in 1876 he married Ann Louise Tuggle. The couple would have three children. He decided to embark on a new path and started a musical supplies company, Sherman, Clay and Company, based in San Francisco. He acquired a fortune which was close to $1,000,000 at the time of his death. In 1886, the family moved to a large estate house in Fruitvale. Charles also owned large ranches in Livermore and Fresno.[127] He died from stomach cancer in 1905 and was buried in the Mountain View Cemetery in Oakland; his gravestone is marked Clement C. Clay.[128]

## FURTHER READING

Beck, Brandon H. *The Battle of Okolona: Defending the Mississippi Prairie.*
Cozzens, Peter. *The Darkest Days of the War: The Battles of Iuka and Corinth.*
Lindsley, John Berien. *The Military Annals of Tennessee. Confederate. First series: Embracing a Review of Military Operations, with Regimental Histories and Memorial Rolls.*
Young, John Preston. *The Seventh Tennessee Cavalry: A History.*

# George Blake Cosby

Brigadier general, Confederate States Army
Born January 19, 1830; died June 29, 1909.

George Blake Cosby was born to Fortunatus and Ellen Cosby on January 19, 1830, in Louisville, Kentucky. He was educated in Louisville, becoming a clerk at seventeen.

He aspired to become a merchant.[129] Garnet Duncan, representative of the Louisville District and family friend of the Cosbys, was able to acquire an appointment for George at West Point. George passed the entrance examination after four years and graduated with honors in 1852.[130] He was made second lieutenant in the U.S. Mounted Rifle Regiment after graduation. He transferred to the 2nd U.S. Cavalry Regiment in 1857. His obituary in the *San Francisco Call* gives an account of his service with the 2nd:

> With his class-mates, Fitzhugh Lee, Phil Sheridan, A.S. Johnson, George B. Thomas, Earl Van dorn, Stoneman and other distinguished American soldiers, he fought through the frontier campaigns in the old Second cavalry. General Winfield Scott recommended him to congress for gallantry at the battle of Lake Trinidad, and he was wounded when Fitzhugh Lee was shot by the indians at Wichita mountain.[131]

George Blake Cosby (courtesy Library of Congress LC-USZ61–1990).

The *Illustrated history of Sacramento County* gives a condensed account of his service to the Confederacy:

> True to his principles and belief as to the calls of duty, he resigned his position on the 12th of May, 1861, and hastened to Montgomery, Alabama, at that time the seat of Confederate government, and tendered his services to President Jefferson Davis, being accompanied in this departure by George B. Anderson and John B. Hood, also of the regular army. He remained in the Confederate service until the capitulation of General Lee, in April, 1865. The stirring events of these years need not be chronicled here, indeed could not be, within the limits of this sketch. Suffice to say that he did his duty, — at Bethel Church, his first battle; at Fort Donelson, where he was captured by the enemy; at Perryville, etc. He served with distinction on the staffs of generals Magruder and Buckner, being chief of staff, and brigadier-general under Van Dorn at the time of the latter's death, engaged in skirmishing duty and guarding the flanks of the army of General Bragg. Later on, toward the close of the war, he was with General Jubal A. Early as Brigadier-Commander in his memorable Virginia campaign.[132]

## CALIFORNIA

George married Antonia Johnson in 1862. They moved to Butte County, California, where for two years he had charge of a stage. For a period, he also was a sutler in Oregon. He held several government positions, including superintendent of construction for the federal headquarters in Sacramento.[133]

George had an attack of paralysis about ten years before his death and spent his later years as an invalid. He committed suicide on June 29, 1909, in Oakland, California, by opening a gas valve. He was buried in the City Cemetery, Sacramento.[134]

## FURTHER READING

Allardice, Bruce S., and Lawrence Lee Hewitt, eds. *Kentuckians in Gray: Confederate Officers and Field Officers of the Bluegrass State.*

*An Illustrated History of Sacramento County, California* by Hon. Wm. J. Davis.
Welsh, Jack D. *Medical Histories of Confederate Generals.*

# Richard William Dancy Crump

Lieutenant and captain, Company E (Sardis Blues), 12th Mississippi Infantry
Born September 25, 1828; died 1903.

Richard Crump was born in Greenville County, Virginia, to Dr. James Robert Crump and his second wife, Mildred Turner Williamson. He moved to the Memphis area at the age of about fifteen with his mother and her family; his father had already passed away. He married Caroline Pierce on October 11, 1850, and moved to Poinsett County, Arkansas, a year later. In 1855 he started to practice law. They moved to Panola County, Mississippi, in the early part of 1860, where he acquired a cotton plantation. He continued planting until the end of the war.[135] When war came, Richard—along with his brother Turner—enlisted in Sardis, Mississippi, in February 1861 and traveled 140 miles to Corinth, Mississippi, to muster into the regiment on April 20, 1861, for 12 months.[136] Richard was voted in as 1st lieutenant of Company E, the Sardis Blues of the 12th Mississippi Infantry. By May, he was elected as captain of Company E, and Turner became 1st lieutenant.[137] Richard had some time to write the Morris sisters of Sardis, thanking them for their contributions to his company:

Camp near Union Mills, VA
November 26, 1861

Miss Callie Morris, Secretary Soldier's Aid Society, Sardis, Miss.

Your note advising me that your society had made for my company a lot of winter clothing, and had kindly furnished us with a sufficiency of blankets to protect us from the keen wintry blasts of this, to us, northern clime, was received some time since. I would have acknowledged its receipt sooner, but awaited the arrival of the goods. They have just been received, after a detention of nearly two months.

To you and the kind friends whom you represent, we owe a debt of gratitude we can never repay. We can only tender you the sincere thanks of hearts that fully appreciate your kindness.

Could you have seen the eagerness with which we gathered around the boxes as they were opened, the smile of satisfaction that played across our features as some package, directed in the well-known hand of some loved one at home, was handed out, and the kindling of the eye with emotion, as the blankets, of which you had deprived yourselves, were distributed to us to protect us from the cold, damp ground, you would have felt that your generous donation was appreciated, and that our hearts spoke thanks that our lips could not utter.

The morning the boxes were opened, the ground was wrapped in a mantle of snow, and we were ordered to go on picket duty. Your gift could not have come more opportunely. We are now, while I write, at our advanced post, expecting daily to meet the Vandal foe who would dare attempt to subjugate freemen, and to make desolate our bright, sunny south. Fear not that he will succeed, while encouraged by the smiles of the fair women of the South, and supplied by their hands with every comfort a soldier needs. We must, we will drive him from our soil. We fight not for conquest; we draw the sword in defense of our firesides, our mothers, wives, sisters and daughters, and until our arms are unnerved by death, or our country is free, we sheath it not again.

Your generous donation, consisting of one hundred pairs excellent blankets, nearly two hundred flannel shirts, one hundred and ninety pairs drawers, over two hundred pairs woolen socks, a large lot of gloves, besides other articles for the soldier's comfort too numerous to mention, have been properly distributed, and in the name of my company I thank you again for them. Very respectfully,

R. W. Crump,
Capt. Sardis Blues, Company E,
12th Mississippi Regiment.[138]

In the spring of 1862, Richard and the 12th were sent to Yorktown, Virginia, and moved up the peninsula. Richard and Turner went into their first fight on May 31, 1862, at the Battle of Seven Pines. The regiment lost 41 killed and 152 wounded.[139] The Confederates were victorious. On June 25 began the Seven Days Battles, beginning at Mechanicsville and ending at Malvern Hill with a series of victories for Lee's army. The "Sardis Blues" lost several men killed, including Richard's brother Turner.[140] The regiment then headed north, missing the Battle of Second Manassas. The next battle Richard and his company fought was at Sharpsburg, Maryland, on September 15, 1862. The regiment lost 6 men killed and 53 wounded.[141] The next great fight for Richard was at the Battle of Chancellorsville in May of 1863. They were part of Posey's brigade during Stonewall Jackson's flanking movement against the federal 11th Corps. The loss of the regiment was 3 killed, 38 wounded, 23 missing.[142]

The regiment's next fight occurred at Gettysburg in July. In Dunbar Rowland's history of the regiment, details are given on the unit's participation at Gettysburg:

> At Gettysburg, Pennsylvania, Posey's brigade was in the attack of A.P. Hill's corps upon the Federal positions in the peach orchard and toward the heights of Little Round Top and the Devil's Den. The Mississippi brigade was ordered to support Wright's Georgia brigade. "Wright's men bore the starry cross on their standards to the crest of the ridge, which they held for ten memorable minutes." They believed that if they had been supported the victory was won. But through some fatality they were not supported in that extreme advance. In fact, Posey had been instructed to send only two of his regiments. The Twelfth was held in reserve through the battles of the 2d and 3d. The casualties of the regiment were seven wounded.[143]

Richard and Company E went into winter quarters at "Orange Court House" on the Rapidan River in the closing months of 1863. The next fighting for the regiment was the Battle of the Wilderness in Virginia in May of 1864. At the Bloody Angle on May 12–13, 1864, the regiment spent twenty hours under fire without food or sleep.[144] The 12th then moved on to Petersburg, Virginia, and was posted about a mile to the right of where the famous mine was exploded.

As Lee's army headed out of Petersburg towards its ultimate end at Appomattox, the 12th Mississippi had only about one hundred and fifty men left. Richard and the regiment were paroled on April 10, 1865.[145]

## CALIFORNIA

Richard's wife Caroline died either during the war or just after, and he married Lenora B. Clanton in the fall of 1871. Richard and family moved to Santa Rosa, California, and then to Lakeport around 1877. He and his wife would raise seven children. In 1875, he was licensed to practice law at the California District Court in Santa Rosa. He did not make law a career until he was elected Lake County district attorney in 1879. Richard also was editor of the Santa Rosa *Daily Democrat* and later became senior editor of the Lake County *Bee*.[146] He died in 1903 and was buried in the Hartley Cemetery, Lakeport.[147]

## Further Reading

Broadwater, Robert P. *The Battle of Fair Oaks: Turning Point of McClellan's Peninsula Campaign.*
Guelzo, Allen C. *Gettysburg: The Last Invasion.*

# Arthur Sinclair Cunningham

1st lieutenant and captain of artillery, P.A.C.S
Major P.A.C.S., assistant adjutant general for General George B. Crittenden
1st lieutenant of artillery, Charleston Arsenal
Lieutenant colonel, 20th Battalion Virginia Heavy Artillery
Lieutenant colonel, 10th Alabama Infantry
Lieutenant colonel, 40th Virginia Infantry
Lieutenant colonel, general inspector, State of Virginia

Born April 1835; died July 26, 1885.

Born in Norfolk, Virginia, to Commodore Robert Barron Cunningham and Ann Starke, Arthur Cunningham followed his father's example of a military career, though not on the same side. He and his six siblings lived in various parts of the United States depending on their father's assignment in the navy. Robert Barron Cunningham was assigned to Mare Island Naval Shipyard as its commandant; he passed away there in 1861.[148]

Ten years earlier, the family was living in Norfolk, Virginia. On July 1, 1851, Arthur became a cadet at the U.S. Military Academy at West Point through his father's contacts. He graduated and was made 2nd lieutenant with assignment to the 10th Infantry at Fort Snelling, Minnesota.[149] The fort was abandoned within a year, and the unit took part in the battle against the Mormons in Utah. Arthur became commander of Company B of the 10th in Utah.[150] On May 1, 1861, Arthur was promoted to 1st lieutenant and resigned from United States service on June 25, 1861.

Being born in Virginia, Arthur considered himself a Southerner and espoused the Southern cause. On July 19, 1861, he was appointed 1st lieutenant of artillery in the Provisional Army of the Confederacy.[151] Arthur's rank varied as he jumped between the Provisional Army and regular army assignments. On August 8, 1861, he was ordered to report for duty to General John H. Winder in Richmond, Virginia, where he was assigned to the 5th Group, Richmond defenses.

Within a month, Arthur was sent to Goldsboro, North Carolina, and ordered to report to General Richard Gatlin. He wrote, "When I arrived at Goldsboro I found General Gatlin's Hdqrs. was at New Bern and proceeded there and reported accordingly."[152] General Gatlin gave Arthur orders to report to General George Bibb Crittenden, then commanding a brigade in the Army of the Potomac (later called the Army of Northern Virginia). On September 12, 1861, Arthur was promoted to the Provisional Army rank of major and assigned as assistant adjutant general to Crittenden. On November 16, 1861, Crittenden promoted Arthur to the temporary rank of lieutenant colonel. Crittenden was soon promoted to command the eastern district of Tennessee, and Arthur continued in the general's service in Knoxville throughout the early part of 1862. In March 1862,

General Crittenden was relieved of duty and arrested for drunkenness. Arthur was out of a job until May 1, 1862, when he was assigned to the Charleston, South Carolina, arsenal with the rank of 1st lieutenant of artillery.[153] During his unemployment he married Helen W. Starke (who may have been a distant cousin) on April 3, 1862, in Richmond. They would have four children. At this point, his rank between the Provisional Army and regular army became confusing. On May 23, 1862, he wrote authorities in Richmond, "Is my provisional appointment as Major expired due to the appointment to an Artillery Company in Charleston?"[154] He received a yes on the question.

On June 8, 1862, Arthur received a promotion to captain (regular service) and was ordered to report to General Samuel Cooper, the highest-ranking officer in the confederacy. On June 12, 1862, General Cooper promoted Arthur to the temporary rank of lieutenant colonel and was ordered to report to Colonel T.S. Rhett, who appointed him temporary commander of the 20th Battalion, Virginia Heavy Artillery, which had just formed on June 21, 1862.[155] The Confederate Congress rejected the first proposed permanent commander, Major Johnston DeLagnel, and he immediately left the battalion. This was Arthur's first field unit. The battalion was assigned to the Richmond Defenses without any fighting. On June 30, 1862, Arthur became the temporary commander of the 10th Alabama Infantry due to the high casualties among its officers.[156] He was wounded during the last day of the Seven Days Battles but continued in command until February 1863.

On June 20, 1863, Arthur was ordered to report to General J.H. Winder, provost marshall and commander of prisons in Richmond, for assignment. He remained under General Winder for the rest of 1863.[157]

On January 4, 1864, Arthur, still lieutenant colonel, PACS, was assigned to general inspection duty, reporting to Colonel Chilton for instruction in Richmond. On January 27, 1864, Arthur requested another field assignment and was given temporary command of the 40th Virginia Infantry. He fought with the unit from May 1864 during the wilderness campaign to the siege of Petersburg, where on September 30, 1864, he was wounded at the Battle of Jones Farm.[158] Arthur was admitted to the hospital in Richmond on October 3, 1864, where he remained for the month. He applied for a position behind the lines in Richmond on October 31, 1864, and wrote, "During this time I may be prevented from rendering my duties in the field on account of wounds received in the battle of September 30, 1864."[159] He was given court-martial duties in Richmond under General Richard S. Ewell and on January 19, 1865, assigned as general inspector of the State of Virginia. On January 27, 1865, Arthur inspected the prison in Danville, Virginia, and on March 20, 1865, started on an inspection of all the cavalry forces in the Army of Northern Virginia, beginning with the divisions of General Lomax. Arthur was officially paroled on May 11, 1865, and returned home.[160]

## CALIFORNIA

In 1866, Arthur and his family moved to San Francisco, where he worked for Wells, Fargo and Company. He married Page Edloe Thompson in Oakland on October 13, 1883, after the death of his first wife. At the time of their wedding, she was only 19. The family decided to leave the city and settle in Eureka, Humboldt County, where Arthur continued to work for Wells Fargo.[161] He died of dropsy and kidney disease at age fifty in 1885 and was buried in Myrtle Grove Memorial Cemetery, Eureka, Humboldt County.[162]

## FURTHER READING

Chernault, Tracy, and Jeffrey C. Weaver. *18th and 20th Battalions of Virginia Heavy Artillery.*
Krick, Robert E.L. *40th Virginia Infantry.*
_____. *Staff Officers in Gray: A Biographical Register of the Staff Officers in the Army of Northern Virginia.*

# Henry Brevard Davidson

Sergeant, Company K, 1st Tennessee Infantry (Mexican War)
Colonel and brigadier general, Confederate States
Born January 28, 1831; died March 4, 1899.

In his book on Confederate military history, Clement Evans gives us an excellent overview of Henry Davidson's military career in the Mexican War as well as the Civil War:

Brigadier General Henry B. Davidson, a true son of the Volunteer State, received his appointment at the United States military academy as a reward for gallant services as a sergeant of Tennessee volunteers at the battle of Monterey, Mexico, September 21 to 23, 1846. He was graduated at West Point in 1853, and promoted to brevet second lieutenant of dragoons. He served at the cavalry school for practice, in garrison duty at Jefferson barracks, Mo.; on scouting duty at Fort Union and Albuquerque; was engaged with Apache Indians in a skirmish on Penasco river, New Mexico, January 18, 1855, and again with hostile Indians in Oregon, March 27, 1856; in the combat of the Four Lakes on September 1st; on the Spokane plains, September 5th, and on Spokane river, September 8, 1858. He was quartermaster of First dragoons from December 5, 1858, to May 13, 1861. Being on leave of absence when

the Confederate war began, he resigned his commission as captain in the United States army and entered the service of the Confederate States, actuated by a sense of duty to his native State, whose command he felt bound to obey. Reporting to the Richmond government, he was assigned in 1862 to the command of the post at Staunton, Va., with the rank of colonel. In August, 1863, he was commissioned brigadier-general, and early in 1864 he was at Rome, Ga., in command of a cavalry brigade belonging to Wheeler's corps. On the 17th of May, as the enemy was approaching Rome, Ector's brigade of French's division, supported by the cavalry of Ross, Morgan and Davidson, had quite a spirited affair, in which Davidson attacked the enemy on the right, driving in their skirmishers. General Davidson did not long remain in Georgia, but was sent back to Virginia and assigned to the command of a brigade of cavalry attached to the division of General Lomax, operating in the valley under General Early. This brigade consisted of the First Maryland and the Nineteenth, Twentieth, Forty-sixth and Forty-seventh Virginia battalions of cavalry.[163]

**Henry Brevard Davidson (*The Photographic History of the Civil War*, vol. 10, by Francis Trevelyan Miller, 1912).**

As part of Wheeler's October 1863 raid into Tennessee, Henry sent messages to Wheeler as he was being pursued:

> Headquarters Davidson's Cavalry Division,
> Aliens House, October 3, 1863
>
> Major General Wheeler, Commanding Cavalry:
>
> General: I am moving down the side of the river. The enemies are following me up. As soon as I can get a position, I will make a stand. I think they are in strong force.
>
> Respectfully,
> H.B. Davidson,
> Brigadier General commanding.

Then he wrote a second note just before the battle:

> Headquarters Davidson's Cavalry Division
> October 7, 1863
>
> To Major General Wheeler, Commanding Cavalry:
>
> General: The enemies are following me. I am now six miles below town, on the south side of the river. I have not yet made a decided stand.
>
> Respectfully,
> H.B. Davidson,
> Brigadier General commanding.[164]

The end of the war found Henry in North Carolina with his small cavalry brigade; he surrendered there with General Joe Johnston. He was paroled at Greensboro, North Carolina, May 1, 1865.

## CALIFORNIA

Henry and his family moved to New Orleans, Louisiana, after the war, where he served until 1867 as deputy sheriff. The couple would have one child. Henry was a U.S. public works director at San Pedro, California, from 1878 to 1886. In 1887 he was named deputy to California's secretary of state.[165] His wife seems to have died before he did, for he died at the home of a relative in Livermore, California, and is buried at Mountain View Cemetery in Oakland.[166]

## FURTHER READING

Miller, Frederic P., Agnes F. Vandome, and John McBrewster. *Henry Brevard Davidson*.
Warner, Ezra J. *Generals in Gray: Lives of the Confederate Commanders*.

# Henry Potter De Veuve, Sr.

Colonel, Planters Guard Regiment, Louisiana Militia
Captain, assistant engineer, to Major General W.W. Loring, 1st Corps, Army of Mississippi.
Captain, Quartermaster's Department
Born July 26, 1831; died April 28, 1900.

Henry De Veuve was born to Daniel De Veuve and Julia Prentiss in West Feliciana, Louisiana. Daniel was professor of modern languages at the University of Louisiana and had practiced law in the state. He passed away before Henry's fifth birthday. Their grandfather, James Prentiss, brought up Henry and his brother Prentiss.[167]

Henry was able to receive a good education, first at Princeton and then during an appointment to West Point. He attended the academy from July 1, 1848, to July 1, 1852.[168] On July 7, 1857, Henry married Laura Sims. They would have six children. By 1860, the family was living in New Orleans. When the war came, Henry decided to form a regiment, with the hopes of being commissioned colonel. In a letter he wrote to General G. Beauregard in 1863, he described his life in the early part of the war:

> Lexington Ga. Feb. 18th 1863
> Genl Beauregard C.S.A.

Dear Sir,

I have arrived here safely having escaped with some peril and much difficulty from the abolitionists in the city of New Orleans in which place I have been shut up since its fall. At the commencement of this war finding that there was a great scarcity of tactical books and a great want of Drill officers I opened a free drill room in the city and devoted myself to drilling and instructing all who desired it. I spent the months of April, May and June 1861 in that manner and instructed several hundred many of whom now hold commissions as Colonels and some higher grades. In July 1861 I tendered President Davis through Genl R. Lee ten companies of infantry to be formed into a regiment under my command. The President declined accepting the same on account of the want of arms and they joined other commands and did good service[.] I thus lost a command to serve under you at Manassas. The President sent me word Through Genl Lee to return to New Orleans and employ myself in raising, arming and equipping troops so as to form another regiment. This duty though very unpleasant I undertook and labored at faithfully until the arrival of the abolitionists and although from many causes I was not able to combine ten companies again under my command and yet I know I was doing good service as I so materially assisted at least twenty companies as to perfect their organization and they have done good service on the field of battle. I also gathered some six hundred stand of arms which were turned over to the government. I have done all in my power to help the cause both by personal exertion and with such means as I possessed, seeking no high rank but simply copying to the best of my ability often the patriotic spirit of the great leaders of our county's cause—When New Orleans was taken, my wife was dangerously ill and one child was at the point of death their means were nearly exhausted and I would have been worse than infidel if I had left them unprovided for when they were able to depart. Butler would not let us go—We both took out certificates of amnesty to the U.S. and suffered all the ills common to registered enemies. In October I got my family off three weeks after I started and had passed the lines but was taken ill and went back and was laid up for weeks—Three weeks again I tried again and with success yesterday met my wife and children for the first time since October—When I applied to Genl Sidney Johnston in Sept. for official recognition, he advised with the President and issued me orders with the title of Colonel but as I never raised a second regiment I know not whether I can claim a commission as above—However as I have always been ready at the call of my country and as you once pleasantly at Sour Lake Texas promised me[,] if fortunes made you a General you would find a place for me. I respectfully request, if it be in your power, that you would find me some position in your department. If possible I should like to have one shot at a Yankee gunboat as all New Orleans refugees have a special hatred towards them and as artillery is my old line of service. If you cannot find a place for me, will you do me the kindness to give such advice as to how I had better proceed together with such assistance as you may be able and willing to grant.

I can only hope that you can excuse this lengthy communication by reflecting that your former kindness has led me to turn to you at this time when I need a friend.

> I am Sir, very respectfully
> Your Obt. Servant Henry De Veuve[169]

Henry wrote directly to the president of the Confederacy on March 12, 1863, asking for an appointment in the artillery or engineers. He told Jefferson Davis that if he did not receive a commission he would like to go back to Texas and join a regiment commanded by a friend in Galveston. Henry got his wish and was appointed as assistant engineer with the rank of captain, reporting to Major-General William W. Loring, commanding the 1st Corps of the Army of Mississippi.[170] During the Vicksburg Campaign, we have a report from Henry to General Loring concerning the terrain near Big Black River:

> Hdqrs., Lanier's House, Baldwin's Ferry Road,
> May 9, 1863. Maj. Gen. W.W. Loring, G.S. Army,
> Commanding:

> Sir: I respectfully offer the following report as to the roads leading into our lines from the Big Black River, at or near the two ferries, Hall's and Baldwin's:
> The ground immediately on the bank of the river, and for an average distance of at least 1 mile, is low and nearly level; then we find a range of hills rising to the height of from 40 to 100 feet. These bluffs or hills meet the river at about a mile or two below Big Black Railroad Bridge. The river can be bridged by the enemy, if he wishes, in a few hours at any point. A little this side of Baldwin's Ferry the road forks; one goes almost in a straight line through P. Nolan's place to the town of Bovina; the other goes to Vicksburg, with a connection to Mont Alban, and also a connection with the first road. From this it is evident that the road to Bovina is the shortest line, and of great importance in connection with the defense of Big Black Railroad Bridge. The nearest point from the Vicksburg road that a good defense can be made on the Bovina road is at least one and a half miles east, on P. Nolan's plantation. The distance from Baldwin's Ferry road to Hall's Ferry is at least 8 miles; to the junction of the Warrenton and Baldwin's Ferry roads to Hall's Ferry, at least 4 miles. There is still a lower road out of the Hall's Ferry road to Warrenton, some 2 miles nearer the ferry. There is also an intermediate ferry between Baldwin's and Hall's which must be watched. It is evident from these facts that an army watching the two ferries (Hall's and Baldwin's) must have a line of at least 6 miles in extent, with its pickets thrown out to the ferries from 1 mile to 2 miles from the main force, with a level country between. There would be two lines, one with its left at a point 10 miles east of the Baldwin's Ferry road, overlooking the river valley and guarding the road to Bovina, with its right some 6 to 8 miles west, at or about the junction of the Warrenton road with Vicksburg and Hall's Ferry road, or the left could be thrown up to Bachelor's place, on the Bovina road, which would give a longer line—one not so convenient, nor so strong.
> I would, in conclusion, state that the roads are very hilly and the surface of the country very irregular. Also that I am of the opinion that the line first mentioned above is the best in every way, provided it is taken upon the other side of the Hall's Ferry road, and extended down the river, and especially if there are troops for the defense of Bovina. I am, sir, very respectfully, your obedient servant,

> Henry De Veuve,
> Engineer on Staff.[171]

On April 30, 1864, Henry asked for a 30-day leave of absence to see his wife and children, who were then residing in the Valley of Virginia.[172] On his arrival back to Confederate headquarters he was assigned as a bonded agent of the Quartermaster's Department and was ordered to report to Captain Winder, in charge of prisoners at Americus, Georgia, where he was to see to the creation of a shoe factory at Oglethorpe, Georgia:

> Quartermaster's Department, Camp Sumter, Ga.,
> June 23, 1864. Henry De Veuve, Bonded Agent,
> Quartermaster's Department:

> Sir: You will proceed without delay to select suitable buildings and materials of all sorts to establish a shoe factory for the Confederate States Government. You will use the utmost diligence

in procuring all necessary machinery and tools to effectually carry this shop into successful operation, and will keep me fully posted in regard to everything connected with it.

You will use your best discretion in making necessary purchases, always keeping in view the best interest of the Government.

R.B. Winder, Captain and Post Quartermaster.

P.S.—Quartermasters will furnish Mr. De Veuve transportation wherever his business may call.[173]

Henry remained in this position until his official parole as a member of the Quartermaster Department, Galveston, Texas, at Salisbury, North Carolina, on May 25, 1865.[174]

## California

After the war, the family resided in Texas; they moved to California in 1870. They initially settled in San Jose, where Henry worked as a civil engineer. In 1876, the governor appointed him to the state board of engineers.[175] Henry was affectionately known as "The Colonel" later in life. He, his wife and his son Henry Jr. all passed away in 1900. They were all buried at Cypress Lawn Memorial Park, Colma, San Mateo County.[176]

## Further Reading

Kautz, Lawrence G. *August Valentine Kautz, USA: Biography of a Civil War General.*
Puckett, Robert M., Major. *Engineer Operations During the Vicksburg Campaign.*

# John Andrew DeVilbiss

Private, Green's Missouri State Guard, Cavalry Regiment
Private, 2nd Northeast Missouri Cavalry (Franklin's Regiment)
Born November 19, 1841; died January 7, 1937.

John DeVilbiss was born in Lewis County, Missouri, to Alexander DeVilbiss and Rebecca Brown. His father, who was an architect and contractor, died when John was eleven months old. Until he was six years old, John lived on his grandfather's farm. His mother remarried, and he lived with her and his stepfather until he was sixteen. In 1858, he moved to his uncle's farm and remained there until the war.[177] It is said that John enlisted in the Missouri State Guard under Sterling Price in 1861, but no records exist except mention of this service in his muster sheets when captured. On July 25, 1862, he enlisted as a private in the 2nd Northeast Cavalry at Camp Fabius in Lewis County.[178] On August 6, 1862, John fought at the battle of Kirkville.[179] Regimental records, though piecemeal, state no casualties; but John is listed in his biography as having been wounded. He was captured and on August 10, 1862, was allowed to tend to his wounds at home with the promise to return to military prison. He wrote:

> I John A. DeVilbiss of Lewis County Missouri a prisoner of war and wounded do hereby sign and give my solemn pledge and point of honor that I will on or about the 31st day of September at the city of Palmyra report myself in person to the commanding officer or Provost Marshall at that

place and this parole is given and if violated will subject me to all of the penalties affixed by Military Law for a violation of a Parole of Honor.

Aug. 11, 1862
John A. DeVilbiss[180]

John returned to Palmyra on October 1, 1862, and was sent to Gratiot Street Prison, St. Louis, on October 4, 1862. He was charged with being a guerrilla under Franklin in 1862 and Sterling Price in 1861. He pleaded guilty to the charge and the military court found him guilty as charged. His sentence was to remain a prisoner until March 1, 1863, and then be released upon oath and bond. While in prison is St. Louis, John wrote to the provost marshall asking to be released early:

John Andrew DeVilbiss (*A Memorial and Biographical History of Northern California*, Lewis, 1891).

November 18, 1862
Gratiot St. Prison,
St. Louis

Sir, I write you a few lines asking you for my release. I have been a prisoner ever since the first of August. I have never taken the Oath. I was paroled for a while when I was first taken and reported myself promptly. I have a very bad cough and I am afraid it has entered my lungs. I want to get out and if you will release me on any terms I shall remember you with the utmost kindest affections. I am willing to take the Oath and give bond and I am willing to be banished to any other state. I am tired of a soldier's life. I am willing to give bond to every dollar I am worth and I have had a trial[.] [Y]ou can call them for my evidence and if there is anything more, call me out. I am ready to meet anything that may be brought up before me. I have wrote home for a petition and what kind of character I have. If you see proper, you can wait for that. I went into the army under a big excitement but now I see my folly and have paid dearly for it. Forgive me if you please and never while waters flow and winds blow will I be in the army again. Set me free once more, from your most obedient servant.

John A Devilbiss[181]

On December 6, 1862, John was sent to military prison in Alton, Illinois. At Alton, he was offered the choice of joining a federal unit in Missouri or banishment. While at Alton he contracted smallpox in prison, and the federal authorities decided they would rather release him than allow him to join a federal regiment. He was discharged on January 2, 1863, on oath and bond to remain north of Springfield, Illinois, and east of the Illinois Central Railroad.[182]

## California

John went to McLean County, Illinois, where until the fall of 1864 he was a farm worker. He met his wife, Esther Cunningham, while there, and they married on November 18, 1864.[183] They soon moved to Lewis County, Missouri, living with his mother until the next spring. Then they started for California. When they reached Virginia City, Nevada, they decided to stay. John worked there in the mines until 1868, when they moved to his Uncle's ranch near Vacaville, California.[184] John first worked in California as a farm hand but soon made enough money to purchase land in the new town of Winters in Yolo County. He planted many acres of fruit and shipped as far east as New York. On July 15, 1890, John opened the Hotel DeVilbiss, which still exists.[185] John lived to the ripe old age of 96 and died in 1937. He was buried in the Winters Cemetery, Yolo County.[186]

## FURTHER READING

Klinckhardt, Wayne. *The War for Missouri.*
McGhee, James E. *Guide to Missouri Confederate Units, 1861–1865.*
Nichols, Bruce. *Guerrilla Warfare in Civil War Missouri.*
Speer, Lonnie R. *Portals to Hell: Military Prisons of the Civil War.*

# Henry "Harry" St. John Dixon

Private, Company H, 11th Mississippi Infantry
Private, Company D, 28th Mississippi Cavalry

Born August 2, 1843; died August 27, 1898.

So much has been written about Harry, and Harry has written so much about himself, that our description of his life will be basic. For more on his life look at the "Further Reading" at the bottom of his section.

Harry was born in Jackson, Mississippi, and grew up on his parent's plantation. Being from the privileged class, he was able to attend college at the University of Virginia in Richmond in 1860. When war came, Harry took up an offer of a general who was a friend of his father, General S.G. French, to be a clerk in the quartermasters.[187] Harry wrote:

> The quiet old soldier was too shrewd to take to himself a stripling for his aide; but consented to give me service under his Quartermaster as a clerk, with the gracious promise that in battle I should be permitted to leave the wagons and act as his aide.[188]

Harry reported for duty on December 10 of 1861 and after just a few days of service became violently ill. He wrote:

> No longer able to stand the mule work of my "staff" position, I had broken with my chief; and although under orders from the governor

Henry "Harry" St. John Dixon ("Dixon in Uniform," Harry St. John Dixon Papers, #2375, Southern Historical Collection, Wilson Library, University of North Carolina at Chapel Hill).

to return home and join a cavalry regiment there, could not refrain joining the 11th Mississippi Infantry, as an independent, on its march through the place, for participation in the Peninsular campaign. Great was my woe and small my glory.[189]

Harry went on: "I do not, although a private, choose to be made a hog of. It is galling to a gentleman to be absolutely subject to the orders of men, who in private life were so far his inferiors. How much a man undergoes for a country."[190]

Not fighting any Yankees, Harry decided to leave the infantry and the Confederate army in the east and join the cavalry in the west, which was intended for him from the beginning. He enlisted in Company D of the 28th Mississippi Cavalry on April 29, 1862, in Richmond, Virginia, taking along a body servant named Dick from his father's plantation.[191] Before getting into any fighting, Harry wrote about this body servant:

I never knew his concern for me until the battle of Thompson's Station, 5th March 1863. I was riding a fiery little pony, acting as courier for General Martin. A missile carried away the end of the scabbard to that same old sabre, leaving its point protruding several inches. It cut the arteries in my horse's foreleg so that the sergeant in command of the couriers ordered me to the rear, to remount myself. The blood had spurted over my boot, so that it looked like I was myself wounded. Galloping around a corner in the little town of Spring Hill, a mile or so in our rear, where our wagons were parked, I halted before Dick, who sat gambling—a favorite pastime of his—with a number of his ebony comrades around a blanket spread on the ground. Reckless of the roar of battle so near, he was so intent on winning our poor promises to pay [three years after the ratification of the treaty of peace between the U.S. and C.S. of America], that he did not see me until I called out, as I dismounted: "Dick, saddle Henry for me—quick!"

Seeing the blood on my leg, as I dismounted, and never comprehending what I said, he threw down his cards, and rushing over blanket, money and companions, without ceremony, caught me in his arms as if I was a child, crying: "By God, Mas' Harry, is yer kilt? Whar's yer hit, honey; whar's yer hit?" When I at last got away from him, and convinced him I was unhurt, he exclaimed, with grotesque satisfaction: O' Lord! won't ole Missus be glad it's de hoss, an' not yon![192]

Dick would die from disease in early 1864. Harry's first combat experience was on the Mississippi River, skirmishing with Yankee gunboats. Harry explains the fight:

Such reflections, however, were soon cut short by the angry growl of the six-pounders on our right, which was the signal to commence firing. Instantly we were answered by a vigorous fire of shell and shot and bullets, which riddled the bushes about us. This was kept up until the boats were out of range. If we had done any damage we did not know it, and had suffered but few casualties ourselves. And how did I act and feel under fire? Like a raw recruit, of course. As soon as I had discharged my rifle, I leaped from behind my good cover, and, shouting the "rebel yell" amid the din, continued firing. Our orderly, a grizzled old veteran of the Mexican War, blurted out at me: "Get down there, you d—d little fool,—you'll get your head blown off!"[193]

In early 1863, Harry's unit was transferred to Cosby's Brigade, Martin's Cavalry Division, under Van Dorn. Harrys' regiment was at the battle of Thompson's Station but did no fighting. They did fight at Franklin on April 10.[194] Again, Harry spoke on the subject:

A force of about 700 infantry was deployed in the plain south of the town, covered by batteries on the north bank of the river. There was offered an open field and a fair fight. The Twenty-eighth was selected to charge, and did so with such gallantry and loss, overcoming their adversaries, that a complimentary field order was issued. The batteries made it impossible to hold the town, however, after taking it; but, though driven back, the "Bloody Twenty-eighth" ever after rejoiced in its name.[195]

Harry became sick again (the medical listing said gonorrhea)[196] and was sent to the hospital at Columbus, Mississippi, from May 13, 1863, to February 1864.[197] On February 6,

Harry went back to his regiment. As a member of the Sigma Chi fraternity from the University of Virginia, Harry kept track of the brothers that he campaigned with. In 1864 he and three other members established the Constantine Chapter of Sigma Chi. Harry was elected president and Harry Yerger, vice president. Also present were members Evan J. Shelby and William H. Bolton.[198] Harry went on to fight the last battles with his regiment until its surrender.

## California

Harry and his family had nothing left in Mississippi, so they moved to California, where Harry became a lawyer and rancher. He married Constance Maynard in 1874.[199] Their son Maynard would become a famous artist. The gonorrhea he had contracted in his younger days resulted in his premature death. Harry passed away on August 27, 1898, and is buried in Mountain View Cemetery, Fresno, California. Some years after his death, fellow members of his fraternity, Sigma Chi, decided to place a large monument over his grave. Unfortunately, in the process they managed to pour cement over and obliterate the graves of his parents.[200]

## Further Reading

Berry, Stephen. *Princes of Cotton: Four Diaries of Young Men in the South, 1848–1860.*
Dixon, Harry St. John, Private. *Recollections of a Rebel.*
Stone, Irving. *Rebel in Sentiment: Family Papers of Harry St. John Dixon.*

# Caleb Dorsey

Captain and colonel, Missouri State Guard
Colonel, Dorsey's Regiment, Shelby's Brigade
Born September 7, 1833; died April 21, 1896.

Caleb was born in Baltimore, Maryland, the fourth son of Edward Worthington and Eleanor Brown Dorsey. In 1834, Edward Dorsey moved the family to Pike County, Missouri.[201] When war came, Caleb joined the Missouri State Guard, where he was promoted from captain to colonel.[202] Little is known of Caleb during the early part of the war. Receipts for back-pay state that he enlisted June 27, 1861.[203] Information does exists of Caleb and his participation in the battle at Mt. Zion Church in December 1861. No official account was published of the Mount Zion, but one of Caleb's soldiers present during the engagement mentions him:

> On December 24, 1861, Col. Dorsey left Pike County, and on the 27th, at Grandview, in Boone County, which is near and west of the church, organized his forces, consisting of six companies, of about 350 men, not all armed. The officers in command were Col. Caleb Dorsey, Lieut. Col. Cole Kent, Maj. Thomas Breckinridge and E.W. Herndon, (now a citizen of Columbia), Surgeon. About 2 o'clock, P. M., of the 27th, this force took up the line of march, intending to camp at Mount Zion church. About a half a mile northeast of the church, the Federals came up and fired on their rear guard, wounding two of Dorsey's men, and then fell back. Dorsey pursued them, and three miles

from the church overtook the retreating force, and fired upon them. A ten minutes' skirmish ensued, in which one Federal was mortally wounded, and Capt. Howland (Federal), was wounded in the thigh, and taken prisoner. Dorsey's surgeon, Dr. Herndon, extracted the ball. None of Dorsey's men were killed or wounded. On the morning of the 28th, the engagement was renewed, the force under Dorsey being about 100 yards east of the church, in the brush and timber. The Federal charge upon them was with both infantry and cavalry, but was repulsed. They again charged, and were again repulsed, after which they made a third charge. The ammunition of Dorsey's command being exhausted, he determined to fall back to his wagons. The Federals advanced upon him, and took some ten prisoners. They then marched on to the church, and seeing soldiers in the building, fired on it, whereupon two of the prisoners who were in the church, ran out and said: "There are no fighting men here; this is a hospital"; hearing which the Federal fire ceased.[204]

After Mt. Zion Church Caleb and his command scattered. In February, Caleb's force regrouped and crossed the Missouri to rejoin Price's army. His muster sheets state:

He was captured while rectg near the Osage River February 15, 1862 and was imprisoned at Alton Ill., Camp chase Ohio and Ft. Warren Mass. and was delivered to the confed agent at Aiken's Landing Va. August 5, 1862 for exchange at which time his age was stated as 28 years, height 6 feet. Subsequently he is mentioned as Capt., as Major & as Col. in command of troops and on Aug 20, 1864, he was authorized to recruit a regt. of Cav for Shelby's Brigade CSA. He appears in November 1864 to have been in command of a body of Confed troops in MO.[205]

On February 2, 1863, federals in White Oak, Arkansas, attacked Caleb and his force.

His men charged the federals, causing them to retreat to Frog Bayou. On April 18, 1863, Caleb and his command were involved in an engagement at Fayetteville, Arkansas. They surprised 1,100 federal cavalry and infantry at six in the morning driving them from their rifle pits to the houses in town. After three hours, the federals ran out of ammunition and fell back. Caleb had one casualty. During the rest of 1863, Caleb fought minor skirmishes and recruited. By 1864, Caleb was under Joe Shelby. Major John N. Edwards, in his 1867 book on Shelby, wrote:

Among the most soldierly and dashing of the young officers interested in keeping their men mounted, and particularly concerned, too, because the orders from department headquarters required all the new recruits to be dismounted, was Lieutenant Colonel Caleb Dorsey, of Slayback's regiment. Dorsey had been very active as a recruiting officer, and was well skilled in the cavalry service. Among his many daring exploits, he had frequently lingered around St. Louis in his numerous scouts, and among the brightest trophies of his service in the enemy's lines, was a magnificent pair of dragoon revolvers, ivory-handled and plated with gold.[206]

**Caleb Dorsey (courtesy Lynne N. Roberts, www.lynnesgenealogy.com).**

It is not know where Caleb and his command ended the war.

## CALIFORNIA

Caleb never married, devoting himself to ranching, raising stock and horses in San Joaquin County. On April 21, 1896, Caleb was shot and killed at a mine by J.T. Newcomer. The *San Francisco Call* newspaper gave the account of the slaying:

> Colonel Caleb T. Dorsey was shot and killed at 1:30 o'clock this afternoon, at a mine fifteen miles from Columbia, by J.T. Newcomer. The latter fired twice, both bullets striking Dorsey. The killing resulted from a dispute over a mine in which the two men were interested. After the shooting Newcomer went to Columbia by the trail leading from the mine to the town. When he arrived there he was almost breathless from the trip, which he made on foot. To Telephone Agent Davis he said that he had killed Dorsey in order to save his own life, but he was too excited to give any further particulars, and hastened on to Sonora, where he surrendered himself into the custody of the Sheriff. The only witness to the killing of Dorsey was the nephew of the murdered man, and he could not be reached at a late hour this afternoon. As soon as the news of the Killing was received at Columbia a number of men started on foot for the mine, among them the Coroner. They had to make the journey over the same trail by which Newcomer came in from the mine.[207]

Newcomer was found guilty and sentenced to San Quentin for eleven years. Caleb was buried in the Dorsey/Ewing family plot in the Rural Cemetery in Stockton.[208]

## FURTHER READING

Nichols, Bruce. *Guerrilla Warfare in Civil War Missouri*, vol. 2, 1863.

Scott, Robert N., United States War Department. *The War of the Rebellion: A Compilation of the Official Records of the Union and Confederate Armies*, series 1, vol. 22, part 1.

Tinkham, George Henry. *History of Stanislaus County California: With Biographical Sketches of the Leading Men and Women of the County.*

Western Historical Company (Saint Louis, Mo.). *History of Boone County, Missouri: Written and Comp. from the Most Authentic Official and Private Sources.*

# Dozier Brothers: Anthony White Dozier, Jr., Edward Charles Dozier, Leonard Franklin Dozier, Peter Cuttino Dozier, and William Gaillard Dozier

## Anthony White Dozier, Jr.

Lieutenant, Company F, 6th South Carolina Cavalry (Aiken's Partisans)
Born January 23, 1842; died October 31, 1874.

## Edward Charles Dozier

Private and 2nd sergeant, Company F, 6th South Carolina Cavalry (Aiken's Partisans)
Born August 17, 1843; died October 9, 1919.

## Leonard Franklin Dozier

Private and lieutenant, Company B, 21st South Carolina Infantry
Assistant surgeon, General Longstreet's staff
Born September 13, 1836; died March 9, 1917.

# Peter Cuttino Dozier

Private, sergeant major (color guard), and lieutenant, Company B, 21st South Carolina Infantry
Born January 12, 1838; died November 24, 1877.

# William Gaillard Dozier

1st lieutenant, Confederate States Navy
Born May 5, 1833; died November 9, 1908.

The Dozier brothers were born to Anthony White Dozier, Sr., and Mary Catherine Cuttino on their plantation on the Pee Dee River in South Carolina.[209] The Doziers were a powerful and large family who had hundreds of slaves to maintain their rice plantation. Anthony was one of the signers of the Ordinance of Secession of South Carolina on December 20, 1860.[210] William, the oldest of the five, went to the Naval Academy and graduated in 1850.[211] Leonard, the next in line, graduated from the South Carolina Military Academy in 1856. In 1859, he graduated from the Oglethorpe Medical College in Georgia.[212] Peter Dozier attended the University of Virginia's College of Law.[213] Anthony Jr. received an appointment to the Citadel Military Academy and became a member of the Cadet Rangers, organized at the school.[214] Younger brother Edward also received an appointment to the Citadel and was also a member of the Cadet Rangers.[215] When the war drums began to beat, all of the brothers answered the call. William was placed in command of the CSS *Lady Davis* and went on to command the CSS *Pamlico*, New Orleans Naval Station, September 2, 1861, through March 1862; and the CSS *Chief*, Charleston Naval Station, plus other commands in and around Charleston.[216] Anthony and Edward enlisted in Company F of the 6th South Carolina Cavalry. Anthony was wounded at Johns Island, South Carolina, captured February 9, 1864, and was held prisoner at Fort Delaware under sentence of death.[217] He was one of four officers selected and mistreated in retaliation for supposed mistreatment of four U.S. officers at Libby prison. He was released to await exchange on February 2, 1865.[218] Edward became a sergeant and was wounded in action at Lee's Mill, Virginia, on April 16, 1862.[219]

Peter and Leonard joined Company B of the 21st South Carolina Infantry. Leonard was promoted to adjutant and lieutenant on January 7, 1863. He served as adjutant of his regiment until after the siege of Battery Wagner, on Morris Island,

**Leonard Franklin Dozier (*History of the State of California and Biographical Record of the Sacramento Valley*, by J.M. McGuinn, 1906).**

Charleston Harbor. During the first day of attack, he was seriously wounded in the right chest. Because of the lack of medical treatment during the siege, he came down with a very severe case of pneumonia.[220] Because of the severity of his illness, he was taken out of the front lines and appointed as surgeon in Longstreet's command on January 26, 1864. He joined Longstreet at Knoxville and surrendered with other members of the Army of Northern Virginia at Appomattox in April 1865.[221] Peter was appointed sergeant major of the color guard on January 7, 1863. At Fort Wagner on Morris Island in Charleston Harbor, Peter was shot through the thigh, captured and sent to the general hospital in Hilton Head on July 13, 1863.[222] He recovered and was exchanged on July 23, 1863, at Morris Island, South Carolina. The regiment was transferred to Virginia, and Peter was promoted ensign on June 17, 1864. In the battle at Weldon Railroad, Virginia, on August 21, 1864, he was again wounded in a charge and was captured.[223]

He was sent to the old capital prison in Washington, D.C., and then sent onto Ft. Delaware on October 21, 1864. Peter took the oath of allegiance on June 17, 1865, at Ft. Delaware and was released.[224]

## California

With the war lost and their plantation and business in ruins, the Dozier family, including Anthony Sr. and his wife, headed to Northern California in March of 1868. The family planted roots in Rio Vista, Napa, and as far north as Ukiah. Anthony Jr. died at the young age of 32 and was buried in the George C. Yount Pioneer Cemetery, Yountville.[225] Leonard kept his medical practice in Rio Vista and died in 1917. He was buried in the Tulocay Cemetery, Napa.[226] Peter practiced law in Fairfield and in Ukiah, where he died and was buried.[227] William died in 1908 and is buried at Cypress Lawn Memorial Park, Colma.[228] Edward became a ranch manager and rancher and died in Rio Vista.[229]

## Further Reading

Allston, Robert Francis Withers. *The South Carolina Rice Plantation as Revealed in the Papers of Robert F. W. Allston*.
Buckley, William H. *The Citadel and the South Carolina Corps of Cadets*.
Conrad, Lee. *The Young Lions: Confederate Cadets at War*.
Johnson, John. *The Defense of Charleston Harbor, 1863–1865*.
Wise, Stephen R. *Gate of Hell: Campaign for Charleston Harbor, 1863*.
Wood, Ira. *Fort Sumter: Where the Civil War Began*.

# John Livingston Estill

Private, Company E (Valley Rangers), 1st Virginia Cavalry
Born September 1833; died September 6, 1905.

John was one of nine children born to Dr. Henry Miller Estill and Mary Jane "Eliza" Patrick in Lexington, Rockbridge County, Virginia. He attended the University of Virginia in 1858.[230] When war came, five of the Estill boys enlisted. William C. Estill enlisted in the

1st Rockbridge Artillery.[231] Charles Patrick Estill was a member of Carrington's Company, Virginia Light Artillery.[232] He would become a captain in the ordnance department of John B. Gordon's division.[233] Henry Miller Estill enlisted as a private in the Richmond Howitzers.[234] Robert K. Estill enlisted in Company C, 1st Virginia Cavalry, on April 18, 1861.[235]

John enlisted the next day, April 19, 1861, in Company C.[236] The company left Waynesboro, Virginia, that same day and reported to Brigadier General William H. Hannan at Harpers Ferry four days later. In early July, under the command of Colonel J.E.B. Stuart, the company became Company E of the newly formed 1st Virginia Cavalry. John experienced his first tangle with the federals at the Battle of Hainesville, July 2, 1861. Company E charged and scattered a federal infantry company, capturing 17 prisoners.[237] At Berry's Ford, John and his comrades crossed the Shenandoah River and scouted the area for signs of federal movement. Because of their assignment, John and his unit were not able to participate in the fight at Manassas. The regiment was camped at Sudley's Springs on July 22 and left the next day for Fairfax courthouse. At Fairfax, they performed reconnaissance and picketing, frequently firing at federal pickets.[238]

Colonel Stuart was promoted to brigadier general in September and given a brigade command, which included the 1st Virginia Cavalry. Colonel William E. Jones was given command of the regiment. In November, John's company commander recommended him for promotion to 2nd lieutenant:

Camp Cooper Fairfax Co. Va. November 28th 61

S. Cooper Adjt. Genl C.S.A.

Sir—I have the honor to request that John L. Estill, a private in Company (E) 1st Regt. Va. Cav. Be commissioned a 2nd lieutenant in the Provisional Army of the C.S.A.

The said John L. Estill is 23 years old, 5 ft. 11 in. high, well formed and free from any physical disabilities for the service. He is well educated being a graduate of Washington College Va. & for the last two years a teacher in Classical schools in which capacity he has exhibited a marked ability to govern men. He has been in the volunteer service of Virginia & the Confederate states as a member of my company of cavalry for nearly eight months, has been during that time, frequently under fire from the enemy & has always in situations trying to men's nerves conducted himself with commendable coolness & courage. I take pleasure in recommending him to you favorable consideration as one on whom a commission will be worthily bestowed.

Respectfully, Wm Patrick Capt.
Co E, 1st Regt. Va. Cav.[239]

This letter went up the chain of command and further recommendations occurred:

Hd 2nd Cavalry Brigade Nov. 29, 1861

Genl

I take pleasure in fully endorsing Capt. Patrick's recommendation. I have frequently noticed Estill's military aptitude and uniform good conduct. He will be an asset to the service.

Your obdt serv
J.E.B. Stuart, Brig. Genl. Comdg.
I take pleasure in joining in the above recommendation.
J.E. Johnston, General[240]

It may be because of politics that John was not promoted. Colonel Jones disliked Stuart, and Stuart felt the same towards Jones. The regiment was divided in their loyalty, with John siding with his old commander; hence, no letter of recommendation exists from Jones. Stuart may have let the decision rest with Jones being that he commanded the unit.

John was sick in the hospital from September 14, 1863, through mid–October and is listed as present through June 1864. This is the last entry in his muster sheets.

## CALIFORNIA

John and his brother Robert are listed as farmers in Fresno County in 1880.[241] They may have moved to California earlier. Robert eventually moved back to Virginia, where he died. John never married and passed away in 1905. He was buried in the Academy Cemetery, Clovis, Fresno County.[242] He was given an obituary in the *Confederate Veteran* magazine:

> John L. Estill, an old Confederate soldier, died in Fresno County, Cal., on the 7th of September. He was a member of Company E, 1st Virginia Cavalry, enlisting in 1861 and served till the close of the war. He was courier under Gens. R.E. Lee, J.E.B. Stuart and Fitzhugh Lee and will be remembered by survivors of his old regiment as a gallant soldier.[243]

## FURTHER READING

Driver, Robert J. *The Confederate Soldiers of Rockbridge County, Virginia: A Roster.*
_____. *1st Virginia Cavalry.*
Longacre, Edward G. *Fitz Lee: A Military Biography of Major General Fitzhugh Lee, C.S.A.*
McClellan, H.B. *I Rode with Jeb Stuart: The Life and Campaigns of Major General J.E.B. Stuart.*

# Oliver Perry Evans

Private, Company B, 22nd Virginia Infantry
2nd cadet sergeant, Company B, Virginia Military Institute
Born June 2, 1842; died May 15, 1911.

Oliver was born near Jackson Court House in what is now West Virginia to Ephraim Sayer Evans and Ruami Wright. When war came, Oliver, then nineteen years of age, enlisted on June 1, 1861, as a private in Company B of the 22nd Virginia Infantry for one year.[244] Oliver trained with his company for the rest of the summer and experienced his first combat at the Battle of Carnifex Ferry on September 10, 1861, in Nicholas County, Virginia (now West Virginia). The battle resulted in a federal victory. Oliver's father was not pleased with his decision to enlist and felt his son should be an officer. Ephraim used his political connections to get Oliver an appointment to the Virginia Military Academy. Oliver received the appointment and was expected to report to the school on January 1, 1862. He took a furlough from his regiment and reported to the school while also writing the senator of his district to obtain a discharge from Confederate service:

> Virginia Military Institute, Lexington Va.
> January 15, 1862
> Senator William W. Newman

Dear Sir,

I have received an appointment to this institute as a State Cadet from the 45th senatorial District, which at the present time you have the honor to represent in the General Assembly of Virginia. I wish to ask you to be kind enough to lay my appointment before the War Department and ask for a discharge for me from the military service of the state from which I am now enlisted in order that I may attend the institute. I am a private in a company of the 22nd Virginia regiment. As I am not formally acquainted with you I will merely say that I suppose you are well acquainted with my father, E.S. Evans of Jackson County. Capt. Lipscomb and Lieut. Col Jackson wrote to the governor for me, recommending my appointment and asking for a discharge for me from the service some 6 or 8 days since. But I did not receive an answer immediately from the governor. Col Jackson & Capt. Lipscomb both told me as there was no doubt about my getting a discharge. That I had better take a furlough of 15 days and report myself to Gen. Smith at the VMI and that the necessary arrangements concerning my discharge would be made during my furlough but Gen. Smith said I had better write to you and ask you to go directly to the War Department and attend to it for me and let me know the result as soon as possible.

I am very respectfully yours
Oliver P. Evans[245]

Oliver was granted his discharge and preceded to immerse himself in the schooling and military drill of the institute. By 1864, Oliver was a 2nd cadet sergeant at the institute.

Oliver was given the honor of color sergeant of the battalion. Jennings C. Wise, in his history of the cadets, described Oliver's actions during the fight at New Market:

Henry Wise ("Old Chinook," beloved of every boy in the command) sprang to his feet, shouted out the command to rise up and charge, and, moving in advance of the line, led the Cadet Corps forward to the guns. The battery was being served superbly. The musketry fairly rolled, but the cadets never faltered. They reached the firm greensward of the farmyard in which the guns were planted. The Federal infantry began to break and run behind the buildings. Before the order to limber up could be obeyed by the artillerymen, the cadets disabled the teams, and were close upon the guns. The gunners dropped their sponges, and sought safety in flight. Lieutenant Hanna hammered a gunner over the head with his cadet sword. Winder Garret outran another and lunged his bayonet in him. The boys leaped upon the guns, and the battery was theirs. Evans, the color-sergeant, stood wildly waving the cadet colors from the top of a caisson. Oliver leapt atop one of the federal guns, waving the Institute flag over his head. Within minutes, the federal line gave way.[246]

The battle was a Confederate victory. Ten cadets lay dead or dying on the battlefield while another 45 were wounded.

Oliver graduated from the institute in 1865 and was remembered by his comrades for leading them in the charge.[247]

**Oliver Perry Evans, Private, Company B, 22nd Virginia Infantry and later VMI cadet flag bearer at the Battle of New Market, 1864 (VMI Archives Photographs Collection, Virginia Military Institute Archives).**

## CALIFORNIA

After graduation, Oliver stayed in Lexington, studying law at Washington College (now Washington and Lee University). In 1868, he moved to San Francisco to practice law; he became a distinguished lawyer, law professor and judge. In 1876, Oliver married Nora M. Ryan. They had four children.[248] Oliver died in 1911 in Berkeley and was buried in Holy Cross Catholic Cemetery, Colma.[249]

## FURTHER READING

Cocke, Preston. *The Battle of New Market and the Cadets of the Virginia Military Institute.*
Johnson, Gerald White. *The Cadets of New Market: A Reminder to the Critics of the South.*
Knight, Charles R. *Valley Thunder.*
Turner, Edward Raymond. *The New Market Campaign: May 1864.*

# Edmund Clare Fitzhugh

Lieutenant, volunteer aide, D.H. Hill's Division
Captain and assistant adjutant general, Garnet's Brigade, Pickett's Division
Captain and inspector, Daniel's Brigade
Captain and assistant adjutant general, Eppa Hunton's Brigade, Pickett's Division
Born abt. 1820; died November 24, 1883.

Edmund led an amazing and adventurous life that ended in an unmarked grave. He was born in Stafford County, Virginia, to Dr. Alexander H. Fitzhugh and Eliza Gibbs Clare. The Fitzhughs were one of the first families of Virginia, with relations to George Washington and the Lee family. The family were also extensive slave owners. By 1850, Edmund owned five slaves himself, one black woman aged 40 and four children who were all mulatto.[250] No proof is given that they may have been Edmund's children by his slave. In 1838, Edmund applied for a cadetship to West Point, which he did not receive due to quotas having been met. This did not deter him, and he sent an application the next year. He received his appointment in 1840.[251] Edmund's rebellious nature did not bode well with the strict discipline of West Point. He seems to have not graduated, and he studied law at Georgetown College.

In 1849, Edmund moved to San Francisco, where he practiced law with A.P. Crittenden and Edmund Randolph. In the early 1850s Edmund became part owner in the Bellingham Bay Coal Mines in Washington territory.[252]

Edmund Clare Fitzhugh (courtesy dandersonclan at ancestry.com).

While in Bellingham, Edmund became an associate justice of the Supreme Court of Washington Territory.[253] In late 1861 Edmund left to join the Confederate war effort and in late May 1862, he was commissioned a 2nd lieutenant and volunteered as an aide to General D.H. Hill.[254] He continued with the general through the Seven Days Battle and later in the year at South Mountain and Antietam September 16–17, 1862, and at Fredericksburg in December. Edmund received promotion to captain and assistant adjutant general early in 1863 and was under Brigadier General Richard Garnett in Pickett's division during the Gettysburg campaign. After Gettysburg, Brigadier General Eppa Hunton was given Garnett's brigade on August 9, 1863. During this period, Edmund seems to have been out of a job. On November 2, 1863, he was re-appointed as a captain in the A.G.'s department and ordered to report to General Robert E. Lee. Five days later Edmund reported to Junius Daniel's brigade as inspector in the assistant adjutant general (AAG) department.[255] He would remain with the brigade for only a short while. On December 29, 1863, Edmund was ordered to duty as inspector and AAG of Eppa Hunton's brigade. He continued with Hunton through Cold Harbor, May 31–June 12, 1864, and the trenches of Petersburg.[256]

On December 29, 1864, Edmund married his first cousin, Ann F. Grayson, in Louden County, Virginia. They would have four children.

On February 5, 1865, Edmund, in the middle of the action at Hatcher's Run, received his first wound of the war. Eppa Hunton wrote in his autobiography:

> I think every man in my brigade acted heroically in that charge, only a short time before the surrender. As we were driving the enemy, Captain E.C. Fitzhugh, my Adjutant, who had succeeded poor Linthicum, was struck in the forehead and down he fell. Colonel Green, of the 56th Regiment, said, "Poor Fitz! Forward, Boys!" and on we went; but not long afterwards we were joined by Fitzhugh, who was only stunned, and he continued in the charge.[257]

Edmund continued with the brigade and surrendered at Appomattox on April 9, 1865. He left for home with two horses and what baggage he had left.[258]

## CALIFORNIA

By 1866, Edmund and his family were living in Iowa, where he continued his law practice. Edmund left for the Washington Territory in 1874, telling them he would be back. He returned for a few months, then abandoned his family and moved to San Francisco. In 1883, he passed away alone in the What Cheer Hotel in San Francisco. His obituary stated:

> About 9 o'clock yesterday morning, E.C. Fitzhugh was found dead in his room at the What Cheer House. While ascending the stairs he fell backwards, striking upon his head, but as he recovered himself immediately, he was supposed not to have been seriously hurt. Mr. Fitzhugh was formerly a law partner of Edward Randolph and A.P. Crittenden, and afterward took charge of the business of the Bellingham Coal Company. Before the breaking out of the rebellion, he removed to Virginia, became a member of the legislature of the state, and afterwards served a Major in the Confederate Army. He has, for several years past been a resident of this state and leaves a wife and children residing in Iowa.[259]

Edmund's burial location in the city is not known.

## FURTHER READING

Gordon, Lesley J. *General George E. Pickett in Life and Legend.*
Greene, A. Wilson. *The Final Battles of the Petersburg Campaign: Breaking the Backbone of the Rebellion.*
Krick, Robert E.L. *Staff Officers in Gray: A Biographical Register of the Staff Officers in the Army of Northern Virginia.*

# George M. Flournoy

Colonel, 16th Texas Infantry
Born November 30, 1832; died September 18, 1889.

George's obituary in the *Sacramento Daily Union* newspaper gives us an account of his early life before the war:

> Colonel Flournoy has a somewhat adventurous history. He was born in Georgia about fifty-seven years ago. His parents died when he was quite young. He engaged in various occupations until twenty one years of age, when he began to study law, and a few years later was admitted to practice in the State Courts of Alabama. Then he went to Texas. During the administration of Governor Sam Houston he was elected Attorney-general of that State. His term of office expired at the beginning of the Civil War in 1861.[260]

In early 1862, George organized the 16th Texas Infantry regiment of Walker's Texas Division.[261] On June 3, 1862, Colonel George Flournoy was assigned to command the Sub-Military District of Houston and established his headquarters in Houston, Texas.[262] On June 7, 1863, George and his regiment fought the Battle of Milliken's Bend. The regiment began the fight on the Confederate right flank. As the regiment was about to move forward, General McCulloch's adjutant stated that the general had ordered them to double-quick to the brigade's left. Colonel Flournoy disagreed but the adjutant replied that that was the order.[263] John Blesington, a member of the regiment, wrote:

> Colonel Flournoy immediately ordered his regiment to double-quick to the left of the brigade. Away they go, pell-mell, along the foot of the levee, led by their colonel, erect and precise in his saddle, towering above his men, calm as a summer morn. It was cheering and inspiring indeed to observe his men, calm and with such determined air, and the unbounded confidence with which they followed him.[264]

The regiment's casualties in the fight were 44 killed, 130 wounded and 10 missing. George and his regiment participated in the Red River Campaign and Camden Expedition, March through May 1864. On April 8, 1864, the regiment fought at Mansfield; the next day they fought in the Battle of Pleasant Hill. The unit had a short respite and then fought at Jenkins' Ferry on April 30, 1864. This ended the fighting for the regiment. George and the 16th were surrendered in Galveston, Texas, on May 26, 1865.[265]

## CALIFORNIA

George's obituary in the *Sacramento Daily Union* concludes with his life after the war:

**George M. Flournoy (*A Comprehensive History of Texas 1685 to 1897*, vol. 2, by Dudley G. Wooten and the Texas State Historical Association, 1898).**

At the conclusion of the war Mr. Flournoy moved to the City of Mexico, where, for several years he practiced law and gained a knowledge of the Spanish language that afterward proved very serviceable. In 1876 he went back to Texas, settling in Galveston, but in 1878 he moved to this city, where, in 1879, he formed a law partnership with John B. Mhoon, son-in-law of the late Justice Samuel B. McKee, and the copartnership has existed ever since. Mr. Flournoy has never held any political office in this State, although he has attended nearly every State Convention for years. In politics he is a stanch Democrat. He has a large interest in the lands allotted by the State of Texas to its pioneers.[266]

George died of Bright's disease in San Francisco on September 18, 1889.[267] He was buried in Mount Calvary Cemetery in San Francisco, and his remains were transferred when that cemetery was shut down to Holy Cross Cemetery in Colma.[268]

## FURTHER READING

Lambert, Will. *"Our Beloved Commander": Tribute of Respect to the Memory of Col. George Flournoy, C.S.A.*
Lowe, Richard. *Walker's Texas Division, C.S.A.: Greyhounds of the Trans-Mississippi.*

# Richard Samuel Floyd

Midshipman, CSS *Florida*
Born 1843; died October 17, 1890.

Richard Samuel Floyd was born in Camden County, Georgia, to General Charles R. Floyd and Julia Ross Boog Floyd. His father had an illustrious career in the military, as did many of the Floyd men, and the family were part of plantation society in Georgia.[269] In keeping up the family military tradition, Richard was appointed to the Annapolis Naval Academy in 1859.[270] When his home state of Georgia seceded from the Union in January 1861, Richard waited until the firing on Ft. Sumter and then resigned from the Academy. On May 16 he was appointed acting midshipman in the Confederate navy. Richard was assigned to the newly commissioned Confederate cruiser CSS *Florida*.[271] On May 3, 1863, the *Florida* captured a federal bark, the *Lapwing*. Lieutenant Maffit gave this report:

> On the 28th March captured the bark Lapwing, loaded with coal, tobacco, and provisions, from Boston, and bound to Batavia. As she seemed to be a fine vessel, I placed two howitzers on board and ordered Lieutenant Averett to command her, furnishing him with two officers and eighteen men.
>
> Lieutenant Averett reported the Lapwing as leaking and totally unfitted for a cruiser. I detached him from the vessel, received on board her armament, and placed Acting Master R.S. Floyd in charge, with Midshipman Sinclair, instructing Mr. Floyd to anchor under the Rocas, 80 miles west of Fernando de Noronha, for the purpose of receiving from him his coal, which was of an excellent quality. I then proceeded on to this place, as it was necessary to have the facility of a machine shop for some important repairs.[272]

The *Florida*'s log for May 3 stated:

> Off Fernando de Noronha. At 9 a. m. the Florida came up with us. Got ready to be taken in tow. At 12:15 in tow of the Florida, heading for the island. Coaling the Florida. Lieutenant Averett, Dr. Grafton, and Acting Master G.D. Bryan were ordered back to the Florida. Acting Master R.S. Floyd took charge of the Lapwing.[273]

Because of the extent of the damage on the *Lapwing* and the crew's shortage of provisions, Richard had the ship burned on June 20, 1863, and they returned to the *Florida*.[274]

The ship was captured not far from Brazil on October 7, 1864. The ship's officers were paroled and the rest of the crew became war prisoners.[275] There are no records that Richard rejoined the service for what was left of the war.

## CALIFORNIA

With nothing left of the plantation life from before the war, Richard embarked on a journey to California in the late 1860s. He married Cora Augusta Lyons in 1871. Richard purchased Quercus Ranch in Lake County and in 1874 started to build a mansion he named "Kono Tayee."[276] Richard would live on through his work with the James Lick observatory on Mt. Hamilton, east of San Jose.[277] He died in October 17, 1890, in Philadelphia Hospital, of pneumonia. He was cremated and placed in Laurel Hill Cemetery, San Francisco, and then removed when the cemetery was destroyed. He is buried in Cypress Lawn Memorial Park, Colma, San Mateo County.[278]

**Richard Samuel Floyd (courtesy Lake County Historical Society).**

## FURTHER READING

Albaug, William A. *Confederate Faces: A Pictorial Review of the Individuals in the Confederate Armed Forces.*
Owsley, Frank Lawrence. *The C.S.S.* Florida: *Her Building and Operations.*
Sanderson, Marcia Bishop, and Maureen Garcia Carpenter. *Lake County.*
Wright, Helen. *James Lick's Monument: The Saga of Captain Richard Floyd and the Building of the Lick Observatory.*
Wyllie, Arthur. *The Confederate States Navy.*

# Robert Chester Foute

Midshipman and captain, Confederate States Navy
Major of artillery, Tucker's Naval Brigade, Mahone's Division
Born April 14, 1841; died July 28, 1903.

Chester Foute (known by his middle name) was one of the eight children born to

Dr. George Washington Foute and Mary Amanda Broyles in Greenville, Tennessee. In 1857 he graduated from Greenville College and entered the United States Naval Academy.[279] When the war came, Chester was the first to resign from the Academy in 1861 and was appointed midshipman in the Confederate navy on June 11, 1861.[280] He was assigned to the Savannah Naval Station between 1861 and '62. He was involved in the fight at Port Royal between Dupont's federal fleet and the Confederate ships and batteries in the area. Later, Chester was appointed senior midshipman to the CSS *Virginia*, the ironclad known as the *Merrimack*, and became captain of Gun #6.[281] Chester was aboard the *Merrimack* during her engagement with the *Monitor* in Hampton Roads on March 8–9, 1862. He wrote an article for the *Southern Historical Society Papers* in 1891 about his experience during the famous battle:

> In our first engagement with the Monitor, our magazines contained only shell and a few round shots for heating; as we were prepared to give battle to wooden vessels only, never once expecting to meet another "iron-clad" on our cruise around Hampton Roads. We went into the dry-dock at once. The one thing now for the "Virginia" to do was to destroy the "Monitor." We believed it could be done. But how? This was the question that occupied officers and crew on watch and off watch continually. What was to be done with the "Monitor"? Well, I'll tell you what we decided to do with her, capture her alive! With this express object in view, and for this very purpose, we organized a boarding party, consisting of four divisions, and each division assigned to its own special part of the work. Volunteers were called for to join in the undertaking. So daring was the enterprise regarded that no one was compelled to join in it.[282]

Chester went on to write:

> These two pioneers of modern naval warfare—the "Virginia" and the "Monitor"—never exchanged shots again, although within sight of each other for weeks. And a few months later they were both destroyed; the former having been burned by her own crew, and the latter foundering at sea off Cape Hatteras, on her way to Charleston.[283]

After this battle, Chester was promoted to lieutenant. He spent some time on the CSS *Georgia* from late 1862 to 1863.[284] In 1863, he was ordered to Liverpool, England, with other officers, for duty on ironclads then being built for the Confederacy on the Mersey River. He soon shipped out, heading back to the United States, running the blockade and landing at Charleston. On the way back out of Charleston, the ship was attacked by the U.S. cruiser *Rhode Island* and sank not far from the Bahamas. We pick up his story written in *The National Cyclopaedia of American Biography*:

> Escaping ashore, he was picked up after two days by a passing schooner, and carried to Bermuda, and sailed thence for Southampton via Havana on the steamer Trent, from which the Confederate commissioners, Mason and Slidell, had previously been taken by the U.S. government on the high seas. He remained abroad fifteen months, waiting for a vessel to be completed; but all of them being seized before getting to sea, he was ordered home at his own request. He sailed from Liverpool on the Cunarder Asia for Halifax, where he took the blockade runner Falcon, and ran the blockade into Wilmington. Ordered thence to Charleston to the steamer Chicora, for the defense of the harbor, he burned her on the evacuation of the city, in February, 1865, himself being the last man on board. Her officers and sailors were then formed into a naval brigade and transferred to Mahone's division, Army of Northern Virginia. Mr. Foute was placed in command at Drury's Bluff, just below Richmond, holding it until Gen. Lee's retreat. By a singular coincidence of nomenclature, the last stand made by his company was at the battle of Sailor's creek. On his way home after the surrender at Appomattox Court House, passing through Washington, Mr. Foute was arrested and thrown into prison, from which he was about two months later released through the influence of his friend, Mrs. Gen. Philip Kearny.[285]

## CALIFORNIA

Chester headed to Rome, Georgia, where his father's family had taken refuge. In 1866, Chester married Mary Stewart De Kantzow and the couple moved to Kentucky, where he took up tobacco farming. The couple soon returned to Rome, Georgia, where Chester prepared for the ministry in the Episcopal Church. In 1873, he was ordained deacon and appointed assistant to the bishop in Christ Church, Savannah.[286] Chester says, of this event, "It was a singular coincidence that in the same city where I began my career thirteen years before as a man of war, I should now have begun my new career as a minister of the Gospel of Peace."[287] In 1874 he was ordained as a priest; he served churches in Kentucky and Georgia. In 1884, Chester became rector of Grace Church, San Francisco.[288] He passed away in 1903 and was buried in Cypress Lawn Memorial Park, Colma, in San Mateo County.[289]

Robert Chester Foute (*Men of the Pacific Coast*, by Pacific Art Company, 1903).

## FURTHER READING

Campbell, R. Thomas, ed. *Voices of the Confederate Navy: Articles, Letters, Reports, and Reminiscences.*
Field, Ron. *Confederate Ironclad vs Union Ironclad: Hampton Roads 1862.*
Holzer, Harold, and Tim Mulligan. *The Battle of Hampton Roads: New Perspectives on the USS* Monitor *and* CSS Virginia.
Luraghi, Raimondo. *A History of the Confederate Navy.*
Marvel, William. *Lee's Last Retreat: The Flight to Appomattox.*
Quarstein, John V., G. Richard Hoffeditz, and J. Michael Moore. *C.S.S.* Virginia: *Mistress of Hampton Roads.*

# Edwin Augustus Garrison

Private and corporal, Company F (Claiborne Volunteers), 2nd Battalion, Mississippi Infantry
Sergeant and chaplain, Company F, 48th Mississippi Infantry
Born February 17, 1841; died April 18, 1894.

Gus, as he was known, was the son of cotton planter and slaveholder Thomas Garrison from Copiah County, Mississippi. His mother was Margaret Mulford Maul. Gus grew up on their plantation near Port Gibson. He studied at Elliot Academy in Mississippi, at Lebanon Academy in Ohio, and at Planters College in Port Gibson. Gus was licensed to preach in 1860.[290] When war came, Gus and his brother Frank considered joining. On September 12, 1861, Gus enlisted at Port Gibson, Mississippi, in Company F of the 2nd

Mississippi Infantry.[291] Frank enlisted in the 36th Mississippi Infantry and would eventually attain the rank of 2nd lieutenant.[292]

Dunbar Rowland's history of the regiment states:

> March 10, 1862, the companies of Mississippi Volunteers commanded by Captains J.R. Hampton and John Kelly, were ordered to join the battalion at Yorktown, and May 17, 1862, Capt. J.E. Martin's company, in the Fourth Tennessee, was detached and ordered to join the battalion. July 10, 1862, the unattached companies of captains J.H. Fields and Rogers, at Columbus, Miss., were ordered to Virginia to be added to the battalion and form a regiment. The battalion, including five companies, left the Rapidan for the James April 6. They were detached from any brigade, with the Second Florida under Colonel Ward, in Early's division, D.H. Hill's corps. April 19 they were reported as 275 effective, armed with Enfield rifles, under General Rodes, in the entrenched line near Yorktown. With the Florida regiment, under Colonel Ward, they made a brilliant sortie from the lines, dislodging the enemy from the Palmentary peach orchard. They evacuated that line May 4, and marched through Williamsburg May 5, but were called back by the Federal attack on Longstreet. The Second Florida and Second battalion were sent to the right of Longstreet's line and the rest of Hill's division to the left. The Second went into the fight at 5 p.m., under Colonel Ward, who was almost immediately killed. The battalion had 5 killed, 30 wounded and 6 missing.[293]

The regiment fought on during the Peninsula Campaign and the Seven Days Battles. With the addition of more soldiers, the battalion was designated a regiment in July 1862.

The son of a cotton planter and slaveholder from Copiah County, Mississippi, Gus Garrison still lived with his parents on their plantation, "Ottawa," near Port Gibson. He became a chaplain in 1863 (courtesy David M. Pierce, San Diego, CA).

Gus was promoted to corporal on August 1, 1862.[294] He was involved in a series of battles and marches from 2nd Manassas to Sharpsburg and Fredericksburg. Dunbar Rowland describes the losses in the three battles:

> In Wilcox's division of Longstreet's corps the brigade took part in the second Manassas campaign, in the battle of August 30, fighting in the vicinity of the stone house. The brigade loss was 26 killed and 142 wounded. The brigade took part in the capture of Harper's Ferry and the battle of Sharpsburg, but there are no official reports. The battalion loss was 5 killed and 55 wounded.... Before the battle of Fredericksburg the battalion was designated as the Forty-eighth Regiment (also for a time called the Forty-sixth), but it was yet unchanged at the time of the battle, and commanded by Lieut.-Col. Manlove. Major L.C. Lee was seriously wounded here, where the men were in line of battle three days, under artillery fire. Loss, 1 killed, 6 wounded.[295]

Gus received his second promotion as 1st sergeant of the company on November 30, 1862.[296] As both armies retired into winter quarters in December, two soldiers from each company of the battalion were granted leave to return home, and although Gus's number did not come up, he was detailed home to go after deserters on

February 7, 1863, during which time the battalion was enlarged and re-designated the
48th Mississippi Infantry Regiment.[297] Gus returned to the regiment by March. The regiment moved towards Chancellorsville, Virginia, in late April of 1863. The 48th fought
at Chancellorsville on May 1, 1863.[298] On May 24, 1863, Gus was presented a chaplain's
commission, which was the result of a petition written by members of the regiment and
approved by brigade command. He refused because he felt he was not initially commissioned as such.[299] In July, Gus fought in the Battle of Gettysburg. Dunbar Rowland tells
us the story of the regiment's fight in the battle:

> The regiment went into battle July 2 on the left of Wright's Georgia brigade, in that part of the
> field where their division, Anderson's of A.P. Hill's corps, attacked the Federal positions at the
> peach orchard and in the vicinity of Little Round Top. Wright reported that he drove the enemy
> from the crest of the ridge before him, a continuation of the Cemetery ridge that Pickett and Petti-
> grew could not carry the next day, and gained the key of the whole Federal line. "Unfortunately,
> just as we had carried the enemy's last and strongest position, it was discovered that the brigade on
> our right (Perry's Floridians) had not only not advanced across the turnpike but actually given
> away and was rapidly falling back to the rear, while on our left we were entirely unprotected, the
> brigade (Posey's) ordered to our support having failed to advance." Often there were such fatali-
> ties. Posey had been instructed by General Anderson to advance but two of his regiments and
> deploy them as skirmishers. When Wright advanced the Forty-eighth, under Colonel Jayne, advanced
> on his left. On the left of the Forty-eighth was the Nineteenth, which pushed up the slope until a
> Federal battery was within sixty yards of the right of the skirmish line. To go further without dis-
> lodging this battery was impracticable, and the dislodging of it occupied the regiment until dark.
> This may explain the failure to more closely follow General Wright. But the want of co-ordination
> was a strange feature of the battle for which the men were not to blame. The casualties were 6 killed,
> 24 wounded.[300]

After Gettysburg, with the unanimous consent of the regiment, Gus became chaplain. He continued to fight for the cause and preach at the battles of the Wilderness and
Spotsylvania in 1864. On November 21, 1864, Gus married his first wife, Mary Melissa
Curtis Hickey. They would have four children. In late 1864 and early 1865, Gus and the
regiment occupied the trenches of Petersburg.[301] On April 6, after retreating with the
Army of Northern Virginia into North Carolina, Gus was taken prisoner at Sailor's Creek
and sent to the Old Capitol Prison in Washington, D.C., on April 14, 1865. He was then
sent to Johnson's Island, Ohio, on May 11, 1865. He officially took the oath of allegiance
on June 14, 1865.[302] Upon returning home, Gus discovered that his brother Frank had
died of wounds while in federal hands in January 1865.

## CALIFORNIA

During the summer of 1865, Gus became a Methodist minister. The shortage of
money found Gus looking for work outside of the church. In 1870, Gus went back to
preaching and became a member of the White River Conference, then transferred to the
Southwest Missouri Conference in 1887.[303] His wife Molly died in 1871, and in December
1873, he married Susan Greenhaw. He would have four children with her. The family
moved to Clinton, Missouri, then on to the Denver Conference, after which he went to
Trinidad. In the fall of 1890, Gus was transferred to the West at Merced, California. In
1893, he came to Colusa to be the Methodist Church minister. He was only able to serve
one year as the Colusa Methodist minister, as he passed away at the age of 53 years. He
is buried in the Colusa Community Cemetery.[304]

FURTHER READING

Brinsfield, J., ed. *The Spirit Divided: Memoirs of Civil War Chaplains: The Confederacy.*
Brinsfield, John Wesley, ed. *Faith in the Fight: Civil War Chaplains.*
Dunbar, Rowland. *Military History of Mississippi, 1803–1898.*
Garrison, E. Augustus. *E. Augustus Garrison Journal 1861–1869.*
Giambrone, Jeff T. *Remembering Mississippi's Confederates.*

# George Washington Gift

Lieutenant, Confederate States Navy
Born March 1, 1833; died February 1, 1879.

George was born in Sumner County, Tennessee, one of the eight children of William Wirt Gift and Elizabeth Dodson. He entered the United States Naval Academy at Annapolis, Maryland, in 1846. He was later assigned as a midshipman to the Pacific Squadron in 1848.[305] The next year George's father moved the entire family to California. He became the federal land registrar for California based in Benicia.[306] William died in 1881 and was buried in Martinez, California.[307] George resigned from the U.S. naval service in 1852 and stayed with his family in California. He became involved in the banking business in Sacramento, California, and then moved to Southern California.

In February 1861, George and others formed the pro–Confederate Los Angeles Mounted Rifles.[308] For his disloyalty to the Union, George was hanged in effigy in Sacramento.[309]

Leaving the Rifles, he stayed with one of his sisters in Tennessee until he was commissioned a lieutenant in the Confederate navy.[310] George describes his experience on one of the many ships he was assigned to, the CSS *Arkansas*:

> In a few moments we see three gunboats round a point in full view, steaming towards us gallantly and saucily, with colors streaming in the wind. The ironclad Carondelet of twelve guns, commanded by Lieutenant Walke was on the right. The A.O. Tyler, the vessel that annoyed our troops at Shiloh, commanded by Lieutenant Gwin, my classmate, was in the center, and the unlucky river ram, Queen of the West, commanded by an army "mustang" named Hunter, was on the left. It was quite probable that they imagined we would take to our heels when we saw the odds, which were against us. They were mistaken. The gunnery of the enemy was excellent, and his rifle boats soon began to ring on our iron front, digging into and warping up the bars, but not penetrating. Twice he struck near my port, and still we could not see him. The first blood was drawn from my division. An Irishman with more curiosity than prudence, stuck his head out the broadside port, and was killed by a heavy rifle bolt, which missed the ship. When another member of the same gun crew was told to throw the headless body over the side, he replied, "Oh! I can't do it sir, it's my brother."[311]

George continued with the story of the CSS *Arkansas* fight:

> When I came on the scene again (not more than ten minutes had elapsed from the first gun), and ran out my gun, the Carmzdelez was right ahead of us, distant about one hundred yards, and paddling down stream for dear life. Her armor had been pierced four times by Grimball, and we were running after her to use our ram, having the advantage of speed. Opposite to me a man was standing outside on the port-sill loading the stern chaser. He was so near that I could readily have recognized him had he been an acquaintance. I pointed the Columbiad for that port and pulled the lock-string. I

have seen nothing of the man or gun since. We were now using fifteen-pound charges of powder and solid shot, which latter were hastily made in Canton, and had very little windage; so that I think we bored the fellow through and through from end to end. It was an exceedingly good thing we had. If his stern guns were not dismounted the crews had deserted them, for they were not used after my gun came into action the second time. I think I had hit four times, and our beak was nearly up to him, when Brady discovered that he was taking to shoal water with the hope of our grounding—we drew four feet more water than she. Therefore, we sheered off, and passed so close that it would have been easy to have jumped on board. Stevens passed rapidly along the port broadside, and saw the guns depressed to their utmost, and bid us wait for a good chance and fire down through his bottom. As we lapped up alongside, and almost touching, we poured in our broadside, which went crashing and plunging through his timbers and bottom. Although his four broadside guns—one more than we had—were run out and ready, he did not fire them. We were running near the left or Vicksburg side of the river (we are now in what is called Old River), and, as soon as passed, we headed for the middle of the stream, which gave Read his first opportunity—and right well did he use it. His rifles "spoke" to the purpose, for the enemy hauled down his colors. In an instant Captain Brown announced the fact from the deck. and ordered the firing to cease; but the ship still swinging, gave Wharton and the others a chance at her with the starboard guns before it was known that he had surrendered. White flags now appeared at her ports, and the news of our victory was known all over the ship in a moment.[312]

George's obituary in the *San Francisco Examiner* provides us with the latter part of his illustrious war-time escapades: "Chased by three Union iron-clads until the engine of his own vessel broke down, he succeeded in running her ashore, there landed his officers and crew, and then fired the train which blew her up, and cheated his pursuers of the capture and prize. With his men he escaped. Soon afterwards he was promoted to the charge of the Naval construction on the Chattanooga River in Georgia and there superintended the building of a fleet of iron-clads and rams."[313]

## California

After the war, George worked for the Arkansas Emigration Company, where his job was to bring Chinese workers back to the United States as cheap labor.[314] He returned to California in 1874 and became the editor of the *Napa Weekly Reporter* and *Napa County Recorder*.[315] He died February 11, 1879, and is buried at Tulocay Cemetery, Napa, California.[316]

## Further Reading

Armistead, Gene C. *California's Confederate Militia: The Los Angeles Mounted Rifles.*
Chaffin, Tom. *The H.L.* Hunley: *The Secret Hope of the Confederacy.*
Smith, Myron J. *The CSS* Arkansas: *A Confederate Ironclad on Western Waters.*
Wyllie, Arthur. *The Confederate States Navy.*

# Morris Greenwall

2nd lieutenant, Company A (Shepherd Guards), 10th Louisiana Infantry
Special and secret detective, Provost Department of Richmond Virginia
Private, Company D, CS Zouave, Louisiana Battalion (Coppens)
Born January 3, 1838; died March 13, 1885.

## 64   Greenwall

Morris Greenwall was born in New Orleans to Abraham and Frederica Greenwall.[317] When war came, Morris and his brothers enlisted. His brother Phillip was a private in the 5th Louisiana.[318] His brother Henry became a 2nd lieutenant in the 2nd Louisiana Militia.[319] Morris, who was working in his brother Henry's clothing store, enlisted in the Shepard Guards forming at Camp Moore on July 22, 1861.[320] He was commissioned 2nd lieutenant at the outset. The company joined others that day to become the 10th Louisiana Infantry Regiment, one of the few Zouave regiments in the Confederate army. Morris and his unit were then ordered to Yorktown on the peninsula of Virginia in defense against possible federal attack, which came in the form of McClellan's invasion. Once the unit reached Richmond, Virginia, Morris resigned his commission, which was authorized by Thomas Overton Moore, governor of Louisiana.[321] Morris may have had connections to the Confederate government, for he was assigned to the provost department in Richmond. He is listed as special and secret detective as early as December 1, 1862, on his pay sheets.[322] The job consisted of capturing deserters and investigating crimes through the confederacy, which was a major upgrade from his earlier investigative position with the provost department. Various correspondence during the war show how important his position was:

SIR: I have respectfully to acknowledge the letter of Secret Detective Greenwall, communicated by you with favorable indorsement.

The services of such a detective, to track out the professional substitute agents in their habitual frauds and the self-styled officers signing papers without commission or authority, and also to expose the criminal disregard of law and orders by company and regimental officers, whether moved by corruption, complaisance, or recklessness, might be eminently useful.[323]

One of his many adventures as a detective were written in *Southern Opinion* newspaper in 1867. Below is an excerpt:

One of those whom we believe suffered imprisonment wrongfully was Captain Greenwall, a young Englishman of the British service, who, like a few others of his countrymen, prompted by a love of adventure, or a real desire to aid the South, came over and landed at Charleston in 1863. Here he found employment in the corps of Topographical Corps of Engineers, but falling under the evil eye of suspicion, was arrested and forwarded to Castle Thunder. Here the writer made his acquaintance, and found him intelligent, and even learned to a degree only attained by the higher classes of English society. He was handsome as he was intelligent. He stated he had served in the Crimean and Indian wars, but unfortunately had nothing to support his professions save his own averments. A long confinement in the dreary Castle followed, varied only by his frequent examinations before the authorities. Nothing was proven, and he was discharged. But his proud spirits were broken; he was thousands of miles from home, penniless, and though his wants would, in a measure, have been supplied by entering the Confederate service, he had not the heart to aid in the defence of a Government that had so unjustly and cruelly suspicioned his first honest intentions, and injured his names and honor. Many is the time we have seen tears come into his fine eyes when any allusion to the subject of his treatment was made in his presence. In his great need he found a good friend in the late A. Judson Crane, of this city, who allowed him the use of a room in his office for a bed-chamber, and supplied him with money. He was a strange young man, and there was a mystery about him that he would not, and nobody else could, explain. One day an English advertisement appeared in one of the Richmond newspapers, calling for information of Captain Greenwall, and warning him, if that notice should reach his eye, to return to England immediately, as a fortune awaited him.—Whether this notice was the genuine emanation from his family, or whether it was a very clever ruse on his part, we never learned; but Captain Greenwald disappeared from his accustomed haunts, and we saw him no more.[324]

We can assume Morris was under cover and was perusing some heinous crime.

Morris remained as a detective through October 1863. Still remaining in Richmond, Morris was conscripted into the Confederate army March 31, 1864, and sent to the trenches of Petersburg.[325] On June 29, 1864, Morris is listed as absent without leave. He did not return to Confederate service.

## CALIFORNIA

Morris headed to Texas after deserting. He later joined his brothers Henry and Phillip in business in Galveston. The brothers invested in a theatre and became agents to stage actors, most notably Lilly Langtree. They expanded, opening theatres in Memphis and Houston as well as in other cities. Morris immigrated to Australia where he continued in the theatre business.[326] He is periodically mentioned in the newspapers of the time:

> Theatrical Notes. Chicago, January 18th.— Morris Greenwall, of California, left here for San Francisco via Portland today. He has engaged Dion Boucicault for a season of ten weeks in Australia next spring. He will play in Sydney and Melbourne, and will leave for Australia in April. Mr. Greenwall has also engaged Langtry for a ten weeks engagement in Australia next spring, but has nothing to do with the Calif, engagement.[327]

**Morris Greenwall (Library of Congress, Prints and Photographs Division, LC-USZ62–134040).**

On his way back to the States in 1885, he became sick and developed pneumonia. Arriving in San Francisco, he passed away on March 13. His obituary read: "GREEN-WALL—On Friday evening, March 13, Morris Greenwall, son of Abraham and Frederica Greenwall, of New Orleans, aged 31 years. The funeral will take place on Sunday, at 10 a.m., from the Occidental Hotel."[328]

Morris was buried in Salem Memorial Park and Garden, Colma, San Mateo County.

## FURTHER READING

Brooks, Thomas Walter, and Michael Dan Jones. *Lee's Foreign Legion: A History of the 10th Louisiana Infantry.*
Jones, Terry L. *Lee's Tigers: The Louisiana Infantry in the Army of Northern Virginia.*
Leavitt, Michael Bennett. *Fifty Years in Theatrical Management.*
Sifakis, Stewart. *Compendium of the Confederate Armies: Louisiana.*

# George Washington Gretter

Cadet 2nd lieutenant, Company B, Virginia Military Institute
1st lieutenant, drill master, Virginia State Reserves under General Kemper
Born June 11, 1845; died January 23, 1919.

George was born in Richmond, Virginia, to David B. Gretter and Martha Winn. In

1861 he entered the Virginia Military Institute and fought with the cadets at New Market.[329] In his book on the Battle of New Market, Jennings C. Wise describes the arrival of George and the cadets:

> The Cadet Battalion was deployed under cover of the rear crest of Shirley's Hill, by the left flank from the pike, and, moving out at double-quick, was soon in line of battle, with its right resting near the road, and concealed from the enemy by the crest of the hill in front. It was while in this position that General Breckinridge with his staff rode by and gave the Commandant of Cadets his orders to the effect that his command would form the reserve, and suggested that he dismount, as that was what all the field officers would do. The Commandant then took occasion to express his hope that the cadets, after so much marching and so many previous disappointments, would not be denied a chance to take part in the action. Whereupon, the commanding general said he did not wish to expose them unnecessarily, but would use them very freely, were developments such as to justify it.[330]

Major Harry Gilmore, a participant in the battle and an eye witness to the charge of the cadets wrote in his book, *Four Years in the Saddle,*

> At one time they advanced on a battery stationed on an eminence covered with cedars, and supported by a full regiment of infantry. They were going up in perfect line, the colors a little in advance. The battery, of four pieces, was pouring canister into them, and two color-bearers were knocked down. When within four hundred yards, the infantry rose and opened upon them. Major Shipp halted and ordered them to fix bayonets, which they did under a terrible fire. While doing this Major Shipp was knocked down by a piece of shell, and lay for a moment breathless, but almost immediately was on his feet, and calling out to the Cadets, "Follow my lead, boys!" started for the artillery, all of which he captured, together with a large part of the infantry, who said they felt ashamed that they had been whipped by boys.[331]

George made it through New Market and graduated from VMI. Upon his graduation, he was commissioned as 1st lieutenant and Drill Master in Richmond under General James Kemper in command of the Reserve Forces of Virginia.[332] George retained his position as drill master until the end of the war and took the oath of allegiance in Richmond on May 2, 1865.[333]

## CALIFORNIA

George moved with his wife to California in 1870, settling in Stockton. They eventually moved to Fresno and then on to the Pajaro Valley in Monterey County. They lived there until 1909, moving to Pacific Grove. He was a teacher in Monterey County for about fifteen years.[334]

An interesting story in the *Santa Cruz Sentinel* in 1879 gives us a story of George and an act of heroism: "PACIFIC GROVE—George W. Gretter, principal of the Pacific Grove Grammar School and chairman of the Monterey County Board of Education is the hero of the hour here, because of his action Monday, when the big public school building caught fire, Single-handed and with only an axe and an ordinary garden hose, he battled with the flames and finally controlled them, so that when the town fire department arrived it was an easy task to extinguish the fire.[335]"

George died in 1919 and was buried in Pioneer Cemetery, Watsonville.[336]

## FURTHER READING

Beller, Susan Provost. *Cadets at War: The True Story of Teenage Heroism at the Battle of New Market.*
Cocke, Preston. *The Battle of New Market and the Cadets of the Virginia Military Institute, May 15, 1864.*

Couper, William, ed. *The Corps Forward: The Biographical Sketches of the VMI Cadets Who Fought in the Battle of New Market.*

Gindlesperger, James. *Seed Corn of the Confederacy: The Virginia Military Institute at New Market.*

# Edward Higgins

Captain, Company I, 1st Louisiana Artillery
Aide-de-camp to Major General David E. Twiggs
Captain, 1st Artillery Regiment, CSA
Lieutenant colonel, 21st Louisiana Infantry
Colonel, Vicksburg River Batteries
Brigadier general, CSA
Born 1821; died January 31, 1875.

Edward's obituary in the *Daily Alta California* newspaper gives us a concise report on his early life:

> Captain Higgins was a native of Norfolk, Virginia, was educated for the Navy, and passed the necessary examination to enter the navy as a midshipman. He served in the navy during the Mexican War, and at its close came to California, being second officer in command when the United States took possession of Monterey in 1847. After that he went to New York and entered the merchant marine, and was placed in command of large ships plying between New York and foreign ports. At one time he was master of the steamer Vanderbilt, now the ship Three Brothers, and made the quickest trip on record on her between New York and Havre, the American residents at the latter port presenting him with a service of silver plate.[337]

When war came, Edward was living in New Orleans. He enlisted in Company I of the 1st Louisiana Artillery and was immediately appointed captain on April 12, 1861.[338] By August he was on detached service as aide-de-camp to General David Twiggs.[339] In early October Edward was detailed to organize a mounted battery.[340] He resigned from the 1st Louisiana Artillery on January 2, 1862, and within a month was promoted to lieutenant colonel of the 21st Louisiana Infantry.[341] Edward was captured on April 28, 1862, at Fort Jackson. Once he was released he gained another promotion, that of colonel and was assigned to the command of General Pemberton at Vicksburg, Mississippi.[342] Edward commanded the river batteries during the siege of Vicksburg.[343] He describes some of the action in this excerpt of his report on the battery's engagements during the siege of the city:

Edward Higgins (*The Photographic History of the Civil War*, vol. 10, by Francis Trevelyan Miller, 1912).

> On the evening of the 19th, the enemy's sharpshooters, having obtained possession of our abandoned line of

outer works, opened a fire upon the upper four-gun water battery, commanded by Maj. F.W. Hoadley, First Tennessee Artillery, thus rendering the battery temporarily untenable. Advantage was taken of the darkness of the night to construct traverses on the flank and in rear of the guns of this battery, and at daylight, there was ample protection afforded to the men while at the guns. The enemy also commenced feeling our batteries, and opened a heavy fire from three of his iron-clads upon Captain [W. C.] Capers' 10-inch columbiad, on the left of my line. Their fire was kept up for several hours, but without any serious damage.

At daylight on the morning of the 20th, the enemy opened fire upon the city and batteries with seven mortars placed under the bank of the river on the Louisiana shore. Three iron-clads also shelled the lower batteries at long range.

On the 22d, at 9 a.m., four iron-clads and one wooden gunboat engaged the lower batteries, and after an engagement of one hour and a half were repulsed. Two of the iron-clads were seriously damaged. This engagement was creditable to the First Louisiana Artillery, who, with ten guns, mostly of small caliber, contested successfully against thirty-two heavy guns of the enemy. Our casualties were only 2 wounded during the fight; one 10-inch columbiad and the 18-pounder rifled gun were temporarily disabled. The Blakely gun burst at the muzzle.

On the 23d, eleven of the light pieces on the riverfront were ordered to the rear, and were there fought by detachments from my command during the remainder of the siege.

From the 24th to the 26th, mortars kept up a steady fire upon the city and batteries. The 8-inch siege howitzer, one smoothbore 32-pounder, the 20-pounder Parrott, and the Whitworth gun were removed to the rear with their detachments.

Soon after daylight on the morning of the 27th, the enemy's iron-clad gunboat Cincinnati, mounting fourteen guns, was observed approaching our upper batteries, while four iron-clads approached the lower batteries. An engagement took place, which resulted in the complete repulse of the enemy, and the sinking of the Cincinnati in front of our guns, after an action of thirty minutes.

Great credit is due to Captains [J.P.] Lynch and [T. N.] Johnston, of the First Tennessee Heavy Artillery, for the handsome manner in which their guns were handled during the engagement.[344]

Edward was praised by General Pemberton for skillful execution of mission at Vicksburg:

> Hdqrs. Dept. Miss. and East LA., Vicksburg,
> May 27, 1863. Col. Edward Higgins,
> Commanding River Batteries in front of Vicksburg:
>
> COLONEL: It affords me pleasure to offer to you, and through you to your gallant artillerists, my grateful acknowledgments of your signal services against the enemy this day on the Mississippi River. In the assurance of his power, the enemy threatened our city of Vicksburg with five of his monster iron-clad gunboats, and seven of his powerful mortar batteries. You manfully worked your guns of the upper batteries against his force, and by your skill sank one of his vaunted champions of the river—the gunboat Cincinnati, carrying fourteen guns, turreted, causing the small surviving crew thereof to ignominiously fly to the distant shore in discomfiture· You drove, too, from their selected point of attack, by your lower batteries, four other iron-clad vessels, and soon after you caused silence to reign around the shore of our beleaguered city. By your gallantry and heroism today you have added to the garland of Vicksburg's victories another bright chaplet. May God speed you in your good work!
>
> Your friend and commander,
> J.C. Pemberton,
> Lieutenant-General, Commanding.[345]

Edward was one of the many Confederates captured at Vicksburg. He was exchanged a few months later and was promoted to brigadier general on October 29, 1863.[346]

He was to report to General Maury in Mobile, where he remained until the end of the war. Edward surrendered at Citronell on May 4, 1865, and was paroled on June 13,

1865.[347] Although he was paroled, he was not pardoned, and was on the list of Confederate officers that had not been pardoned. He wrote President Andrew Johnson:

> New Orleans July 7, 1865
> To His Excellency
> Andrew Johnson
> President of the United States
>
> Sir,
>
>    I have the honor to ask a release from my position as one of those excluded from the benefits of the amnesty proclamation.
>
> Very respectfully
> Edward Higgins
> Late Brigadier General CS Army[348]

It took a few more letters from prominent individuals for the president to react and pardon Edward.

## CALIFORNIA

We end Edward's story as we began, with his obituary: "Soon after the close of the war he returned to New York and found employment with an Insurance Company. About two years ago, on the recommendation of ship-owners in whose employ he had been, he was appointed Agent of the Pacific Mail Company at this port, which position he held for a number of months. Latterly he has been engaged in business as a stock broker. He was about 53 years of age, and leaves a wife and brother in this city."[349]

Edward was first buried in Mount Calvary Cemetery, San Francisco. When that cemetery was shut down, his remains were removed to Holy Cross Cemetery, Colma, California.[350]

## FURTHER READING

Bearss, Edwin C. *The Campaign for Vicksburg*, vol. 3.
Campbell, R. Thomas, ed. *Voices of the Confederate Navy: Articles, Letters, Reports, and Reminiscences.*
Confederate States of America War Department. *Official Reports of Battles.*
Derry, Joseph Tyrone. *Story of the Confederate States.*
Ericson, Peter. *Running the Batteries.*
Hearn, Chester G. *Mobile Bay and the Mobile Campaign: The Last Great Battles of the Civil War.*
Hewitt, Lawrence L., and Arthur W. Bergeron, eds. *Confederate Generals in the Western Theater: Essays on America's Civil War.*
Pierson, Michael D. *Mutiny at Fort Jackson: The Untold Story of the Fall of New Orleans.*
Porter, David Dixon. *The Naval History of the Civil War.*
Smith, Timothy B. *Champion Hill: Decisive Battle for Vicksburg.*
Warner, Ezra J. *Generals in Gray: Lives of the Confederate Commanders.*

# Horace Antonio Higley

Ordnance sergeant, 40th Alabama Infantry
Major, staff of General William Whann Mackall
Major, chief of commissary, General Braxton Bragg's staff, Army of Tennessee
Born May 29, 1928; died November 24, 1873.

Horace Higley, the eldest son of Horace Loomis Higley and Eualine Collins, was born in Pensacola, Florida. In the year 1849, when gold was discovered in California, he decided to head West to make his fortune. Horace was well educated and knew he could work as a surveyor while he pursued mining. In the 1850s he became surveyor of Alameda County. His fame as a surveyor grew, and he was soon elected surveyor-general of the State of California.[351] In Mary Coffin Johnson's book on the Higley family, she quotes a letter written by Andrew J. Moulder, mayor of San Francisco, concerning the popularity of Horace: "General Higley was well-known to all of the leading old Californians, and was universally admired by the women and beloved by the men. He was the very type of a high-toned Southern gentleman, the soul of honor, generous, and brave to rashness."[352]

When war came, young Horace and his three brothers all fought for the Confederacy. He left California in late 1861 and went back to Mobile, Alabama. Horace's brother John was colonel in the 40th Alabama Infantry, and Horace enlisted in the regiment on August 1, 1862, in Mobile and was made ordnance sergeant of the regiment.[353]

On February 2, 1863, Horace was promoted to major and ordered to report to General William Mackall as a member of the commissary.[354] On April 17, 1863, General Mackall was appointed chief of staff to General Braxton Bragg. It seems that he recommended Horace for a position on Bragg's staff, for Horace was made chief of commissary on April 30, 1863.[355] Horace was ordered on detached service to John Hunt Morgan's Division and accompanied it during the Battle of Salineville, July 26, 1863. Mary Coffin Johnson gives an account of Horace's capture:

> After General Morgan had started on his famous cavalry raid through Kentucky into Ohio, Higley was sent post-haste with instructions to overtake him and deliver orders from his commanding general. He came up with Morgan just after he had crossed the Ohio River. The Union forces were pursuing so closely that he could not get back to his command. He told me describing his adventure in stirring terms that he had an all night race for life. Morgan and his troops were captured, utterly worn out. Higley was taken prisoner among the number, and confined at Columbus, O. He complained bitterly afterward that he was not treated as a prisoner of war, but was treated as a felon, closely confined in a narrow cell and put on prison fare. Ladies who were friends of his family in Louisville, Ky., came to his aid cheered, comforted, and supplied him with luxuries.[356]

**Horace Antonio Higley (Alabama Department of Archives and History Q4295).**

On June 25, 1864, Horace was transferred to Hilton Head, South Carolina.[357] He was exchanged in Charleston on August 3, 1864. Given a 30-day leave, he left for his home in Mobile, Alabama. He seems to not have returned to the service and was paroled at Gainesville, Alabama, on May 14, 1865.[358]

## CALIFORNIA

By 1869, Horace was back in California. Two years later he married Sallie Phole. They would have no children. His health began suffer soon after his return to California, caused by heavy drinking during and after the war. He was taken to the Sisters of Mercy hospital in San Francisco on March 3, 1873.[359] He died at age 44 and was buried at Holy Cross Catholic Cemetery, Colma.[360]

## FURTHER READING

Blomquist, Ann Kicker. *The 40th Alabama Infantry: Confederate States Army.*
Crute, Joseph H., Jr. *Confederate Staff Officers 1861–1865.*
Martin, Samuel J. *General Braxton Bragg, C.S.A.*
Simmons, Flora E. *A Complete Account of the John Morgan Raid Through Indiana and Ohio, in July 1863.*
Warner, Ezra J. *Generals in Gray: Lives of the Confederate Commanders.*

# Henry St. George Lyons Hopkins

Assistant surgeon, 2nd Battalion, Virginia Artillery
Assistant surgeon, 3rd Battalion, North Carolina Artillery
Assistant surgeon, Richmond hospitals
Surgeon general, staff of General Daniel Ruggles (military prisons)
Born October 21, 1834; died May 25, 1914.

Henry Hopkins was born to attorney John Hopkins and Abby Byrd Hopkins on his family's estate near Winchester, Virginia. His grandfather was a colonel in the American Revolution.[361] Once Henry was of age he attended the University of Virginia; he went on to receive a medical degree from the University of Pennsylvania in 1855.[362] He later was employed by the government as a surgeon in the North Atlantic passenger service. Once this service was done, Henry worked as a surgeon in Philadelphia.[363] In 1860, he married Katherine Christina Brown, a woman of a wealthy Philadelphia family, and a child was born. When the war started, Henry headed to the South without them. A detective agent arrested Henry in a hotel in Annapolis, Maryland, and he was imprisoned at Fort McHenry as a state prisoner.[364] During his imprisonment, his wife filed for divorce, stating that he was a traitor to the United States and she was a loyal unionist.[365]

While in prison, Henry requested to be allowed to write his lawyer in reference to the divorce proceedings.[366] The marriage was annulled by the state. It may have been one of the first cases where an annulment was issued because of the couple's political sympathies. Because it was an annulment and this was the Victorian era, Katherine's reputation was at stake, for the child was considered as illegitimate. Therefore, Henry's father adopted the child as his own.[367] Henry was soon released and immediately again headed for the South. It is stated that he enlisted as a private in the 27th Virginia Infantry, but no record has been found of this. The first records on Henry list him as an assistant surgeon (appointed June 11, 1862) in the 2nd Battalion, Virginia Artillery, and then mention his transfer to the 3rd Battalion, Virginia Artillery.[368] During the Seven Days Battles in Virginia between June 25 and July 1, 1862, Henry is mentioned in the official reports:

> Of our medical staff, Surg. J.E. Page and Assistant Surgeons Greene, Perrin, Semple, Monteiro, and Hopkins were called upon for the exercise of their skill, and with exemplary fidelity devoted themselves not only to the relief of our own wounded, but to alleviating the injuries of other sufferers.[369]

He was also mentioned in the report of Major William Nelson, commanding the 3rd Battalion Artillery: "I cannot too fully express my thanks for and appreciation of the conduct on the occasions referred to of Surg. J.R. Page and assistant Surgeons Perrin and Hopkins; also Lieutenant Massie and my young aide Mr. R.R. Jones. These gentlemen all did much to excite my grateful remembrance."[370]

On January 16, 1863, Henry was transferred to the 3rd North Carolina Artillery Battalion as assistant surgeon.[371] This may have been just temporary, to assist the battalion's surgeons, since he is not listed on the muster sheets of the unit. Henry was relieved from this duty by Special Order 21, issued by the Confederates States medical director on April 15, 1863, ordering him to report to a surgeon Sutton in charge of a smallpox hospital for assignment to duty.[372] He was then sent to General Hospital No. 11 (also called Florida Hospital) in Richmond, Virginia.[373] Henry was relieved from that duty and ordered on July 13, 1863, to report to Surgeon R.F. Baldwin in charge of the general Hospital at Mt. Jackson in the Blue Ridge Mountains for assignment.[374] The stress of the war and multiple assignments was one of the reasons why Henry's name appeared on the hospital list for General Hospital No. 4 in Richmond, Virginia, on September 21, 1863, with "nervous debility."[375] Henry was given a furlough of 60 days beginning October 6, 1863.[376] By November 21, 1863, Henry was to report to surgeon John Wilkens in charge of General Hospital #21 in Richmond for assignment. He was still there as assistant surgeon on duty as of January 1864. On March 21, 1864, Henry relieved surgeon J.G. Cabell on duty with the ambulance committee of Richmond.[377] He had been in this position for only a month when he was sent to Hospital No. 21, at the Confederate military prison in Richmond.

Henry was ordered to the surgical reserve corps on May 5, 1864, and then re-assigned to the military prison hospital on May 29, 1864.[378] He was relieved from duty by the medical director on July 27, 1864, and was told to proceed immediately to surgeon W.A. Davis, at Mt. Jackson, for duty; he stayed there until September.[379] In October 1864, Henry was listed as belonging to the reserve surgical corps and by late November was back on duty at General Hospital No. 21, the military prison hospital in Richmond. On January 30, 1865, he was given a short leave of absence. By May 24, 1865, Henry was listed as staff surgeon general for General David Ruggles, head of military prisons in Augusta, Georgia, where he was paroled.[380] During his service for the Confederacy, Henry received the rare Confederate Cross of Honor.[381]

## CALIFORNIA

Henry practiced in Baltimore after the war and in 1866, married Katherine Dunnington. Four years later the couple had moved to Virginia City, Nevada. Henry eventually moved his

Henry St. George Lyons Hopkins (*History of Fresno County, California*, by Paul E. Vandor, 1919).

family to Oakland, Alameda County. Within two years his wife died, leaving Henry to tend to their four children. He married his third wife, Annie M. Foster, after moving to Fresno. Three more children were added to the family.[382] He lived in Fresno for the rest of his life and was buried at Mountain View Cemetery, Fresno.[383]

## FURTHER READING

Bergner, George. *The Legislative Record 1862: The Debates and Proceedings of the Pennsylvania Legislator.*
Sohn, Anton P. *Healers of 19th Century Nevada: A Compendium of Medical Practitioners.*
United States War Department. *List of Staff Officers of the Confederate States Army: 1861–1865.*
Vandor, Paul E. *History of Fresno County, California, with Biographical Sketches of the Leading Men and Women of the County Who Have Been Identified with Its Growth and Development from the Early Days to the Present,* vol. 2.

# Irvine Brothers: Landon C. Irvine and Robert Hugh Irvine

## Landon C. Irvine

Private, Kirkpatrick's Company, Virginia Light Artillery (Amherst Artillery)
Born February 6, 1842; died January 17, 1918.

## Robert Hugh Irvine

Sergeant and private, Company I (Amherst Rifle Greys), 19th Regiment, Virginia Infantry
Born May 24, 1840; died May 1, 1926.

Landon and Robert Irvine were born in Amherst County, Virginia, to John Rose and Lucy Hobsons Irvine. The couple had five children. John Rose Irvine was a merchant and farmer, born in Lynchburg, Virginia, in 1799. He passed away in 1867.[384] Robert Hugh Irvine and his brother Samuel Rose Irvine enlisted in the Amherst Rifle Greys on April 29, 1861, in Buffalo Springs, Virginia.[385] Robert was elected 4th sergeant of the company, and the boys were officially mustered into service on May 29, 1861, in Charlottesville, Virginia. The regiment would serve in every major battle involving the Army of Northern Virginia.

In March of 1862, Robert became sick and was sent to the hospital. It is not noted what he was suffering from, but he spent the next five months in there.[386] When he returned to the regiment, his rank had been reduced to private, probably because of the amount of time he had been absent. By June 1862 it was Landon's turn to enlist, and he joined the Amherst artillery battery on June 13, 1862, in Richmond.[387] The army was fighting McClellan at the time, and that same day, Landon was thrown into battle at Garnett's Farm. The fighting continued on June 26 and 27, with the battalion under fire all day on the 27th. This continued for the next two days.[388]

By September 1862, both brothers and their units had crossed the Potomac River into Maryland, leading to the Battle of Antietam. Meanwhile Landon and the Amherst

Artillery were guarding the Potomac River fords near Williamsport and Shepherdstown and did not fight at Sharpsburg. At this time, the unit had two 12-pound Howitzers and two 6-pounders.[389] By winter, the boys were in front lines of Fredericksburg, Virginia, with little fighting.

By early summer 1863 the Army of Northern Virginia was headed north in a campaign that would culminate in the Battle of Gettysburg. Robert left his unit and was assigned courier to Brigadier General Garnett in June 1863.[390] Landon was part of General Richard Ewell's 2nd Corps Artillery during the battle. The unit carried one 3-inch rifle and three Napoleons to the battlefield. Landon and the Amherst Artillery arrived in Gettysburg late on July 1, 1863. The next day the unit moved about several times and spent most of the day in the rear of Pennsylvania College.[391] By the afternoon, Robert and Garnett's brigade, Pickett's Division, had arrived, but they were told they were not needed that day. The boys' units were in close proximity to each other, and it was possible that they were able to meet on July 2.

On July 3, 1863, Robert, as courier to Brigadier General Garnett, was part of Pickett's charge. He wrote years later about the death of Garnett during the attack. His story is presented here in its entirety:

As an eyewitness to the death of General Garnett, I am able to give the attending circumstances and the reasons why his body was not identified and why his friends never knew what became of it. At the beginning of the War Between the States I was a student at Roanoke College, Virginia. Returning to Amherst County, where I was born, I joined a Volunteer company of that county which became Company I. 19th Virginia Regiment of Infantry. The commander of this regiment was Col. John B. Strange, who was killed in the battle of Boonsboro Gap, Md. September 14, 1862. I continued with my company and regiment until June, 1863, when the Army of Northern Virginia began its march to Pennsylvania. I was then detailed as a courier for General Garnett commanding one of the brigades of Pickett's Virginia Division.

In the early morning of July 3 the three brigades of the division—viz., Kemper's, Armistead's, and Garnett's—were moved forward in battle line into position on the slope of Seminary Ridge into an open field some four hundred yards in the rear of the Confederate batteries, occupying the crest of the ridge and a little more than fourteen hundred yards from the Federal battle lines on Cemetery Ridge. The aggregate strength of General Garnett's brigade that morning was not above fourteen hundred, of which only about three hundred came back from the battle.

The artillery duel, which began at about 1:30 p.m., lasted nearly an hour and a half. During this artillery fire the men lay on the ground flat on their faces under a broiling July sun, and many were killed and wounded by shell and shot.

An exploding shell in the ranks of the 19th Regiment killed Lieutenant Colonel Ellis, of that regiment, and a fragment of it slightly wounded me in the arm. During this fearful artillery combat General Garnett rode to and fro along the line of his brigade until induced to dismount. At the close of the artillery duel the advance began, Kemper's Brigade on the right. Garnett's on the left, with Armistead's close up on the left rear of Garnett's. The advance was made with spirit and in splendid order through open fields, obstructed at the Emmitsburg road by a post-and-rail fence, which the men were forced to climb in order to keep the line. General Garnett rode close behind his line of battle; and as it met the fire of the enemy and men fell, killed or wounded, he continually called out; "Steady, men! Close Up! A little faster; not too fast! Save your strength!" When within close musket range the Federal infantry delivered a tremendous volley, which struck down a very large number of men and killed, wounded and unhorsed the whole of the staff and couriers except General Garnett and myself, but wounding our horses.

The men in their headlong rush had reached the stone fence behind which the Federal infantry was posted and were driving and pushing them back, when I was ordered by General Garnett to rush to the rear and hurry up Armistead's men. Returning quickly from this mission, I was again at the General's side, the struggle still close and bloody. Discovering that the troops on the left of his brigade were giving way and the enemy flanking his brigade, the General ordered me to go to the left (he went to the right) and tell the officers to fall back. I was quickly back at his side, finding him within fifteen or twenty paces of the rock wall, a little to the right of the point of the angle known as the "Bloody angle" as we faced the enemy. Just as the General turned his horse's head slightly to the left he was struck in the head by a rifle or musket ball and fell dead from his horse, and almost at the same moment a cannon shot from a Federal battery on the right struck my horse immediately behind the saddle, killing him and throwing his body over the General's body and me upon the ground. Immediately springing to my feet, I dragged the body from between my horse's fore and hind feet, took the General's watch from his pocket, and gave it to Adjutant General Linthicum, who just then came up wounded and who said to me: "We had better get away quickly, or we will be killed or captured." We ran away as rapidly as we could but were halted as we went in aiding a wounded comrade, a former schoolmate of mine, to a ditch or depression in the ground where there was shelter. I hurried to the rear for a litter to remove General Garnett's body, but when I returned with the litter I found that the enemy had the ground, and I could not reach the body.

Since the war I met an ex–Federal soldier, Smith by name, who said he was a sharpshooter on the day of this battle and had shot General Garnett and that as soon as the Confederates retreated from the ground he went to the body and with his knife ripped from the General's collar his insignia of rank and took his sword.

In as much as General Meade refused us permission to remove our wounded and bury our men who died within his line, I have no doubt that, as all evidence of his rank had been removed, General Garnett was unknown to the Federal burial squads and that his body was undoubtedly buried near the spot where he fell in the common grave of dead Confederates who lay around him. Captain Linthicum, adjutant general of the brigade, was afterwards killed in the battle of Cold Harbor, 1864.[392]

Robert continued as courier for Brigadier General Eppa Hunton, the final commander of the brigade, until September 1864. Robert is listed as receiving a transfer to Company E, the Amherst Mounted Rangers of the 2nd Virginia Cavalry, on February 24, 1865, but no record exists of his muster sheet. Landon continued through the rest of the war with the Amherst Artillery. There is no record of his surrender.

## CALIFORNIA

After the close of the war, Landon moved to Pike County, Missouri, in 1867, and after four years moved to San Francisco, living there until 1872, when he moved to Washington State and farmed near Farmington. He married Adelia Ann Ladd on October 26, 1878, in Walla Walla. The couple had five children.[393] At some point, he left his family and moved to Kelseyville in Lake County, California. It is not known if he divorced; his wife was buried in Spokane, Washington. Landon died in 1918 and was buried in the Hartley Cemetery in Lakeport, Lake County.[394]

After the war, Robert married Sarah E. Russell. The couple had five children. They lived in Montana, where Sarah passed away. Robert and a few of his children later moved to Lodi, San Joaquin County. He passed away in 1926 and was buried in Harmony Grove Cemetery, Lockeford, San Joaquin County.[395]

## FURTHER READING

Gallagher, Gary W., ed. *The Shenandoah Valley Campaign of 1864.*
Hess, Earl J. *Pickett's Charge: The Last Attack at Gettysburg.*
Jordan, Ervin L., and Herbert A. Thomas. *19th Virginia Infantry.*
Sherwood, William Cullen, and Richard Ludlum Nicholas. *Amherst Artillery, Albemarle Artillery, and Sturdivant's Battery.*

# James C. Kane

Private, Company C, 1st Maryland Infantry
Private, Shank's Company, Virginia Horse Artillery (Pelham/Breathed)
Private, Company D, 43rd Virginia Battalion Partisans (Mosby's Rangers)
Born January 1842; died November 15, 1916.

James Kane was born into a prominent family of Baltimore, Maryland. His uncle, George Proctor Kane, was head of the Baltimore Police during the riots of 1861. George was imprisoned as a Southern sympathizer and eventually released. He would become mayor of Baltimore after the war.[396] The Kane family were pro-secession, and with the advent of war, James would do his part for the Confederacy.

James crossed over into Virginia and headed to Richmond, where on June 15, 1861, he enlisted for a year in Company C of the 1st Maryland Infantry.[397] On July 21, 1861, James fought in the first major battle of the war at Manassas. In his book on the Maryland Line, William Worthington Goldsborough wrote of the first combat of the unit:

> From high overhead of the command there came a screaming sound. None of the troops had ever before heard such a strange sound, but, as if by intuition, all knew that it was a shell, and for the first time felt what was really meant. "Bang!" "Bang!" went two more, and then they came literally in showers. It seemed as if that little brigade was the target for all the artillery of the Union Army. Then it began to dawn upon the wondering men that the clouds of dust which they were raising on their march had told the Federals that Confederate reinforcements were moving to the front. And still General Smith rode grimly and sternly forward.
>
> Now rifle balls begin to "zip" on every hand, and many a man who had sworn never to bow his head at the sound of a bullet found himself doing so involuntarily; and there were some who, when they raised their faces in shame, expecting to meet the jibes and laughter of their comrades, found them all making a like obeisance.
>
> And now came a critical moment. The First Maryland was on the right of the advancing column, with General Smith riding silently at its head, when suddenly, as it entered a strip of wood, a fierce volley of musketry was poured into it at short range. General Smith fell from his horse desperately wounded, and several of the men in the First Maryland were also injured, Sergeant John B. Berryman, of Company C, being shot in the groin and rendered a cripple for life.
>
> This was the First Maryland's baptism of fire, but it never faltered. Instinctively, and as it seemed without an order, with steady precision, it calmly swung into line.[398]

James fought in two more battles, Front Royal on May 23, 1862, and Winchester on May 25, 1862, before his enlistment was up. William Worthington Goldsborough again describes the unit's actions at Winchester:

> Before daylight in the morning of May 25 the First Maryland was ordered forward by General Ewell to open the battle in his front. Colonel Johnson deployed a portion of his regiment as skirmishers, and steadily they moved through the darkness toward Winchester. But as the day dawned a fog arose so dense that objects could be seen only a few feet away. Not knowing where he was, and fearing that he might run into a superior force of the enemy, Colonel Johnson wisely assembled his men and ordered them to lie down in an orchard. And it was well he did, for when the fog lifted in a measure right in front of him, not over two hundred yards away, lay a large body of the enemy behind a stone fence. It would have been folly for Colonel Johnson to have attacked them with his little command, for it would have meant their destruction.
>
> But the spattering fire of musketry was heard on the left, and it was evident that Jackson was moving forward to the attack. Suddenly the fog disappeared entirely, and the sight that met the gaze of

the Maryland boys was, indeed, inspiring, although for the moment they were compelled to hug the ground closely for fear of being seen by the enemy, for they were completely isolated from the remainder of Ewell's command. In front of them, and off to their left was a long line of Federal troops drawn up on the outskirts of Winchester. Their skirmishers were falling back before those of Jackson. Suddenly there emerged from the woods a long line of Confederates. They moved with the most beautiful precision, although their trail was marked by dead and wounded men at every step. It was General Dick Taylor's glorious Louisiana brigade and the Tenth and Twenty-third Virginia.

Beautifully the line advanced upon the doomed Federals, and as the right of Taylor's Brigade brushed by the First Maryland, Colonel Johnson could remain a passive spectator no longer, and he led his Marylanders in the headlong charge along with the men from Louisiana and Virginia. The enemy could not withstand the attack, but broke and fled through the streets of Winchester in dire confusion, closely pursued by the victorious Confederates.[399]

James C. Kane (*left*) and his brother John as members of Company D, Mosby's Rangers (*Mosby's Rangers*, by James Joseph Williamson, 1909).

James had enough of the infantry and transferred to the artillery on June 1, 1862.[400] As a member of Stuart's Horse Artillery, James fought in all the battles of the Army of Northern Virginia through late 1864: Antietam, September 1862; Fredericksburg, December 1862; Chancellorsville, May 1863; Brandy Station, June 1863; and Gettysburg, July 1863. At Gettysburg the battery consisted of four 3-inch rifled guns and sustained 6 killed, 4 wounded and 10 horses killed or disabled.[401] James remained on the unit's roster until September 30, 1864. While in the valley, he had learned of the exploits of Colonel John Mosby's partisan rangers. His brother John was a member of the unit, and James applied for a transfer. He officially became a member of the rangers in Fauquier County, Virginia, on October 11, 1864.[402] James and his brother participated in raids by the rangers in late 1864 and early 1865 before being officially paroled at Winchester, Virginia, on April 22, 1865.[403]

## CALIFORNIA

Little is known of James's life after the war. He had gone west and by 1870 was living in San Francisco. He married Mary K. (last name not known) in the city. The couple had 8 children. His wife passed away in 1910.[404] James died in 1916 and was buried in the Holy Cross Cemetery, San Francisco. He was moved to Colma, San Mateo County, when the cemetery in the city was closed.[405]

## FURTHER READING

Alexander, John H. *Mosby's Men.*
Goldsborough, William Worthington. *The Maryland Line in the Confederate Army, 1861–1865.*

# John Kolb Law

Cadet lieutenant, South Carolina Military Academy, Class of 1863
Drill master, Beauregard's Corps, Army of the Potomac (Confederate)
Aide-de-camp to Colonel Evander McIver Law
2nd lieutenant, assistant enrolling officer, Conscript Department, Darlington District

Born January 19, 1841; died December 14, 1913.

John Law was born in Darlington County, South Carolina, to Ezekiel Augustus Law and Sarah Elizabeth McIver Law.[406] His grandfather, William A. Law, was a plantation owner in the county.[407] John was one of eight siblings; his brothers would also go on to fight for the Confederacy.[408] His brother Junius August Law became colonel of the 6th Alabama Infantry; Evander McIver Law became a brigadier general, and A.E. Law died in the trenches of Petersburg. Like his brother Evander, John became a cadet at the South Carolina Military Institute. When South Carolina seceded, he was one of the cadets man-

**John Kolb Law (*History of the State of California and Biographical Record of the Sacramento Valley*, by J.M. McGuinn, 1906).**

ning the battery on Morris Island, which fired the first shots of the war in January 1861 and stopped the federal steamship *Star of the West* from resupplying Fort Sumter.[409] John continued with his studies at the Academy and spent the summer of 1861 as drill master in the Army of the Potomac (Army of Northern Virginia) under General Beauregard.[410] By the summer of 1862 he was back in the field as aide to his brother Evander, then colonel in charge of a brigade in Lee's Army.[411] John participated in the Battle of South Mountain and Antietam on September 14 and 17, 1862. At Antietam, Law's Brigade advanced from the woods at the Dunkard Church early on the morning of the 17th. In his report General Law wrote:

Soon after daylight on the 17th, the attack of the enemy commenced. The battle had lasted about an hour and a half, when I was ordered to move forward into the open field across the turnpike. On reaching the road, I found but few of our troops on the field, and these seemed to be in much confusion, but still opposing the advance of the enemy's dense masses with determination. Throwing the brigade at once into line of battle, facing northward, I gave the order to advance.[412]

During their advance, John was hit by a Minié ball in the left ankle. He spent the next 18 months with crutches.[413] Evander reported, "The members of my staff—Lieutenant Terrell, assistant adjutant-general, Captain Kirkman, Lieutenant Law, of the Citadel Academy, and Private Smith, Fourth Alabama—as usual, performed every duty bravely and efficiently."[414]

John went back to school and graduated in the spring of 1863. At home recuperating, John applied for a position behind the lines:

Darlington S.C. Aug. 24th 1863
Major C.D. Melton Commandant of
Camp of Instruction Columbia S.C.

Dear Sir,

Having been disabled by a wound received in the Battle of Sharpsburg by a Minnie ball which went through my left ankle joint and thus rendered unfit for active service in the field and being desirous of serving my country in her present struggle for independence to the extent of my humble ability, I would be glad to obtain the appointment of enrolling officer for this district. My wound is still unhealed and requires constant care and attention but I feel able and willing to undertake the duties of the position which I seek, as I am a resident of this town and could remain near my home.

At the commencement of the present war I was a cadet in the South Carolina Military Academy of which institution I am a graduate. Not wishing to leave the Academy until I had finished the course of study prescribed, I did not join the army regularly but served on Morris Island when the state first seceded; was one of the party of Cadets who fired on the Star of the West; During my summer vacation of 1861 I served as Drill Master in the Army of the Potomac under Genrl Beauregard; returned to my studies until the summer of 1862, when I again joined the army as aide to Col. (now Genrl) E.M. Law in which capacity I was serving at the time I was wounded. As to my conduct while in service I would refer you to Genrl Law's reports of the Battles of Boonsboro and Sharpsburg and as to capabilities to Genrl Law, the board of directors and faculty of the Military Academy.

Hoping that these statements sufficient to procure
the appointment I remain yours truly John K. Law.[415]

On October 3, 1863, he was appointed 2nd lieutenant in the service of the Confederacy as assistant enrolling officer in the Williamsburg District South Carolina.[416] He remained in this position for the rest of the war. His biography states that he was made captain and commanded a mounted unit participating in repelling Potter's raid in South Carolina in 1865. No record exists of John commanding a unit.[417]

## CALIFORNIA

After the war, John studied law and practiced in South Carolina's supreme court, after which he practiced with his father.[418]

John and his wife, Mary L. James, moved to California in 1869, where John taught in private and public schools. The family moved to Merced in 1873, where he became county superintendent of schools. In 1876, he was elected district attorney; he served until 1878. John was elected superior court judge in 1890. In 1896, he was re-elected and served until April 27, 1900, when he resigned, going back to practicing law.[419] John died in 1913 and was buried in the Merced Cemetery District, Merced, Merced County.[420]

## Further Reading

Baker, Gary R. *Cadets in Gray: The Story of the Cadets of the South Carolina Military Academy and the Cadet Rangers in the Civil War.*
Bostick, Douglas W. *The Union Is Dissolved!: Charleston and Fort Sumter in the Civil War.*
Krick, Robert E.L. *Staff Officers in Gray: A Biographical Register of the Staff Officers in the Army of Northern Virginia.*
Sears, Stephen W. *Landscape Turned Red: The Battle of Antietam.*

# Leconte Brothers: John Eatton Leconte and Joseph Quarterman Leconte

## John Eatton Leconte

Major, superintendent, Nitre and Mining Bureau, CSA
Born December 4, 1818; died April 29, 1891.

## Joseph Quarterman Leconte

Major, chemist, Nitre and Mining Bureau, CSA
Born February 26, 1823; died July 6, 1901.

Much has been written on the LeConte brothers. Of Huguenot descent, the boys were born in Liberty County, Georgia, on the plantation of their father, Louis Le Conte.[421] Being of wealth, John and Joseph were well educated. Joseph graduated from Franklin College, University of Georgia, in 1841.[422] He later went to medical school in New York and then studied under the famous scientist Louis Agassiz at Harvard University.[423] In 1851, he was elected chairman of natural science at Oglethorpe University in Georgia.[424]

John studied under Alexander H. Stephens during his early education and began his college studies at Franklin College, the same as brother Joseph.[425] He followed in Joseph's footsteps and graduated from medical school at the same school in New York. After graduation he married in New York.[426] John later practiced in Savannah, Georgia, and then became head of the physics department at Franklin College. In 1855 he became head of the chemistry department in the College of Physicians and Surgeons in New York.[427]

During the war, both brothers worked for the Confederate Nitre and Mining Bureau at Columbia, South Carolina.[428] Though their biographies state that they were commissioned as majors, their muster sheets have them listed as 1st lieutenants for the duration of the war.[429] In Joseph's autobiography, he writes about his reasons for joining the cause:

> I felt that I must do something in support of the cause that absorbed every feeling. Just as I was asking myself how I could turn my scientific knowledge to some useful account, a large manufactory of medicines for the army was established in the suburbs of Columbia, and I was asked to be the chemist. I accepted, and for about eighteen months was engaged in the manufacture on a large scale of many kinds of medicine, alcohol, nitrate of silver, chloroform, sulfuric ether, nitric ether, podophyllin, etc. The whole army was supplied by this laboratory with all medicines, except those that could be had more easily by running the blockade.[430]

*Left:* John Eatton Leconte. *Right:* Joseph Quarterman Leconte (both photographs from *The Autobiography of Joseph Le Conte*, by Joseph Le Conte and William Dallam Armes, 1903).

He went on to say:

> My business was to test all nitrous earth, whether from caves or niter beds. My laboratory was that of the College, and I was given an accomplished analyst as assistant. In the summer I visited all the niter caves in northern Georgia, Alabama, and Tennessee, all the niter beds in South Carolina, Georgia, and Alabama, and the iron mines and blast-furnace at Shelbyville, Alabama.[431]

Towards the end of the war, Union general Sherman began his march through Georgia. Joseph left Columbia to retrieve his family. He writes in his autobiography:

> Then we heard that Hood had gone around to Sherman's rear and invaded Tennessee, leaving the door open to the south for Sherman to march through Georgia, from the mountains to the sea, an easy thing to do, since there was no force to oppose him. Next we heard that Hood's army had been met and shattered by Thomas and that the remnants were hastening to South Carolina again to get in front of Sherman. In the meantime his army was nearing Savannah and would certainly ravage the whole coast. My widowed sister, her two girls, and my own fourteen-year-old daughter were at Halifax, my sister's plantation, some thirty-five miles south of Savannah, with no one to protect them but faithful negroes. I hastened to their rescue, leaving Columbia on the ninth of December.[432]

Once back in Columbia, the brothers decided they had to leave for fear of the Union army headed in their direction. Joseph went on to say in his biography:

> Full of these sad tidings, I went to see my brother John, and found him and Captain Ashbell Green consulting about leaving at once. The military authorities had at last confessed that they could not hold Columbia, and had advised them to save what Niter Bureau stores they could. We decided to

go as soon as possible. By Mr. Davis's advice we packed all our valuables, manuscripts, lecture-notes, etc., and sent them to the Niter Bureau to go out with the stores, and then took a sad, heart-breaking leave of our families, commending them to the tender mercy of God, our common Father.[433]

Joseph went on in his autobiography about life just after the war and his attitude towards slavery:

As a result of the war I lost everything I had in the world, for, except the eight thousand dollars in bonds lost at the capture of the wagons, all my property was in lands and negroes. But this total loss did not in the least dishearten me; I did not lose a wink of sleep. This was partly because everybody else had suffered in the same way, partly because I felt sure that I could make my living somehow, partly, and perhaps chiefly, because I had always been oppressed by the ownership of slaves. Not because I felt any conscientious scruples about it, but because I felt distressingly the responsibility of their care; because I felt that those who own slaves ought personally to manage them, as my father did. This I could not do without sacrificing all my ambition in life and the health of my family. The income from my land, on account of its situation, had always been far smaller than its market value warranted, and I could at any time during the twenty years previous to the war have sold it and changed the form of investment with great advantage to myself. This I refused to do purely out of kindness to the negroes and because of a sense of responsibility for their welfare. By their emanci-pation, therefore, I felt that an intolerable burden had been lifted from my shoulders. To the aston-ishment of all my friends, I asserted that, although practically it might be and in this case undoubtedly was, the freeing of slaves was not necessarily any loss of property at all; that it certainly was not loss of property in the sense in which the burning of a house is. This was only saying that slaves were not property, chattels, in the sense in which other things are, and in fact they were never so treated in the South. The right claimed was to their labor and the change was simply from a slave-system to a wage-system. I contended that, if the labor remained reliable, the market value of the slaves would be transferred bodily to the land. For, I argued, under the wage-system, if the negroes were reliable, the income of the land would certainly be as great as ever. This was admitted. Now, the value of land, as of every other investment, is determined wholly by the income. Q.E.D. The great impoverishment of the South was due wholly to the complete disorganization of the labor as a nec-essary consequence of the sudden change.[434]

Joseph and John had little left in the South and were open to starting a new life.

## CALIFORNIA

An article in the *Mariposa Gazette* in 1921 speaks of the LeConte brothers' move to California:

Therefore when in September 1869, the University of California extended a call to Joseph LeConte and also to his brother, John LeConte both accepted and came west. The University of California had just been established as a University and John LeConte became acting president of the new institution. Both were closely identified with its progress and their character and ability gave power to the college which is now the largest in number of students in America. Professor Joseph LeConte was for 30 years professor of geology, botany and zoology, and it was in geology that he won fame as a scientist.[435]

Joseph died in Yosemite Valley on July 6, 1901.[436] He was brought back to Berkeley and buried in the Mountain View cemetery, Oakland.[437] In the memoirs of John LeConte, Joseph gives us an account of John's last years:

In June, 1889, his strength visibly failing, he was given a year's leave of absence for travel, recreation, and sorely needed rest. Unfortunately, on the eve of his intended departure for Europe, where he expected to visit personally his many correspondents, his wife was prostrated with protracted illness. For nearly a year he scarcely left her bedside, and only his tender, unremitting care nursed her back to life and comparative health. The opportunity of recreation was lost. Unrefreshed at the beginning of the session, August, 1890, he took up again the burden of duties, and would have been able to bear it to the end of the session, when it was arranged he would be permanently relieved, but an attack of la grippe easily overcome his weakened frame, and after an illness of a few days he died, April 29, 1891.[438]

John was buried in the Mountain View Cemetery, Oakland.[439]

## FURTHER READING

Anderson, Richard LeConte. *LeConte History and Genealogy*, 2 vols.
Donnelly, Ralph W. *Scientists of the Confederate Nitre and Mining Bureau.*
Green, Edwin Luther. *A History of the University of South Carolina.*
LeConte, Emma. *When the World Ended: The Diary of Emma LeConte.*
LeConte, Joseph. *Autobiography of Joseph LeConte.*
_____. *Memoir of John LeConte 1818–1891.*
_____. *Ware Sherman: A Journal of Three Months' Personal Experience in the Last Days of the Confederacy.*
Lucas, Marion Brunson. *Sherman and the Burning of Columbia.*
Trimpi, Helen P. *Crimson Confederates: Harvard Men Who Fought for the South.*

# John Wickham Leigh

Major, Company F and Company S, 4th Regiment, Virginia Heavy Artillery
Born July 11, 1825; died November 18, 1904.

John Leigh was one of 12 children born into the prestigious Leigh family of Virginia. On February 25, 1847, he was commissioned as 1st lieutenant and was breveted captain for gallantry in fighting guerillas at Paso Ovejas National Bridge and Cerro Gordo, Mexico, on August 10, 12 and 15, 1847. He mustered out on August 31, 1848.[440] By 1849, John continued his law studies in New York.[441]

Using the modern term, John was suffering from post-traumatic stress because of the war and needed a new start, so he went to California in 1850, arriving in San Francisco in July.[442] Still stressed and unable to work in the Mariposa County mines for a year, he returned to San Francisco and obtained work on the *San Francisco Herald*.[443]

Still restless, John quit journalism and became stock grower in Santa Clara County and then Monterey County.[444] In 1861, John married in San Francisco. When war came in the East, John felt he needed to serve his country again, since he considered Virginia home. He hired an agent, whose name is lost to the past, and headed back East with the notion that his wife would follow once the agent sold all of their property off; she would use the money to travel safely.[445]

Once back in Virginia, John wrote the Confederate secretary of war, volunteering his services and stating the experience he had in the Mexican War.[446] On May 15, 1862, John was appointed major of the 4th Regiment, Virginia Heavy Artillery.[447]

The regiment was formed that May to serve as either artillery or infantry. John and the regiment's first fight was at Seven Pines on May 31, 1862, where they retreated under fire, leaving the 5th Alabama vulnerable. The 5th Alabama started to take many casualties because of this. General Rodes, in his official report, said:

At this time a portion of the Heavy Artillery Battalion [serving as infantry] retired and, I regret to say, headed by their officers, took refuge in the ditches in front of the enemy's redoubt, a position from which I had much difficulty in dislodging them, when they were called upon to man the redoubt. It was evident that nothing could be effected toward an advance while the right wing of the brigade was so exposed.[448]

The battle ended McClellan's offensive on the peninsula. While in camp, John waited for news of his wife and the outcome of the sale of his property in California. Not hearing anything, he wrote a letter of resignation to George Randolf, then secretary of war for the Confederacy, on October 12, 1862:

> George W. Randolf Richmond October 12, 1862
> Secretary of war
>
> Sir,
>
> I find myself under the necessity of resigning the position, which I hold in the service of the Confederate states. When in December last I left the state of California for the purpose of rendering service to the C.S. Government. I made certain disposition of my property for the comfort of my wife who was unable at the time to accompany me I thought such was sufficient until I might be able to bring her to me. It was in my power as I imagined to maintain correspondence with San Francisco. In the interval the experience of the past eight months have proved the utter impracticality of this last plan. During the whole time I have been in the confederacy I have not received a single letter from my wife or the agent settled with the charge of my property. Once I found reason to believe when I crossed the line last month that the agent in question rendered no account either to my wife or myself. She is therefore now dependent upon her mother who cannot afford the charge. The property I might be coerced to give up if I could find means to convey my wife to me but that being myself on [illegible] the line there is no mode of accomplishing. My sympathies are deeply with the country in the struggle it is now engaged in but have to thus protest my reluctance to leave my colors under any pretext but I do not see how I can reconcile [illegible] with that care of my wife and child which nature demands of me. The latter no other person than myself can perform.
>
> Very respectfully your obedient servant
> Jno W. Leigh
> Major 4th arty[449]

On October 28, 1862, John was officially resigned from Confederate service by Special Order 252, issued by Secretary of War George W. Randolf.[450]

## CALIFORNIA

Returning to California, John reunited with his wife and went into the stock-raising business. He ended this work because of drought in 1863-64. John's first son was named after his half-brother Benjamin Watkins Leigh, who had been a major in the army of Northern Virginia and who was killed at Gettysburg on July 3, 1863, leading a charge on Culp's Hill. He is one of the only Confederates buried in the National Cemetery of Gettysburg.[451]

In 1865 John and his family went back to live in Virginia but soon left, preferring California. He soon gained employment with the *Stockton Gazette* as editor.[452]

In December 1868, the family moved to Monterey, where John ran the *Monterey Democrat*.[453] He also was appointed receiver of the United States Land Office in San Francisco by President Cleveland.[454] John died in 1904 and was buried in the Garden of Memories Cemetery, Salinas.[455]

## FURTHER READING

Elliott and Moore. *History of Monterey County, California: With Illustrations Descriptive of Its Scenery, Farms, Residences, Public Buildings, Factories, Hotels, Business Houses, Schools, Churches, and Mines: With Biographical Sketches of Prominent Citizens.* 1881.

Schroeder, Rudolph J., III. *Seven Days Before Richmond: McClellan's Peninsula Campaign of 1862 and Its Aftermath.*

Smith, Gustavus Woodson. *The Battle of Seven Pines.*

# Henry Schultz Lubbock

Captain, CSN Steamer *Bayou City*
Born April 2, 1823; died December 7, 1909.

Henry Lubbock was born in Charleston, South Carolina, to Henry W. Lubbock and Susan Lubbock.[456] He went to California in 1850 by way of the Isthmus of Panama, arriving in San Francisco with his brother William. William became captain of the steamer *American Eagle,* and Henry was chief engineer.[457] The vessel was sold after two years, and Henry headed east to bring out the steamer *Bay City.* Returning, the ship was scuttled in Rio de Janeiro. Henry then took over the steamer *Sophia,* running her until 1859.[458] Henry's obituary in the *San Francisco Call* gives us a condensed version of his service to the Confederacy:

> At the commencement of the civil war Lubbock returned to the south and enlisted in the Confederate army. He served on the staff of General Magrudcr and was in command of the Confederate gunboat Bayou City, —which attacked and captured the union gunboat Harriet Lane in Galveston harbor. Frank R. Lubbock, a brother of Henry L. Lubbock, was the Confederate war governor of Texas and was an aid to Jefferson Davis. He was captured with the president of the confederacy and was for a time in Fortress Monroe under sentence of death. Another brother, Thomas Lubbock, was the head of the Texas rangers and was killed in a battle with the union forces in Tennessee. Henry L. Lubbock was a personal friend of General Grant, and when his brother, the governor of Texas, was a prisoner in Fortress Monroe he besought the head of the union armies to assist him in obtaining a pardon for his relative.[459]

Henry, who was in command of the *Bayou City*, gave a complete report on the fighting at Galveston:

> "At last came the expected signal," says Capt. Henry S. Lubbock, "first from a heavy cannon, and then from smaller pieces. We could not mistake the clear ring of the little cannon, which we at once recognized as the Nichols guns. Then came the boom, boom, of the heavy guns of the enemy, telling plainly that the fight had begun. Our boys replied with a deafening rebel yell, and our vessels were at once put in motion and steamed briskly down the bay towards the hostile fleet." The Bayou City, in the van, was equipped with boarding planks, — one on the larboard and one on the starboard side, —under the special charge of Commodore Smith.
>
> "When within about two miles of the enemy, our gun was discharged without effect. The Lane was then engaged with a shore battery. She immediately paid attention to us, but we were not touched, and kept rapidly advancing. After one discharge from our cannon, it was again loaded. The shot, when rammed half-way down, stuck in the barrel. When the match was applied the gun burst, instantly killing Captain Weir and two of the gunners who were working it. The body of Captain Weir was found on the deck after the explosion; those of the men were doubtless blown overboard,

as they were nowhere to be seen. Unexpected and tragic as this event was we could bestow little attention upon it. We were now approaching the Lane at a lively rate of speed, high steam and a strong ebb tide sweeping us down the bay.

"When about 800 yards off, I shaped our course for the docks, abreast of which the Lane was anchored. I wished to run below the vessel, turn, and come up, with the tide against us; but perceiving there was too much risk in that movement, and being only about 500 yards from the Lane, I pointed the Bayou City directly for her. The swift current carried us past the Lane, the two vessels grazing, and our wheel-house being torn off. At the critical moment the guy-rope holding our grappling device was not cut, and to make matters worse it was cut when too late. As we drifted past the Lane our men poured a deadly fire into her, a perfect fusillade being kept up for about a minute. It was at this time that the casualties occurred on the Lane. We drifted down with one wheel fouled. This was soon cleared, and we backed into a slip, which enabled us to turn quickly, and we then headed for the Lane, with the current on our bow, and our boat, consequently, under complete control.

"By this time the Neptune (Captain Sangster) had come up to and in collision with the Lane in an effort to ram her, but without damage to the Lane. The Neptune, however, stove in her own prow, and, commencing to sink rapidly, drifted past the Lane and sunk near the wharf. In passing, Captain Harby, with his little brass pieces, fired away with no appreciable result. The infantry on the Neptune did not prevent the gunners of the Lane from discharging two twenty-pound Dahlgrens which she carried on the after-deck as stern-chasers, creating fearful havoc on the Neptune. The sinking of the Neptune left the Bayou City to battle single-handed with all the Federal vessels in the harbor. The Bayou City made a rush, under a full head of steam, for the Lane. When within easy rifle range the order was given 'shoot at will,' and our men opened a brisk and effective fire, and a moment later the sharp stem of the Bayou City struck the Lane, carrying away a three-inch wrought-iron brace attached to the guard-beam and hull, and cutting into the iron water-wheel of the enemy. At this time, while we were fouled with the Lane, the Owasco came up within 200 yards and opened on us with shrapnel. We lost one man killed by a shrapnel bullet. Quite a number of shrapnel burst on our decks, embedding balls in our engine frame, and our heater was broken. A ten-inch solid shot from the Owasco passed through the Lane's cabin, striking the water pitcher on the sideboard, and, coming out of the port window, struck the broken gun-carriage on the Bayou City's deck, and there remained. I called on Capt. J. Martin and his sharp-shooters to attend to the Owasco. One round from them and the Owasco retired. A white flag was then raised on the Harriet Lane, and immediately afterwards white flags were raised by the other vessels."[460]

The Confederates recaptured Galveston. General Magruder, in his official report of the battle, commended Henry and the others involved in taking the city:

The gallant Captain Wainright (Federal) fought his ship admirably. He succeeded in disabling the Neptune and attempted to run down the Bayou City, but he was met by an antagonist of even superior skill, coolness and heroism, Leon Smith, ably seconded by Capt. Henry S. Lubbock, the immediate commander of the Bayou City.[461]

The Trans-Mississippi Department, of which Henry was a part, was the last Confederate force to surrender, signing terms at Galveston on June 2, 1865.

## CALIFORNIA

In 1868, Henry returned to California, where he married Mary Haughout; they eventually had four children. He farmed in San Jose until 1871 and then ran the Flora Springs Water Works of Nevada. In 1876 they moved to Utah, living there for only a few years. They moved back to San Francisco when Henry was appointed superintendent of dock repairs.[462] His last position was supervising inspector of steam vessels, which he held until his death in 1909. Henry was cremated and buried in the San Francisco Columbarium, San Francisco.[463]

## Further Reading

Campbell, R. Thomas, ed. *Voices of the Confederate Navy: Articles, Letters, Reports, and Reminiscences.*
Cotham, Edward T. *Battle on the Bay: The Civil War Struggle for Galveston.*
Lewis, Oscar, Bailey Millard, and Lewis F. Byington. *The Bay of San Francisco*, vol. 2. Lewis Publishing Co., 1892.
Lubbock, Francis Richard, Cadwell Walton Raines, and William E. Howard. *Six Decades in Texas; or, Memoirs of Francis Richard Lubbock, Governor of Texas in War Time, 1861–63.* 1900.

# Egbert Joseph Martin

Lieutenant and captain, aide-de-camp to General Edward Johnson
Born 1842; died June 9, 1908.

The life of Egbert Martin, known as Joe by family and friends, was tough at the outset. He was born in Louisville, Kentucky, and moved to New Orleans as a child.[464] His uncles were Philip Johnson and Edward A. Johnson, who would gain fame in the war. Joe's father died after the family moved to St. Louis, Missouri. We first hear of Joe's appearance in the war in May of 1863 as serving on the staff of one of his uncles, Major General Edward Johnson.[465] Johnson was given the Stonewall division after the death of Stonewall Jackson at Chancellorsville. General Johnson immediately wrote the Confederate authorities, stating that he needed an aide-de-camp (ADC) and suggesting Joe for the position.[466] Joe remained by his uncle's side through the Battle of Gettysburg as a volunteer ADC. In an after-action report Johnson commended his nephew: "Mr. E.J. Martin, my volunteer aide-de-camp, rendered valuable service by his prompt transmission of orders."[467] On December 4, 1863, Joe was officially appointed ADC with the rank of lieutenant, backdated to July 1, 1863. Joe retained this position through the winter of 1863 and spring of 1864. During the Battle of Spotsylvania Court House, on May 12, 1864, Johnson was captured with most of his division and was imprisoned.[468] Joe was wounded in the leg and sent to the general hospital in Richmond.[469] He returned to duty on May 28, 1864. He was then granted a 30-day leave of absence on August 4, the day after his uncle was exchanged from prison. The two may have gone back to Salisbury Estate for rest and recuperation. The general was then sent west to join Lt. Gen. John Bell Hood's Army of Tennessee, where he commanded a division in the corps of Lt. Gen. Stephen D. Lee. Joe followed along as the ADC.[470] During the Franklin-Nashville Campaign at the Battle of Nashville, on December 16, 1864, Johnson was captured again.[471] He again spent months in a federal prisoner of war camp. Joe was paroled in May of 1865. Through correspondence between the general, still in prison, and Joe's mother, Joe found out that she was gravely ill and was at a curative spring in Elmira, New York. We are not sure what she was suffering from, but Joe wrote a letter from Richmond to the federal authorities asking for permission as a paroled prisoner to go to her side:

Richmond VA
May 1st, 1865
Brig. Gen. J.C. Kilton
A.A. Gen

General

I respectfully submit the following statement and ask that permission be granted me to visit the state of New York.

Two days since I received a letter from my uncle, Maj. Gen. Edward Johnson, who is a prisoner of war at Ft. Warner of which the following is an extract, "Since writing the other day I have received another letter from your mother—she is very unwell but better than when she wrote a few days before—she is still very anxious to see you. I shall write to her today and calm her anxiety in regard to yourself and assure her that every step will be taken in order to allow you to visit her, as soon as it is safe and the authorities will grant passports to visit the north. You had better apply to Gen Halleck for permission to visit your mother, stating all the circumstances that render it proper that you should do so, her illness and peculiar situation, her husband a prisoner for more than eleven months and she entirely among strangers. I know Gen. Halleck and I believe that if you will appeal to him with a candid statement of facts, he will allow you to visit your mother. Do all that an Honorable man can do to effect it, for your mother is ill, very ill and her anxiety to see you very great."

I called on General Halleck yesterday and he directed me to make my application in writing. My mother is in the Elmira Water Cure, New York. If permission to visit her is granted me I shall wear citizen's clothes in the north and conduct myself as becomes a prisoner on parole.

I am, General, Very respectfully
Your obd. Servt.
E.J. Martin
1st Lieut and A.D.C.
Paroled Prisoner[472]

It is assumed that Joe was allowed to go north and comfort his ailing mother. There is no record of the nature of her illness.

## California

At the close of war Joe moved to Brunswick, Georgia, and entered into partnership with General John B. Gordon, in the sawmill business. In Georgia, Joe became an alcoholic; he states in a testimonial:

My first drinking commenced in Georgia, where I was planting rice with General Gordon. That was in 1867. I did not drink during the war at all except that I might have taken a drink occasionally when I met with friends. My uncle would not permit liquor about his headquarters.[473]

It was many years before Joe became a reformed alcoholic. He went to New York and later to Colorado, where he thought a change of climate might help him kick the alcohol. He remained a year and married his wife, Helen W. Martin. They would have two children. The couple went to San Francisco in 1881. Joe became a manager at the Harbor Electric Light Company, which soon consolidated with the San Francisco Gas and Electric Light Corporation.[474] He made $3,000 a year at the job. Joe stated, "They wanted to make a contract with me for five years, giving me three thousand dollars a year, if I would bind myself not to drink during the five years. I found it was not such an easy thing to quit drinking."[475] He was an authority on electricity and was frequently consulted on such matters. Joe eventually took the family back to Virginia, to settle some land matters, and then to New York again.[476] They moved back to California, and Joe retired in Berkeley. Joe died in 1908 and was buried in Mountain View Cemetery, Oakland, Alameda County. If the reader would like to read the full testimonial of Joe Martin, Rev. Gross Alexander's book listed below is recommended.

## FURTHER READING

Alexander, Rev. Gross. *Steve P. Holcombe, the Converted Gambler: His Life and Work.* 1891.
Clemmer, Gregg S. *Old Alleghany: Life and Wars of General Ed Johnson.*
Gleason, Rachel Brooks, and Silas Orsemus Gleason. *Circular of the Elmira Water Cure.*

# John Edgar McElrath

Private, lieutenant, captain, and quartermaster, Company B, 3rd Tennessee Mounted Infantry
Captain and quartermaster, Allston's Brigade, Major General E. Kirby Smith's
Department of East Tennessee
Major and quartermaster, Tracy's Brigade, Carter L. Steven's 2nd Military District,
Lt. Gen. John C. Pemberton's Department of Mississippi and East Louisiana
Major and quartermaster, Stevenson's Division, Hardee's Corps, Army of Tennessee
Born January 2, 1844; died May 9, 1907.

John McElrath was born in Citico, Monroe County, Tennessee, to Hugh McDowell McElrath and Elizabeth Lowrey Morgan. He was a member of an illustrious family from Tennessee and was able to live a privileged life, becoming a student at Harvard.[477] In May 1861, John enlisted as a private in the 3rd Tennessee Mounted Infantry.[478] His father was a captain and assistant quartermaster in the same regiment (Hugh would be relieved on March 24, 1862).[479] The regiment was under General Edmund Kirby Smith's command. John and his unit marched to western Virginia, where they would "see the elephant" in a skirmish on June 19, 1861, at New Creek, West Virginia. At five in the morning, John and his regiment attacked the federal troops at the bridge over the Potomac.[480]

They were able to capture it and two artillery pieces, with one man wounded.[481] John's next battle was at First Manassas on July 21, 1861. In his after-action report, General Joseph Johnston wrote:

General E.K. Smith arrived with three regiments of Elzey's brigade. He was instructed to attack the

**John Edgar McElrath (McElrath Family Private Collection).**

right flack of the enemy now exposed to us. Before the movement was completed he fell, severely wounded. Colonel Elzey at once taking command, executed it with great promptitude and vigor. General Beauregard rapidly seized the opportunity thus afforded him, and threw forward his whole line. The enemy was driven back from the long contested Hill and victory was no longer doubtful.[482]

John was soon commissioned an officer in Company B. The Harvard College *Secretary's Report* gives a concise account of John's service:

He was elected, February 9, 1862, Second Lieutenant of his company; April 10, First Lieutenant; and, on May 14, Captain. He was appointed, June 1, Assistant Quartermaster, with the rank of Captain of Cavalry, and ordered to report to General Kirby Smith, and was assigned to the Cavalry Brigade, commanded by Colonel Benjamin Alston, and took part in Bragg's Kentucky campaign. On December 11, 1862, he was appointed Quartermaster, with rank of Major of Cavalry, and ordered to Vicksburg, and was in all the battles around that city, surrendering July 4.[483]

John was then reassigned to General Carter L. Stevenson's staff and served with him through the Vicksburg campaign. In Stevenson's report on the siege he commended John: "Major McElrath, acting quartermaster of my division during the siege, has placed me under many obligations by his ready anticipation of the wants of the command and his untiring energy in supplying them."[484]

John surrendered with Pemberton. He was paroled at Vicksburg on July 4, 1863, and was exchanged on September 11, 1863. He continued with the Army of Tennessee and was paroled on April 26, 1865.[485]

**John Edgar McElrath in uniform (McElrath Family Private Collection).**

## California

After the war, John began the study of the law and practiced in Cleveland, Tennessee.[486] On June 23, 1869, John moved from Tennessee to San Francisco, and continued his practice until 1887, when he moved his office to Oakland. On September 23, 1875, John married Elsie Ann Alden; together they had eleven children. In 1907 while visiting his family in Tennessee, he passed away. John was brought back to California, where he was buried in the Mountain View Cemetery, Oakland.[487]

## Further Reading

Davis, William C. *Battle at Bull Run: A History of the First Major Campaign of the Civil War.*
Groom, Winston. *Vicksburg, 1863.*
Hess, Earl J. *Kennesaw Mountain: Sherman, Johnston, and the Atlanta Campaign.*
Hughes, Nathaniel Cheairs. *Bentonville: The Final Battle of Sherman and Johnston.*
Trimpi, Helen P. *Crimson Confederates: Harvard Men Who Fought for the South.*
United States War Department. *List of Staff Officers of the Confederate States Army: 1861–1865.*

# Edward "Ned" McGowan

Major, Herbert's Battalion of Arizona Cavalry, CSA
Born March 12, 1818; died December 8, 1893.

So much has been written about Edward McGowan, known as Ned, that we can only give the essentials in this brief profile. We will let Ned do the talking:

> I was born in the district of Southwark in this city in 1818, and took quite a prominent part in politics at one time. In 1838, I was elected Clerk of the Moyamensing District of Philadelphia County and was re-elected to the same position for five successive years. In 1842, I was returned to the Pennsylvania Legislature, and in the fall of 1844 was appointed by Governor Porter Superintendent of the State magazine for the Eastern District of Pennsylvania. While one of the county members in the State Legislature I was one of those who voted to send James Buchanan, "old Buck," as we called him, to the United States Senate. Not long after this I became involved in a difficulty with a man named Bratton, State Printer, in the House while in session. I cut him with a knife. This naturally led to the loss of my seat. Not long after this I went to California, and while there got mixed up in the killing of James King of William by James P. Casey, at which time I was falsely accused of having passed to Casey a derringer. This was in 1856. Though I was entirely innocent in the matter, there is no reasoning with the blind fury of a mob, so that after remaining a long time in hiding, and after a number of hairbreadth escapes, for if the vigilantes had caught me my doom was sealed, I reached Sacramento and had a bill passed, unanimously, in both houses giving me a change of venue, and was acquitted of any complicity in the taking off of Mr. King. I afterward started a newspaper called the Phoenix, a sheet devoted to attacks upon the outlaws, who, under the name of vigilantes, had inaugurated a reign of terror in California. Life in California becoming unendurable, I went to Fraser's River, in British Columbia, at that time the scene of a tremendous mining excitement.[488]

Ned got in more trouble in British Columbia and headed back to California. He continues:

> I secured passage on a Sardinian schooner, the Giletta, but, thinking it unwise to return to San Francisco so soon after the late unpleasantness, was put off at the Golden Gate and remained three weeks at San Rafael. From there I went to Guaymas, in the Mexican State of Sonora, where I met Captain Stone, who afterwards distinguished himself in the Union and Egyptian armies. Stone was in command of a surveying party of forty men. Among other Americans who had drifted down there was Philemon T. Herbert, the California member of Congress who killed Keating, the Irish waiter at Willard's Hotel in Washington, for which he was afterwards acquitted, and my son, James McGowan. Pescara, the Mexican governor, was silly enough to take us for filibusters and gave Stone, with his party, and the rest of us forty days to leave the country. We stood not upon the order of our going, and I found myself, in 1859, in Arizona.[489]

When the war came, Ned and Phil Herbert organized the Arizona Battalion for the Confederacy. During the battle at Bayou Teche, the Confederates fought off the federal flotilla with a captured gunboat, the *Diana*, for hours. Ned continues the story:

> Just after the breaking out of the war Granville H. Oury, Phil Herbert and myself organized a battalion for service in the Confederate Army, under the auspices of General Sibley of Louisiana, who afterwards served in the army of the Khedive. Our service was as much naval as military. One company manned a gunboat we had on the Teche. Captain Semmes, a son of Raphael Semmes of Alabama fame, fought the battery.[490]

Thomas P. Ochiltree wrote an article in the *San Francisco Examiner* giving details of the fight:

The boat was absolutely riddled with shot and shell. The boiler had been smashed, and the escaping steam mingled with the smoke of battle. But above all was heard the voice of Ed McGowan calling upon his men to continue the fight. I went up to him and told him that General Taylor was of the opinion that if he could hold the passage half an hour longer he believed everything would turn out all right. It seemed then as though we were winning the battle. He said that things were in pretty bad shape but he would try. I said my further instructions to him were that when he found that he could no longer hold the position he was to blow up the boat, sinking it in midstream if possible, so as to obstruct the passage. He said he would do so, and I left him.[491]

Ned continues the story:

We were captured by Union vessels, but not until we had blown up the ship. Semmes, the first mate, I and sixty of our men were put on board a vessel and taken to New Orleans, where they kept us in close confinement in the old slave pen. The New Orleans ladies, who could see us from the street, made such a demonstration in our favor that we were transferred for safe keeping to the Custom House. After an imprisonment of two or three months we were notified that we were to be taken to Johnson's Island, and were put on board a steamer in charge of a detachment of Billy Wilson's Zouaves, who, I must admit, treated us very kindly. At Fortress Monroe we were transported to another steamer called the Maple Leaf. On the second day out, I communicated with Semmes and some of the others, and, managing to get possession of some arms, we overpowered the guard, consisting of a lieutenant and twenty men of a Pennsylvania regiment, and ran the vessel ashore about eight miles from Cape Henry light, but did not destroy the vessel. We arrived at Richmond with a maple leaf in our hats, and were at once returned to our commands.[492]

No records exist of Ned's oath of allegiance and parole at the end of the war.

## California

Ned tells the story of his life after the war:

After the surrender, I made a flying visit to Philadelphia. Lived several years in the City of New York, and, in 1875, drifted back to the Pacific Coast, as is usual with old Californians. I am now 71 years of age, and have, since a short time, lived in Washington, where I hold a position under the door-keeper of the House of Representatives. Of my Philadelphia relations Captain John McGowan, my eldest brother, 79 years of age, is on the retired list of the Revenue Marines, and my son, John McGowan, an officer in the United States Navy, is at the naval rendezvous in this city.[493]

Edward "Ned" McGowan (*Narrative of Edward McGowan*, by Edward McGowan, 1857).

Ned passed away in St. Mary's Hospital in San Francisco on December 8, 1893. He was buried three days later in Holy Cross Catholic Cemetery, Colma, San Mateo County.[494]

## Further Reading

McGowan, Edward. *Narrative of Edward McGowan.* 1857.

Miller, Edward F. *Ned McGowan's War.*

Witt, Jerry V. *Escape from the Maple Leaf: Including Roster of Confederate Officers on the Maple Leaf, and Discussion of System of Exchanges and Paroles.*

# Lewis David McKissick

Colonel, Confederate military governor, and provost marshal of Memphis, Tennessee.
Born March 17, 1828; died October 2, 1903.

Lewis McKissick was born in Henderson County, Tennessee. His mother died in 1836, and he and his brother went to live with his grandparents in Alabama. In 1841, the boys returned to Tennessee and went back to their schooling.[495] After graduating in 1850 Lewis taught school and studied law. Three years later, he was accepted to Cumberland University, and after graduating he was admitted to the bar of the supreme court of the state.[496] At this time, the assumption is that he became acquainted with and a close friend to Isham G. Harris, who would become war governor of the state and would figure prominently in Lewis's future. Lewis practiced in Lexington, Paris, Tennessee, and finally Memphis in 1857.[497] Just before the outbreak of war, Governor Isham G. Harris was an extreme advocate for secession, and it is assumed that once the state left the union he proceeded to put his friends in positions of authority. Lewis may have been recommended by Governor Harris to General Braxton Bragg, who was the military commander of Tennessee, for he was given the position of military governor and provost marshal of Memphis with the rank of colonel. It is not known when Lewis took the position, and records are scarce of his day-to-day operations. Some orders issued by Lewis did survive and are presented below:

Col. L.D. McKissick, Military Governor of Memphis, presumably acting under orders from the Department of War at Richmond, issued an order commanding the destruction of the vast surplus of sugar, molasses, and cotton which had been accumulated at Memphis. Cotton had no present merchantable value, the first grades of molasses only commanded 2 cents per gallon, one dollar per barrel of forty gallons; the best grade of brown sugar two cents per pound. The vacant commons on the bluff in front of the city was covered with molasses barrels; when the heads of the barrels were knocked out floods ran out in streams to the river like lava from a volcano. Cotton estimated at three hundred thousand bales were hauled to the suburbs and burned. Night was as lurid as flames could make it, and the day as hazy with the clouds of smoke as a fog on the river. These commodities would have been of vast utility to the population, the cotton alone commanded forty cents per pound the 6th of June, 1863, the day the city was taken by the Federals. The one hundred and forty millions of pounds consumed in that patriotic fire would have brought $54,000,000 to the city. The molasses and sugar destroyed would have increased the revenue to $75,000,000, all of which went up in smoke and ashes, on the idiotic idea that its destruction would cripple the North far more than it would injure the South.[498]

**Lewis David McKissick (courtesy the Kleinsorge-McKissick families).**

The Memphis *Daily Dispatch* wrote on May 22, 1862:

> The Provost Marshal has received instructions from the military authorities to require the Banks at Memphis to take Confederate notes as currency in the transactions of their business, and to arrest as disloyal all persons who refuse Confederate money in ordinary business transactions. These instructions the Provost Marshal will vigilantly and rigidly enforce.[499]

After the Battle of Shiloh, General Braxton Bragg declared martial law in Memphis. As the federal army came closer to Memphis, Lewis issued orders to remove all gold and monies from the bank in Memphis:

> Office of Civ. Gov. and Pro. Mar. May 27, 1862
>
> To the Cashier, Officers and Directors of the Union Bank at Memphis
>
>   Gentlemen, by command of General Beauregard, you are hereby ordered to place the books, papers and assets of your bank, in a condition to be removed from the city forthwith. They will be removed on a special train tomorrow evening
>
>   Yours, L.D. McKissick
>   Civ. Gov. and Prov Mars'l.[500]

Confederate forces eventually left Memphis, and the local government resumed control. On July 14, 1862, Special Order #14 was issued by General Grant, stating in part:

> All persons holding state, county, or municipal offices, who claim allegiance to said so-called Confederate government, and who have abandoned their families and gone south, would be given safe conduct to leave, upon application to the Provost Marshal of Memphis which was now a Federal officer.[501]

Nothing is known of what Lewis did after the taking of Memphis by the federals.

## CALIFORNIA

Lewis remained in Memphis after the war until 1879, when he moved west to California. He first lived in San Jose and later became a lawyer for the Pacific Railroad Company in San Francisco. His biography states:

> As a lawyer Judge McKisick [*sic*] has won an enviable reputation, and in society he is alike popular. A lover of classic literature and a student of various branches of knowledge as well as the science of law; always unselfish, kind and true; with a stateliness of manner that repels undue familiarity, and an earnestness of character that does not invite jesting, his society is sought and his friendship warmly appreciated.[502]

He died in 1903 and was buried in the Olivet Memorial Park in Colma, San Mateo County.

## FURTHER READING

Cottrell, Steve. *Civil War in Tennessee.*
Dowdy, G. Wayne. *A Brief History of Memphis.*
Hallum, John. *Diary of an Old Lawyer: Scenes Behind the Curtain.*

# Thomas Jefferson McQuiddy

Captain and major, Company B, 3rd Battalion Missouri Cavalry
Born March 6, 1828; died February 10, 1915.

Thomas McQuiddy was born in Woodford County, Kentucky, one of six children of John McQuiddy and Achsah Dale. His great-grandfather was a wealthy Virginian who had fought with George Washington. Thomas's grandfather left Virginia for Kentucky and settled in Woodford County.[503] About 1840, the family moved to Bedford County, Tennessee, where they farmed and raised stock.[504]

Thomas married Jane M. Ruth in 1847. They would have seven children before she passed away at the age of thirty-five.[505] By 1859 the family was living in Nodaway County, Missouri, where Thomas was made sheriff, holding the office until the beginning of the war. He raised a company and was made captain on January 29, 1862.[506] The company initially served as General Sterling Price's body guard. The battalion fought at Bentonville and Elkhorn tavern. The company was reorganized on May 15, 1862, and became Company B of the 3rd Battalion, Missouri Cavalry; Thomas was re-elected captain.[507] General Van Dorn dismounted all cavalry units before embarking for Memphis, Tennessee, around April 14. Thomas and his boys reluctantly gave up their mounts and left for Tennessee. On June 12, 1862, Thomas was promoted to major of the 3rd Battalion. The battalion's first major battle was at Corinth on October 3–4, 1862. The battalion was involved in the route of the federals on the first day and participated in the charge on Battery Powell on the second day. The battalion losses were 12 killed, 62 wounded and 26 missing.[508] Thomas received gunshot wounds to the arm and thigh and was furloughed for 30 days to recuperate. When Thomas returned to the battalion, he participated in the Vicksburg Campaign. The battalion did not do any more major fighting until May 16 at Champion Hill, where the unit lost 9 killed, 15 wounded and 15 missing.[509] Thomas and the battalion retreated to the defenses of Vicksburg, where they surrendered on July 4, 1863. Once furloughed, Thomas headed back to Tennessee, where he was captured. There are no records of his imprisonment and he never returned to the battalion. On September 15, 1863, he was dropped from the battalion rolls and labeled as a deserter.

## California

In 1866, Thomas married Mary J. Huffman; his first wife had passed away while he was in the service of the confederacy. In 1874 the family moved to Cali-

**Thomas Jefferson McQuiddy** (*History of Tulare County, California*, W.W. Elliott, 1883).

fornia and settled in Tulare County. He bought government land in the Mussel Slough District, and then more land from the Southern Pacific Railroad Co. In McQuiddy's biography, the full story is given of the problems that occurred. Southern Pacific made promises that

> upon securing title, the land should be graded at from $2.50 to $5 per acre, improvements made by settlers not to be considered in fixing the valuation. Relying upon the word of the railroad company, about two hundred and fifty families settled on the lands, which were then nothing but an arid sand plain, and cultivated them at an enormous expenditure of time, money and patience. Banding together in a common cause, they organized the Settlers' Ditch Company, diverted water from the Kaweah river, a distance of twenty miles, and in time witnessed the transformation of their desert home. In 1877 the railroad was built through, and in 1878 the company graded lands at from $5 to $45 an acre, thus completely ignoring its former promise. A spirit of intense bitterness prevailed among the settlers, and a league was formed to protect their homes and lands. The company, however, gave no heed, but secured indictments, in many instances evicting holders and selling to other settlers. Their spirit of vindictiveness and persecution resulted in the killing of seven men. May 11, 1880. During this affair Major McQuiddy was the means of saving the lives of United States Marshal Pool and land grader Clerk. Litigations continued through the courts until 1887, when the settlers were obliged to pay for their land according to the assessed value. Major McQuiddy was one of the foremost who exerted strenuous efforts for fair dealing, but he also was obliged to pay the exorbitant demand, and continued to live on his farm until removing to Hanford in 1889.[510]

Thomas lived on his ranch until October 1889, at which time he bought a house in the town of Hanford.[511] In 1915, he died at age 86 and was buried in the Hanford Cemetery, Hanford, Kings County.[512]

## FURTHER READING

McGhee, James E., ed. *Guide to Missouri Confederate Units, 1861–1865.*
Shea, William L. *Pea Ridge: Civil War Campaign in the West.*

# Thomas Richard Meux

Private and asstant surgeon, Company C, 9th Tennessee Infantry
Assistant surgeon, Company F and Company S, 34th Tennessee Infantry
(4th Tennessee Infantry)
Born August 6, 1838; died December 2, 1929.

Thomas Meux was born near Stanton, Tennessee, one of eight children born to John Oliver Meux and Anne P. Tuggle Meux. Thomas's father was born in Virginia in 1809 and raised in Huntsville, Alabama; he later moved to Tennessee.[513] Thomas received his schooling at the University of Virginia and in 1859 studied medicine at the University of Pennsylvania. He graduated in 1860 and started his practice back in Stanton and later in Covington, Tipton County.[514] On May 24, 1861, Thomas and his brother John W. Meux enlisted in Captain David J. Woods's "Southern Confederates"—Company C of the 9th Tennessee Infantry in Jackson, Tennessee—for 12 months.[515] Thomas and John would "see the elephant" at the Battle of Shiloh on April 6–7, 1862. On the first day, the regiment made a charge with Maney's 1st Tennessee. General Cheatham wrote in his after-action report:

> The Ninth Tennessee Regiment (Colonel Douglass) being at hand and having to this time suffered less than the others of the Second Brigade, was, with his (Maney's) battalion of the First Tennessee, selected to move forward with him across the field fronting the wood, while Colonel Cummings, Nineteenth Tennessee Regiment (properly of General Breckinridge's command, but which had been with Colonel Maney on his detached service during the morning), was placed to his right and between General Breckinridge and myself, with instructions to move forward in concert with the First and Ninth Tennessee. With these dispositions I pressed the final attack upon the position in question. Colonel Maney advanced his First and Ninth in excellent order across the field, and was so fortunate as to almost reach the shelter of the woods before the enemy opened fire on him. Pressing forward to this point, he ordered his line to lie down until a general fire from the enemy's line had been delivered, and then promptly resumed his advance. The next instant I knew (from the lively cheering in his direction) that his charge had begun and the enemy routed and driven by it.[516]

**Thomas Richard Meux (courtesy Meux Home Museum).**

Being a doctor in civilian life, Thomas helped attend to the wounded. Though not officially commissioned as a military surgeon, he may have assisted the regimental surgeons after the battle. He would continue in this capacity. John W. Meux died on June 25, 1862, in Tupelo, Mississippi, from wounds received at Shiloh.[517]

Thomas's surgical skills were tested at the Battle of Perryville on October 8, 1862. He was officially commissioned assistant surgeon to the regiment with the rank of captain on December 4, 1862, which was backdated to August 22, 1862, when he was unofficially performing surgeries.[518] On their way back south after treating the wounded at Perryville, Thomas and his fellow surgeons were arrested by federal authorities and held. The captives wrote a message to federal general J.T. Boyle, military governor of Kentucky, addressing their situation:

> Military Prison Hospital, October 29, 1862.
>
> General J.T. Boyle.
>
> Sir: We take the liberty of addressing you today to call your attention to a change in our situation, ordered yesterday by Doctor Head, medical director. Confederate surgeons, we were on our arrival here (on our way South from attending to our wounded in Perryville) arrested and sent to the prison hospital to be held (so we were informed) as hostages for a Federal surgeon said to be confined in Knoxville, Tenn. We are now to be sent to the military prison by order of Doctor Head. While we ask leave to doubt the truth of any Federal surgeon being confined merely for being a Federal surgeon, we would respectfully request of you if we are held as prisoners to be confined to some other quarters more comfortable to us as non-combatants and more suited to our condition. We will cheerfully give our parole of honor not to leave any premises or house you may confine us to, or give you bond here in the city if released on parole to return here in a specified time if the

Federal surgeon should prove to be confined. We respectfully request that if we are to be held as prisoners we be assigned quarters better suited to our condition than the military prison, provided we have to leave the hospital.

> Respectfully,
> K.C. Divine, J.M. Alexander, H. Hinkley, Brigade Surgeons. T.W. Leak, Surgeon. T.R. Meux, N.D. Phillips, J.S. Fenner, A.T. Clark, Assistant Surgeons.[519]

Their letter made its way up through channels, reaching one of the highest levels of authority, General U.S. Grant:

> Headquarters District of Memphis, Memphis, November 3, 1862.
>
>    Dr. J.B. Cowan, C.S. Army; Doctor Hinkley, C.S. Army; Doctor Phillips, C.S. Army; Doctor Clark, C.S. Army; Doctor Leak, C.S. Army; Doctor Divine, C.S. Army; Doctor Fenner, C.S. Army, and Doctor Meux, C.S. Army, are hereby permitted to proceed southward to the Confederate lines pursuant to instructions from Maj. Gen. U.S. Grant. They will proceed by the Hernando road today.
>
> By order of Major-General Sherman:
> J.H. Hammond, Assistant Adjutant-General[520]

Brigade Surgeon Alexander Hinkley wrote a letter to General Braxton Bragg afterwards, explaining what had taken place. He stated:

> We were referred to Colonel Dent, provost-marshal, who informed us we were under arrest and must go to the prison hospital "as hostages for a Federal surgeon who was reported to be confined in a dungeon at Knoxville, Tenn., on bread and water." We were courteously allowed by Colonel Dent to return to our friend's house to supper and report at the prison at 8 p.m., which we did, protesting, however, against our imprisonment. We were assigned beds in the hospital wards and ate at the surgeons' table. We found in the hospital as hostages like ourselves Surgeons Alexander and Leak and Assistant Surgeon Meux, C.S. Army, who had been confined to the prison but transferred to the hospital.[521]

Thomas wrote of his experience on the front lines at the Battle of Chickamauga in his memoirs after the war:

> While in the line of battle on the afternoon of the 19th, I rode along in front of my Regiment giving instructions to litter bearers. Emory Sweet called out, "Remember me today." I bowed and two hours afterwards he was brought to my field hospital all covered with blood, shot through the right cheek and shoulder as he was taking sight. I told him we could save his life, but he would lose his arm. And so he did at the shoulder where the ball went through. He lived to return home, and at the close of the war, married and raised a nice family of children.[522]

Thomas continued as assistant surgeon with the 9th until he was reassigned on May 31, 1864, to the 34th Tennessee Infantry, also known as the 4th Tennessee, which became the 1st consolidated Tennessee in April of 1865. He was discharged by surrender at Greensboro, North Carolina, on May 3, 1865.[523]

## California

On June 3, 1874, the doctor married Mary E. Davis in Brownsville, Haywood County, Tennessee.[524] Thomas decided to move his family to the Central Valley of California. In December 1887, the Meux family registered at the Southern Pacific Hotel in Fresno. Thomas purchased land in the city of Fresno and the family moved into the newly built house in January 1889.

Thomas established his medical practice in Fresno and served the community until his retirement. He died in 1929 and was buried in the Mountain View Cemetery, Fresno, Fresno County.[525]

## FURTHER READING

Broadwater, Robert P. *The Battle of Perryville 1862: Culmination of the Failed Kentucky Campaign.*
Cunningham, Horace Herndon. *Doctors in Gray: The Confederate Medical Service.*
Daniel, Larry J. *Shiloh: The Battle That Changed the Civil War.*
Fleming, James Rodger. *Band of Brothers: Company C, 9th Tennessee Infantry.*
_____. *The Confederate Ninth Tennessee Infantry.*
Goodspeed Publishing Co. *Haywood County History of Tennessee.* 1886.

# John Brown Moore

Captain and major, Company L (Calhoun Guards), Orr's 1st South Carolina Rifles
Born March 21, 1835; died November 22, 1926.

John Moore was born in South Carolina. He studied law at the University of Virginia, graduated, and started to practice law in Anderson, South Carolina. His wife was Clara J. Jones, a member of a wealthy Georgia family.[526] John answered the call of his home state of South Carolina when war broke out and enlisted on July 20, 1861, for three years or the duration of the war, just a few months after the surrender of Fort Sumter.[527]

He was immediately elected as captain of the Calhoun Guards because of his education level. The unit's first casualties in battle occurred at the Battle of Gaines's Mill on June 27, 1862, part of the Seven Days Battles. During the battle, the 1st Rifles attacked a battery but were repulsed by federal Zouaves firing on their flanks, which resulted in 81 killed and 234 wounded.[528] The battle resulted in a Confederate victory during the Peninsular campaign and Robert E. Lee's first victory as commander of the Army of Northern Virginia. John and the Calhoun Guards next fought at the Battle of Second Manassas (Bull Run) on August 28–30, 1862. Captain George Miller, commanding the regiment at the battle, gave these reports on the regiment's two days of action:

September 30, 1862.

Sir: In obedience to orders I hereby transmit a report of the part taken by the First South Carolina Rifles in the battle of Manassas on Friday, August 29:

On Thursday evening, August 28, the enemy were engaged by General Ewell on the turnpike leading to Centreville. Colonel Marshall, being in command of the regiment, which was in position on the unfinished railroad of the Independent line of the Alexandria and Manassas Gap Railroad, was ordered to his support, but before reaching the ground the battle had ceased; it was now dark. Having upon inquiry ascertained that our forces occupied the battle-field, the regiment was ordered to stack their arms and bivouac for the night.

Early the next morning (Friday) the regiment was ordered to take position on the above-named railroad some half mile in advance and to the left of the position occupied the evening previous. Having crossed the railroad and advanced some distance in the woods beyond we came suddenly upon the enemy, when a fierce engagement took place, which, lasted only a few minutes, when the enemy gave back. We were then ordered to the south side of the railroad, with instructions to hold that position during the day. Here we were repeatedly charged by the enemy and as often repulsed them, until 4 p.m., when the regiment was ordered to charge the enemy. Colonel Marshall gave the command, when he received a mortal wound in the head and expired in two hours. About the same time Colonel Ledbetter received a mortal wound in the left side. The command then devolved upon Capt. J.J. Norton, who conducted the charge and drove the enemy some distance beyond the railroad, when the regiment was ordered by him to fall back to its former position. Being informed by Acting Adjutant (W.W.) Higgins, (Company G), that I was the senior officer present, I took command of the regiment. The regiment was then ordered to the support of Colonel Simpson, of the Fourteenth Regiment South Carolina Volunteers, who occupied a position in the open field on the left, where we remained until after dusk, when hostilities had ceased for the night. The regiment was then ordered to the woods a few hundred yards to the rear, where it bivouacked for the night.

Enclosed you will find a list of the casualties of the day.

All of which is respectfully submitted by—

> G. Mod. Miller, Captain, Commanding First South Carolina Rifles.
> Col. J.W. Livingston,
> First South Carolina Rifles.[529]

September 30, 1862.

Sir: I hereby transmit a report of the part taken by the First South Carolina Rifles in the battle of Manassas on Saturday, August 30:

The regiment was ordered to a position some 400 yards to the left of the one occupied by it on Friday, with orders to send forward pickets some 200 yards in advance, then remain and watch the movements of the enemy. Constantly during the day our pickets were fired upon by those of the enemy and the fire returned. About 12 m. the enemy advanced in considerable force, driving our pickets back, when they were repulsed by McIntosh's battery, which was in position immediately in our rear. The regiment was then ordered to change its front by a left half-wheel and advance some 150 yards into the corn field, where we remained until after dark, when I was ordered to withdraw my pickets and retire to the old field in rear and bivouac for the night.

Casualties of the day: Killed, none; wounded, none.

All of which is respectfully submitted by—

> G. Mod. Miller, Captain, Commanding First South Carolina Rifles.[530]

On September 1, 1862, the regiment was again engaged in combat at the Battle of Ox Hill (Chantilly) in Fairfax County, Virginia. Captain Joseph Norton of the Rifles made this report:

It was a supporting regiment when the brigade was led into action, and as such about an hour by sun was marched in line of battle across the field to a hollow, and here halted and caused to lie down 30 or 40 yards in rear of the position at the fence which was occupied by the left of the Fourteenth and right of the Twelfth South Carolina Regiment. It remained in this position exposed to the enemy's fire a short time, until those two regiments were withdrawn and the enemy were found to be advancing on the position from which they had been withdrawn. Then, in pursuance of previous orders, the regiment rose, delivered a volley, and charged up the fence, and continued to fire upon the enemy, who kept up a brisk and well-directed fire with musketry and a battery. In the meantime a heavy shower of rain fell, which wet and prevented two-thirds of our guns from firing. In this condition, some half or three-quarters of an hour after taking the position, the regiment was retired about 100 yards into the wood in rear of its position, when other regiments of the brigade were held in reserve. It was not again engaged, but remained on the field until 11 o'clock that night. The principal loss sustained by the regiment was while in position at the fence. The aggregate carried into this action was 218 men and officers ... 3 killed, 24 wounded, and 1 missing. No field officer of the regiment being present, I, as senior captain, took command thereof, and was assisted in this action by Capt. G. McD. Miller, acting lieutenant-colonel, and Capt. John B. Moore, acting major.[531]

John and the Calhoun Guards went on to fight at the Battle of Antietam on September 17, 1862.

At the battle of Fredericksburg, the regiment was on the Confederate right flank and defended against George Gordon Meade's attack. The regiment was in reserve and not expecting an attack. The story unfolds in the history of the brigade:

Had not the enemy been as ignorant of our position as we of theirs, this knowledge might have come in time to give us an easy victory. But they, never dreaming of an obstacle, blundered on rapidly, until, all at once, they fell upon the Rifle regiment. They immediately opened upon the latter. These sprang to their arms to oppose them. But Gen. Gregg, who was rather deaf, not being able to see the true state of affairs, and anxious to prevent firing into the first line of our own troops, (who must, in reason, fall back over us before the enemy could reach us,) rode rapidly to the right and ordered the men to quit the stacks and refrain from firing. In fact, he rode in front of the line, and used every effort

**John Brown Moore as captain of the Calhoun Guards (courtesy South Carolina Library, University of South Carolina, Columbia).**

to stop them. By this time the Federal line was right upon the Rifles, and before one could scarcely reason, much less act, they precipitated themselves upon the stacks of arms. Then ensued a scramble and hand-to-hand fight. The issue may be easily conjectured. The Rifle regiment was, as a body, broken, slaughtered and swept from the field. Gen. Gregg was, of course, an object of note, riding, in full uniform, in front of the regiment. The enemy fired upon him, and he fell, mortally wounded through the spine. It is pretty well ascertained that the man by whose hand he fell met a speedy death at the hands of the brigade. The left company of the Rifles, under Lieut. Charles, and such men as could be rallied from the rout, closed upon the First regiment, which, with the other three regiments, Twelfth, Thirteenth, and Fourteenth, stood their ground. Gen. Hill says they stood firm as on parade! Sergt. Pratt, of Company B, Orr's Rifles, is mentioned as bravely rallying a squad of men, and fighting upon the right of the First regiment.[532]

The 1st Rifles did not see action again until May of 1863. On May 5, 1863, John was appointed major of the regiment. From late September 1862 through the spring of 1863, John suffered from chronic dysentery, being in and out of the hospital. It is not sure if he actually participated in Antietam, Fredericksburg or Gettysburg. He did fight with the regiment at Chancellorsville and finally resigned because of his debilitating condition:

Hart County GA
July 26, 1863

Col.

For over (10) months past I have had Chronic-diarrhea to such an extent as to render me unfit for duty during which time I have received about four months furlough on Surgeon Certificate of disability. The other portion of the time I have spent in hospitals at the regt. and with the exception of the battle of Chancellorsville I have done but little duty. I am still laboring under the same disease and have no hopes of a speedy cure.

I therefore offer the government my resignation to which I respectfully ask you to approve and forward.

Your Obt. Servt.
John B. Moore
Major, Orr's Regt Rifles S.C.V.[533]

John's resignation was official as of August 28, 1863. There are no other records indicating he served in any other capacity in the Confederate service.

## CALIFORNIA

After his discharge, John went home to his wife and children. Soon after the war, he entered politics. He was elected to the South Carolina Legislature. John fought a duel with E.B. Murray on September 15, 1885, a newspaper editor. The two fired at least five times at each other, with John being wounded slightly.[534] The men were charged, John pleading guilty to two counts and Murray pleading innocence per self-defense on count one and guilt on count two. John was fined fifty dollars on the charge of fighting with pistols on a public square and twenty-five dollars on a second charge—carrying a concealed weapon. Murray was fined twenty-five dollars on count two. The fight had been over whiskey, with Murray standing for total prohibition and John, the freedom to imbibe. Murray had the newspaper and was able to besmirch John's good name.[535] John left the South Carolina Legislature the next year. The family relocated to California, settling in Colusa, where John served as the justice of the peace for Colusa Township.[536] John passed away at the age of 91 years and is buried in the Colusa Community Cemetery, Colusa County.[537]

## FURTHER READING

Bigham, John Mills. "The 1st South Carolina Rifles: An Album of Officers in Orr's Regiment." *Military Images* 10, no. 3 (Nov./Dec. 1988): 23–27.
Burton, Brian K. *Extraordinary Circumstances: The Seven Days Battles.*
Crute, Joseph H., Jr. *Units of the Confederate States Army.*
Langellier, John. *Second Manassas 1862: Robert E Lee's Greatest Victory.*
O'Reilly, Francis Augustin. *The Fredericksburg Campaign: Winter War on the Rappahannock.*
Southern Historical Society, Southern Historical Society Papers, Vols. 27–28, "Orr's South Carolina Rifles," by J.W. Mattison, 1899.
Welker, David A. *Tempest at Ox Hill: The Battle of Chantilly.*

# George Washington Mordecai

Private, Company K, 1st Virginia Artillery
Private and corporal, 2nd Company, Richmond Howitzers (Watson's Battery)
Born April 18, 1844; died June 14, 1920.

George Mordecai was born to Augustus Mordecai, a tobacco trader and plantation owner, and Rosina Young at Rosewood plantation near Richmond, Virginia.[538]

When war came, George's brother John was the first to enlist in the 1st Virginia Artillery.[539] Though being only 17 and under age for military service, George was mustered into the 1st Virginia by special order of General Robert E. Lee on May 17, 1861.[540] By March of 1862, another brother, William, enlisted in the same unit.

Organized before the war as the Virginia Howitzers Artillery Battery, the battery was divided and formed three companies of the newly named Richmond Howitzers Artillery Battalion.[541]

The brothers were members of the second company. Though the companies of the battalion were considered as one unit, they rarely fought together as one.

George and his brothers fought at Big Bethel on June 10, 1862. This was the only time that the Richmond Howitzers Battalion fought as a unit during the war.[542] In the history of the Richmond Howitzers, William S. White, a member of the unit, recalled the battle:

> For nearly two hours the fight was confined to the artillerists almost exclusively, but so soon as the enemy came in musket range our infantry gave them a reception worthy of Southern hospitality. About this time one of Captain Brown's howitzers, the one in front and to the right of the main battery, became spiked by the breaking of a priming wire in the vent, and was rendered ineffectual during the rest of the engagement. By reason of this, three Virginia companies of infantry on the right front flank were in a measure unprotected, and were withdrawn by Colonel Magruder to the rear of the church.
>
> The New York Zouaves seeing the gun disabled charged upon the works in which this howitzer was placed, and our men retired slowly, discharging their pistols as they fell back upon the North Carolina infantry. Colonel Magruder immediately ordered Captain Bridges of the "Edgecombe Rifles" to retake the lost position, which 'tis said he attempted to do by himself, failing to order his company to follow him, in his eagerness to obey orders. But his company did follow him in gallant style and drove the Zouaves off at a double-quick. The two howitzer guns of Stanard's Third Company now coming up from the rear, under the command of Sergeant Powell and Lieutenant Edgar F. Moseley, were immediately placed in position, and again the battle raged. Major Winthrop, aid to General B.F. Butler, in command at Fortress Monroe, having come up with reinforcements wearing our badges, white band around the cap, made an ineffectual attempt to carry our works, and lost his life in the endeavor. After his fall the enemy fled in disorder, having also lost a valued artillery officer. Lieutenant Greble, who commanded his battery with great bravery. Badly crippled and much worse frightened, they now were in precipitate flight toward Hampton, hotly pursued by a small squadron of Virginia cavalry, who reached the field just as the fight ended. If Magruder had have had a thousand cavalry we could have taken the whole force prisoners. Our loss has been comparatively small—one killed and ten wounded, three of the wounded belonging to the Second Howitzers.[543]

Next, the boys fought at Second Manassas; they then were sent to Sharpsburg on September 17, but arrived after the battle. On November 9, 1862, George was appointed corporal. On December 13, 1862, the 2nd company fought in the Battle of Fredericksburg. Colonel J. Thompson Brown, commanding the battalion, reported:

Headquarters First Virginia Artillery,
December 10, 1862.

Captain A.S. Pendleton, Assistant Adjutant General:

Captain: In obedience to orders, I beg leave to submit the following report of the operations of my command in the late engagement before Fredericksburg:

About ten o'clock, Saturday morning, my batteries were ordered to a position in rear of Hamilton's house, ready to be called on as occasion might require. About twelve o'clock, by order of Col.

Crutchfield, I sent two Parrott rifles from Captain Poague's battery, under command of Lieutenant Graham, and two similar pieces from the third Howitzers, under Lieutenant Utz, to report to Major Pelham, on the right of the railroad. Shortly afterwards, I was ordered to send to the same point four other rifle guns, viz: two ten-pounder Parrotts and one brass rifle from second Howitzers, and one three-inch rifle from Captain Dance's battery, all under the command of Captain Watson, (second Howitzers). These eight guns were actively engaged, and suffered severely from the enemy's artillery and sharpshooters. I have to lament the loss on this part of the field of a gallant and most excellent officer, Lieutenant Utz, commanding third Howitzers. The ammunition of most of the pieces was exhausted before dark, and the pieces themselves withdrawn. Having obtained ammunition for the two rifles of the third Howitzers, I sent them back to the field, where they remained, in company with the three pieces of Captain Watson's battery, until about nine o'clock. About two o'clock, by order of Colonel Crutchfield, I placed in position, on the hill to the extreme right of our infantry line, the two twenty-pounder Parrotts of Captain Poague's battery. These two pieces, unaided, engaged the enemy's artillery, and afterwards opened upon the infantry. The exact range of the hill having been obtained by much previous firing, our loss at this point was heavy. Among the killed was Lieutenant McCorkle, a brave soldier and estimable gentleman. Later in the evening, Lieutenant Colonel Coleman brought up two howitzers from Captain Dance's battery, and placed them on the left of Captain Poague's pieces. Lieutenant Colonel Coleman was severely wounded at this point, but remained on the field until after dark. I fear I shall lose the assistance of this valuable officer for several months. Late in the evening, two pieces of Captain Hupp's battery, under Lieutenant Griffin, were ordered to the right of the railroad, and were successfully engaged with the enemy's sharpshooters. Captain Brooke's battery, although not actively engaged, was exposed to the enemy's fire on Saturday and Sunday. I cannot refrain from expressing my high admiration for the conduct of the officers and men of my command in the action before Fredericksburg. After marching all of the previous night, they came upon a field strewn with the wrecks of other batteries, and behaved in a manner which elicited the praise of all who saw them. I append a list of casualties: Lieutenant Colonel Coleman, wounded in leg. Poague's battery, six killed and ten wounded. Watson's second Howitzers, one killed and seven wounded. Smith's third Howitzers, three killed and three wounded. Dance's battery, none killed, two wounded. Hupp's battery, none killed, one wounded. Brooke's battery, none killed, two wounded, Total killed, ten. Total wounded, twenty-six.

I beg leave to call attention to the fact that but few of the shell for Parrott rifles exploded, owing to imperfect fuses. Respectfully submitted,

J. THOMPSON BROWN,
Colonel First Virginia Artillery.[544]

By February 1863, George was suffering from chronic diarrhea. He remained on sick leave from February 3, 1863, until the beginning of 1864. He did not fight with his unit at the battles of Chancellorsville or Gettysburg. George reported back to the Howitzers on April 24, 1864. On May 14, he was admitted to General Hospital #9 with a gunshot wound to the thigh that he had received at the Battle of Spotsylvania Court House.[545] Brother William reported the incident in his diary: "May 12.—Rainy. Hard fighting. The Yankees the attacking party. We had Davy Clarke, Joe Cocke, George Christian, George Mordecai, John E. Uett, Burnley, and Trent wounded. Left the field after firing all our ammunition."[546] The wound was slight, and George returned to the unit and followed to the end at Appomattox Courthouse.

## CALIFORNIA

George came to California in 1868, where he bought land in Fresno County; the land later became part of Madera County. His ranch consisted of 4,000 acres, with grain as the majority. George also raised stock, including cattle, sheep and horses. He married

Louise Dixon, and they had four children. George was elected to the state legislature and nominated as state senator but was not elected.[547] George died of a heart attack in 1920 and was buried in the private cemetery at his ranch in Madera, Madera County.[548]

## FURTHER READING

Bingham, Emily. *Mordecai: An Early American Family.*
Hartwig, David S. *To Antietam Creek: The Maryland Campaign of September 1862.*
Manarin, Louis H., and Lee A. Wallace. *Richmond Volunteers: The Volunteer Companies of the City of Richmond and Henrico County, Virginia, 1861–1865.*
Marvel, William. *Lee's Last Retreat: The Flight to Appomattox.*
Sears, Stephen W. *To the Gates of Richmond: The Peninsula Campaign.*
Wallace, Lee A. *The Richmond Howitzers.*

# Thomas Pleasant Nelson

Captain and major, Company G (Nelson Grays), 4th Mississippi Infantry
Born June 1, 1824; died January 1, 1910.

Thomas Nelson was born in Murfreesboro, Tennessee, and as a young boy moved with his family to Durand, Mississippi.[549] On August 24, 1861, Thomas enlisted at Grenada, Mississippi, in the 4th Mississippi Infantry for 12 months.[550] He was appointed captain of the company on the same date, and the men became known as the "Nelson Grays."

He and his men, along with the rest of the Fort's Donelson's defenders, surrendered the fort and became prisoners. Thomas is listed as being sent to Camp Chase, Ohio, and then with the other officers was sent on to Johnson's Island near Sandusky, Ohio, on April 17, 1862.[551] He was exchanged and proceeded with the regiment to Vicksburg, Mississippi. The regiment defended Vicksburg, fending off federal attacks and hunger until the surrender of the city on July 4, 1863.

The unit was surrendered and paroled on the same day, and on July 16, 1863, Thomas was promoted to major of the regiment.[552] The regiment went on to reinforce General Johnston's army in Georgia and fight in all of the battles in and around Atlanta. Thomas continued with the regiment through the fighting at Nashville, Franklin and Murfreesboro. In January 1865, Thomas had had enough of war and sent a letter of resignation to authorities in Richmond, Virginia:

**Thomas Pleasant Nelson (courtesy Morgan S. Blasingame).**

4th Mississippi Infantry January 21, 1865

Genl. S. Cooper, Richmond Va.

   Genl. I respectfully tender my resignation as Major of the 4th Mississippi regiment of infantry unconditional and immediate. The effective total of the regiment is only fifty seven (57) including one company detailed as provost guard and without that company forty two (42). Col Adair, the Col. of the regiment is absent at present but will be with the command in a few days. There are no charges against me. I am indebted to the Confederate States.

Genrl. Respectfully
Thomas p. Nelson Comdr. 4th Mississippi Infantry[553]

Either Thomas reconsidered or his resignation was not accepted, for he continued as major of the regiment. The muster sheets in March 1865 show the brigade commanded by Colonel Thomas N. Adair and the 4th Mississippi Regiment by Thomas. Thomas was captured and appears on a roll as a prisoner of war received at Ship Island, Mississippi, on April 16, 1865.[554] He was transferred to Vicksburg on April 28 and then New Orleans on April 30; he was exchanged on May 1, 1865.[555]

## CALIFORNIA

   In 1868 Thomas and his wife came to California, spending two months at Sonoma and then living in Fresno's Mississippi district, where many from that state had moved after the war.[556] He worked in the cattle and stock business and also entered politics on the county board. He was also elected under-sheriff.[557] In later years, Thomas talked about the war and in particular the battle of Franklin Tennessee: "At that fight were lost hundreds of the bravest boys that ever marched, many of whom I buried with my own hands, and I wept bitter tears over what seemed to me my own sons."[558] Thomas died in 1910 and was buried in the Mountain View Cemetery, Fresno, Fresno County.

## FURTHER READING

Knight, James R. *The Battle of Franklin: When the Devil Had Full Possession of the Earth.*
Massey, Steve. *Broken Sword: The 4th Mississippi Infantry at Fort Donelson and in Captivity.*
Massey, Steve, Rod Martin, and Charles Bradford. *Foremost: The 4th Mississippi Infantry in the Civil War.*
Richard, Allan C., and Mary Margaret Richard. *The Defense of Vicksburg: A Louisiana Chronicle.*
Rowland, Dunbar. *Military History of Mississippi, 1803–1898.*

# Edward and Patrick Noble (Father and Son)

## Edward E. Noble

Private and 1st lieutenant, Company G, 19th South Carolina Infantry
Major, 5th South Carolina Reserve
1st lieutenant and drill master, PACS
1st lieutenant and chief enrolling officer, 4th Congressional District, Abbeville

Born December 9, 1823; died April 14, 1889.

# Patrick Noble

Private, South Carolina State Troops, CSA
Born January 14, 1849; died October 2, 1920.

The Noble family were one of the prestigious first families of South Carolina, which included their relations, the Calhoun and Pickens families. Edward's father was Patrick Calhoun Noble, governor of South Carolina 1838–1840, who died while still in office.[559] Edward graduated from South Carolina College in 1844 and practiced law in Abbeville and Charleston.[560] He owned five slaves in 1850.[561] By 1860, he had nineteen, and his estate was valued at $29,000.[562] Patrick was the oldest of five children born to Edward and his wife Mary Means Bratton in Abbeville. He was a student when the war began. Edward, a supporter of South Carolina's secession, introduced a resolution calling for the state's separation: "Resolved, that in the opinion of the people of Abbeville district the election of Abraham Lincoln ... must be promptly and sternly resisted by the State of South Carolina and that the secession of the State from the Federal Union is the proper mode of resistance."[563] He was the second signer of the South Carolina Ordinance of Secession.

Wanting to do more, Edward enlisted as a private in Company G of the 19th South Carolina Infantry on December 19, 1861.[564] Within a month, he was promoted to 1st lieutenant on January 11, 1862, and was signing the roll as company commander with the rank of captain, though he had not been promoted to the captaincy.[565] Edward was relieved of command during the reorganization of the army. He went back to Abbeville, where he secured a major's position in the 5th South Carolina Reserve, which was activated for service from November 5, 1862, to February 1863.[566] With the end of the 5th's active service, he was again without a unit. He decided to use his political connections to gain a position:

> Camp of Instruction, Columbia South Carolina
> March 24, 1863
> Brig. Gen. G. Rains, Superintendent of Conscription
>
> Gen.
>
> Captain Edward Noble late of the 19th Regiment SCV was not re-elected in the reorganization of the army and becomes liable to conscription. He is an officer of great merit, a lawyer of eminence and a man of energy and general intelligence. He would be admirably suited for enrolling service as Congressional enrolling officer. He is willing to take the position with the commission of any grade the department may grant. I very respectfully ask that he be so commissioned and ordered to report to me.
>
> Col. J. Preston[567]

On March 30, 1863, Edward was appointed drill master under Colonel Preston at Abbeville. Within a few days, he was promoted again and was appointed chief enrolling officer of the 4th Congressional District, with his headquarters in Abbeville.[568]

Over a year later, Edward was in want of field duty and went to his brother-in-law for a position:

> Hdqrts, Bratton's Brigade
> August 5, 1864
>
> General,
>
> I have the honor to recommend and request that 2nd Lieutenant Edward Noble be appointed

# GREAT
# Mass Meeting

## AT ABBEVILLE C. H., S. C., NOVEMBER 22, 1860.

At a meeting of the citizens of Abbeville, held in the Court House on Wednesday the 14th inst., On motion Edward Noble, Esq., was requested to act as Chairman; and Capt. J. C. Calhoun was requested to act as Secretary. On motion of Dr. Wardlaw, it was

*Resolved,* That a mass meeting of the citizens of Abbeville District be held at Abbeville Court House on Thursday the 22d., to consult as to the course to be pursued by our District in the crisis, and that a Committee of twenty-one be appointed to make all necessary arrangements.

Distinguished Speakers have been invited to address the people on that day---Hon. Robt. Toombs, of Georgia; Hon. James Chesnut, Hon. James H. Hammond, Hon. M. L. Bonham, Hon. A. G. Magrath, Hon. W. F. Colcock, James Connor, Esq., and others.

A Band of Music has been engaged, which will play during the day, and also at night.

At a meeting of the Committee of arrangements, the following Resolution was adopted:

*Resolved,* That we recommend for the purpose of securing unanimity in the District, that the nomination of Delegates to the Convention should be made by the people of the District; and that in our opinion, the 22d Inst., the day of the Mass Meeting of the citizens, will be the best time to make such nominations.

| | | |
|---|---|---|
| Dr. J. J. Wardlaw, | J. H. Wilson, | D. F. Jones, |
| J. S. Cothran, | Wm. Hill, | R. A. Fair, |
| Hon. T. C. Perrin, | J. C. Calhoun, | S. H. Jones, |
| Col. J. A. Calhoun, | A. H. McGowan, | John Knox, |
| A. J. Lythgoe, | J. H. Cobb, | R. J. White, |
| Hon. A. Burt, | J. T. Moore, | H. W. Lawson. |
| R. H. Wardlaw, | W. H. Parker, | |

Committee of Arrangements.

Edward Noble was a signer of the South Carolina Ordinance of Secession and a Confederate officer. He retired to San Francisco (courtesy Phil Noble, Jr.).

assistant adjutant General and appointed to duty with this brigade. He is at present enrolling officer for one of the congressional districts of South Carolina. His appointment will bring into the
field again the services of a valuable man. Abbeville SC is his post office.

> I am General, with much respect your obedient servant.
> Jno Bratton, Brigadier General.[569]

It doesn't seem that Edward was granted the appointment, for no records exist of this
duty.

Meanwhile, Patrick had left school in 1865 and served with the South Carolina State
Troops until the close of the war.

## CALIFORNIA

Patrick finished his studies at Charleston College after the war and in 1868 traveled
to San Francisco.[570] He got a job with the Pacific Rolling Mill Company and eventually
was promoted to the general manager. In 1898, he took over the entire business and
remained president of the company until his death.[571] When Edward's wife passed away
and he decided to retire, he left South Carolina for California, joining his son Patrick in
the 1880s. Edward passed away in 1889 and was buried in San Francisco. When the San
Francisco Cemeteries were closed, his body was moved to Cypress Lawn Memorial Park
in Colma.[572] Patrick passed away in 1920 and was buried near his father.[573]

## FURTHER READING

Capers, Ellison. *Confederate Military History—South Carolina.*
Channing, Steven A. *Crisis of Fear: Secession in South Carolina.*

# William Newton Mercer Otey

Drill master, Richmond, Virginia
Private and 1st lieutenant signal officer, Graham's Company, Rockbridge Artillery
Chief signal officer, General Leonidas Polk's Corp, Army of Tennessee
1st lieutenant, Signal Corps, General Nathan Bedford Forrest's staff
1st lieutenant, Signal Corps, Department of Alabama, Mississippi and East Louisiana
1st lieutenant, Signal Corps, Army of Tennessee
Born April 15, 1842; died December 15, 1898.

William Otey, or Mercer, as everyone knew him, was born in Columbia, Maury
County, Tennessee, to J.H. Otey, the first Episcopal bishop of the state, and Eliza Davis
Pannill.[574] Mercer was educated at the Virginia Military Institute.[575] The cadets were called
upon to guard the hanging of the abolitionist John Brown. Mercer described the scene
in his later years for *Confederate Veteran* magazine:

> Our first awakening to war's rude alarms was in November, 1859, when two hundred of the corps
> cadets were ordered to proceed to Charleston, Va., under the command of Maj. T.J. Jackson, to pre-
> serve the peace and dignity of the commonwealth in the execution of John Brown. We were a merry
> crowd, and enjoyed it as youngsters naturally would under the circumstances. How little did we

dream of what was in store for us in so short a time! For three weeks we stood guard over the advance agent of emancipation, and on the morning of December 2, 1859, we were drawn up at the foot of the gallows and within forty steps thereof witnessed the hanging of John Brown, captured October 18, 1859, by United States marines under Capt. Robert E. Lee. He was tried October 29, 1859, by the laws of the United States, and executed by the officers of the State of Virginia.[576]

**William Newton Mercer Otey (*History of Nevada*, 1881).**

Mercer went on to say:

John Brown rode to the place of execution, where the gallows had been erected in an old sedge field about three-fourths of a mile from town, seated in an open wagonette and surrounded by an escort. Observing the military display of some two thousand troops ordered up by Gov. Henry A. Wise, he remarked to the sheriff that it was all unnecessary as no attempt would be made to rescue him or his associates. He mounted the few steps leading to the gallows platform with arms pinioned behind him, and after he bade the sheriff and Jailors good-by the death cap was adjusted, and at a signal with a handkerchief by Professor Francis H. Smith, Superintendent of the Virginia Military Institute, the drop was sprung, and after a few convulsive motions the body spun round two or three times. Soon all signs of life were extinct. The physician in attendance placed his ear to the chest, and, with finger on pulse, pronounced him dead.[577]

Mercer only spent two years at the institute before war broke out and the cadets were commissioned early. Mercer's first position was as a drill master for the new recruits coming into the Confederate service.[578] He then enlisted in Graham's Company of the Rockbridge Artillery on August 17, 1862.[579] Mercer gained a promotion to 1st lieutenant of the Signal Corps on October 10, 1862. On November 12, 1862, he was ordered to report to General Bragg for duty with General Leonidas Polk.[580] Mercer reported for this duty on November 30, 1862. He was soon promoted and from December 9, 1862, to August 19, 1863, he is listed as chief signal officer, headquarters, Polk's Corps, Army of Tennessee.[581]

On August 19, 1862, Mercer was relieved as chief signal officer and ordered to report to headquarters, Army of Tennessee, for further instructions and assignment. On November 2, 1863, he was relieved from duty in the Department of Tennessee and ordered to report to General Polk. Mercer remained on Polk's staff until March 7, 1864, when he was assigned to General Nathan Bedford Forrest's staff as a 1st lieutenant in the Signal Corps.[582] Mercer worked closely with Forrest and was responsible for the delivery of Forrest's orders:

Headquarters Forrest's Cavalry,
Jackson, Tenn., March 29, 1864.

Brigadier General J.R. Chalmers, Commanding Division:

General: The major-general commanding directs me to say that he desires you to assume command of your division, and to move with the same to Brownsville, Tenn., via La Grange, keeping in communication with him by courier-line to Salisbury. You will report to him the time that you will reach La Grange. You will bring only such wagons with you as may be necessary to transport your ammunition and cooking utensils. You will leave the Fifth Mississippi Regiment and Nineteenth Mississippi Battalion to scout the country in the direction of Memphis, and any movement of the enemy will be reported at the earliest moment.

Captain Rodgers will be allowed to proceed with the organization of his company, and when completed will report to Lieutenant-Colonel Crews. Six hundred prisoners are now in transit for Corinth, and you will keep an eye that no move of the enemy is made to recapture them; and in case of any such movement, you will use every exertion to prevent its accomplishment, and communicate the fact to me at this place, and to officers in command of the guard from this point to Corinth, or from Corinth to Tupelo.

I am, general, very respectfully, your obedient servant,
W. N. Mercer Otey[583]

On June 30, 1864, Mercer was transferred from Forrest's staff. Having been in the position of 1st lieutenant for so long, he requested a promotion on July 16, 1864. In the request, Mercer claimed to have been in the 1st Virginia Cavalry and to have been 1st lieutenant and adjutant in the 13th Arkansas Infantry. No record or muster sheets exist stating this was the case. Mercer did not receive the promotion and was ordered to report to General Taylor as lieutenant, Signal Corps, Department of Alabama, Mississippi and East Louisiana.

On October 29, 1864, Mercer was relieved from duty in the department and reported to the war department as per the orders of Lieutenant General Taylor.[584] On November 2, 1864, while in Macon, Mississippi, Mercer was ordered to General Beauregard, commanding the Military Division of the West, for assignment to duty with the Army of Tennessee, and he signed as a 1st lieutenant in the Signal Corps. After his report on December 1, 1864, no other record is found until his parole in 1865.[585]

## California

After the war, Mercer worked in the mercantile business in Memphis, Tennessee. In 1872, he moved to San Francisco, gaining employment with the *San Francisco Chronicle*.[586] In July 1878, Mercer moved to Virginia City, Nevada, and worked for the Yellow Jacket Silver Mining Company. Mercer married Geraldine Goger on June 22, 1876. The family moved back to the San Francisco Bay Area and resided in Oakland, where Mercer passed away, after an amazing life, in 1898 at the young age of 56.[587]

## Further Reading

Bradley, Michael R. *Nathan Bedford Forrest's Escort and Staff.*
Driver, Robert J. *1st Virginia Cavalry.*
Hughes, Nathaniel Cheairs. *The Battle of Belmont: Grant Strikes South.*
McMurry, Richard M. *Virginia Military Institute Alumni in the Civil War: In Bello Praesidium.*
Mitchell, Robert Raymond. *The Rockbridge Artillery, C.S.A.*
Parks, Joseph Howard. *General Leonidas Polk, C.S.A., the Fighting Bishop.*
Schraff, Anne E. *John Brown: We Came to Free the Slaves.*

# William Wood Porter

1st lieutenant and aide-de-camp to General George B. Crittenden
Volunteer aide-de-camp to General Polk
Volunteer aide-de-camp to General Beauregard
Captain and aide-de-camp to General Joe Johnston
Born September 8, 1826; died January 17, 1907.

William Porter was born in Orange County, Virginia, and moved to Mississippi as a youth. His biography gives us an account of his life before the war:

> [Porter] graduated from Centenary College, Mississippi, in 1845; studied law at Jackson, Mississippi, for two years, and was then admitted to practice in all the Courts of the State; entered at once upon the practice of law in Coahoma County, Mississippi; emigrated to California in 1850; in 1852 was elected District Attorney of San Joaquin County, California; after the expiration of the term of office, removed to Calaveras County, California; in 1855 was appointed, by the governor, County Judge of Calaveras County, to fill a vacancy; in 1856 was elected to the same office for a full term of four years.[588]

In June 1861, William was involved in a challenge to a duel with H.G. Worthington. William's friend Judge David Terry was to be his second, but the duel never happened.[589] When war came, William went back east to serve the Confederacy. On November 18, 1861, William was appointed aide-de-camp to General George B. Crittenden with the rank of 1st lieutenant.[590] Crittenden had been promoted to major general just nine days earlier.

Crittenden commanded the 2nd Division of the Army of Central Kentucky in 1862, but he was relieved on March 31 and arrested the next day on charges of drunkenness. William was out of a job. During the battle of Shiloh he volunteered as aide-de-camp for General Polk on April 6 and then as aide-de-camp for General Beauregard on the next day of the battle.[591] Beauregard had Crittenden released and restored to his position on April 18. William wanted a field position with the army, and on July 14, 1862, he applied for an appointment to command a battalion of sharpshooters, stating in his letter that he would prefer them to be Mississippians.[592] He did not get the position. Crittenden left the army, and William was without a position. On November 11, 1862, he wrote to Jefferson Davis seeking a position as minister of military courts. It was a long shot, but William had nothing to lose. Again he did not receive the position, and again he wrote the authorities in Richmond, this time on November 25, 1862, stating he had been without a position since Crittenden resigned:

> Richmond Nov 25th 1862
>
> General
>
> I have the honor of addressing you to ask to be appointed Major in the Adjutant & Inspector General's Department. I beg leave to state that I have been aid-de-camp to Maj Genl Geo B Crittenden for more than a year and by reason of his resignation am now out of the service. Permit me to call attention to the accompanying letter from Col L [illegible]. If deemed necessary I will submit other letters on my behalf.
>
> > Respectfully your Obt. Svt
> > W.W. Porter
> > Genl Cooper
> > Adgt & Inspt Genl
> > Richmond VA[593]

On December 12, 1862, William was appointed captain and enrolling officer at the Camp of Instruction in Brookhaven, Mississippi, and ordered to report to a Major Clark at that location. For some reason William felt he deserved a more prominent position at the camp, so on January 6, 1862, he wrote the authorities in Richmond requesting to be placed in command of the camp at Brookhaven. He did not receive the job. By July 19, 1863, William was on a leave of absence.[594]

We next find him writing from Meridian, Mississippi, on October 25, 1863, to the authorities in Richmond, stating that General Joe Johnston has recommended him as lieutenant colonel of a regiment being organized. This was the truth, for we do have the note written by Johnston:

> Walton Jany 17th 1864
> Maj Gen S D Lee
>
> Jackson
>
> I recommend Cap W.W. Porter for Lieut Col of Millers regiment. The Secty of War promised the appointment as soon as the regiment should be formed and reported at Richmond. This by telegraph to me.
>
> J.E. Johnston[595]

Three days later, letters were sent from Major Steede, commanding the battalion—which was forming into a regiment—protesting the possible appointment of William as lieutenant colonel of the new regiment. On January 31, 1864, a letter was sent from Major General S.D. Lee to Richmond stating that to give William command of the regiment would displace the current commanders higher in seniority than he. William gave up the hope of attaining this position and decided to write the authorities in Richmond about other positions in the field:

> Richmond Va. 8th Feby 1864
> Honorable E. Barksdale
>
> Sir
>
> I have been for some time reporting to Col. H.H. Miller, by order of Genl JE Johnston and recommended by Genl Johnston as Lt. Col. of the regiment to be organized. The war department telegraphed the general that I should receive the appointment when the muster rolls of the companies were received. The matter of the organization was committed to Genl SD Lee who formed the regiments of two battalions and three other independent companies. On account of such formation the Secy of war decided that the officers commanding said battalions should have precedence. There are other independent companies, which the Secy of war has directed Lt. Genl Polk to organize into regiments and I respectfully request that you will make application to the president to have me appointed a field officer in one of the regiments. I am anxious to be relieved from duty out of, and be placed in the field.
>
> Respectfully,
> Your Obdt Srvt W.W. Porter[596]

On February 25, 1864, William was in Richmond, applying to the secretary of war for an appointment as lieutenant colonel of a cavalry regiment; he stated that General Joseph Johnston strongly recommended it. By March, William was in Cahaba, Alabama, and still without a position; and he requested to be appointed a field officer in a regiment. Finally, on May 16, 1864, though not in command of combat troops, William was appointed aide-de-camp to General Johnston, Army of Tennessee.[597] Still wanting a combat field position, Williams wrote to Major General Melton at headquarters, Army of Tennessee, on August 2, 1864, stating that Major General Wheeler had recommended him as a judge of a military court for the cavalry being formed and that General Hood concurred. No record exists of William's gaining the position. This seems to be the last we hear of William until he was surrendered at Citronelle by Lieutenant General R. Taylor to General Canby, USA, on May 4, 1865, and was paroled on May 15 at Jackson, Mississippi.[598]

## CALIFORNIA

After the war William lived with his father in Jackson, Mississippi. He soon went to Mexico for a short time and returned to Jackson to practice law in 1866. That same year he married Elizabeth "Lizzie" Osborne Dabney. They would eventually have five daughters. In 1872, William and his family returned to California, settling first in Merced and later in Santa Rosa, where he continued the practice of law.[599] In October 1885, President Cleveland appointed him as associate justice of the supreme court of the Territory of Arizona.[600] In 1890, William retired to his home in Santa Rosa. He passed away in 1907. He is buried in the Santa Rosa Rural Cemetery, Santa Rosa, Sonoma County.[601]

## FURTHER READING

Drake, Rebecca Blackwell. *The Battle of Raymond and Other Collected Stories.*
Herringshaw, Thomas William, ed. *Herringshaw's National Library of American Biography.*
Sanders, Stuart W. *The Battle of Mill Springs, Kentucky.*

# Pressley Brothers: Harvey Wilson Pressley, James Fowler Pressley, John Gotea Pressley, and William Burrows Pressley

## Harvey Wilson Pressley

Williamsburg County Defense Force (old men and boys)
Born February 21, 1850; died 1928.

## James Fowler Pressley

Captain, Company E (Black Mingo Rifles), 10th South Carolina Infantry
Lieutenant colonel and colonel, 10th and 19th South Carolina Infantry
Born August 30, 1835; died February 13, 1878.

## John Gotea Pressley

Captain, Company E, 1st South Carolina Infantry (Hagwood's)
Lieutenant colonel, 25th South Carolina Infantry
Born May 24, 1833; died July 5, 1895.

*Left:* James Fowler Pressley (courtesy Bruce Tognazzini, great-grandson of Col. Pressley). *Right:* A native of South Carolina, Lieutenant Colonel John Gotea Pressley graduated from the Citadel in 1851. In 1860, he was a signer of South Carolina's Articles of Secession. He moved his family to Santa Rosa, where he is buried (courtesy Bruce Tognazzini, great-grandnephew of Lt. Col. Pressley).

## William Burrows Pressley

Cadet private, Company B, South Carolina Military Institute

Born October 18, 1847; died October 17, 1930.

Much has been written about the Pressley family and most of it by the pen of John Gotea Pressley. The family were of the privileged Southern planter society of the Williamsburg District near Charleston, South Carolina. Ten children were born to John B. Pressley and Sarah Gotea. Sons John, James and William benefited from a military education at the South Carolina Military Institute, now called the Citadel. John graduated in 1851 and went on to practice law.[602] In February 1854, he married Julia Caroline Burckmyer. The couple had ten children.[603] John was instrumental in the secession of South Carolina while representing the Williamsburg District in the state legislature.[604]

When war came, the Pressleys defended their way of life. All five of the Pressley boys fought for the South. Brother Hugh McCutcheon Pressley joined the 25th South Carolina Infantry.[605] John formed a company, which become Company E of the 1st South Carolina Infantry, on September 11, 1861.[606] He served as captain until April 23, 1862, when he resigned his position and was appointed lieutenant colonel of the 25th South Carolina Infantry on July 22, 1862.[607] John remained colonel of the 25th during the duration of the war. On May 7, 1864, near Petersburg, Virginia, he was wounded in the left arm just below the shoulder.[608] He received a furlough because of his wound, and because the rest of the brothers were off fighting in the war and his father had died in May 1863, he requested a discharge to handle his parents' estate, which he received.

The next oldest, James Fowler Pressley, was elected and commissioned lieutenant colonel of the 10th South Carolina Infantry on May 31, 1861.[609] James was promoted to colonel on April 26, 1863. During a charge against the federal batteries on the Georgia railroad near Atlanta, July 22, 1864, he was severely wounded. He never returned to duty with the 10th regiment.[610]

The next in line was William Burrows Pressley. When the war started, William was a cadet in the South Carolina Military Academy. In 1864, he and his fellow cadets under Major J.B. White were ordered to the field. In late 1864, they were stationed on James Island until Charleston was evacuated.[611] In February 1865, William and the cadets were ordered to North Carolina but were soon back in South Carolina. William was at home on furlough when the end of the war came.[612]

John Gotea Pressley wrote in an 1898 history of the family that the youngest, Harvey Wilson Pressley, was a schoolboy during the war, but was in a unit known as "the old men and boys." He writes that they were involved in some confederate service. No record exists of this service.

## California

With the war lost and their livelihoods in ruins, the family, including their mother Sarah, left South Carolina and came to California in 1869.[613] They arrived in San Francisco, then moved to Suisun, Solano County. John practiced law in Suisun, then moved to Santa Rosa, where he continued his practice. He became city attorney of Santa Rosa and then was elected judge of Sonoma County.[614] John died in 1895 and was buried in the Santa Rosa Rural Cemetery.[615]

James also settled in Suisun City in Solano County with his wife, Emma Wilson Pressley, and practiced medicine. James passed away at a young age in 1876 and was buried in the Suisun-Fairfield Cemetery.[616]

William married twice. His first wife, Nina Dozier, gave him two children and passed at an early age. He then married Mary Hard. The family were blessed with the addition of two more children. He first was a rancher in Suisun and then moved to Berkeley.[617] He passed away in 1930 at the age of 83 and was buried in the Rio Vista Masonic and Odd Fellow Cemetery, Solano County.[618]

Harvey Wilson Pressley became a successful farmer, owning a ranch in Shasta Valley. He died in 1928 and was buried in the Anderson District Cemetery, Anderson, Shasta County.[619]

## Further Reading

Fonvielle, Chris Eugene. *Fort Anderson: Battle for Wilmington.*

Lee, J. Edward, Ron Chepesiuk, and Edward J. Lee, eds. *South Carolina in the Civil War: The Confederate Experience in Letters and Diaries.*

Walker, Cornelius Irvine. *Great Things Are Expected of Us: The Letters of Colonel C. Irvine Walker.*

# William Bond Prichard

1st lieutenant and captain, Company B (Pittsylvania Vindicators), 38th Virginia Infantry
Born February 17, 1842; died November 16, 1915.

William was born in Petersburg, Virginia, to William Irwin Prichard and Mary Margaret Hammett. William's father was a banker in Petersburg and all of their children, eight boys and four daughters, benefited from his wealth.[620] William Bond Prichard was a cadet at the Virginia Military Institute when the war broke out. He and his other classmates were drillmasters at Camp Lee, near Richmond, Virginia.[621] Later, William became 1st lieutenant of Company B of the 38th Virginia Infantry on July 7, 1861.[622] The regiment immediately left Camp Lee for Winchester, Virginia. On July 18, they were ordered to Manassas but did not reach the battlefield until the July 22, too late to participate in the action.[623] The first fight of the regiment occurred at Williamsburg, Virginia. William made it through the battle without a scratch. He would not be so lucky in the next fight. He received his first wound, though slight, at the Battle of Seven Pines on May 31.[624] During the Battle of Second Manassas in August, William encountered the son of a famous politician. The story was written in *Confederate Veteran* magazine in 1912:

> It was Capt. W.B. Prichard, of the 38th Virginia Regiment of Infantry, Pickett's Division, that discovered Col. Fletcher Webster, son of Daniel Webster, soon after he was mortally wounded. Kneeling over his enemy, he asked if he could be of any service, and received the reply: "Water! Water!" Captain Prichard brought him a canteen of water and asked if he could be of further service. Webster replied: "I am dying!" Captain Prichard assured him that he would see his body delivered to his friends. Webster handed Captain Prichard his eyeglasses and a ring, which Prichard restored to Webster's wife in Boston after the close of the war.[625]

William and the 38th Virginia, as part of Armistead's brigade, Pickett's Division, continued the fight at Sharpsburg (Antietam) and Fredericksburg before the year's end. William was promoted to captain of Company B on December 10, 1862.[626]

On June 11, 1863, Lee started north on a campaign that would end at the Battle of

Captain William Bond Prichard, Company B (Pittsylvania Vindicators), 38th Virginia Infantry (VMI Archives Photographs Collection, Virginia Military Institute Archives).

Gettysburg. Lee had requested that Pickett's Division rejoin the Army of Northern Virginia, and it headed north with the army. Colonel George Griggs kept a diary during the war and wrote of the Gettysburg Campaign:

> At 3 a.m. on morning of 3d the division was ordered forward to the right of Gettysburg and formed line of battle in front of ——; the troops remained under partial shelter by a small strip of woods until the order of advance, when they moved forward as steadily as when on drill. The Fifty-seventh Virginia regiment of the brigade was immediately to left of the regiment; Thirty-eighth charged the enemy across a wide plain—they being sheltered behind a rock fence, earthworks, &c.—and though unprotected and having to climb two high fences in the face of a concentrated fire from the masked number of the enemy's artillery, the troops moved steadily forward, driving the enemy from his strong position, capturing all his guns, but only for a moment; having no reinforcement, and the enemy in strong force on our left and rear, the few surviving men cut their way back. The loss was irreparable to the regiment as well as division; the noble and beloved Colonel E.C. Edmonds killed; Lieutenant-Colonel Whittle, who had lost an arm at Malvern Hill, was seriously wounded in thigh; Captain Towns killed, and all the other company officers more or less seriously wounded. Never did men more than these on that day. In retiring, the regiment with the division had the difficult duty of escorting the prisoners captured into Virginia, arriving at Williamsport on 7th July.[627]

After Gettysburg, the regiment moved back to Virginia and on into North Carolina. On January 30, 1864, the regiment and the division were ordered to Newbern. On the morning of February 1, 1864, the regiment fought at the Battle of New Bern, North Carolina, which ended in a Confederate defeat on February 3.[628] William had been lucky so far during the war, with only a minor wound, but his luck started to run out. On May 10, 1864, he and the 38th fought in the Battle of Chester Station. In his diary, Col. George K. Griggs, commanding the regiment, reported:

> At this point I found my left entirely unprotected and the enemy upon a line with my own. I immediately reported the fact to Colonel Cabell and one of General Barton's staff and deployed my left, Company K, Lieutenant W.G. Cabaniss commanding, perpendicular to my line of battle and continued the advance, breaking and driving back three lines of battle the depth of my regiment, capturing two pieces of artillery. My ranks having in this time been so much depleted from casualties, and the enemy on my left having passed around and in my rear, I was ordered by Captain Thom, Acting Adjutant and Inspector General, to fall back, and turning about, fought its way out, killing about fifteen, wounding many, and capturing fifty of the Thirteenth Indiana regiment. My loss in this action was heavy, and none more regretted than that of the brave and noble Colonel Cabell, who fell mortally wounded in the early part of the action.[629]

William was one of the casualties of the battle. He was shot in the thigh and also lost a finger. He received a 30-day furlough after his time in the hospital, returning to the regiment in time to take part in the fighting near Bermuda Hundred, Virginia, on June 17. William continued with his regiment through the Petersburg Campaign and the retreat to Appomattox Courthouse, where he surrendered with Lee on April 9, 1865.

## CALIFORNIA

When the war ended, William was offered and accepted a department head position at the Virginia Military Institute. He remained there only for a few years when he decided to make San Francisco his home. In 1876, he married Margaret Johnston, daughter of General Albert Sidney Johnston. They would have one child. A highlight of his work was the planning and laying out of Golden Gate Park. William died in 1915 and was buried in Cypress Lawn Memorial Park, Colma, San Mateo County.[630]

## FURTHER READING

Gallagher, Gary W., ed. *The Fredericksburg Campaign: Decision on the Rappahannock.*
_____. *Third Day at Gettysburg and Beyond.*
Gregory, G. Howard. *38th Virginia Infantry.*
McKenzie, Jake. *Civil War Comes Home: The Battle of Williamsburg.*
Patchan, Scott C. *Second Manassas: Longstreet's Attack and the Struggle for Chinn Ridge.*
Sears, Stephen W. *Landscape Turned Red: The Battle of Antietam.*
Smith, Gustavus Woodson. *The Battle of Seven Pines.*

# Robert Hazon Rhodes

Private, Company A, 5th North Carolina Cavalry (63rd State Troops)
Sergeant major, Company C, 11th North Carolina Infantry (Bethal Regiment)
Born May 17, 1845; died June 2, 1874.

Robert was born in Galveston, Texas, to E.A. Rhodes and his second wife, Mary Woodman Kimball Driggs. The family originated in Bertie County, North Carolina, and moved back to North Carolina after Robert's birth. They soon moved to Stockton, California, where Robert's mother Mary worked, providing for the family due to his father's having had a stroke and becoming an invalid.[631] The family were wealthy enough to allow the children a good education. Robert's brother Edward Averitt Rhodes attended the Virginia Military Institute and was commissioned a 2nd lieutenant at the outbreak of the war.[632] He became an officer and acting adjutant of the 11th North Carolina Infantry.[633] The younger brother, Robert, left California and enlisted on March 20, 1863, as a private in Company A of the 5th North Carolina Cavalry.[634] Robert was detailed as courier to Brigadier General Beverly Robertson.[635]

Robert's first encounter with the federals was at Middleburg on June 17, 1863.[636] Within two weeks the Battle of Gettysburg was fought, and Robert's brother Edward was in the thick of it. Charles D. Walker, in his book on the cadets of VMI, gives us a vivid account of Edward's final hours:

> In the great battle of July 1, 1863, he fell. In a charge of his regiment, on the afternoon of that day, the color-bearer was wounded in the ankle; as he fell, Lieutenant Rhodes seized the colors, and was in the act of advancing, cheering the men, when he was struck in the head by a Minie-ball, and fell, murmuring, "Oh, God !" into the arms of his captain. His two young friends, Cooper and Lowrie, fell nearly at the same moment, and were buried that night by the officers on the spot where they fell, near the "Seminary." Colonel Leventhorpe, in a letter to Mrs. Rhodes, written soon after her son's death, speaking of this day's battle, says, "I saw Eddie for a moment, just as we were nearing the enemy, when he remarked to me, with a smile, "We are marching in excellent line." Even in the moment of peril of life, the brave young officer could not repress this feeling of soldierly pride in the troops he had so patiently and faithfully drilled. The surgeon of the 11th, a prisoner at Norfolk, also wrote to Mrs. Rhodes, telling her of her son's death. Going at once to Gettysburg, she identified the graves of the three friends, Rhodes, Cooper, and Lowrie, their names being written on a barrel-stave at the head of the grave, and in the following spring had their remains removed to "Greenmount," Baltimore.[637]

Edward was buried on Seminary Ridge where he fell. It is not certain if Robert, arriving at Gettysburg on the morning of July 3, went in search of his brother or knew he had been killed. Edward's body was not returned to California.[638]

From September to December 1863, Robert was detailed as courier to the new brigade commander, James B. Gordon. The regiment participated in the Bristoe Campaign and in the Mine Run Campaign before moving into winter quarters. Robert decided to accept a position in his brother's old regiment and on February 9, 1864, was appointed sergeant major of the 11th North Carolina Infantry.[639] He fought with the regiment during Grant's Wilderness Campaign and on May 8–9, 1864, at Spotsylvania. The regiment then moved into the trenches at Petersburg. During the Confederate army's breakout of Petersburg on April 2, 1865, Robert was captured. He was sent to Fort Delaware, arriving on April 4, 1865. He spent what was left of the war as a prisoner, being released upon his oath of allegiance on May 4, 1865.[640]

## CALIFORNIA

Robert returned to California. He is listed in the 1869 voter registration as a conductor in San Francisco. He, along with his brother William, became writers and had their works published. Since little is known of Robert, we will let his work speak for him:

> Farewell, life! my pulses thrill
>   In the grasp of giant Death, Heavier is the labored breath, Keener airs the senses chill. Press, oh, press thy lips to mine, That at last my soul may be, E're it pass beyond the sea, thrilled by one fond kiss of thine. When the other shore is won, Crowded with its silent ships, With thy kisses on my lips I shall know a Heaven begun.[641]

Robert never married. He died of tuberculosis at the age of 29 in 1874 and was buried in the Stockton Rural Cemetery, Stockton, San Joaquin County.

## FURTHER READING

Brown, Kent Masterson. *Retreat from Gettysburg: Lee, Logistics, and the Pennsylvania Campaign.*
Dixon, Sam H. *The Poets and Poetry of Texas.* 1885.
Hartley, Chris J. *Stuart's Tarheels: James B. Gordon and His North Carolina Cavalry.*
Venner, William Thomas. *The 11th North Carolina Infantry in the Civil War: A History and Roster.*

# Miles Carey Selden, Jr.

1st lieutenant, captain, and aide-de-camp to General Henry Heth
Born January 9, 1836; died June 29, 1899.

The Selden family of Virginia were one of the state's most respected and prosperous families, with connections to many famous Virginians. Miles Jr. was born to Miles Carey Selden, Sr., and his first wife, Harriet Heth. Harriet was a first cousin of Brigadier General Henry Heth, who would marry her daughter Harriet—his second cousin and Miles Jr.'s sister. Another prominent individual who married into the Selden family was Colonel Walter Herron Taylor, Robert E. Lee's adjutant during the war. Walter, a close friend of Miles Jr., married Miles's cousin Bettie Selden Saunders.[642] Miles Carey Selden, Sr., was a plantation owner in Goochland County, owning 58 slaves by 1850.[643] Miles Jr. gained an appointment to the Virginia Military Institute class of 1859, where many of the Seldens attained their education, but is listed as only remaining a year and a month. Miles seemed to yearn for adventure, for he left the school and headed west.

By 1860, he was living in the town of Kearney, Nebraska Territory, and was listed as a merchant.[644] When war started in the east, Miles saw the opportunity for excitement and headed home. Because of family connections, he was appointed 1st lieutenant and aide-de-camp to his cousin and brother-in-law, Brigadier General Henry "Harry" Heth, on January 28, 1862.[645] Already on the fast track, Miles was promoted to captain four months later in May 1862. Miles remained under Heth for the rest of the war, assisting him during Heth's service under Kirby Smith and then back in the Army of Northern Virginia in March 1863. In Heth's report on the Battle of Gettysburg, he mentions Miles:

> My thanks are also due to my personal staff—Major [R.H.] Finney, assistant adjutant-general; Major [H.H.] Harrison, assistant adjutant and inspector general; Lieutenants [M.C.] Selden, jr., and [Stockton] Heth, my aides-de-camp, and acting engineer officer, William O. Slade—for their valuable services in carrying orders and superintending their execution.[646]

In 1864 Mile's younger brother was of age to join in the fight and enlisted in the 4th Virginia Cavalry. On January 29, 1865, Miles was granted a 20-day sick leave. He came back to the army and took the oath of allegiance on April 19, 1865.

## CALIFORNIA

Not much is known of Miles after the war. In 1876, he was living in San Mateo and was listed as a clerk. Within two years, he had moved to San Francisco.[647] Miles died in 1899 and was buried in the now defunct Masonic Cemetery in San Francisco.[648] The burials were moved to Woodland Memorial Park in Colma, San Mateo County, after 1931.

## FURTHER READING

Krick, Robert E.L. *Staff Officers in Gray: A Biographical Register of the Staff Officers in the Army of Northern Virginia.*
Taylor, Walter Herron, R. Lockwood Tower, and John S. Belmont. *Lee's Adjutant: The Wartime Letters of Colonel Walter Herron Taylor, 1862–1865.*

# Henry Bloom Shackelford

Private, Company F (Atlanta Greys), 8th Georgia Infantry
Private, Company G (Amelia Light Dragoons), 1st Virginia Cavalry
Courier for Brigadier General Fitzhugh Lee
Born July 10, 1848; died June 25, 1903.

One of the youngest in these profiles to serve the Confederacy, Henry was born in Charleston, South Carolina. By 1860, the family were living Georgia.

When war came Henry's brother Frank, who was seventeen, decided to enlist, and Henry followed, though only thirteen. The brothers enlisted in Company F of the 8th Georgia Infantry on May 22, 1861, in Atlanta.[649] The company, under the command of

Captain T.L. Cooper, was ordered to Richmond, Virginia, where it was mustered into Confederate service.[650] The brothers and their regiment moved directly to the area of Manassas, where the Confederate army was massing. On July 21, 1861, at Manassas, Henry and Frank fought in their first battle. A correspondent for the *Richmond Dispatch* followed the regiment into battle, describing the action in the July 29, 1861, edition:

> They were first ordered to support Pendleson's Virginia Battery, which they did amid a furious storm of grape from the enemy's.—Inactive as they were, compelled to be under this fire, they stood cool and unflurried.
>
> They were finally ordered to charge Sherman's Battery. To do this it was necessary to cross an intervening hollow, covered by the enemy's fire, and establish themselves in a thicket flanking the enemy's battery. They charged in a manner that elicited the praise of Gen. Johnston. Gaining the thicket, they opened upon the enemy. The history of warfare probably affords no instance of more desperate fighting than took place now. From three sides a fierce, concentrated, murderous, unceasing volley poured in upon this devoted and heroic "six hundred" Georgians. The enemy appeared upon the hill by the thousand. Between six and ten regiments were visible. It was a hell of bullet-rain in that fatal grove. The ranks were cut down as grain by a scythe. Whole platoons melted away as if by magic. Cool, unflinching and stubborn, each man fought with gallantry, and a stern determination to win or die. Not one faltered. Col. Bartow's horse was shot under him. Adjutant Branch fell mortally wounded. Lieut. Col. Gardner dropped with a shattered leg. The officers moved from rank to rank, from man to man, cheering and encouraging the brave fellows. Some of them took the muskets of the dead and began coolly firing at the enemy. It was an appalling hour. The shot whistled and tore through trees and bones. The ground became literally paved with the fallen. Yet the remnant stood composed and unwavering, carefully loading, steadily aiming, unerringly firing, and then quietly looking to see the effect of their shots. Mere boys fought like veterans—unexcited, save with that stern "white heat," flameless exhilaration, that battle gives to brave spirits.
>
> After eight or ten rounds the regiment appeared annihilated. The order was reluctantly given to cease firing and retire. The stubborn fellows gave no heed. It was repeated. Still no obedience. The battle spirit was up. Again it was given. Three volleys had been fired after the first command. At length they retired, walking and fighting. Owing to the density of the growth, a part of the regiment were separated from the colors. The other part formed in an open field behind the thicket. The retreat continued over ground alternately wood and field. At every open spot they would reform, pour a volley into the pursuing enemy and again retire.[651]

For bravery in the battle of Manassas, both Henry and Frank were recommended for promotion to lieutenant in January 1862. Promotions usually ran slow, and by April 1862 the Confederate government instituted the Conscript Act, which prohibited individuals below the age of eighteen to serve. Henry was dismissed from service but he vowed to find a way to serve the Confederacy. Frank followed him, but being of military age, he accepted a transfer to the Amelia Light Dragoons in July 1862. The Shackelfords had kin in Amelia County, Virginia, and Henry followed Frank on September 29, 1862.[652] However, being only fourteen years of age, Henry may have been allowed to stay if he was watched over by his older brother Frank. They were kept out of the actual fighting by both being assigned as couriers for Brigadier General Fitzhugh Lee.[653] Lee had been promoted to brigade command in July 1862. It is not known if their family back in Georgia knew of the Brother's enlistments. The boys served as Lee's couriers throughout the fighting at Fredericksburg, Chancellorsville, Gettysburg and the Wilderness Campaign. The only known reference to Henry during the war was in Lee's after-action report of the Battle of Kelly's Ford, March 17, 1863. Lee wrote:

> All of the couriers praised for their good conduct were from the 1st: Privates John H. Owings and Otho Scott Lee of Company K, John A.K. Nightingale of Company A, and Henry Shackleford of

Company G. The conduct of Couriers Owings, Lee, Nightengale, and Henry Shackelford deserves the highest praise.[654]

Fitz Lee was promoted to major general in August 1864. We last hear of the brothers in service in late August 1864, with Frank in a Richmond hospital.

## CALIFORNIA

Henry became a civil engineer after the war. In 1869, he went to Sacramento and worked for the railroad engineering corps. In 1873, he move to Red Bluff, Tehama County, and became county surveyor. On July 9, 1884, he married May McCommins. The couple had three children. Henry worked for Senator Leland Stanford, holding various positions, including laying out the extensive grounds that would become Stanford University.[655] Henry died in 1903, the result of a stroke, and was buried in Oak Hill Cemetery, Red Bluff, Tehama County.

## FURTHER READING

Driver, Robert J. *1st Virginia Cavalry.*
Longacre, Edward G. *Fitz Lee: A Military Biography of Major General Fitzhugh Lee, C.S.A.*

# George David Shadburne

Private and sergeant, Company A (Natchez Cavalry), Jeff Davis Legion, Mississippi Cavalry
Chief of scouts (Iron Scouts), under General Wade Hampton
Born June 13, 1842; died March 25, 1921.

Much has been written about George Shadburne, and much more is undocumented because of the shadowy nature of his career as a famous scout for the Confederacy. He was born in Brenham, Texas, to William Henry Harrison Shadburne and Eliza Wheeler As a boy, George heard amazing tales of the Texas revolution from his father, who had fought in the Battle of San Jacinto. George received a good education and as a young man was a student at St. Mary's College, Kentucky.[656] On December 19, 1861, he enlisted in the Natchez Cavalry, which would become Company A of the Jeff Davis Legion of Mississippi Cavalry.[657] George's first tangle with the federal army was during McClellan's Peninsula Campaign in the spring of 1862. At the Battle of Williamsburg on May 5, 1862, George and the legion participated in Jeb Stuart's ride around McClellan's army.[658] On October 15, 1862, George was promoted to 4th corporal.[659] Within six months he was promoted to 1st corporal. He fought with the legion through the Gettysburg Campaign. The company's muster roll tells the story of the actions during the campaign:

The Company was engaged in the Cavalry fight near Brandy Station, June 9 also in the fight near Upperville June 21st and was in the Brigade (Hamptons) on the raid from Upperville via Fairfax C.H. into Maryland and Pennsylvania. The Company was engaged in the severe cavalry fight near Hunterstown Penn. On July 3, 1863—and in all the skirmishes of the Brigade from that time till it crossed the Potomac at Williamsport. Also in the cavalry Battle near Brandy Station Aug. 1st, 1863.[660]

On August 9, 1863, George was promoted to 5th sergeant. He was gaining a name for himself. When Hampton took command of the Army of Northern Virginia's cavalry corps, he ignored George's rank and made him chief of his scouts.

Wade Hampton said of George:

> as soon as a fight began he was instantly transformed into the dashing cavalryman, his whole soul seemed to be in the battle…. Armed with at least two pistols and often three, he would dash against the enemy firing with a rapidity and precision not surpassed by even Mosby who was very handy with his pistol.[661]

During the summer of 1864, George became the leader of Hampton's "Iron Scouts." He was wounded twice, twice captured and twice escape from the federals.[662]

While on a reconnaissance George discovered a herd of federal cattle. He reported to Hampton on the situation:

Near Black Water, September 5, 1864.

General: I have just returned from near City Point. The defenses are as follows, viz: At Wormley's Point, one mile northeast of City Point, are 1,200 dismounted cavalry. One mile southwest of City Point, and on the railroad, is an immense hospital and ambulance and wagon train. At the Old Court-House, three miles from the Point, is a very large pontoon train. At the old Frog-Hole Bridge is a small party getting our timber for beast-works and other purposes. At Cedar Level Station, three miles from the Point, is an immense amount of supplies; there is besides about one regiment of infantry acting as guard. The nearest point of picket-line you could strike is Colonel Green's farm, on the stage road; or, rather, the line is half a mile this side of Green's, on the stage road, running from Mount Sinai Church to Hite's place, thus cutting off a large bend in this road. Southeast of the Court-House, about five miles from City Point, is a small force of infantry, about one large regiment (Negroes). The stream this side of City Point, about three miles, is impassable below Frog-Hole Bridge, which they could burn before it could be attained. At Coggins' Point are 3,000 beeves, attended by 120 men and 30 citizens, without arms. At Sycamore Church is one regiment of cavalry (First District of Columbia), about 250. This is the nearest point of the picket-line to Coggins' Point, about two miles. Sycamore Church is eight miles from Hines' Bridge, on the Blackwater; Hines' Bridge, three miles from Gee's Bridge, on Warwick Swamp, and five miles from Gee's residence. Enemy's cavalry are northwest of the Court-House. The greatest danger, I think, would be on the Jerusalem plank road in returning. The enemy are constructing a railroad from the City Point railroad to the Fifth Corps; it intersects the City Point road about six miles from City Point at a place called Jordan's. It is near this place they have their large mortar, which was firing last night; it is very large, placed on car wheels, and seems to be moved as the road progresses, which is fast. The Tenth Corps is on the right (this side Appomattox); Ninth, center; Fifth, next; Second on extreme left. I hear that they have a Fifteenth [Eighteenth] Corps, commanded by Ord. From best information Birney commands the Tenth Corps. This fifteenth [Eighteenth] and Tenth Corps are on

**George David Shadburne (*History of the Bench and Bar of California*, by J.C. Bates, 1912).**

**General Wade Hampton and George D. Shadburne's famous cattle raid, September 14–17, 1864. Sketch by Alfred Waud (Library of Congress, LC-DIG-ppmsca-22447).**

the other side of Appomattox. Butler has just returned (yesterday) from convention. It is thought more cavalry is about returning. Colonel Spear is under arrest for drunkenness, I understand; Stratton in command.

> Your obedient scout,
> Shadburne.[663]

David Cardwell, a member of the Stuart Horse Artillery, was witness to the beefsteak raid:

> We ran them out and took them prisoners in their night clothes. It was the First District of Columbia Cavalry, and I think we took the most of them, with their camp and splendid horses. I remember how forlorn they looked as we mustered them out later in the day, many sitting on bare-backed horses with nothing on but their shirts. General Rosser, it appears, had about as much as he could attend to. He encountered Colonel Spears, Eleventh Pennsylvania Cavalry, the same command that had made a name for itself as a fighting regiment. They made a good fight for their meat, but Rosser finally whipped them and they fell back, leaving their dead and wounded in the field, as well as their camp. General Bearing, on the right, made his attack according to programme, and was entirely successful. General Rosser without delay began to drive out the cattle, and General Hampton says "there were 2,486 head of them." General Hampton says in his report to General Lee that he withdrew all forces before 8 A.M., and the different columns were united before reaching the Blackwater.[664]

In his after-action report General Hampton wrote:

> I cannot close my report without notice of the conduct of the scouts who were with me. Sergeant Shadburne, of the Jeff. Davis Legion, who gave me the information about the cattle, acted as guide to General Rosser, accompanied the leading regiment in its charge, kept his party always in the front, and acted with conspicuous gallantry.[665]

George was captured on March 6, 1865, near Fredericksburg. He offered his guards $3,000 apiece to release him. Colonel S.H. Roberts of the 139th New York described the capture:

> Cavalry pickets were thrown out on the principal roads to prevent all persons from leaving the city. While posting the latter, Capt. C.S. Masten, of the First New York Mounted Rifles, arrested two rebel soldiers, who fired six shots at him without effect. The two prisoners on being searched were found to be two rebel scouts of Jeff. Davis Legion, by name of Shadburne and Taylor. The former is a notorious guerrilla, and is well known to the Army of the Potomac as a desperado, whose capture has long been desired. It is proper to state that after being taken he offered $3,000 to each of his three guards if they would release him. The names of the guards who refused this tempting bribe are Privates Vandervoort, Holmes, and Glutz, of Troop M, First New York Mounted Rifles.[666]

George was sent to Fort Monroe, Virginia, and then to Wallkill, a federal prison barge at City Point.[667] Charged with being a spy, he faced hanging, but escaped. George continued with Hampton for what was left of the war.

## CALIFORNIA

After the war, George, not wanting to be a part of the "Yankee Kingdom," attempted to leave for Brazil but for some reason never made it. He then moved to Bardstown, Kentucky, where he studied law. In 1867, George started to practice law in Louisiana. On June 13, 1867, he married his first wife, Ada M. Grivot. A year later the family arrived in San Francisco, where George continued his practice.[668] Ada died at a young age and on July 1, 1905, George married Florence Earle McKay.[669] George died in 1921 at his home in Alameda and was buried at Holy Cross Catholic Cemetery, Colma.[670]

## FURTHER READING

Pinnell, Eathan Allen. *Serving with Honor: The Diary of Captain Eathan Allen Pinnell, Eighth Missouri Infantry.*
Weant, Kenneth E. *Civil War Records, Missouri Confederate Infantry: 8th Through the 11th Regiments plus 8th and 9th Battalions and Clark's Infantry Regiment*, vol. 2.

# Shearin Brothers: Mark Harvel Shearin, Jr., and William Shearin

## Mark Harvel Shearin, Jr.

Private, Captain John West's Company (Independent-Missouri)
Born November 17, 1839; died May 10, 1919.

## William Shearin

Private, Captain William H. Myers's Company, Dorsey's Regiment (Missouri)
Born 1837; died 1865.

The Shearin family lived in Halifax, North Carolina, before they moved to Montgomery County, Missouri.[671] When the war came, two of the five Shearin brothers enlisted (as far as records show)—William and Mark Jr. Both brothers became Confederate guerrilla fighters and both left papers explaining their service. William joined Captain Bill Myers's Partisan Rangers. They were technically under Sterling Price but acted independently. The company was loosely connected, with men joining and leaving at various times. William states:

> I live in Audrain County Missouri, 27 years of age. Born in Warren County North Carolina. Was in Montgomery County Missouri when war began. Never in the rebel army. I left Montgomery County Missouri December 1, 1861 intending to join the rebel army. We got about 30 miles when we were

attacked by Federal troops and scattered. We numbered 25 or 30 recruits for Price. This was on the third day after leaving home I went back home. I was at home two or three weeks when I went to Danville, gave myself up to the Colonel of the 81st Ohio Infantry. Took the oath of allegiance and escaped. The soldiers guarding me said that I would be released and I could leave the Guard house if I thought proper. They could have stopped me if they wished. I had been paroled several times and was not on parole when I escaped. This on the 13th of March 1862. The militia were searching for me and went to my sister's house in Audrain County. Went to Audrain County and remained there until the 9th of June 1863. Went to St. Charles and gave myself up. Took Oath and was paroled and released in August 1863. Went to Montgomery County, worked for 13 months on family farm until the spring of 1864. Came back to Audrain County. Remained there until Tuesday, 12th of July 1864. Went to the town of Mexico on business. Was arrested by Provost Marshall's office and kept till Friday evening, 16th day of July 1864 and sent to Gratiot Prison in St. Louis.[672]

He was released on parole and bond of $5,000 on September 15, 1864. His parole papers state he would report for trial when called for.[673] It is not sure if he ever did.

Brother Mark was in a similar situation but claims he was forced to join the rebels:

I originally took the Oath of Allegiance in St. Louis on December 1, 1861 and received a pass to go home. I was conscripted while at work at my sister's in Audrain County Missouri about the 15 Oct. 64.

Some seven of Captain West's men armed came to me and West told me to be ready in three days. I did not leave the house since the county was full of Rebels. On the night of the third day West and seven armed men came to my house and took me with them. I objected to go and they took me by force. Had been in a skirmish in Pike County Missouri near Frankford while on picket duty. The Federals came upon us and we fired at them and ran into camp. The Federals exchanged shots with us before and after we got to camp. I did not shoot but once. I did not see anyone killed on either side. I learned after the fight that the Confederates lost one man killed. After the fight we went to Audrain County and then Boone County where we intended on crossing the Missouri River and go south to look for the main rebel army. Finding we could not cross the river we went back to Audrain County where we disbanded. Captain West took my gun when we disbanded. I and William Mason in the company of 3 or 4 others started to go to Nebraska City, Nebraska as above stated (Iowa). I decided to go to Nebraska instead of reporting to the Federal authorities thinking I would be a prisoner and I would live there. I was captured in Iowa where I remained at Bloomfield Iowa 4 to 5 weeks and then Macon County Mo. for 5 days and then sent to Gratiot St. Prison on the 25th Day of December 1864.[674]

Mark was sent to Alton, Illinois, for exchange on February 10, 1865, and never returned to Confederate service.

## California

Just after the war, the entire Shearin family, led by Mark Harvel Shearin, Sr., left Missouri for a new life in California. Renegade Indians killed William just as the family left Missouri. He buried along the way.[675] Mark Jr. ended up in Maxwell, Colusa County, where he married Roeann B. Kennedy. They had four children. Mark died in 1919 and was buried in the Maxwell Cemetery, Maxwell Colusa County.[676]

## Further Reading

Beilein, Joseph M. *Bushwhackers: Guerrilla Warfare, Manhood, and the Household in Civil War Missouri.*
Erwin, James W. *Guerrillas in Civil War Missouri.* Civil War Series.

# Rufus Shoemaker

Private and captain, Company H (Claiborne Guards), 12th Mississippi Infantry
1st lieutenant and aide-de-camp to General Earl Van Dorn

Born January 5, 1830; died March 9, 1893.

Rufus was born to Doctor David Shoemaker and Martha Holliday in Linden, Copiah County, Mississippi. The family had moved between various places, settling in Linden, where David practiced medicine until he moved the family to Grass Valley, Nevada County. That year Rufus had graduated Oakland College in Mississippi; staying in Mississippi, he obtained a job as newspaper editor in Port Gibson.[677] While in Port Gibson, Rufus married Sarah Overton Lacy, niece to the future Confederate general Earl Van Dorn. A year later the couple left for Grass Valley, California, where Rufus obtained worked as county clerk, edited a newspaper and was commissioned captain of the local militia. He invested in the *Grass Valley Telegraph* in July 1858 and worked as chief editor for a year.[678] In 1859 they moved back to Port Gibson, Mississippi. When the war came, Rufus enlisted as a private in the Claiborne Guards on March 23, 1861, mustering in Corinth on May 12 as Company H of the 12th Mississippi Infantry.[679] He was immediately made 1st sergeant of the company, probably because of his education.

The unit was then sent on to Union City, Tennessee, remaining there until July 18, 1861, when they were ordered to Manassas, Virginia, arriving a day after the battle.[680] Rufus and the regiment remained at Manassas for three weeks. The remainder of the year was spent on duty near Alexandria, Virginia. Rufus was promoted to 1st lieutenant on September 1, 1861, and within two months was made captain of the company on November 18, 1861.[681] In early 1862, the regiment, as part of Rhodes's Brigade, moved to the Virginia peninsula to stop McClellan's advance and to help in the defense of Richmond.[682]

During his stay near Yorktown, Rufus applied for a position as aide-de-camp to his wife's uncle, Major General Earl Van Dorn. Although under heavy fire at Williamsburg on May 5, 1862, Rufus and his comrades actually fought their first major battle at Seven Pines on May 31–June 1, 1862. E. Howard McCaleb, sergeant major of the regiment, wrote:

> For eight long, consecutive hours the 12th Mississippi Regiment was under fire in the hottest and thickest of the fight, capturing the Federal fortifications and an excellent battery of artillery. But the victory was dearly won, for of the 446 men we carried into this engagement, 204 were killed and wounded.[683]

**Rufus Shoemaker (*Grass Valley Morning Union*, March 10, 1893).**

Rufus fought in two more battles, Gaines' Mill on June 27 and Frasier's Farm on June 30, before being appointed as aide-de-camp to Van Dorn on July 24, 1862.[684] He lost his captaincy and was reduced in rank to 1st lieutenant, which was the norm for aides-de-camp.[685] Rufus remained with General Van Dorn until May, when a jealous husband shot and killed Van Dorn.[686] Rufus was out of a job and spent months looking for a position in the Confederate service. He finally wrote to Confederate Chief of Staff Colonel B.S. Ewell:

Head Quarters, Cosby's Brigade October 10, 1863

Col. I have the honor to ask of you an order to go to Richmond to report. In the event that an order cannot be given to me I ask for a report to Richmond.

My case is this: I was Aide-de-camp to Late General Van Dorn and after his death I received from you a leave to go to Port Gibson Miss. to await orders. I have reported by letter several times and have received no orders; and being tired of inactivity I make the request above mentioned. Please answer to Maj. H.L. Boone at General Cosby's Headquarters.

I have to honor to be very respectfully You Obt. Svt.<br>R. Shoemaker[687]

Rufus does not appear in any rolls after this, and it is presumed he was not given another position.

## CALIFORNIA

In 1866, the family returned to Grass Valley, and Rufus became editor of the *Grass Valley Union*. He was a member of the California Constitutional Convention in 1879 and in 1889 started the *Evening Telegraph* newspaper.[688] Rufus died in 1893 and was buried in Greenwood Memorial Cemetery, Grass Valley, Nevada County.[689]

## FURTHER READING

Carter, A.B. *The Tarnished Cavalier: Major General Earl Van Dorn, C.S.A.*
United States War Department. *List of Staff Officers of the Confederate States Army: 1861–1865.*

# George William Shreve

Private, Pelham's Battery, Virginia Horse Artillery<br>Private and sergeant, G.W. Brown's Company, Chew's Battalion, Virginia Horse Artillery<br>Born May 9, 1844; died October 19, 1940.

Born in Falls Church, Fairfax County, Virginia, to William Henry Shreve and Mary Southern, George and his brother Richard (known as Dick) enlisted in the service of the Confederacy in Yorktown, Virginia, joining Captain John Pelham's artillery battery on April 15, 1862, during the beginning of McClellan's Peninsular Campaign.[690] Pelham advanced in rank rapidly, gaining fame as an artillery commander and dying in battle early in 1863. George's brother Richard later joined the unit, being commissioned as 2nd lieutenant because of his college education at Dickenson College.[691] The first battle that

George fought in was at Williamsburg, Virginia, on May 5, 1862. Captain Pelham, in his after-action report, stated:

> I fired 286 rounds of spherical case and 4 of canister from the 12 pounder howitzers and 40 percussion shell and 30 solid shot from the Blakeley gun. Total of 360.
>
> During the entire engagement both officers and men acted with commendable calmness and courage. The example of cool, conspicuous bravery set by Lieutenants Breathed, McGregor, and Elston was emulated by my non-commissioned officers and men.
>
> Casualties as follows: 2 men wounded, Summers and Gibson; 4 horses killed, 3 wounded, and 13 escaped from horse-holders, all of which have since been found except two.[692]

George contracted measles and was hospitalized at Camp Winder Hospital, reporting back to the battery before 2nd Manassas on August 28–30, 1862. In Stonewall Jackson's after-action report he commended the unit: "Owing to the difficulty of getting artillery through the woods I did not have as much of that arm as I desired at the opening of the engagement; but this want was met by Major Pelham, with the Stuart Horse Artillery, who dashed forward on my right and opened upon the enemy at a moment when his services were much needed."[693]

George William Shreve (*The Genealogy and History of the Shreve Family from 1641*, by Luther Prentice Allen, 1901).

In December the unit fought in the Battle of Fredericksburg. George wrote of his experience in the fight years later in the *Santa Cruz Sentinel* newspaper:

> On December 11th Federals attempted to place the pontoons across the river in front of the town, but were repulsed by sharpshooters, stationed on the river bank and behind and within the buildings on the waterfront. After repeated attempts and the loss of many men, the project was given up for the day. However, on the 12th they succeeded and Sumner's Corps crossed and occupied the town, capturing about 50 sharpshooters. About a mile and a half below the town two pontoon bridges were placed and Hooker's and Franklin's grand divisions crossed, the latter 40,000, and occupied the plain. On the morning of the 13th a heavy fog enveloped the locality, so dense that could hardly be observed over 25 or 30 yards. Two guns of the Stuart Horse Artillery, to which the writer was attached moved cautiously down through the fog and succeeded in reaching a position behind a cedar hedge, in front of and within about 200 yards of Franklin's infantry, unobserved by them, where we waited in silence for developments. At about 10 o'clock the fog lifted, and peering through the hedge we had a clear view of our assailants, all spread out on the plain. Of course we were not expected to do more than to feel the enemy and gain information. We commenced firing thus opening the great battle. Their guns responded at once, both those with the infantry and also the big guns on the north side of the river, making it too hot for our little detachment, but fortunately for us most of the shells exploded beyond us. Our loss was quite heavy. For some reason the federals did not advance until near noon, when Franklin's infantry march out in magnificent order, their bright uniforms and glistening bayonets reflecting the sun's rays, making a superb spectacle. We could not but admire them. They immediately

engaged our infantry and our artillery, and finding a gap in our lines, undefended, rushed through it and separated our extreme right from the main line, imperiling our safety, but fortunately at that moment General Ewell of the reserve came up and soon drove the Federals and reestablished the line. The loss on both sides during these operations, in officers and men was heavy. To our surprise Franklin remained comparatively inactive during the rest of the day, while on our left the Federal Grand Division of Sumner, assisted by Hooker, were charging repeatedly the stonewall. Sumner occupied the town, the troops being concealed from our view by the houses. A short distance from the town a canal or ditch passes through the plain, about 500 yards from the base of the hills. French's division debouched from the streets of the town, in grand formation and apparently unadvised about this canal, were delayed in crossing it, and had to reform beyond it. They pressed forward in a grand charge, firing as they got nearer the stonewall; our artillery from the crest of the hills, poured in a deadly avalanche of shot and shell into their ranks; still they pressed on in most gallant manner until reaching within 200 yards of the stonewall; the Confederate infantry opened on them a withering fire which, with the force of the artillery, was so effective that they could not endure it longer, but were obliged to retreat. No troops on earth could have acted with greater courage.[694]

In early June, Lee began his move north with the army, culminating in the Battle of Gettysburg on July 1–3, 1863. George missed the battle because of being wounded on the way north.[695]

George and Richard fought at Spotsylvania and continued in constant fighting through the end of May. That spring, George was promoted to sergeant. By June, the battery was in the trenches of Petersburg. Richard was wounded in action, though not seriously. He caught up with George and the unit on their way to Appomattox and ended the war with his brother.

## CALIFORNIA

After the war, George went back to school in Baltimore, then got a job in a St. Louis, later moving to New York.[696] Richard and his wife died together from a bolt of lightning entering their house on June 15, 1874.[697] George married his first wife, Matilda Shreve, on March 11, 1875, and moved to San Francisco in 1878. The couple had two children. In San Francisco, George established a gun and sporting goods store.[698] After the death of Matilda, George married his second wife, Jesse, and a few years later they moved to Fresno. They were living in Santa Cruz by 1938. George died in 1940 and was buried in the Mountain View Cemetery, Oakland, Alameda County.[699] He was the last surviving member of the Stuart Horse Artillery Battalion.

## FURTHER READING

Moore, Robert H. *The 1st and 2nd Stuart Horse Artillery.*
Neese, George Michael. *Three Years in the Confederate Horse Artillery.*
Trout, Robert J. *Galloping Thunder: The Story of the Stuart Horse Artillery Battalion.*
_____, ed. *Memoirs of the Stuart Horse Artillery Battalion.*

# Robert C. Smith

Lieutenant colonel, 13th Battalion Virginia Reserves
Born March 1, 1819; died December 23, 1899.

Robert C. Smith was born in Jacksboro, Campbell County, Tennessee. Little is known of his early life. In 1839 at age 20, he married Dorinda W. Cecil in Tazewell County, Virginia, and took up farming.[700] On June 3, 1864, as protection for Tazewell County and southwest Virginia, the 13th Battalion, Virginia Reserves, was formed. Robert was elected lieutenant.[701] Robert's battalion became famous at the first Battle of Saltville, October 2, 1864. In his history of Tazewell County, Virginia, William C. Pendleton gives an account of the unit's participation:

> The 13th Battalion held the line in front of the residence of "Governor" (James) Sanders. Every attack made by the Federals was repelled, and the battalion did such valiant service that Summers, writing about the part the reserves took in the battle, says: "It was though at the time that the bravery exhibited in this contest by the reserves from Southwest Virginia was equal to the bravery exhibited by the citizens of this county at King's Mountain in 1780."[702]

Robert's troops were given furloughs after the fight but requested more. Robert wrote the assistant adjutant general with their request:

Hdqrts. Mountain Grove Tazewell County Va.
February 18, 1865
Capt. H.J. Stanton a.a.g.

Dear Sir

I am requested by the old men of my Battalion to ask for an extension of their furloughs if it is consistent with the Military interest of the dept. for the purpose of enabling them to make preparations for putting in a crop the weather has been such since they have been home that nothing in that way could be done if it can be granted they will respond to any notice at any time from your hdqrts.

I am your Obd servt.
R Smith Lt. Col Commanding[703]

Four days later the battalion was renamed the 6th Virginia Reserves Battalion and disbanded on April 12, 1865.[704]

## CALIFORNIA

Robert and his family remained in Tazewell County until 1871, when they moved to California, first settling in San Joaquin County. In 1874, they moved to Watsonville, Santa Cruz County. In 1890, Robert was elected justice of the peace for Watsonville and served until 1898, when failing health resulted in his retirement.[705] After his wife died, his health declined even more. Robert died in 1899 and was buried in the Pioneer Cemetery, Watsonville, Santa Cruz County.[706]

**Robert C. Smith (*History of Tazewell County and Southwest Virginia*, by William C. Pendleton, 1920).**

## Further Reading

Mays, Thomas Davidson. *The Price of Freedom: The Battle of Saltville and the Massacre of the Fifth United States Colored Cavalry.*

Pendleton, W.C. *History of Tazewell County and Southwest Virginia, 1748–1920.*

# Robert Press Smith, Jr. and Sr.

## Robert Press Smith, Jr.

1st lieutenant, Company B and Company C, 1st (Butler's) South Carolina Regular Infantry
Captain, Company E, 1st (Butler's) South Carolina Regular Infantry

Born October 10, 1839; died October 19, 1899.

## Robert Press Smith, Sr.

Captain and quartermaster, Company F (Union Light Infantry Volunteers), 1st (Charleston)
Battalion South Carolina Infantry (Gaillard's Battalion)
Captain and quartermaster, Company C, 27th South Carolina Infantry

Born January 6, 1814; died May 24, 1887.

The Smiths were of English and Huguenot descent and a prestigious family of Charleston, South Carolina. Robert Press Smith, Sr., was born in Charleston and was the grandnephew of Bishop Robert Smith of the Episcopal Church.[707] He was a graduate of Charleston College. Robert Sr. married Mary Mazyck Gaillard of another very prestigious family.[708] After college, he worked in the wholesale hardware business until 1843, when he left the city and acquired rice and cotton plantations in St. Stephen's Parish, on the Santee River. He was a successful planter, and bought and sold plantations until the start of the war.[709] Robert Jr. was born into the world of Charleston high society. He was schooled by private teachers at home and then graduated from the South Carolina Military Academy (the Citadel) in March 1859. Robert Jr. then studied medicine at the South Carolina Medical College and graduated in the first week of March 1861.[710]

During this time, war fever had hit Charleston and secession seemed imminent. As soon as he graduated, Robert Jr. enlisted in the newly forming 1st South Carolina Infantry on March 4, 1861.[711] The unit trained as infantry but was utilized as an artillery unit and served in the Department of South Carolina, Georgia, and Florida. Robert Jr. was elected 1st lieutenant of Company B. He was transferred to Company C sometime between April 30 and May 17, 1861, and then was put on detached service as quartermaster between July and August of 1861. On October 23, 1861, Robert Jr. was promoted to captain of Company E. By November, Robert Jr. and his company were stationed at Edisto Island, south of Charleston.[712]

On November 19, 1861, the unit moved to Ft. Moultrie on Sullivan's Island near the mouth of Charleston Bay.[713] Meanwhile back at home in St. Stephens' Parish, Robert Sr. answered the call of the Confederacy and enlisted in the 1st Battalion South Carolina

*Left:* **Robert Press Smith, Jr.** *Right:* **Robert Press Smith, Sr. (both photographs courtesy David R. DuBose, 4th great-grandson of Robert Press Smith, Sr.).**

Infantry on May 5, 1862.[714] His brother-in-law Peter C. Gaillard organized the unit. Their first fight was at Secessionville, South Carolina, on June 21, 1862. During the battle, Robert was severely wounded. None of his muster sheets detail his wounding and it seems he was not capable of returning as a foot soldier.[715] He wanted to serve in some capacity, and Lt. Colonel Gaillard commissioned him as a captain and appointed him as quartermaster on July 16, 1862, at Secessionville.[716]

On May 3, 1863, Robert Jr. went on sick leave for ten days. No record exists of the reason for the leave. On September 8, sixteen men of Robert Jr.'s company were killed and twelve wounded by an explosion of ammunition chests. Major Robert DeTreville, commanding Fort Moultrie, gave this after-action report of the incident:

> I regret to announce here an accident most terrible in its effect, and but for which our casualties would have been but slight. A 15 inch shell from the Weehawken struck the muzzle of an 8-inch Columbiad, and, glancing off, exploded among a number of shell-boxes and ammunition chests which had been placed behind a traverse (and at which a number of the men of Captain Smith's company were stationed), killing instantly 16 men and wounding 12 others. Captain [R.P.] Smith, Jr., himself narrowly escaped by leaping from the parapet into the ditch in front of the fort.[717]

The men of Company E continued trading shots with the federals, and Robert Jr. reported daily on their skirmishes:

> Headquarters Brooke Gun Battery,
> November 20, 1863.
>
> Sir: I have the honor to report that between 2.30 and 3 o'clock this morning rapid and heavy discharges of small-arms were seen and heard in and around Fort Sumter. I fired the Brooke gun

three times with shrapnel and once with a hollow shot, in the manner prescribed in case of an assault on Fort Sumter. The Brooke gun was also fired twice during the day with hollow shot for the purpose of getting the range around Fort Sumter. The mortars were fired eight times this morning at Cumming's Point.

> Very respectfully, your obedient servant,
> R. Press Smith, Jr.,
> Captain, Commanding Post.
> Lieutenant E.C. Edgerton,
> Acting Assistant Adjutant-General.[718]

Robert Sr. went on sick furlough from September 1863 to March 1864 because of the wound he had received at Secessionville in 1862. Robert Jr. received a leave of absence for 30 days starting on December 11, 1863; the reason is also not known. Both father and son had a brief respite from the war.

The muster roll of Robert Jr. and his company on April 30, 1864, gives Battery Marion, Sullivan's Island, as the company's station, adding: "This Company has been engaged in frequent practice at the enemies works on Morris Island; The enemy returning the fire Sometimes."[719]

Robert Sr. reported to the 27th South Carolina and resumed his duties until August 1, 1864, when he was admitted to the Episcopal Church Hospital, Williamsburg, Virginia. He received a furlough on August 29, 1864, because of acute dysentery, for 30 days. He did not return to the unit and officially resigned on September 8, 1864.[720]

On October 6, 1864, Robert Jr. and his company relieved Company B at Battery Marshall at Fort Sumter.[721] On March 16, 1865, Robert Jr. and the regiment fought at the Battle of Averasboro, North Carolina. He was wounded and admitted to Confederate General Hospital in Greensboro, North Carolina, on March 19, 1865.[722] He remained in the hospital until his parole at Chester, South Carolina, May 5, 1865.

## California

After the close of the war, Robert Jr. went back to the practice of medicine in Charleston. He moved to Santa Rosa, California, in March 1868.[723] After the war, Robert Sr. was appointed as auditor of Berkeley County, South Caroloina, leaving the post in 1886 and moving to California, where he lived with his son and his family.[724] Robert Sr. died the next year and was buried in the Santa Rosa Rural Cemetery.[725] Robert Jr. only outlived his father by 12 years, passing away in 1899. He was buried near his father.[726]

## Further Reading

Brennan, Patrick. *Secessionville: Assault on Charleston.*
Fowler, Malcolm. *The Battle of Averasboro.*
Phelps, W. Chris. *Charlestonians in War: The Charleston Battalion.*
Poole, W. Scott. *South Carolina's Civil War: A Narrative History.*
Seigler, Robert S. *South Carolina's Military Organizations During the War Between the States: The Low Country and Pee Dee.*
Wise, Stephen R.. *Gate of Hell: Campaign for Charleston Harbor, 1863.*

# John Snow

Private and quartermaster sergeant, Company F (Lumsden's Battery),
2nd Battalion, Alabama Light Artillery

Born May 24, 1844; died June 29, 1921.

John Snow's family originally were from Massachusetts. The family moved to northern Alabama, where John was born on a large cotton plantation near Tuscaloosa to Dr.
Charles Snow and Virginia Penn, a member of an old distinguished family from Virginia.[727] John learned the cotton trade from his father and studied other agriculture pursuits. As the war clouds gathered, he enlisted as a private on November 29, 1861, in
Tuscaloosa for the duration of the war.[728] By the time the battalion was formed in Mobile
in January 1862, John was elected quartermaster sergeant. The battalion was stationed at
Fort Gaines on Dauphin Island until after the Battle of Shiloh in April 1862.[729] John and
his battery were given six guns and then placed at Tupelo, Mississippi. On May 9, 1862,
one section of two guns opened fire on the enemy near Farmington. A federal battery
fired at John and his guns, and a skirmish began. This was the first time John and the
battery were commended for their action in a fight.[730]

On July 26 John and his comrades left Tupelo, arriving at his hometown of
Tuscaloosa on August 8, 1862, where he
spent a week at home. By September, the
battery was in Kentucky and fought in the
Battle of Perryville. The history of the
battery, published in 1905, gives us a brief
account of the battle:

On Tuesday 7th, the command retraced its march
back to within two miles of Perryville, sleeping at
their guns during the night. Next morning Lumsden's and Selden's (Montgomery, Alabama) Batteries opened the fight in a duel with two Yankee
batteries, Lumsden going forward into the battle
and unlimbering under fire of the enemy, losing
one horse from the fourth gun. The fighting was
severe during two hours, 4:00 p.m. to dark. Sims
and another man were wounded in the head by
pieces of shell and Goodwyn by rifle ball. The 4th
piece was dismounted and two more horses killed,
then our infantry charged and drove the enemy for
two miles with considerable loss to the Federals.
The battery fired about 2000 rounds, the distance
being about one half mile and after the battle, the
battery opposing us was seen knocked all to pieces,
horses piled up and haversacks and canteens strewn
over the ground, while in rear was a long line of
knapsacks and overcoats laid down by the infantry
before going into battle and left in their hurried
retreat. Many of our men secured blue overcoats
which they wore until the close of the war. Sergt.

**John Snow (*History of Mendocino and Lake
Counties, California,* by Aurelius O. Carpenter and Percy H. Millberry, 1914).**

Little says he saw a thousand of them but never thought of securing any booty, but that night as it was very cold, paid a member of the company $7.00 for one which he wore until it was shot off him at Nashville. Eventually Yankees fell back nine miles. The ground was strewed with Yankee dead, overcoats, canteens, muskets etc. Lumsden got wheels from Captain Greene to fix up the dismounted gun and remained in field until noon the next day. This was Lumsden's first battle with the whole battery.[731]

Their next fight occurred at the Battle of Stones River on December 31, 1862–January 2, 1863. As part of Brigadier General John K. Jackson's Brigade, the battery shot 250 rounds of ammunition, doing damage to the federals. John spent most of the next year near Murfreesboro, Tennessee.[732] The Battery fought at Chickamauga on September 19–20, 1863. John and his comrades were removed from the front lines and reported to General Longstreet.[733]

The battery followed John Bell Hood to Nashville and fought a battle on December 15–16, 1864, where they lost all its guns. Again we pick up the story through the printed history of the battery:

It was about 12 o clock that Capt. Lumsden sent orderly Sergeant J. Mack Shivers on horseback to report to General Stewart that all Confederate infantry had been driven into the fallen timber at our front, and that it was evident the enemy would soon rush us with a charge. That we could leave the guns and get away with all the men. Shivers returned with the orders, "Tell Captain Lumsden it is necessary to hold the enemy in check to the last minute regardless of losses." This was about 12:30 P.M. They overwhelmed us about 2 P.M. So that Lumsden's Battery alone had stopped the advance of A.J. Smith s federal Corps for 3 hours during which Confederate troops had been moved from right wing to a new line behind the Hillsboro pike several hundred yards in our rear, which was all important, to the Confederates.[734]

What was left of the battery was sent back to Alabama. John and the battery were first stationed at Mobile and then placed in Spanish Fort, Baldwin County, where from March 27 to April 8, 1865, they were under siege. The battery was moved nearer the river, from where they were transported by rail to Meridian and surrendered on May 4, 1865.[735]

## CALIFORNIA

After the war John succeeded first as a grocer and then owner of a general store. He then created the J. Snow Hardware Company of Tuscaloosa. John became wealthy and spent his winters in Tuscaloosa and his summers at his estate on the Hurricane River. He sold everything around 1890 and moved west to Mendocino County, where he served as the town of Willits's justice of the peace.[736] John moved to Ukiah, where in 1921 he died and was buried in the Russian River Cemetery, Ukiah, Mendocino County.

## FURTHER READING

Bobrick, Benson. *The Battle of Nashville.*
Broadwater, Robert P. *The Battle of Perryville 1862: Culmination of the Failed Kentucky Campaign.*
Daniel, Larry J. *Battle of Stones River: The Forgotten Conflict Between the Confederate Army of Tennessee and the Union Army of the Cumberland.*
Hearn, Chester G. *Mobile Bay and the Mobile Campaign: The Last Great Battles of the Civil War.*
Woodworth, Steven E., ed. *The Chickamauga Campaign.*

# John Meredith Spencer

Private, Company G (Cumberland Light Dragoons), 3rd Virginia Cavalry
Private, Company E (Black Eagle Rifles), 18th Virginia Infantry
Private, Company C, 43rd Battalion Virginia Cavalry (Mosby's Rangers)
Born July 4, 1842; died February 6, 1909.

John Spencer was one of the eight children born to Nathan Spencer and his second wife, Martha G. Spencer, in Buckingham County, Virginia. On May 14, 1861, he enlisted in the 3rd Virginia Cavalry.[737] John was discharged eleven days later with a surgeon's certificate of disability.[738]

He soon volunteered in the Black Eagle Rifles, Company E of the 18th Virginia Infantry. *Confederate Veteran* magazine states, "He served with conspicuous gallantry through the war, and in the battle of Gaines's Mill he was wounded while carrying the flag up the ramparts after five color bearers had been shot in the attempt."[739] John was wounded in the battle, though not severely. He recovered and, wanting to continue his service to the confederacy, joined Mosby's Partisan Rangers on September 7, 1863.[740] The Rangers were officially called the 43rd Battalion Virginia Cavalry. John was captured April 15, 1864, in Louden County, Virginia. He was sent to Lieutenant Colonel H.H. Wells, provost marshall at Alexandria, Virginia.[741] John was then sent to Fort Warren, Boston Harbor, September 30, 1864.[742] He spent the next eight months at Fort Warren and was released on oath of allegiance on June 12, 1865.[743]

H.E. Wood, who had been a color sergeant in the 18th Virginia Infantry, mentioned John in an article he wrote for the Southern Historical Society:

> There is another instance of patriotic devotion and loyalty to the Southern cause, that of John M. Spencer, of Buckingham county, Va. Spencer was too young at the beginning of the hostilities to be enrolled as a soldier, but being very patriotic, he volunteered his services with the color guard of the Black Eagle Company for the battle of Seven Pines, Va. He passed through that baptism of fire and leaden hail unscathed, which nerved him to try his luck again at Gaines' Mill, VA. He was more fortunate this time when he received his mark of honor: was wounded and afterwards joined Mosby's command. He was captured and confined at Fort Warren, Mass., till the cruel war was over, and is now living at Berkley [*sic*], California, as patriotic as ever—a good old rebel yet.[744]

## CALIFORNIA

After the war, John married Georgia Spencer (maiden name not known). The couple had seven children. The family lived in Chariton County, Missouri, in 1870, where John was a grocer. They moved to Oakland, Alameda County, in 1899. John is listed as a grain shipper in 1908.[745] He passed away in Oakland in 1909 and was buried in the Mountain View Cemetery, Oakland, Alameda County.[746] His obituary reads:

> SPENCER—In Oakland. Cal. February 6, 1909. John Meredith Spencer, beloved father of Meredith L. and Julian Spencer and Mrs. I.N. Breedlove. Buckingham County, Va. was in Pickett's division at the battle of Gains Mill in 1862, and a color bearer at the age of 18. Funeral at home. 71 Thirty-Second Street, this (Monday) afternoon. February 6, at 1:30 o'clock, and will be strictly private.[747]

## FURTHER READING

Keen, Hugh C., and Horace Mewborn. *43rd Battalion Virginia Cavalry, Mosby's Command.*
Robertson, James I. *18th Virginia Infantry.*

Williamson, James Joseph. *Mosby's Rangers: A Record of the Operations of the Forty-third Battalion of Virginia Cavalry from Its Organization to the Surrender.* 1909.

# Waverley Thompson Stairley

Private, Company B (Brooks Troop), Hampton's Cavalry Battalion
Private, Company K, 2nd Regiment South Carolina Cavalry
Born August 3, 1845; died June 10, 1932.

Waverley Stairley could trace his lineage through the leading families of Virginia. Through his grandmother he was a distant cousin of "Light Horse Harry" Lee and his son Robert E. Lee.[748] Born in Greenville, South Carolina, Waverley's father, Benjamin Franklin Stairley, was a very successful plantation owner. Benjamin felt that Northern schools were better at educating young boys and decided to send Waverly to school in New York City at the New York City College, where he was when his home state seceded.[749]

Waverley went back to South Carolina and enlisted in a cavalry troop just forming. He joined them on June 14, 1861, in Columbia, South Carolina, for 12 months.[750] As a cavalry man, his distant cousins Rooney and Fitzhugh Lee near Richmond trained him.

Their first fight as the newly designated 2nd South Carolina was at Second Manassas on August 28–30, 1862. Waverley and his unit then moved on to fight at Antietam on September 17, 1862. Wade Hampton, commanding the brigade, commended the unit's conduct in battle: "I beg to commend most favorably the conduct of the Second South Carolina Regiment on this occasion. They were ably and gallantly led by Colonel Butler. Especial praise is due to the squadron of Lieutenant Meighan, which had never been under fire before, and yet no troops could have behaved better."[751]

On November 13, 1862, Waverley was discharged under Confederate regulations for being under 18 years of age. He went home and waited until he turned 18 eight months later. On July 27, 1863, just a few days before his 18th birthday, he rejoined his company in Greenville, South Carolina, having just missed the Battle of Brandy Station and Gettysburg.[752]

On March 26, 1864, Waverley's horse died; he remained dismounted for eight more days before he was given 30 days to procure a horse and meet up with the regiment.[753] After 30 days, word was sent to his commander that he was very sick at home. By the July–August muster of the

**Waverley Thompson Stairley (*Pacific Wine and Spirit Review*, San Francisco, 1894).**

regiment, Waverley still had not returned. The November–December 1864 muster reports that Waverley was present for duty. The reason for his long absence is not known and did not have any effect on his standing with the unit. The regiment went on to fight in the Carolinas at Goldsboro and at Bentonville. The remnants of the 2nd South Carolina surrendered with Johnson's army.

## CALIFORNIA

With the war over, Waverley returned to New York City and finished his schooling. In 1866, he was offered a position with a company in San Francisco and came West. In 1868, he was working for the Southern Pacific Railroad Company; he later worked in banking and at a stock brokerage firm. By 1882 he was working for a lumber company in Red Bluff, California. A year later he married Mary Ridgely Tilden. The couple had two children.[754] By 1894 Waverley was working for the Internal Revenue Service in Sacramento. By April, the family was living in Richmond, California, and Waverley was in the business of banking. He eventually left to become postmaster of Richmond, Contra Costa County. Towards the end of his life, he was living in Berkeley with one of his children. He lived a long life, reaching the age of 87. Waverley died in 1932 and was buried in the Sunset View Cemetery, El Cerrito.[755]

## FURTHER READING

Douglas, David G. *A Boot Full of Memories: Captain Leonard Williams, 2nd South Carolina Cavalry.*
Williams, Leonard. *The Civil War Letters of Captain Leonard Williams: 2nd South Carolina Cavalry, Hampton's Legion, Company K, Brook's Troop, 1861–1865.*

# John Adolph Steinbeck

Private, Company B (the St. Augustine Blues), 3rd Florida Infantry
Born November 27, 1832; died August 10, 1913.

John was born Johann Adolph Grossteinbeck in Dusseldorf, Nordrhein-Westfalen, Germany. At age 17, he and his brother moved to Palestine (now Israel), where he worked as an interpreter and wood worker. In 1855, Johann met Almira Ann Dickson in Palestine. They married on June 1, 1856.[756]

On January 11, 1858, Johann's brother and a man named Walter Dickenson were murdered on Dickenson's ranch in Jaffa by Arab robbers.[757] Four individuals were arrested and imprisoned, but a fifth individual, who actually killed John's brother, was still at large.[758] Johann's brother's killer was never apprehended.

Johann and his family decided to move to America, where he changed his name to John Adolph Steinbeck. The family first settled in Massachusetts, where Almira's family lived, but then decided to move to the warmer climate of Florida. In 1860, the family was living in St. Johns County, Florida.[759]

When the war came, John enlisted on October 1, 1861, in the St. Augustine Blues, commanded by Captain John Lott Philips, which became Company B, 3rd Florida Infantry.[760]

Stories exist about John being conscripted into the army but nothing has been proven since conscription was enacted later in the war and the 3rd's muster sheets show his enlistment. Whether his family headed north during his service is speculation and family tradition. On October 8, 1862, John fought his first and last battle at Perryville, Kentucky. General Bragg in his official report stated:

> The action opened at 12.30 p.m. between the skirmishers and artillery on both sides. Finding the enemy indisposed to advance upon us, and knowing he was receiving heavy re-enforcements, I deemed it best to assail him vigorously and so directed. The engagement became general soon thereafter, and was continued furiously from that time until dark, our troops never faltering and never failing in their efforts. For the time engaged it was the severest and most desperately contested engagement within my knowledge. Fearfully outnumbered, our troops did not hesitate to engage at any odds, and though checked at times, they eventually carried every position and drove the enemy about 2 miles. But for the intervention of night we should have completed the work. We had captured 15 pieces of artillery by the most daring charges, killed 1 and wounded 2 brigadier-generals and a very large number of inferior officers and men, estimated at no less than 4,000, and captured 400 prisoners, including 3 staff officers, with servants, carriage, and baggage of Major-General McCook. The ground was literally covered with his dead and wounded. In such a contest our own loss was necessarily severe, probably not less than 2,500 killed, wounded, and missing.[761]

John was listed as missing in Kentucky by October 15, 1862. Some stories suggest he put on the uniform of a dead federal soldier and deserted and others that he was captured. By March 30, 1863, John was reported as deserted and was dropped from the roll on May 1, 1863.[762]

**John Adolph Steinbeck (courtesy Martha Heasley Cox Center for Steinbeck Studies, San Jose State University).**

## CALIFORNIA

John returned home to his family, whether still in Florida or back in New England. Eventually they were in New England. For ten years, John was a woodworker, making pianos in Massachusetts. The family decided to head back to warm weather, this time, California. In 1872 the family headed west and settled in Hollister.[763]

In 1878, John bought a Victorian home and ten acres in Hollister and started a dairy ranch. John's son Ernst settled in the Salinas Valley and married Olive Hamilton; they had a baby they named John Steinbeck in honor of John Adolph Steinbeck.[764] The boy grew up to become the famous Nobel Prize–winning author. John Adolph Steinbeck died in 1913 and is buried in Woodlawn Memorial Park, Colma San Mateo County.[765]

## FURTHER READING

Broadwater, Robert P. *The Battle of Perryville, 1862: Culmination of the Failed Kentucky Campaign.*
Daniel, Larry J. *Soldiering in the Army of Tennessee: A Portrait of Life in a Confederate Army.*
Sheppard, Jonathan C. *By the Noble Daring of Her Sons: The Florida Brigade of the Army of Tennessee.*

# Edward Bernard Stonehill

Private, Company I, 2nd Tennessee Infantry (Robison's)
Private and sergeant major, Company A (Confederate Rangers),
17th Battalion (Sander's) Tennessee Cavalry
Captain and aide de camp, Brigadier General Frank Crawford Armstrong
Captain and aide de camp, Major General Joseph O. Shelby

Born 1829; died February 5, 1898.

Edward Stonehill was born in Germany and moved to New York when he was a boy. He fought in the Mexican War as a member of the 1st New York Volunteers. After the war ended, Edward returned to New York. He then went on to Missouri and, in the early 1850s, moved to Nevada, where he worked as a miner. In Washoe, Nevada, Edward became a member of the Nevada County Rifles and fought in the Piute Indian war.[766]

In August 1861, after the breaking out of the war, Edward went east and enlisted as a private in the 2nd Tennessee Infantry on April 25, 1861, at Camp Holmes, Virginia, for three years.[767]

On October 1, 1861, Edward re-enlisted for 12 months. On February 9, 1862, the regiment was transferred to the Western Theatre to serve with the Army of Tennessee. Edward and the regiment were given a brief furlough, which lasted from February 13 through April 1, 1862.[768] When the men of the regiment returned, it reorganized and moved to Corinth, Mississippi. Edward and his comrades fought in the Battle of Shiloh, April 6–7, 1862.

Edward and his regiment were in the Siege of Corinth, Mississippi, from April 29 to May 30, 1862. Five days before the end of the siege on May 25, 1862, Edward received a transfer to Sander's 17th Battalion Tennessee Cavalry.[769] He reported for duty on June 1, 1862. On September 15, 1862, Edward was promoted to sergeant major.[770] By the end of 1862 or early 1863, Edward was pro-

**Edward Bernard Stonehill (*San Francisco Call* newspaper, 1898).**

moted to captain and was moved up to brigade headquarters as aide-de-camp to Brigadier General Frank Crawford Armstrong, with the rank of captain.[771] He is listed in various biographies as also aide-de-camp to Major General Joseph Shelby, "having served under Armstrong until the fall of Atlanta, when he was transferred to the Trans-Mississippi Department and assigned to duty under Shelby."[772] Information seems to be sketchy on the Shelby connection.[773] On June 16, 1865, Edward was surrendered and paroled by Kirby Smith and the Army of the Trans-Mississippi Department.

## CALIFORNIA

In 1868 Edward returned to Nevada, where he practiced law.[774] Edward was elected a Nevada delegate to the Democratic National Convention in Cincinnati, which nominated General Winfield Scott Hancock for president. In 1880 he was appointed assistant district attorney of San Francisco; six years later he was elected district attorney.[775] Edward died suddenly in 1898 and was buried in Cypress Lawn Memorial Park, Colma, San Mateo County.[776]

## FURTHER READING

Daniel, Larry J. *Shiloh: The Battle That Changed the Civil War.*
Hotard, Patrick Michael. *The Campaign (Siege) of Corinth, Mississippi, April–June 1862.*
Joslyn, Mauriel, ed. *A Meteor Shining Brightly: Essays on the Life and Career of Major General Patrick R. Cleburne.*
Warner, Ezra J. *Generals in Gray: Lives of the Confederate Commanders.*

# Thomas Porcher Stoney

Private, Parker's Company, South Carolina Light Artillery (Marion Artillery)
Born April 25, 1835; died December 19, 1891.

Thomas Stoney was descended from Huguenots who emigrated the United States and settled in South Carolina.[777] His parents were Peter Gaillard Stoney, a rice planter, and Anna Maria Porcher. He went to Mount Zion College in Winnsboro, South Carolina, in preparation for his higher education. Thomas then went on to the South Carolina College at Columbia, South Carolina, and studied law at the University of Virginia in 1855.[778] In 1856 he moved to San Francisco, then moving on to El Dorado County, where he ventured into quartz mining. He soon left the mines and moved to Napa, where he practiced law. He then started his own firm.[779]

In 1860, Thomas married Kate M. Allen, and the couple remained in Napa until the breaking out of the war in 1861, when he and his wife left for the East and lived with her family in New York. Four of his brothers and his father fought for the Confederacy. John Safford Stoney served as a Confederate surgeon in 1862 in the 1st and then the 6th South Carolina Infantry.[780] Capt. William Edmund Stoney was inspector general on the staff of Hagood's Brigade.[781] Pierre Gaillard Stoney, Jr., was a private in Company A, State Cadet Battalion, and then a private in the South Carolina Cavalry. J. Dwight Stoney was in the 27th South Carolina Infantry.

In May 1863, leaving his family in New York, Thomas headed South to join the Confederate service. Arriving in Charleston, he at once enlisted in Captain Parker's Company of the Marion Artillery on January 9, 1864.[782] The unit had been assigned to the Department of South Carolina, Georgia and Florida in the 6th Military District under Brigadier General Henry Wise. In early March 1864, Thomas's wife Kate gave birth to their first child, a girl. His biography states:

**Thomas Porcher Stoney (*Historical and Contemporary Review of Bench and Bar in California*, by the *Recorder Printing and Publishing Co.*, San Francisco, 1926).**

> His wife, who, with the only one of their children then born, was left for safety with her relatives in New York, had resolved that "his country should be her country," and that even grim-visaged war should not separate her and her child from the husband of her choice, went to Nassau, on the Island of New Providence, then the great entrepot for the Confederate fleet of merchant vessels engaged in running the blockade. Orders had been given by the Confederate Government at Richmond, forbidding the taking of ladies and children on board of vessels engaged in the service of that government. Mrs. Stoney found that she and her child would not be taken. After great difficulty and much urging on her part, a kind captain agreed to make an exception in her case if she would consent to share all the dangers and hardships incidental to the hazardous service in which this adventurous seaman was engaged. She was told that the vessel would be burnt rather than allowed to be captured by Federal cruisers. She cheerfully agreed to risk all the danger's of the voyage and embarked on board a blockade-runner. She reached Wilmington, North Carolina, safely, and soon joined her husband in the land of Sumter and Marion.[783]

On April 11, 1864, Thomas was given a 48-hour leave, presumably to rejoin his wife and see his child.[784] This is pure speculation but coincides with her arrival back in Charleston. Thomas rejoined his unit and continued in the defense of Charleston. The unit joined Johnston's Carolina Campaign and surrendered with the army.[785]

## CALIFORNIA

Thomas and his family moved back to New York for a year and then in 1866 moved back to Napa. Not being able to practice law because of his Confederate service, he was employed as a law assistant. When the law was repealed, he formed a law partnership with W.W. Pendegast.[786] Thomas was soon elected Napa County judge for two terms. In 1879, he was nominated for associate justice of the California Supreme Court, but lost. Thomas and his family then moved to San Francisco the next year, where he continued his law practice.[787] Thomas died in 1891 at age 57 of bronchitis that had turned to pneumonia.[788] He was buried in Laurel Hill Cemetery, San Francisco, and removed after its closure to Cypress Lawn Memorial Park, Colma, San Mateo County.[789]

## FURTHER READING

Broadwater, Robert P. *Battle of Despair: Bentonville and the North Carolina Campaign.*
Johnson, John. *The Defense of Charleston Harbor.*
Seigler, Robert S. *South Carolina's Military Organizations During the War Between the States: The Lowcountry and Pee Dee.*

# Charles Fletcher Taylor

2nd lieutenant, Quantrill's Partisan Rangers
Born May 19, 1842; died April 22, 1912.

Much has been written of the guerrilla exploits of Fletch Taylor during the war. He fought closely with such infamous men as "Bloody Bill" Anderson, Frank and Jesse James, and the Youngers, as well as his first commander, William Quantrill. Charles Fletcher Taylor was born in Zanesville, Muskingum County, Ohio, to William Taylor and Mary A. Ross. Fletch's father was born in London, England, and moved to Virginia, where he was married. In 1833, the family moved to Ohio, and just after Fletch was born, they moved to Missouri. The family moved to Hannibal, Missouri, in 1844 and then to the town of Paris, Missouri. In 1851, the family went to Independence, Missouri. Fletch's father was a teacher and school commissioner of Jackson County, Missouri, in 1858. William tought Fletch and his two siblings in school. William Taylor died in 1862.[790]

When the war came, Fletch was one of the first recruits in William Quantrill's band, initially created to defend their families and homes. On August 7, 1862, Quantrill is officially listed as being paid by the Confederate Quartermaster's Department.[791] Bill Anderson ("Bloody Bill") is listed in Quantrill's muster sheets but not Fletch.[792]

By August 1863, the federals in Missouri were tired of the guerrilla tactics of Quantrill and his men. They resorted to capturing and imprisoning the female

**Charles Fletcher Taylor (Wilson's Creek National Battlefield, WICR 30209).**

family members of the guerrillas. These women and young girls were jailed in Kansas City in a civilian's home. When this did not work to roust Quantrill's men, the federals allegedly caused the collapse of the house. Several of the women were maimed and killed. This caused outrage among the citizens and guerrillas of western Missouri. Calling for revenge, Quantrill organized the raid on Lawrence, Kansas.[793]

As 1863 ended, many of the raiders disagreed with Quantrill's methods of defeating the federals. "Bloody Bill" Anderson split off from Quantrill and formed his own guerrilla group, one that was much more violent to the federals and anyone who sympathized with the Union cause. Fletch left Quantrill and formed his own command in June 1864, leading some of Quantrill's former guerrillas (including Frank and Jesse James) into the Platte County, Missouri, area to provide security to Confederate colonel John Calhoun. On several occasions, Fletch's band worked with John Thrailkill's Partisan Rangers and Bloody Bill's men.[794]

On August 8, 1864, when Fletch was returning to his band after attending a guerrilla council of war, somewhere in north Lafayette County the local militia there fired at his party, severely wounding him in the left arm. Two local doctors, Murphy and Regan of Wellington, had to amputate the arm three days later in the woods.[795] Fletch recovered and in September 1864 led his band in operations supporting General Price's Missouri raid. They continued in Missouri until the end of the war. No record exists that Fletch ever signed the oath of allegiance to the United States or was ever paroled. John N. Edwards in his 1877 book *Noted Guerrillas* described Fletch at the height of the war:

Fletch Taylor was a low, massive Hercules, who, when he had one arm shot off, made the other all the more powerful. Built like a quarter horse, knowing nature well, seeing equally in darkness and light, rapacious for exercise, having an anatomy like a steam engine, impervious to fatigue like a Cossack, and to hunger like an Apache, he always hunted a fight and always fought for a funeral.[796]

*Left to right*: Charles Fletcher Taylor, Frank James and Jesse James. Photograph taken around 1864 (Dr. Richard S. Brownlee Photograph Collection, P0070. Identifier #023823. The State Historical Society of Missouri).

## CALIFORNIA

Fletch's obituary gives a short synopsis of his life after the war, saying that he "went to Missouri and later to Nebraska. He was a native of the former state, and during his later years was connected with the operation of stage lines there. He was engaged in similar business in Humboldt county, California."[797] Fletch is quoted as having said: "I have never been ashamed of anything I did in that war. I simply fought for my own people and their homes, and I suppose if I had been born and raised in Kansas a few miles away I would have been just as strong on the other side."[798]

He died in Oakland at the age of 70 of natural causes and was cremated. Fletcher was buried in the Odd Fellows Cemetery, San Francisco, but was later disinterred and moved to Green Lawn cemetery, Colma, San Mateo County.[799]

## FURTHER READING

Banasik, Michael E., ed. *Cavaliers of the Brush: Quantrill and His Men.*
Castel, Albert E., and Thomas Goodrich. *Bloody Bill Anderson: The Short, Savage Life of a Civil War Guerrilla.*
Edwards, John N. *Noted Guerrillas, or, the Warfare of the Border.*
Erwin, James W. *Guerrillas in Civil War Missouri.*
Fellman, Michael. *Inside War: The Guerrilla Conflict in Missouri During the American Civil War.*
Petersen, Paul R. *Quantrill of Missouri: The Making of a Guerrilla Warrior.*
Stiles, T.J. *Jesse James: Last Rebel of the Civil War.*

# David Smith Terry, Sr.

Private, 1st Texas Mounted Rifles (Mexican War)
Colonel, Terry's Regiment, Texas Dismounted Cavalry
Born March 2, 1823; died August 14, 1889.

David Terry's father and mother had died by the time David was thirteen. His obituary gives us a thorough description of of his life before the civil war:

David Smith Terry was a Kentuckian. He was born on March 2, 1823, in Gold county of that State, and was, therefore, at the time of his death sixty-six years old. He was of Scotch-Irish descent, his ancestors having settled in Virginia in early days. The Terry family was famous during the war of the Revolution. The father of David S. Terry was a planter in Kentucky, but afterward lived in Mississippi, and, moving from there to Texas, died there in 1835. The widow followed her husband a year later, leaving her thirteen-year-old boy to look out for himself. Young Terry grew up wild and independent. He took an active part in the movement which secured the independence of Texas. He never had much schooling and acquired all his knowledge by his own exertions, principally through reading while a soldier on the frontier. After the independence of Texas was assured David Terry studied law in Houston and was there admitted to the bar. At the outbreak of the Mexican war he enlisted under Taylor and was with him at Monterey. In 1849 Terry led a company of Texans across the plains to California, having one or two fights with Indians on the way. He commenced mining in Calaveras county, but after a few months went to Stockton and began the practice of law. He at once entered into politics, and ran for Mayor of Stockton in 1850, but was defeated by Samuel Purdy. At this time he formed a partnership with D.W. Purley, which continued until 1855. In the fall of that year Terry was elected Justice of the Supreme Court for the short term, on the Native American ticket. He took his seat January, 1856. His decisions are considered terse logical and sound. In 1856 Judge Terry, then Chief Justice of the Supreme Court, had his adventure with S.A. Hopkins. Terry was an antagonist of the Vigilance Committee. A shipment of arms intended for State troops in this city had been seized on a schooner in the straits between San Pablo and San Francisco bays. A man named Reuben Maloney was supposed to know all about the matter, and the vigilantes desired his testimony. He refused to testify. S.A. Hopkins, Vigilance sergeant, was sent with two men to take Maloney by force. They found him in a room over Palmer, Cook and Co's bank, with Judge Terry and others. Seeing that he could not take Maloney with his small force, Hopkins went for re-enforcements and on his return met Terry, Maloney and the others, all armed with guns. Hopkins attempted to arrest Maloney. A fight ensued. Terry drew a knife and stabbed Hopkins in the neck. Afterward they all took refuge in the armory. The vigilantes surrounded the place and demanded the surrender of the fugitives. Promising not to injure Terry and Maloney, the two were surrendered. They were lodged in Fort Gunnybags and Terry, after remaining there some weeks, was released. Hopkins in the meantime having recovered.[800]

In 1859 Terry and David Broderick, a California senator, got into a disagreement concerning Terry's re-election.[801] On September 13, 1859, the two met for a duel. Just before they were both to fire, Broderick's pistol discharged early, allowing Terry a clear shot. Terry shot Broderick, who died three days later. Terry was acquitted of the murder.[802]

When the war came, David was still in California. Though a slavery and state's rights advocate, he remained in the West. David decided in 1863 that his time had come to serve the Confederacy. A.E. Wigstaff tells us of his David's war years:

After leaving Monterey they went to Comorgo and thence to Kings Ranch, Columbus and Richmond on the Brazos. Here the party stopped and rested two weeks at the plantation of Colonel Frank Terry, the judge's oldest brother, who was killed at the head of his regiment at Green River, for the purpose of recruiting their jaded animals, previous to proceeding to Tennessee, where they proposed joining Bragg's army. It was the wish of Judge Terry to enlist in the Eighth Texas Cavalry regiment, originally recruited and commanded by his brother Frank. After recruiting, they proceeded on horseback to Shreveport, La., thence to Natchez, Miss., and from there to Jackson, where General Jo. Johnson was commanding a small army, attempting to raise the siege of Vicksburg. While here Judge Terry and others of the party were introduced to General Johnson by Captain W.W. Porter, who was on the general's staff as assistant adjutant general. Terry was invited by General Johnson, with others of the party, to accompany him on his staff, where they remained for a short time, going with him to the Big Black in the rear of Vicksburg, and retiring with him to Jackson after the surrender of that stronghold. They remained with him during the seven days' siege of Jackson, and after the evacuation of that city and its occupation by Sherman and his forces on the 22nd of July, there being no more active operations. Judge Terry proceeded to Richmond to offer his services to the Confederate Secretary of War. The writer has been informed by a person who was in the confidence of the Confederate Secretary of War that when asked by the head of the department what he wanted, he demanded a commission as major general and the command of a department. He was told that this was out of the question; that such positions were reserved for those who had borne the heat of the conflict and earned such honors by distinguished services. However this may be, he was granted authority to raise a regiment in Texas, and after visiting President Davis, whom he had known while in the Mexican War, he started for the West. On his way to Texas

**David Smith Terry, Sr.** (*Life of David S. Terry,* by A.E. Wagstaff, 1892).

he fell in with the Confederate army, under Bragg, just a few days before the battle of Chickamauga. Here Terry was in his first and last battle. His brother's old regiment, the Eighth Texas Cavalry, then commanded by Colonel Harrison, of Texas, was in General Wharton's division, and he volunteered his services on the general's staff. In this engagement he received a flesh wound in the right arm, near the shoulder. After the battle of Chickamauga he proceeded to Texas, in company with Major S.B. Brooks and Duncan Beaumont, and they formed a regiment of conscripts, and he was chosen colonel, and Brooks's lieutenant colonel. Soon after he was commissioned brigadier general. The immediate department was under command of General Wharton, a brave and gallant officer, and the assignment of Terry to the command of the brigade incensed the military spirit of the senior colonel, named Bayler, who made some remarks while angry derogatory to the fighting qualities of General Wharton. Some unpleasant words passed between them, and, when the general visited the headquarters of Bayler to settle the dispute, in a friendly way, and while the two were alone, General Wharton was shot dead. Colonel Bayler was arrested and tried, and, having presented a clear case of self-defense before a civil tribunal, he was acquitted. General David S. Terry remained in command of the brigade in Texas until the close of the war, and his command was included in the surrender of troops under General E. Kirby Smith.[803]

## CALIFORNIA

David and his wife Cornelia moved back to California in 1869. He was unable to re-enter the political field. In 1884 Cornelia died. David became involved in a strange divorce case that same year. A woman named Sarah Althea Hill claimed that she was the legal wife of silver millionaire William Sharon and wanted a divorce. Sharon claimed they were never married. David became her lawyer. He lost the case and eventually wound up marrying her.[804] They appealed, and United States Supreme Court Justice Stephen J. Field, a former friend of Broderick's, ruled against them and jailed them both on contempt of court. David vowed he would get even. On August 14, 1889, he assaulted the Supreme Court justice at a train station in Lathrop, near Stockton. Field's bodyguard shot and killed David.[805] He was buried at Stockton Rural Cemetery, San Joaquin County.[806]

## FURTHER READING

Allardice, Bruce S. *Confederate Colonels: A Biographical Register.*
Buchanan, Albert Russell. *David S. Terry of California: Dueling Judge.*
Wagstaff, Alexander E., ed. *Life of David S. Terry.*

# John Thompson

Sergeant and captain, Company A (the Floyd Guard), 45th Virginia Infantry
Born July 8, 1839; died February 2, 1882.

John Thompson was one of eight children born to James Thompson and Rebecca Louisa Harrison in Tazewell County, Virginia. He enlisted on May 29, 1861, in Company A, 45th Virginia Infantry, and was elected sergeant.[807] The regiment was formed under Henry Heth, who was appointed colonel. In August, John and his regiment were moved to Kanawha Valley in present-day West Virginia, where on August 26, 1861, they experienced their first fight, leaving one wounded.[808]

On September 10, 1861, John and his comrades fought in the Battle of Carnifex Ferry. He was elected captain of Company A on October 16, 1861.[809] In December, the regiment became part of a new brigade under their old commander Henry Heth.

The regiment fought at the Battle of White Sulfur Springs on August 26–27, 1863, under the brigade command of Colonel George S. Patton (grandfather of WWII's General Patton), who wrote: "Repeated charges were now made on the right and left, which were in every instance handsomely repulsed. Desperate efforts were made to dislodge the Forty-fifth Regiment, but the steadiness of that regiment and the courage and skill of its commander foiled them all."[810] Colonel William Browne, commanding the regiment, wrote in his after-action report:

> During the engagement I repulsed eight separate and distinct charges of the enemy, besides frequent engagements with his skirmishers. In a majority of these charges the enemy came within the distance of fifteen or twenty paces of my line, and I am well satisfied I did him great damage, capturing some, killing and wounding large numbers. Notwithstanding the long marches my men had made (having marched about 100 miles during the four days preceding the engagement), I had no stragglers or scullers. I have never on any battle-field seen men act cooler and braver; they fought with a determination to do or die.[811]

John and his comrades spent the winter near Saltville. On May 9, 1864, the regiment resumed fighting at the Battle of Cloyd's Mountain. Colonel Browne again gives us the account of the battle:

> My center was the highest point of the ridge, running parallel with the mountain, and descending to the right and left of the center. The right being repulsed, the enemy occupied this high point and gave an enfilading fire to the left, which being also hotly assailed in front was driven back. My regiment fell back about 200 yards and rallied on the left of the Thirty-sixth Virginia Regiment, which had been brought from the extreme left to that point, the Sixtieth immediately rallying on my left. We maintained our position here under a very heavy fire for about fifteen minutes, when the enemy appeared in force on a hill on the left of the road, within 150 yards of the left of the Sixtieth Regiment. The whole line then moved back in tolerable order, and on arriving at the skirt of wood in rear of this last position made another stand for a short time and then continued to retreat. Some confusion ensued in consequence of the commands becoming intermingled. My loss in this battle was 20 killed, 93 wounded, 46 captured, and 6 missing; total, 174.[812]

John Thompson (*History of Tazewell County and Southwest Virginia*, by William C. Pendleton, 1920).

The regiment participated in Jubal Early's threat on the federal capital. John was wounded on September 22, 1864, at Fisher's Hill, New Market Valley, and sent to a hospital.[813] He reported to the regiment in November 1864. In early 1865, the regiment was ordered to Petersburg but the unit only got as far as Waynesboro,

Virginia, where John was captured.[814] He was sent to Fort Delaware via Harpers Ferry, arriving there on March 12, 1865. John remained at Fort Delaware for three months, took the oath of allegiance, and was released on June 14, 1865.[815]

## CALIFORNIA

John was elected Tazewell County sheriff in 1867.[816] With the death of his mother, the family, including his father and siblings, moved to Northern California by 1876. John and his family lived in Watsonville, eventually moving to Woodbridge, San Joaquin County, where he passed away in 1882 and was buried in the Woodbridge Masonic Cemetery.[817]

## FURTHER READING

Lardas, Mark. *Shenandoah 1864: Sheridan's Valley Campaign.*
Noyalas, Jonathan A. *The Battle of Fisher's Hill: Breaking the Shenandoah Valley's Gibraltar.*
Patchan, Scott C. *The Battle of Piedmont and Hunter's Raid on Staunton: The 1864 Shenandoah Campaign.*
Pendleton, William Cecil. *History of Tazewell County and Southwest Virginia: 1748–1920.*
Robertson, James I., Jr., ed. *Soldier of Southwestern Virginia: The Civil War Letters of Captain John Preston Sheffey.*

# Harry Innes Thornton, Jr.

Lieutenant and aide-de-camp to Major General George B. Crittenden
Captain and assistant adjutant general to General William W. Mackall
Captain and assistant adjutant general to General Braxton Bragg
Major, 32nd and 58th Consolidated Alabama Infantry
Born 1834; died February 25, 1895.

Harry Thornton, Jr., was the son of Harry Innes Thornton, Sr., a judge and member of the Alabama Legislature.[818] In 1854, Harry and his family moved to San Francisco, California, after President Pierce appointed Harry Sr. to the position of government land commissioner. Harry Jr. became an attorney and politician.[819] Although the family lived in California, they remained loyal to Alabama and the South, so when war came Harry Jr. resigned his position as a California state senator and traveled back to Alabama, where his cousin George B. Crittenden, a major general in the Confederate service, made Harry his aide-de-camp with the rank of lieutenant on September 6, 1861.[820] George Crittenden commanded the District of East Tennessee and was defeated at the Battle of Mill Springs. Harry was mentioned in the general's after-action report: "My aides, Lieuts. W.W. Porter and H.I. Thornton, displayed throughout the action intelligence, activity, and courage, and were of great service to me."[821] Crittenden was relieved on March 31, 1862, and arrested the next day on charges of drunkenness. General Braxton Bragg ordered a court of inquiry in July 1862 and Crittenden resigned as a general, reverting to colonel in October 1862. Colonels were not allowed to have aides-de-camp, and Harry was made assistant adjutant general with the rank of captain on the staff of General William W. Mackall on November 27, 1862.[822] On April 17, 1863, Mackall became chief of staff to General Braxton Bragg in the Army of Tennessee. Mackall may have recommended Harry for the job of Bragg's assistant adjutant general, for on June 10, 1863, he was assigned the position. Harry hoped for a field position and on July 25, 1863, he was commissioned as major in the 58th Alabama Infantry.[823] Harry's first action in a combat unit was in the Battle of Chickamauga on September 19–20, 1863. Harry was wounded slightly in the shoulder and ankle. At Resaca, Georgia, on May 15, 1864, Harry was again wounded. Colonel Jones in his after-action report stated: "I regret to state that Major Harry Thornton is among the number of the wounded, but his wound, though disabling for several weeks, perhaps is not dangerous. He endeavored to remain with the regiment, but after a trial of several days he was compelled to go to the rear."[824]

**Harry Innes Thornton, Jr.** (*Breeder and Sportsman*, **vol. 26, no. 9, 1895**).

Harry and his comrades went on to fight in the battles around Atlanta, and on July 22, 1864, Harry was wounded a third time though not seriously. C.C. Goodwin, a comrade of Harry's, wrote years later of an incident he witnessed involving Harry:

> One day, when General Sherman was before Atlanta and Bragg was in command of the Confederate army in his front, Bragg sent a flag of truce to Sherman. Thornton heard the order given and begged to go along. The little company passed through the union lines and came upon Sherman's headquarters. One side of Sherman's tent was thrown back and Sherman was seen within bending over a map and talking to a group of officers around him and gesticulating in his impetuous way. As the flag of truce was announced, all in the tent stood at attention. The ranking officer approached General Sherman. They had been friends before the war. Sherman greeted him cordially and presented him to the officers around him. Then the Confederate officer presented those who had accompanied him, until it came to Thornton, when Sherman said: "One moment." Looking intently at Thornton in his colonel's uniform, he said: "I had the honor of being associated with you in the trial of the case of Lucas Turner & Company versus Langston's Express Company, in Downieville, California. The trial began on the 16th day of February 1854, and lasted four days. It was a hot fight, but we licked 'em. I am glad to see you, Colonel Thornton." Then added, "Colonel Harry I. Thornton." Then he turned to his officers and introduced Thornton as an old California friend.[825]

Harry went on to fight at the battle of Franklin. His obituary, written in the *Breeders and Sportsman* periodical of 1895, stated:

> Col. Thornton at the battle near Franklin, Tennessee, specially distinguished himself. All the brigade officers higher in rank than he being killed, including General Jack Adams, he took command of the brigade and led it over the Harpeth Bridge against General Schofield and captured the celebrated Gin (Cotton Gin) house on the other side of the river. Seven times he led his men to the charge and seven times were they repulsed, the Harpeth was red with the blood of the Fifty-eighth, and scores of them lay dead on either bank. As they were preparing for another charge an order came which carried the regiment to another part of the battlefield.[826]

Harry and his regiment surrendered at Meridian, Mississippi, and were paroled on May 10, 1865.

## CALIFORNIA

C.C. Goodwin, mentioned earlier, wrote an interesting story about Harry just after the war:

> When the war closed Thornton prepared the necessary papers and went to Washington. He went to Secretary of War Stanton's office next morning and waited his turn to speak to him. When the others were disposed of, Thornton went to the rail, which separated the outer from the inner office, and Stanton asked in his brusque way what he could do for him. Thornton, pushing forward his papers, replied: "I have come, Mr. Secretary, with a petition for pardon." Stanton looked down upon him for an instant and then said: "You had better go about your business. We are not spending our time in pardoning boys." I suspect that hurt Thornton more than would a blow.[827]

Harry married his cousin Katherine Marshall Thornton on June 17, 1868, in Greene, Alabama.[828] The couple lived in Texas, Montana, Utah, Nevada and finally San Francisco, where Harry continued to practice law, specializing in mining litigation and criminal defense.[829] He died in 1895 and was buried in Cypress Lawn Memorial Park, Colma, San Mateo County.[830]

## FURTHER READING

Arnold, James. *Chickamauga 1863: The River of Death.*
Crute, Joseph H., Jr. *Confederate Staff Officers 1861–1865.*
Hewitt, Lawrence L., and Arthur W. Bergeron, eds. *Confederate Generals in the Western Theater: Essays on America's Civil War.*
Jody, Iosias. *58th Regiment Alabama Infantry.*
Secrist, Philip L. *The Battle of Resaca: Atlanta Campaign, 1864.*

# James Ellis Tucker

Private and color sergeant, Company K, 2nd Virginia Cavalry
Born October 25, 1844; died February 26, 1924.

Jim Tucker's life reads like an adventure novel. He was born in Virginia to Nathanial Beverley Tucker and Jane Shelton Ellis.[831] He attended school in England while his father was consul-general at Liverpool.[832] Jim also attended school at Vevey, Switzerland.[833] On January 7, 1863, he enlisted in the Albemarle Light Horse, a company that had formed in Albemarle County, Virginia, where Jim was listed as residing.[834]

On March 17, 1863, Jim fought his next battle at Kelly's Ford in Culpeper County, Virginia. General Fitzhugh wrote in his after-action report:

> My whole command acted nobly; sabers were frequently crossed and fences charged up to, the leading men dismounting and pulling them down, under a heavy fire of canister, grape, and carbine balls. Had I my command in the order it arrived in this enervating section of country, and not weakened by the absence of four squadrons on picket, guarding a line stretching from Griffinsburg, on

the Sperryville turnpike, to Richard's Ford, and by the large number of horses unfit for duty by exposure to the severe winter, with a very limited supply of forage, I feel confident the defeat of the enemy would have been changed into a disorderly rout, and the whole brigade resupplied with horses, saddles, and bridles.[835]

On June 17, 1863, while serving as color bearer, Jim was wounded in the leg at Aldie, Virginia. His wound was severe enough to warrant admission to the hospital in Richmond, where he remained until he was granted a furlough on August 20, 1863, to recuperate at home.[836] Jim missed the fighting at the Battle of Gettysburg, July 1–3, 1863. He returned to the regiment on November 15, 1863, participating in the Battle of Mine Run on November 27–December 2, 1863, before the regiment went into winter camp.

On March 24, 1864, Jim was admitted to the hospital in Richmond with furuncles on his feet and legs. He recovered and fought with his regiment at the Battle of Spotsylvania Courthouse on May 7, 1864, where he had his horse shot from under him and received a wound in the left thigh.[837] Jim was admitted to Chimborazo Hospital in Richmond and returned to the regiment on September 6, 1864. While he was in the hospital, his uncle tried to get him a cadetship to the Virginia Military Institute. The Confederate government could pull soldiers from the ranks whom it deemed fit to become military students. Even General Fitzhugh Lee sent a letter of recommendation:

> July 18, 1864
> General S. Cooper
> Adjt & Insp. General
>
> General,
>
> I have the honor to recommend for the appointment of cadet in the C.S. Army Private James E. Tucker 2d Va Cavalry. Private Tucker has been serving during the war as a soldier in the ranks and has been twice wounded at the head of his Regiment. No one in the command enjoys a higher reputation for gallantry, and from my personal knowledge of his character and merits, I do not think any of our young men are better qualified for, or more deserving, an appointment of this kind.
>
> I am respectfully Your Obd. Servant
> Fitz Lee
> Major General[838]

Unfortunately, he was not selected.

On December 15, 1864, Jim was officially made color sergeant of the regiment. At some point in December 1864, he was wounded by a saber cut to his right shoulder. The muster sheets

James Ellis Tucker, color bearer, Company K, 2nd Virginia Cavalry. James was wounded three times and had five horses shot from under him during the war (*Tales of the Tuckers*, by Beverly Randolph Tucker, 1942).

Chimborazo Hospital, Richmond, Virginia (Library of Congress, LC-DIG-ppmsca-33629).

**James Ellis Tucker (*Tales of the Tuckers*, by Beverly Randolph Tucker, 1942).**

for December do not give a specific date or location. He was hospitalized in Charlottesville, Virginia, but requested to be moved to Richmond:

> Harris House Hospital
> January 28th 1865

Dr.

> I respectfully ask to be transferred from this hospital to one in Richmond where my mother resides.

> Very respectfully
> Your obedient servant
> James E. Tucker
> Sergt. Co K, 2nd Va Cav[839]

Jim was transferred to the hospital in Richmond and returned to the regiment on March 21, 1865. He surrendered, carrying the flag, on April 9 and was paroled that day with the rest of the Army of Northern Virginia.

## CALIFORNIA

In 1869, Jim headed for California. He spent twelve years working for the Pacific Mail

Steamship Company.[840] In 1879, he married Laura Harris, his first wife, and they had two children.[841] Jim became chief appraiser at the customs house under Cleveland.[842] In 1895, Jim married his second wife, Mary Champney Bourn, in San Francisco.[843] Jim died in 1924 in San Francisco and was buried in Saint Helena Public Cemetery, Saint Helena, Napa County.[844]

## FURTHER READING

Driver, Robert J., and Harold E. Howard. *2nd Virginia Cavalry.*
Lardas, Mark. *Shenandoah 1864: Sheridan's Valley Campaign.*
Longacre, Edward G. *The Cavalry at Appomattox: A Tactical Study of Mounted Operations During the Civil War's Climactic Campaign, March 27–April 9, 1865.*
Parker, Robert W. *Lee's Last Casualty: The Life and Letters of Sgt. Robert W. Parker, Second Virginia Cavalry.*

# Henry Clay Tupper

2nd lieutenant, Company E (Helen Johnstone Guards), 24th Mississippi Infantry
1st lieutenant and aide-de-camp to Lieutenant General John C. Pemberton
Captain and assistant adjutant general, Brantley's Brigade, Anderson's Division

Born December 29, 1842; died February 29, 1928.

Henry Clay Tupper (Anne S.K. Brown Military Collection, Brown University Library).

The Tupper family could trace their lineage back to Plymouth, Massachusetts, and England. Henry's father, Tullius Cicero Tupper, was a lawyer in Canton, Mississippi, and an Episcopal layman. A man of considerable wealth, he was able to give his children the best education. Henry graduated from Princeton University, class of 1861, with a law degree.[845] He enlisted in the Helen Johnstone Guards (named after the woman who financed the company) on September 15, 1861, and was mustered into service on October 21, 1861.[846] Within the next month, because of his education, he was appointed 2nd lieutenant of the company. On November 22, 1861, at Savannah, Georgia, he reported to General Robert E. Lee, who was then in command of that department. Henry and his regiment returned to Mississippi in early 1862 and participated in their first battle at the siege of Corinth, Mississippi, April 29 to May 30, 1862. The unit was in the charge that swept back the federal forces at Perryville on October 8,

1862.[847] It is stated in his biography that Henry was wounded three times during the battle and that during his recuperation he was detailed to conscript soldiers for the regiment in Mississippi.[848] Not being satisfied with this detail, Henry may have used his father's connections to obtain a staff officer position. In late 1862, he wrote General Bragg:

> Canton Mississippi
> December 13th 1862
> General Braxton Bragg
> Commanding the Army of Tenn.
>
> General,
>
> I am directed by Lieut. General Pemberton commanding the Dept. of Miss. & East La, to inform you that it is his request that I be relieved from duty, detached from my command (in the 24th Regt. Miss. Vols.) and ordered to report to him for duty, as he desires my services temporarily on his staff.
>
> I deem it proper to state that the Captain, 1st and 2nd Jr. Lieutenants are on duty with the company to which I belong.
>
> I am very respectfully, Yr. obt. Svt.
> H.C. Tupper
> 2nd Lieut. Co E, 24th Miss Regt[849]

On January 29, 1863, Henry was appointed 1st lieutenant and aide-de-camp to General Pemberton in Vicksburg, Mississippi. He remained with the general though the Siege of Vicksburg, participating in the Battle of Baker's Creek (Champion Hill) on May 16, 1863. He was ordered to write a report on his position in the battle:

> Lieut. Gen. J.C. Pemberton.
> Headquarters, Demopolis, Ala., July 29, 1863.
>
> General: I have the honor to report the part taken by myself in the battle of Baker's Creek, on May 16.
>
> Soon after the skirmishing commenced near Mrs. Ellison's house, I was ordered to report to General Loring that you had been informed that a large column of the enemy were approaching on his right. About an hour after this I was ordered to direct General Loring to collect all the spades and picks and cut down the sides of the banks of the ford at Baker's Creek, on the road leading from Mrs. Ellison's to Colonel Withers' plantation. About 10 or 11 a.m. I was directed by you to order General Stevenson to halt his command until further orders. I found General Stevenson at the houses about 200 yards to the left of your headquarters in the field, and the order was immediately executed.
>
> Soon after the skirmishing began in front of General [S.D.] Lee, I was sent forward to ascertain if he could maintain his position, or if he needed re-enforcements. His reply was, "he thought he could hold his position for the present." His skirmishers were at that time falling back, but soon afterward went forward again. Soon after this I was ordered to order up one brigade of General Bowen's division to reinforce General Stevenson. Just before the command was ordered to fall back, and just after you had seen General Stevenson, where the battle was raging most terribly, I was directed by you to indicate the line of battle for Brigadier-General Buford, who came up with his brigade. I directed him to go forward to the road in which you saw General Stevenson at the time he informed you there were between 60,000 and 80,000 men in his front. When you and staff were retiring from the field, you ordered me to direct General Tilghman to halt his command, and I had just given the order when you rode up. I gave no more orders until you and staff arrived at the bridge which crosses the railroad at Edwards Depot, where you were informed by Major [Howell] Webb, adjutant and inspector general to Major-General Stevenson, that two brigades were approaching Edwards Depot, on the road running parallel with the railroad from Edwards Depot (the road taken by the command in marching out toward Clinton), one of these commanded

by Brigadier-General Barton; the other commander I do not remember. You then directed me to order General Barton to form a line of battle, with his right resting on the railroad in such a manner as to protect the depot. Immediately after you left for the entrenchments at Big Black, Major Webb informed me that this was a mistake; that no troops of ours were on this road. About this time an officer in command of six companies of the Twentieth Mississippi (mounted) reported to me that he had been sent to Edwards Depot to guard the wagon trains, which were at that time retreating across Big Black. I directed this officer to deploy his men as skirmishers, and keep the enemy in check as long as possible. I then rode to the entrenchments at Big Black, and informed you what I had done. This includes the verbal orders conveyed by me on the 16th. I carried none on the 17th.

> Very respectfully, your obedient servant,
> H.C. Tupper, Aide-de-Camp.
> Lieutenant-General Pemberton.[850]

Pemberton surrendered Vicksburg on July 4, 1863. Henry was paroled on July 6, 1863, and went home. He was still officially under the command of Pemberton even though the general was a prisoner. In August 1863, Henry wrote to the adjutant general in Richmond asking for an appointment as a captain and AAG because of his experience under Pemberton. When Pemberton was exchanged, he sent a letter of recommendation to Richmond on behalf of Henry.

Henry was officially relieved of staff duty under Pemberton on March 24, 1864, and was ordered to report to his regiment. He spent the next three months waiting for Richmond's decision on his promotion.[851]

On June 21, 1864, Henry was appointed assistant adjutant general of Brantley's Brigade, Anderson's Division, with the rank of captain.[852] Henry and his brigade participated in the Atlanta campaign where at the Battle of Jonesboro (August 31–September 1, 1864) he was severely wounded. He recovered and again was wounded at the Battle of Franklin, Tennessee, on November 30, 1864.[853] To rest and recuperate Henry was given a 30-day leave of absence.[854] In February 1865, Henry returned to the brigade and the remnant of the Army of Tennessee and participated in the Carolinas Campaign, where he surrendered along with the rest of the Army of Tennessee in North Carolina on April 26, 1865. He was paroled on May 31 from Greensboro and returned home to Canton, Mississippi.[855]

## CALIFORNIA

After the war, Henry studied law and began practicing in Mississippi. In July 1877, he moved to Fresno and started to practice law in California.[856]

On December 25, 1878, Henry married Elizabeth Johnson in San Francisco. They had nine children. Henry passed away in 1928 and was buried in Mountain View Cemetery, Fresno, Fresno County.[857]

## FURTHER READING

Daniel, Larry J. *Soldiering in the Army of Tennessee: A Portrait of Life in a Confederate Army.*
Knight, James R. *The Battle of Franklin.*
Martin, David G. *Vicksburg Campaign: April 1862–July 1863.*
Noe, Kenneth W. *Perryville: This Grand Havoc of Battle.*
Smith, Timothy B. *Champion Hill: Decisive Battle for Vicksburg.*

# Tazewell Tyler

Assistant surgeon, 22nd Battalion Virginia Infantry (formerly part of 2nd Virginia Artillery)
Assistant surgeon, General Hospital, Camp Winder, Richmond, Virginia
Surgeon, 13th South Carolina Infantry
Surgeon, 18th North Carolina Infantry
Surgeon, Jackson Hospital, Richmond, Virginia
Surgeon, 19th Battalion Virginia Heavy Artillery
Born December 6, 1830; died January 8, 1874.

Tazewell Tyler was the youngest of eight children born to John Tyler, the tenth president of the United States, and Letitia Christian Tyler, his first wife. "Taz," as he came to be called, followed the call of medicine and graduated from Jefferson Medical College in Philadelphia in 1853.[858] Taz decided to put his medical talent to work when the war came, and he was requested by the commander of the 22nd Battalion Virginia Infantry to join the unit as assistant surgeon because of a measles epidemic in the unit. On March 1, 1862, he enlisted and was assigned the duty.[859] He assisted the unit, helping attend to the casualties from the Battle of Cedar Mountain on August 9, 1862, and then on to Antietam on September 17, 1862. The unit was not actively engaged in that battle.[860]

By the winter of 1862-63, Taz was assigned as assistant surgeon at the general hospital at Camp Winder in Richmond. On January 26, 1863, he passed his exam for the position of full surgeon and was ordered to A.P. Hill's division, where he was assigned as surgeon in the 13th South Carolina Infantry on March 29, 1863.[861] He had spent only a month with the regiment when he was assigned surgeon duties with the 18th North Carolina Infantry on April 9, 1863.[862] This unit saw much heavier action at battlefields such as Chancellorsville and Gettysburg than had Taz's previous regiments. Taz performed many amputations once assigned to this regiment. During this period Taz may have started drinking heavily, for by April 1864 it was found that he was suffering from heart disease.[863] On April 23, 1864, Taz reported to Dr. William A. Carrington, medical director of General Hospitals in Virginia, and was assigned to duty on May 5, 1864, at the Jackson Hospital in Richmond, Virginia. Most of the soldiers received at Jackson were from Georgia and South Carolina. On May 15, 1864, Taz was assigned temporary duty in the medical division at Drewry's Bluff with reserve surgical corps.[864]

On September 7, 1864, Taz was temporarily assigned as surgeon for the 19th Battalion Virginia Heavy Artillery, stationed in the defensive positions around Richmond. He remained in this position for one month. By December Taz was surgeon-in-charge of the 3rd Division at the General Hospital at Camp Winder in Richmond.[865] He was not in very good health because of his drinking and heart disease, so he was given a 15-day furlough on January 15, 1865.[866] Taz returned on the 28th and continued his work at the hospital. On April 3, 1865, Taz was captured at the Jackson Hospital in Richmond by federal forces. He was officially paroled on April 16, 1865.[867]

## CALIFORNIA

After the war, Taz practiced medicine in Virginia and then move the family to Baltimore, Maryland.[868] By 1867, Taz finally headed west and moved with his family to San

Francisco, where he continued to practice medicine. Taz passed away in 1874 and was buried at Olivet Memorial Park, Colma, San Mateo County.[869] His obituary gives us a glimpse into his personality:

> All who knew him appreciated his many noble qualities and admired his brilliant intellect, which made him a most agreeable companion. He had for everyone a kindly greeting and welcome smile, and was untiring in his efforts to relieve the suffering; and, though not blessed with fortune, was ever ready to share his purse with a friend in distress. Where his services were required he was prompt at his post, and "Fideles ad mortem" was his motto.[870]

## FURTHER READING

Calcutt, Rebecca Barbour. *Richmond's Wartime Hospitals.*
Cunningham, Horace Herndon. *Doctors in Gray: The Confederate Medical Service.*
Gillispie, James. *Cape Fear Confederates: The 18th North Carolina Regiment in the Civil War.*

# Joseph P. Vaughn

Major and lieutenant colonel, 2nd Infantry Regiment, 3rd Division, Missouri State Guard
Private and major, Company E, 3rd Battalion Missouri Infantry (Erwin's)
Major, 6th Missouri Infantry

Born March 1830; died October 3, 1862.

Joseph Vaughn's father, Singleton Vaughn, originally came from Kentucky. He married and moved to Missouri, where he gained wealth.[871] Joseph and his siblings were privileged to receive good educations as children. In 1837, a slave family escaped Singleton and settled in Hamilton County, Indiana. Singleton went to Indiana, receiving a warrant to bring them back. He was stopped because they were now residing in a free state and Missouri was not considered an original slave state. In 1845, the court found for the individuals who stopped Singleton.[872] This occurred 13 years before the Dred Scott decision.

In 1850, Singleton moved his family. The Mexican war had started, and Joseph stayed in Missouri, joining Colonel Alexander W. Doniphan's 1st Regiment Mounted Missouri Volunteers.[873] After the war, Joseph headed west to Benicia, California, where his family had settled, and he studied law. When war came again, Joseph, now practicing law in California, decided to go back to Missouri to fight for the South. He joined the 2nd Regiment, 3rd Division of the Missouri State Guard and was elected major on August 20, 1861.[874] His first encounter with the federal army was at the Battle of Lexington on September 12–20, 1861.[875] Joseph did not fight again until the Battle of Elk Horn Tavern on March 7, 1862. General Sterling Price praises Joseph, now a lieutenant colonel, in his official report:

> Lieutenant Colonel James P. Vaughan [Price got his first name wrong] deserves especial consideration, for whose careless indifference to danger, where duty called him, was observed by everyone in the command. He never ceased to urge and encourage the men as long as the enemy held their position. His bearing was that of a true soldier and worthy the cause for which he fights so gallantry [sic].[876]

On March 17, 1862, the Missouri State Guard were dissolved, and the men joined the regular Confederate army. Joseph, now without a regular army commission, enlisted as a private in Company E of Lt. Colonel Andrew Eugene Erwin's 3rd Battalion Missouri Infantry on March 25, 1862, in Van Buren, Arkansas.[877] Lt. Colonel Erwin, realizing the background Joseph had in the guard, made him a major on May 15, 1862.[878] William McKendree Gwin, a former senator from California, wrote to Jefferson Davis in August requesting a brigadier generalship for Joseph, but it was turned down.[879] With the addition of companies, the battalion became the 6th Missouri Infantry and Joseph continued as its major.[880]

The regiment's first real fight came at Corinth, Mississippi, on October 3–4, 1862. Around 4 pm, Joseph was killed in a charge against the enemy works.[881]

## California

Joseph's body was sent back to California with his personal effects, including the $64.37 on him when he died.[882] He was buried in the family plot in the Benicia City Cemetery, Benicia, Solano County.[883]

## Further Reading

Cozzens, Peter. *The Darkest Days of the War: The Battles of Iuka and Corinth.*
Hanna, H.L., ed. *The Confederate Official Reports of the Battle of Elkhorn Tavern: 7th and 8th of March 1862.*
McGhee, James E. *Guide to Missouri Confederate Units, 1861–1865.*
Wood, Larry. *The Siege of Lexington, Missouri: The Battle of the Hemp Bales.*

# James Richard Waggener

Chaplain, 56th Virginia Infantry
Born January 24, 1830; died December 30, 1900.

From his childhood, James Waggener knew he wanted to be a preacher. He was born in Clarke County, Virginia. (The last name had various spellings, for example Waggoner and Wagoner, but Waggener seems to be the most common.) He became a Methodist preacher in Rockbridge County.[884]

In early 1862, James felt the need to preach the word of god to the Confederate army in the field and wrote to Daniel Coleman DeJarnette, Sr., who represented Virginia in both the First Confederate Congress and the Second Confederate Congress. He figured with the right backing he would be able to gain a chaplain's position in a regiment. DeJarnette had met James before and forwarded on his letter:

> Richmond
> April 3rd 1862
> Hon. G.W. Randolph
> Secretary of war

Sir

Permit me to call your attention to the enclosed letter of the Rev. J.R. Waggoner asking the appointment of Chaplain to some regiment now in the field. In my opinion no man can be more devoted to our cause or better fitted for the post.

Most respectfully
Hon D.C. DeJarnette[885]

James wrote:

Louisa C.H.
April 2nd 1862
Hon. D.C. DeJarnette

Dear Sir,

Having concluded to enter the army in the character of chaplain, I write to request you to apply for the appointment if it meets with your approval. I can supply the best recommendations as to character and qualification from this county if needed. My friend the Hon John Good jr. from Bedford co. will have no doubt unite with you in the application. It is not necessary to specify any particular [illegible]. I wish however to be in the Army of the Potomac (Confederate). Attention to this request would be profusely appreciated.[886]

On June 1, 1862, James was appointed chaplain of the 56th Virginia Infantry. Private John Holt of the regiment was overjoyed to finally have a chaplain for the regiment. He wrote to his wife on July 29, 1862:

We now have a chaplain to our regiment, the first we have had since we have been a regiment. He is a Methodist preacher and his name is Waggoner. He preaches for us twice on the Sabbath, in the morning and at night, and every Wednesday night. He holds prayer meetings every other night and distributes tracts and religious newspapers to us. He is a fine preacher, and I hope his service among us may be blessed with good consequences. If any people need religious instruction it certainly is soldiers.[887]

James preached to the men of the regiment through Second Bull Run, Antietam, Fredericksburg, Chancellorsville and finally Gettysburg, where the regiment received absolution by James before stepping off to attack the federal center in what became known as Pickett's Charge. Having seen so much death and destruction in his one year of service, James had had enough and resigned on July 10, 1863, just a week after Pickett's Charge.[888]

## CALIFORNIA

James went home to Lynchburg, Virginia. He continued as a preacher and by 1880 had settled in Santa Rosa, Cali-

**James Richard Waggener (Sketches and Portraits of the Virginia Conference, Methodist Episcopal Church, South, by John J. Lafferty and D.S. Doggett, 1890).**

fornia, where his son continued his legacy as a preacher in the Methodist Church. James died in 1900 and was buried in the Santa Rosa Rural Cemetery, Sonoma County.[889]

His funeral notice is here in full:

> The funeral of the late Rev. J.R. Waggener took place on Tuesday morning from the Fifth street M.E. church and was very largely attended. The pulpit and front of the organ loft were draped in black out of respect to the memory of the aged minister, who for nearly half a century occupied a pulpit in the Virginia conference of the M.E. Church, South. The choir rendered appropriate singing. The Rev. Dr. J.E. Moore of San Francisco conducted the funeral service and delivered an eloquent address and paid a tribute to the honored career of the deceased. There were many floral pieces.[890]

## FURTHER READING

Holt, John Lee. *I Wrote You Word: The Poignant Letters of Private Holt.*
Rollins, Richard, ed. *Pickett's Charge: Eyewitness Accounts at the Battle of Gettysburg.*
Young, William A., and Patricia C. Young. *56th Virginia Infantry.*

# William Thomas Welcker

Captain of artillery, CSA
Born June 24, 1830; died November 3, 1900.

William was born in Athens, McMinn County, Tennessee, to the notable attorney William L. Welcker. William became an orphan while a child and was raised on his grandfather's cotton plantation until age twelve, when he became a laborer on a farm in Tennessee. William's early schooling included the Rittenhouse Academy in Kingston.[891]

William graduated West Point in 1851 and was commissioned a lieutenant in the Ordnance Corps with duties in Benicia, California, Vancouver Ordnance Depot, Watervliet Arsenal and St. Louis Arsenal. On July 23, 1857, he married Katie W. Adair.[892]

William resigned his service in 1861 to serve Tennessee and the Confederacy. William could not reach the South because he was suspected of being disloyal to the Union and having the intention to join the Confederacy. He moved his family to Victoria, British Columbia, and there received a commission of captain of artillery in the Confederate army in 1864. The family eventually found their way into Texas by way of the Rio Grande by April 1865, after the armies of Lee and Johnston had surrendered. In July 1865, William, being considered a commissioned Confederate officer, was surrendered with Kirby Smith and Magruder's commands.[893] Never having fought against the Union but being commissioned, William sent a letter to the secretary of war asking for amnesty:

> New Orleans
> July 24, 1865
> Hon. W.H. Seward
> Secretary of State

Sir:

I have the honor hereby to make application that the President's amnesty may be extended to myself. I find myself in the excepted classes by reason of having been an officer of the army and tendering my resignation on the breaking out of the war. I am a native of Tennessee and in the year 1847 that state having eleven cadetships in the Military Academy at West Point conferred one of them upon me. I was graduated in 1851 and served in the ordnance department until Tennessee separated herself from the Union and engaged in the war. Having been educated as a soldier by her or through her instrumentally I felt that as a man of honor my services were due her. Accordingly after having turned over to my successor my money, property and closing my accounts with the U.S. Treasury, I resigned. But I did not succeed in reaching the South and in 1862 I went to live in the British Colony of Vancouver Island. Here I engaged exclusively in private pursuits until the autumn of 1864 when the Confederate government, having sent me a Captain's commission and funds to make the journey with, I proceeded to the South arriving in Texas by way of Matamoras in April 1865. Soon after the Trans-Mississippi Department was surrendered and I along with it.

   I have been financially ruined by the war and it is necessary for the support of my wife and children that I should get to work immediately. I therefore trust that the President will be pleased to extend to me the full benefits of his amnesty.

Respectfully your Obdt. Serv.
Wm. T. Welcker
Capt. Conf Artillery C.S.A.[894]

William received his amnesty before the month had ended.

## CALIFORNIA

   William returned to California but was not allowed to practice law because he had been a commissioned Confederate officer. Later he took the family to Idaho, where he practiced law for a short time. He then moved the family again to British Columbia, where he mined and was a steamship company agent.[895]

   In 1868, the family moved to San Francisco, where he looked for work; in 1869 he became professor of mathematics at the University of California in Berkeley. He also went into politics and was elected state superintendent of public instruction. In 1899, the University of California elected William emeritus professor of mathematics.[896] He died in 1900 and was buried in the Mountain View Cemetery, Oakland, Alameda County.[897]

**William Thomas Welcker (Annual Report of the Association of the Graduates of the United States Military Academy, 1901).**

## FURTHER READING

Eliot, Ellsworth. *West Point in the Confederacy.*
Patterson, Gerard A. *Rebels from West Point.*
Welcker, William T. *Advanced Algebra.*
_____. *Military Lessons: Military Schools, Colleges and Militia.*

# Milton Edward White

Private, 3rd Arkansas Infantry Battalion
Private and corporal, Company F, 21st Arkansas Infantry (McRae's)
Private and corporal, Company F, 15th (Northwest) Arkansas Infantry
Private, Company H, 1st Arkansas Cavalry (Crawford's)
Born September 4, 1838; died January 9, 1923.

Milton White's parents were James A. White, born in North Carolina on August 5, 1801, and Matilda Lawder, who was born in Tennessee.[898] The couple settled in the Arkansas Territory just after the birth of Milton. Milton enlisted in the 3rd Arkansas Infantry Battalion on October 1, 1861, in Bentonville for nine and a half months.[899] The unit was later designated the 21st Arkansas Infantry.

On February 13, 1862, Milton was made 2nd corporal and fought in his first battle at Elkhorn Tavern on March 6–8, 1862.[900] The regiment sustained heavy losses, with the company losses at 3 killed and 2 wounded out of 70.[901] Milton was detailed as a teamster. He continued in this position during the Battle of Corinth in June 1862. He was promoted to wagon master on August 31, 1862, and continued this job through the Siege of Vicksburg.[902] He surrendered with the unit on July 4, 1863. Milton was released and sent home to await parole camp and final release to join the regiment again. The unit never formed again, and Milton enlisted in Crawford's 1st Arkansas Cavalry, which formed in December

1863 in Camden, Arkansas.[903] He fought with the 1st during the Red River Campaign, March–May 1864, and during Sterling Price's raid through Arkansas, Missouri and Kansas, during which Milton received a gunshot wound. He was captured at the Battle of Mine Creek, Kansas, on October 25, 1864.[904] He was sent to the Mound City, Kansas, hospital on November 1, 1864, discharged from the hospital on December 17, 1864, and sent to Ft. Leavenworth, Kansas, arriving on December 21, 1864. No record exists of his release at the end of the war.

## CALIFORNIA

Milton married Eunice Melvina Harvey sometime during the war. The marriage probably occurred in the interim between his return home from Vicksburg in July 1863 and his second enlistment in December 1863.[905] The couple had seven children and divorced in 1879. Milton died in 1923 at the San Joaquin General Hospital

**Milton Edward White fought through most of the war in multiple Arkansas units. He received a gunshot wound and was captured at the Battle of Mine Creek, Kansas, on October 25, 1864 (courtesy Joyce Kay Espinosa).**

in French Camp of chronic Bright's disease. He was buried at Park View Cemetery, Manteca, San Joaquin County.[906]

## FURTHER READING

Apostolis, Dismas Reinald. *21st Arkansas Infantry Regiment.*
Bailey, Anne. *Civil War Arkansas: Beyond Battles and Leaders.*
Hanna, H.L., ed. *The Confederate Official Reports of the Battle of Elkhorn Tavern: 7th and 8th of March 1862.*
Hoehling, A.A. *Vicksburg: 47 Days of Siege.*

# Richard Owen Whitehead

Captain and lieutenant colonel, Company A (Marion Rangers), 16th Virginia Infantry
Born December 27, 1830; died March 4, 1911.

The Whitehead family had been in Virginia since the mid 1600s. Richard was born in Suffolk, Nansemond County, Virginia. He was able to gain a good education because of his family's wealth and in 1851 graduated from the Virginia Military Academy.[907] He went on to attend the University of Virginia Law School.[908] When Abraham Lincoln was elected, Richard felt compelled to write him and ask that he resign the office of the presidency in Charleston, South Carolina:

> Suffolk, Virginia
> Jan 6th 1861.

Dear Sir:

I love my Country, as well, I believe, as I love my life; and I love every man who is willing to risk his life to save his country.

The Union is sick unto death, if not dead already; you are the only man who lives, who can restore it to life. Mr. Lincoln, do not regard this proposition as an idle one.

Will it be too great a humiliation to you, to go in your closet, & on your bended knees, read the proposition over once? Remember, it is to him you humble yourself not to man. If there is any good in it, he will show it to you; if there is no good, he will show it to you.

The action proposed may cost you your life but what of that? It will save your Country from civil war, and it places you as a moral hero in the estimation of the whole world, next to Washington, if not by his side.

No moral spectacle, in the whole history of man, would be so grand as yours, and I humbly believe, that it would enshrine you with unparalleled love, as the chosen President, in the hearts of the whole American People. But, if you were struck down, the next minute after you did it, by the fury of madmen, North or South, it would win for you an immortality of the purest fame, worth a hundred Presidencies. Will you go to Charleston? You must go in disguise, not from fear, but no one must know what you intend to do and there, throwing off your disguise, upon the chasm of the Earthquake of terror, which trembles beneath the nation, resign, fully, to the will of the nation. God designs to humble this people, and you, its head, must bow first.

He will then still the raging of the people, as he stilled the raging of the sea, and closed the mouths of the lions for Daniel.

I am, Dear Sir, an humble young lawyer & citizen of Virginia, a pupil of Colonel Francis H Smith, of the Military School of Virginia, was an elector for Bell & Everett, am an admirer of patriotism unto death, whether called by the name of Republican, Whig, or Democratic. And if you will treat this appeal, made in humility & prayer, with that respectful consideration which is due to the spirit & purpose with which it is penned.

> I am Dear Sir,
> Your obedient, humble Servant:
> R.O. Whitehead.
> Suffolk, Virginia[909]

In March 1861, Richard started to gather men for the upcoming war and formed the Marion Rangers.[910] They were mustered into the Confederate service as Company A, 16th Virginia Infantry, on July 1, 1861.[911] Richard was commissioned captain of Company A and the regiment was assigned duty through the winter in Norfolk. Richard and his company fought at the Battle of Malvern Hill and the Second Battle of Manassas, where Richard received a gunshot wound to the right toe. While convalescing he was promoted to major.[912] He remained on leave through March 6, 1863, missing the battles of Antietam and Fredericksburg. On May 16, 1863, Richard was commissioned as lieutenant colonel and commanded the regiment.[913] He commanded the unit at the Battle of Chancellorsville. Richard was second in command under Colonel Joseph H. Ham at the Battle of Gettysburg.

By the spring of 1864, Richard was back in command of the regiment and fought in the Battle of the Wilderness. He was at Petersburg with the regiment, witnessed the mine explosion, and participated in the bloody Battle of the Crater. He wrote:

> When the artificial earthquake caused by the explosion of General Grant's mine awakened Petersburg in the early morning of July 30, 1864, the 16th Virginia were sleeping the sleep of the dead just in the trenches at Wilcox's barn, about a mile to the right of the explosion. If the 16th heard the thunder, they probably turned over and went to sleep, for it was too early to fry fat pork and get peanut coffee; but if they thought that it was only a bigger gun than usual firing from Fort Hell, or Hare's Hill upon the doomed city, the wide awake pickets soon undeceived them.
>
> It might have been an hour or more after the explosion when we received orders to get under arms as quietly as possible, and proceed by the ravines and covered way towards the mine. Just before reaching it, the regiment was halted and ordered to unsling knapsacks, fix bayonets and leave everything behind except arms and ammunition. The 16th knew what that meant, for it was not their first bayonet charge.[914]

Richard went on to say:

> The Confederates were upon the Union troops with fixed bayonets and loaded muskets, almost before they knew we were coming. They had either to kill us all or surrender and they laid down their arms.
>
> Many were killed who would not surrender, in trying to escape back to the Union lines. Hundreds sought shelter in the crater and were either killed or captured a few moments later. General Mahone came up though the firing was exceed-

**Richard Owen Whitehead (*The Story of American Heroism*, 1897).**

ingly dangerous and joined the right of the 16th to the left of 8th Georgia, I believe, so as to cover the gap made by the crater. My regiment stretched across the front of the crater and beyond it on each side, and had orders to reform our torn and broken line of defense. So great had been the power of the explosion, it was said to have killed three hundred men outright and a thousand men could have been buried in the mine.[915]

The Confederate Congress listed Richard on the "Roll of Honor" for his capture of a federal flag at the battle.[916]

On October 27, 1864, Richard, still in command of the regiment in the trenches at Petersburg, Virginia, fought in the Battle of Hatcher's Run. Again he was wounded, and was given furlough November 2, 1864. The wound was not serious, and he returned to the Petersburg defenses. Richard's next wounding occurred on January 30, 1864, with a wound to the left shoulder.[917] He was admitted to the CSA General Hospital in Charlottesville and did not return to duty until April 6, 1865, three days before the surrender at Appomattox Court House.[918]

## California

After the war, Richard left Virginia and practiced law in Knox, Tennessee, where he met Amanda Wharton Seay and married.[919] By 1881, the family were living in Oakland, California, where Richard continued his law practice. Richard died in 1911 of apoplexy and was cremated.[920] No cemetery is listed, so his ashes may have remained with the family.

Richard wrote about an interesting incident that happened on his way home from war:

> When I was returning home as a paroled prisoner from Appomattox an officer stepped up to me on the steamer between Richmond and Old Point Comfort. He proved to be the same General Henry G. Thomas of Maine. I did not know him. He made himself known, and just before we reached Old Point, he made the following proposition: "You are sick," he said. "The battle has gone against you. Come, go with me to Portland. Here are my fine horses, we can ride around the city; I have a nice yacht, we can sail around the bay. Then. I have a beautiful little farm near Saccarappi—plenty of cows, milk, sugar and brandy—go with me and get well, and when you are well, if you need me I will be glad to try and help you build up your fortunes."
>
> I have known since that day that "Southern hospitality" in excellent form is found also north of Mason and Dixon's line, and though I have never been able to accept the general's offer I have never ceased to feel grateful.[921]

## Further Reading

Schmutz, John F. *The Battle of the Crater: A Complete History.*
Trask, Benjamin H. *16th Virginia Infantry.*
Wallace, Lew. *The Story of American Heroism: Thrilling Narratives of Personal Adventures During the Great Civil War, as Told by the Medal Winners and Roll of Honor Men.*

# Peter Singleton Wilkes

Private, sergeant major, and assistant quartermaster, Company C, 3rd Battalion Missouri Cavalry
Private, Company A, 3rd Missouri Cavalry
Born February 8, 1827; died January 2, 1900.

Peter Singleton Wilkes led an interesting and privileged life before and during the war. His father, Edmund Wilkes, was a Virginian and mother, Cynthia Houston, was from North Carolina. Edmund slowly moved west with his wife, first to Maury County, Tennessee, where Peter was born, and then into Missouri.[922] In 1850 Lanceford Wilkes, Peter's older brother, and Peter became students at the University of Missouri at Columbia. He and his brother received bachelor of arts degrees in 1852 and master of arts degrees in 1855.[923] Lanceford became a Baptist minister and lived near Peter in California.

When the war came, Peter, torn between serving the Confederacy as a politician or soldier, chose the latter and enlisted as a private on March 25, 1862, in Van Buren, Arkansas, in the 3rd Battalion Missouri Cavalry. Because of his advanced education he was immediately promoted to sergeant major on that same day.[924] On May 7, 1862, Peter was promoted to assistant quartermaster and on June 15, 1862, was transferred to Green's regiment of Missouri Volunteers, which became Company A of the 3rd Missouri Cavalry on November 4, 1862.[925] The muster sheets list him as a private. Attacking a federal outpost near Clark's Mill in Missouri on November 7, 1862, Peter saw his first action with the unit. The federals submitted after a short battle.[926] Peter and his comrades were trapped in an ambush at the Battle of Hartville on January 11, 1863, leading to six dead and nineteen injured.[927] The regiment next fought at Helena, Arkansas, on July 4, 1863, with regimental losses of three killed and six wounded.[928] Peter and his comrades went on to fight almost continuously during the defense of Little Rock in August and September 1863 with battles at Brownsville, Bayou Metoe, Reed's Bridge and Bayou Fourche. On October 25, 1863, at Pine Bluff, Arkansas, the regiment attacked while dismounted and were repulsed with casualties amounting to three killed and seven wounded.[929]

On January 1, 1864, Peter was put on detached duty to the commissary department. During this time, he may have been garnering votes for a run as a Missouri representative in the Confederate Congress. In May 1864, Peter was elected to the Confederate House of Representatives as the representative from Missouri in the 2nd Confederate Congress. He may have won the election because he had been a soldier and had gained their votes. He took the seat on November 8, 1864, and continued as a representative until the end of the war.[930]

## CALIFORNIA

One of Peter's obituaries gives us a description of his life after the war:

> After the close of the war, he went to Mazatlán, Mex., and later came to Stockton, where he formed a law partnership with Judge Joseph H. Budd, father of ex–Gov. Budd, and later became associated with David S. Terry under the firm Terry, Carr and Wilkes. Wilkes was 72 years of age, and although he acquired considerable wealth through his marriage, he lost it in the financial collapse, which wrecked many people in this city.[931]

Peter died in 1900 and was buried in the Stockton Rural Cemetery, Stockton, San Joaquin County.[932]

## FURTHER READING

McGhee, James E. *Guide to Missouri Confederate Units, 1861–1865.*
Mudd, Joseph Aloysius. *With Porter in North Missouri.*
Nichols, Bruce. *Guerrilla Warfare in Civil War Missouri.*
Warner, Ezra J., Jr., and W. Buck Yearns. *Biographical Register of the Confederate Congress.*

# Ambrose Rucker Woodroof
## (a.k.a. John Miller)

Private and 1st lieut., Kirkpatrick's Company, Virginia Light Artillery (Amherst Artillery)
Born 1835; died October 8, 1896.

Born to Pitt Woodroof, a Methodist minister, and Margaret McDaniel Rucker, Ambrose led an unusual and tragic life. The family's first tragedy occurred in 1857, when Ambrose's mother and six of his siblings died of typhoid fever. The Reverend Woodroof survived and during the war ran a Confederate hospital from his home.[933] Ambrose married June Churning Pleasants in Amherst County. His brother Alfred married Jennie's sister. Ambrose and his brother Alfred became business partners in Lynchburg and shared a farm in Amherst County. The brothers' business went downhill as the war approached.[934] When war came, Alfred enlisted in the 2nd Virginia Cavalry. Also feeling he needed to do his duty to Virginia, Ambrose enlisted as a private in the Amherst Artillery on March 28, 1862, in Orange Court House.[935] His brother John enlisted a few days later in the unit. On May 15, 1862 Ambrose was elected 2nd lieutenant.[936] The unit experienced its first fight at Garnett's farm on June 13, 1862.

On October 11, 1862, Ambrose was promoted to 1st lieutenant.[937] By November, the artillery was in the defensive lines of Fredericksburg, Virginia.

In May 1863, Ambrose's brother Pitt enlisted in the company. He joined John and Ambrose in moving north with the army in its advance into Pennsylvania. We have some insight into how the men of the unit felt about Ambrose. Henry Robinson Berkeley's diary, *Four Years in the Confederate Artillery,* describes an incident in camp: "Today Lt. Woodruff [Woodroof] attempted to arrange the gun crew and messes in our company to suit his notion. He suited no one, not even his own brother Pete [Pitt]. Lt. Hobson and the Capt. [Kirkpatrick] came to our rescue and we all soon got back into our old places."[938]

At Gettysburg, the battalion arrived too late to fight on July 1, 1863, and were in position on Seminary Ridge near the college the next day. On July 3, the unit was on the extreme left of the Confederate line. The Amherst Artillery had no casualties and used no ammunition during the battle.[939] On July 4, 1863, Ambrose and twelve men of the unit became prisoners. He was confined at Fort McHenry, Maryland, on July 6 and sent to Fort Delaware four days later.[940] Set for exchange on July 18, 1863, the order was rescinded, and Ambrose was sent to Fort Monroe on February 6, 1864. He was finally exchanged for a Lieutenant Doughty of the 53rd Indiana on February 26, 1864.[941]

Ambrose returned to the unit and continued the fight until he was wounded and captured a second time on July 9, 1864, at the Battle of Monocacy.[942] As of January 5, 1865, Ambrose was listed as wounded and a prisoner of the federals. We can assume he remained captive until the end of the war.

## CALIFORNIA

Ambrose's life after the war became complicated. Because of his financial losses, he left his wife and family to try to make his fortune in California. Whether he told his wife he would send for her is not known. Ambrose assumed the name of John Miller and got a job in Sacramento working as a clerk for the Central Pacific Railroad Company. He eventually was appointed secretary of the Contract and Finance Company. After the offices were moved to San Francisco, Ambrose, a.k.a. John Miller, was accused of embezzlement of $800,000.[943]

He was arrested on June 21, 1875, and sent for a lawyer, who in turn contacted one of his brothers in Lynchburg, who received $60,000 to compensate Ambrose's company. The railroad also was given the mansion owned by Ambrose. The company in the end did not prosecute.[944] In 1896, Ambrose killed himself. Part of his obituary reads: "Miller has been in ill health for some time and has been suffering from severe pains in his head, which at times have affected his mental equilibrium, and it is thought that, believing death to be but a matter of a few weeks, and living in dread of insanity, he ended his sufferings with a bullet from his pistol."[945]

Ambrose was buried in the Sacramento City Cemetery, Sacramento, Sacramento County.[946] His second wife, Elizabeth, remained at his side to the end and passed away in 1900.[947]

## Further Reading

Berkeley, Henry Robinson. *Four Years in the Confederate Artillery: The Diary of Private Henry Robinson Berkeley.*

Sherwood, William Cullen, and Richard Ludlum Nicholas. *Amherst Artillery, Albemarle Artillery, and Sturdivant's Battery.*

# Edmund Platoff Zane

Private and 1st lieutenant, Company I and F, 12th Virginia Cavalry
1st lieutenant and adjutant, field and staff, 19th Virginia Cavalry
Born 1835; died May 7, 1893.

Edmund Zane was born in Wheeling, West Virginia, to Ebenezer Zane and Mary M.S. McGovern. Edmund's father died in 1843, leaving the family very well off. His wife's net worth was $100,000 dollars in 1850.[948] By 1860 it had grown to real estate valued at $83,000 and personal estate at $29,000.[949]

Edmund was able to have a good education, receiving a law degree at Georgetown University in the classes of 1855 and 1860.[950] In June 1862, he enlisted in Rippon, then West Virginia, as a private in Company I of the 12th Virginia Cavalry, commanded by Colonel Ashur W. Harman.[951] The history of the Laurel Brigade gives a good account of the unit's participation in Robertson's brigade during Second Manassas:

> In the meantime Robertson's brigade had reached the Lewis house on the ridge overlooking Bull Run. The Second Virginia, under Colonel Munford, was in front. A small body of Federal cavalry was seen. Lieut.-Col. J.W. Watts of the Second, with one squadron charged and routed it, but before he had gone far discovered Buford's brigade of cavalry drawn up. The rest of the Second now coming up, the whole regiment was soon engaged with the enemy, meeting their charge with a countercharge. Here a terrible hand-to-hand fight ensued, and the Federals with greatly superior numbers began to force back the Confederates, when the Seventh, under Capt. S.B. Myers; the Twelfth, under Col. A.W. Harman, and the Sixth, under Colonel Flournoy, coming up to the rescue, the Federals were

soon forced from the field, and the Seventh and Twelfth continued the pursuit until the enemy were driven beyond the turnpike at Stone Bridge. Says Stuart in his report, "Nothing could have equaled the splendor with which Robertson's regiments swept down upon a force greatly outnumbering them." In this fight Colonel Brodhead of the First Michigan was mortally wounded by Lieut. Lewis Harman, adjutant of Twelfth Cavalry. Three hundred prisoners with many horses, arms, and equipments were captured. The loss in Robertson's brigade was five killed and forty wounded.[952]

At Antietam, the unit was on the extreme right of the Confederate line, arriving the day before the battle. They experienced no action the next day.[953]

On November 20, 1862, Edmund was appointed 2nd lieutenant of Company F. He commanded the company in the absence of Captain Harry W. Gilmor, who had been captured just before Antietam. Eight days later, he led the company in a skirmish at Berryville, Virginia, which was used against him. By the spring 1863 those who felt they had been passed up for the command of the company given to Edmund persuaded General Jones to bring up charges against the lieutenant:

12th VA Cavalry April 2, 1863

Charges and specifications against Lt. E.P. Zane Co. F, 12th VA Cav
Charge-Drunkenness on duty
Specifications—In this that the said Lt. E.P. Zane on the 20th day of March 1863 while on a march and in command of his company was himself under the influence of intoxicating [sic] and remained under its influence largely the whole day. Witness Asst. Surgeon Williams 12th Va. Cav., Sergeant Hansberger, Private Bozin[954]

Edmund was also charged with cowardice, which was claimed to have occurred at Second Manassas. He asked for an inquiry by General Jones and it never happened. Within a month, he sent a letter of resignation to the secretary of war:

Camp near Harrisonburg May 27, 1863
Hon James A. Seddon, Sec. of War

Sir,

I respectfully tender to you my resignation as 1st Lieutenant in Co F, 12th Regt. VA Cav. which I am influenced to do for private reasons and have a desire to be connected with Col. William L. Jackson or some other command in Northwestern Va. my native portion of the state.

Edmund P. Zane 1st Lieut. Co F, 12th VA Cav.[955]

Edmund received reinforcement in a letter sent to Secretary Seddon by Charles W. Russell (delegate from Virginia to the Confederate Provisional Congress, 1861–62, and representative from Virginia in the Confederate Congress, 1862–65):

Richmond June 11, 1863
Hon. Jas. A. Seddon, Secy of War

Dear Sir,

About the beginning of this year, you appointed E.P. Zane 1st Lieutenant of a company in the 12th VA Cavalry. He was recommended for promotion by Col. A.W. Harman. Afterward Brig. Gen. W.E. Jones wrote to you protesting against the appointment and you suspended it. Gen Jones made two accusations against Lt. Zane one of which was serious—being that of cowardly behavior in an affair at Berryville. He had derived his information from others, I believe the letter of Col. Harman now on file, and the papers, which I now enclose, will satisfy you that the charges were wholly unjust. Lt. Zane is furious that he was not provided a hearing from Gen Jones who at one time advised him to ask for a court of inquiry but afterwards it could not be had probably because the command was too actively deployed. Finally, Lt. Zane finding his position for several reasons intolerable (as he informs me) tendered his resignation.

I feel quite confident that Gen. Jones has done injustice to a young gentleman of high standing at home who served faithfully and gallantly as a private until he was promoted. Under the circumstances, I do not know how he is to pursue any redresses. I can only ask on his behalf that his resignation be accepted and that the enclosed papers may be filed with the letters of Gen Jones and Col Harman on this serious subject.

Very Respectfully Charles W. Russell[956]

Edmund went further and contacted Colonel William L. Jackson, who wholly endorsed the young lieutenant:

Hdq. Huntersville December 1, 1863
Hon. James A. Seddon Sec. of War

Sir,

Enclosed find letter of Lt. Col. Thompson commanding the 19th Regt. Va. Cav. recommending E.P. Zane as Drill Master of the 19th Regt. Va. Cav. I respectfully approve said recommendation. Lt. Z is a gallant officer and has for some time discharging officially the duties of Drill Master to my cavalry. Hoping you will confer the appointment for him.

I am very respectfully You Obdt. Servt.
William L. Jackson, Colonel[957]

On December 9, 1863, Edmund was appointed 1st lieutenant and adjutant of the 19th Virginia Cavalry.[958] Edmund fought with the unit in Early's Campaign against the federal capital. On October 9, 1864, he was wounded in the left arm at the Battle of Tom's Brook in Shenandoah County, Virginia. Edmund was sent to the Confederate general hospital in Danville, Virginia, where he received a 40-day furlough on November 10, 1864.[959] He returned just before Christmas, missing the Battle of Cedar Creek, Virginia. Edmund was officially paroled in Danville, Virginia, on May 8 and took the oath of allegiance on May 25, 1865.

## California

Edmund married Mary Louise Loughborough in Wheeling around 1868, and the couple moved to Baltimore, where he left law and became a grocer and merchant.[960] They had three children. By 1871, the family had moved to San Francisco, where Edmund continued as a merchant.[961] Later in life, he became a real estate agent. Edmund died prematurely of a fractured skull from a fall off a steep stairway in 1893.[962] He was just 57 years old. Edmund was buried in Holy Cross Cemetery, Colma, San Mateo County.[963]

## Further Reading

Armstrong, Richard L. *19th and 20th Virginia Cavalry.*
Frye, Dennis E. *Twelfth Virginia Cavalry.*

# Notes

1. *An Illustrated History of Sonoma County, California: Containing a History of the County of Sonoma from the Earliest Period of Its Occupancy to the Present Time* (Lewis Publishing Co., Chicago, IL) 1889, 534.

2. John Peyre Thomas, *The History of the South Carolina Military Academy: With Appendixes* (Walker, Evans & Cogswell Co., Charleston, SC) 1893, 107.

3. https://www.fold3.com/image/20/83573927, NARA M267. Compiled service records of Confederate soldiers from South Carolina units.

4. United States War Dept., *The War of the Rebellion: A Compilation of the Official Records of the Union & Confederate Armies*, Series 1, Vol. LIII (Government Printing Office, Washington, D.C.) 1902, 36.

5. *An Illustrated History of Sonoma County, California: Containing a History of the County of Sonoma from the Earliest Period of Its Occupancy to the Present Time* (Lewis Publishing Co., Chicago, IL) 1889, 534.

6. Find A Grave, database and images (https://www.findagrave.com: accessed 11 July 2019), memorial page for James Seale Austin (1838–26 Oct 1917), Find A Grave Memorial no. 28327775, citing Santa Rosa Rural Cemetery, Santa Rosa, Sonoma County, CA, USA; Maintained by Jeanie Leete (contributor 47019987).

7. http://www.fold3.com/image/8275204/, NARA M311. Compiled service records of Confederate soldiers from Alabama units.

8. William Calvin Oates, *The War Between the Union and the Confederacy, and Its Lost Opportunities, with a History of the 15th Alabama Regiment and the Forty-Eight Battles in Which It Was Engaged* (Neale Publishing Co., New York and Washington, D.C.) 1905, 212–216.

9. William Calvin Oates, *The War Between the Union and the Confederacy, and Its Lost Opportunities, with a History of the 15th Alabama Regiment and the Forty-Eight Battles in Which It Was Engaged* (Neale Publishing Co., New York and Washington, D.C.) 1905, 246.

10. California, Voter Registers, 1866–1898 [database on-line]. Provo, UT, USA: Ancestry.com.

11. California, Voter Registers, 1866–1898 [database on-line]. Provo, UT, USA: Ancestry.com.

12. Find A Grave, database and images (https://www.findagrave.com: accessed 15 April 2019), memorial page for Alvis Early Averrett (13 Nov 1846–27 Mar 1894), Find A Grave Memorial no. 117950975, citing Pioneer Cemetery, Watsonville, Santa Cruz County, California, USA; Maintained by Find A Grave (contributor 8).

13. Oswald Garrison Villard, *John Brown 1800–1859: A Biography Fifty Years After* (Houghton Mifflin Co., Boston, MA) 1910, 671.

14. https://www.fold3.com/image/20/13579541, NARA M324. Compiled service records of Confederate soldiers from Virginia units.

15. https://www.fold3.com/image/20/13582043, NARA M324. Compiled service records of Confederate soldiers from Virginia units.

16. *Colusa Daily Sun*, Vol. XII, No. 41, 18 February 1896, retrieved from https://www.newspapers.com, Newspapers made available courtesy of Chronicling America & University of Tennessee.

17. *San Francisco Call*, Vol. 107, No. 134, 13 April 1910 pg. 9, retrieved from https://www.newspapers.com, Newspapers made available courtesy of Chronicling America & University of Tennessee.

18. http://www.fold3.com/image/92872133/, NARA M319. Compiled service records of Confederate soldiers from Kentucky units.

19. Edwin Porter Thompson, *History of the Orphan Brigade* (L. N. Thompson, Louisville, KY) 1898 pg. 211.

20. Edwin Porter Thompson, *History of the Orphan Brigade* (L. N. Thompson, Louisville, KY) 1898 pg. 214.

21. The Papers of Abraham Lincoln: Doc 283272 Almareane W. Baker to Abraham Lincoln 1865-01-15 Images from the National Archives and Library of Congress 1865-01-15 Images from the National Archives and Library of Congress.

22. Find A Grave, database and images (https://www.findagrave.com: accessed 16 June 2019), memorial page for Almareane Wellborn Baker (7 Jul 1843–17 Aug 1905), Find A Grave Memorial no. 23421157, citing Ono Cemetery, Ono, Shasta County, California, USA; Maintained by Ancestry Seeker (contributor 46913946).

23. Year: 1860; Census Place: Petersburg East Ward,

Petersburg (Independent City), Virginia; Roll: M653_1342; Page: 171; Family History Library Film: 805342 at Ancestry.com.

24. http://www.fold3.com/image/10307559/, NARA M324. Compiled service records of Confederate soldiers from Virginia units.

25. http://www.fold3.com/image/13120894/, NARA M324. Compiled service records of Confederate soldiers from Virginia units.

26. http://www.fold3.com/image/13333823/, NARA M324. Compiled service records of Confederate soldiers from Virginia units.

27. http://www.fold3.com/image/13334020/, NARA M324. Compiled service records of Confederate soldiers from Virginia units.

28. J. Ogden Murray, *The Immortal Six Hundred: A Story of Cruelty to Confederate Prisoners of War* (Stone Printing and Manufacturing Co., Roanoke, VA) 1911 pg. 1.

29. J. Ogden Murray, *The Immortal Six Hundred: A Story of Cruelty to Confederate Prisoners of War* (Stone Printing and Manufacturing Co., Roanoke, VA) 1911 pg. 155.

30. Find A Grave, database and images (https://www.findagrave.com: accessed 15 April 2019), memorial page for Peter Vernon Batte (1841–21 Nov 1893), Find A Grave Memorial no. 10346586, citing Stockton Rural Cemetery, Stockton, San Joaquin County, California, USA; Maintained by J. Rubio (contributor 47507413).

31. Marguerite Hune, *History of Solano County, California* (S.J. Clarke Publishing Co., Chicago, IL) 1926 pg. 281.

32. http://www.fold3.com/image/67612742/, NARA M320. Compiled service records of Confederate soldiers from Louisiana units.

33. https://www.fold3.com/image/20/67610792, NARA M320. Compiled service records of Confederate soldiers from Louisiana units.

34. http://www.fold3.com/image/72861712/, NARA M320. Compiled service records of Confederate soldiers from Louisiana units.

35. https://www.fold3.com/image/72861722, NARA M320. Compiled service records of Confederate soldiers from Louisiana units.

36. United States War Dept., *The War of the Rebellion: A Compilation of the Official Records of the Union & Confederate Armies*, Series 1, Vol. XXXIV (Government Printing Office, Washington, D.C.) 1902 pg. 564.

37. Find A Grave, database and images (https://www.findagrave.com: accessed 29 November 2019), memorial page for Col James Hamilton Beard (28 Jul 1833–8 Apr 1864), Find A Grave Memorial no. 10485829, citing Evergreen Cemetery, Frierson, DeSoto Parish, Louisiana, USA; Maintained by David Hill (contributor 46626495).

38. Find A Grave, database and images (https://www.findagrave.com: accessed 17 June 2019), memorial page for Lieut Edward Derrel Beard (30 Sep 1844–14 Jun 1927), Find A Grave Memorial no. 82274185,

citing Tulocay Cemetery, Napa, Napa County, California, USA; Maintained by Clayton Lord (contributor 46949960).

39. Jay Guy CisCo., *Historic Sumner County, Tennessee, with Genealogies of the Bledsoe, Gage and Douglass Families and Genealogical Notes of Other Sumner County Families* (Folk-Keelin printing Co., Nashville, TN) 1909 pg. 225.

40. Jay Guy CisCo., *Historic Sumner County, Tennessee, with Genealogies of the Bledsoe, Gage and Douglass Families and Genealogical Notes of Other Sumner County Families* (Folk-Keelin printing Co., Nashville, TN) 1909 pg. 225.

41. http://www.fold3.com/image/69462346/, NARA M268. Compiled service records of Confederate soldiers from Tennessee units.

42. Jay Guy CisCo., *Historic Sumner County, Tennessee, with Genealogies of the Bledsoe, Gage and Douglass Families and Genealogical Notes of Other Sumner County Families* (Folk-Keelin printing Co., Nashville, TN) 1909 pg. 225.

43. Jay Guy CisCo., *Historic Sumner County, Tennessee, with Genealogies of the Bledsoe, Gage and Douglass Families and Genealogical Notes of Other Sumner County Families* (Folk-Keelin printing Co., Nashville, TN) 1909 pg. 225.

44. http://www.fold3.com/image/65614373/, NARA M331. Compiled service records of Confederate officers and enlisted men who did not belong to any particular regiment, separate company or comparable unit, or special corps.

45. *Confederate Veteran* Magazine, Vol. 22 (Nashville, TN) 1914 pg. 420.

46. Clement Anselm Evans, ed., *Confederate Military History: A Library of Confederate States History*, Vol. 8 (Confederate Publishing Co., Atlanta, GA) 1899 pg. 297.

47. Clement Anselm Evans, ed., *Confederate Military History: A Library of Confederate States History*, Vol. 8 (Confederate Publishing Co., Atlanta, GA) 1899 pg. 297.

48. *Confederate Veteran* Magazine, Vol. 5 (Nashville, TN) 1897 pg. 363.

49. *Confederate Veteran* Magazine, Vol. 22 (Nashville, TN) 1914 pg. 420.

50. Jay Guy CisCo., *Historic Sumner County, Tennessee, with Genealogies of the Bledsoe, Gage and Douglass Families and Genealogical Notes of Other Sumner County Families* (Folk-Keelin printing Co., Nashville, TN) 1909 pg. 225.

51. Find A Grave, database and images (https://www.findagrave.com: accessed 17 June 2019), memorial page for Isaac Thomas Bell (17 Jul 1844–3 Jun 1914), Find A Grave Memorial no. 146422647, citing Visalia Public Cemetery, Visalia, Tulare County, California, USA; Maintained by Bill Lee (contributor 46838557).

52. *Daily Alta California*, Vol. 36, No. 12476, 13 June 1884 pg. 4, California Digital Newspaper Collection, Center for Bibliographic Studies and Research, University of California, Riverside, http://cdnc.ucr.edu.

53. http://www.fold3.com/image/307202613/, NARA M616. Card index to service records of volunteer soldiers who served in the Mexican War, arranged alphabetically by state or territory.

54. Works Progress Administration (WPA) in conjunction with the office of the Adjutant General and the California State Library, "California Militia and National Guard Unit Histories: Benham Guard," 1940, http://www.militarymuseum.org/BenhamGuard.html.

55. James O'Meara, *Broderick and Gwin: The Most Extraordinary Contest for a Seat in the Senate of the United States Ever Known* (Bacon & Co., Printers, San Francisco Ca.)1881 pg. 245.

56. *Sacramento Daily Union*, Vol. 22, No. 3330, 29 November 1861 pg. 2, California Digital Newspaper Collection, Center for Bibliographic Studies and Research, University of California, Riverside, http://cdnc.ucr.edu.

57. United States. War Dept., *The War of the Rebellion*, Vols. 1–8 [serial no. 114–121] (Government Printing Office, Wash. D.C) 1902 pg. 1020.

58. http://www.fold3.com/image/64980192/, NARA M331. Compiled service records of Confederate officers and enlisted men who did not belong to any particular regiment, separate company or comparable unit, or special corps.

59. J. H. Segars (Editor), Charles Kelly Barrow (Editor), *Black Southerners in Confederate Armies: A Collection of Historical Accounts* (Pelican Publishing, Gretna, LA) 2007 pg. 13.

60. https://www.fold3.com/image/64980287, NARA M331. Compiled service records of Confederate officers and enlisted men who did not belong to any particular regiment, separate company or comparable unit, or special corps.

61. http://www.fold3.com/image/64980192/, NARA M331. Compiled service records of Confederate officers and enlisted men who did not belong to any particular regiment, separate company or comparable unit, or special corps.

62. *San Luis Obispo Tribune* (Weekly), Vol. 11, No. 525, 6 September 1879, pg. 1, California Digital Newspaper Collection, Center for Bibliographic Studies and Research, University of California, Riverside, http://cdnc.ucr.edu.

63. San Francisco Area, California, Funeral Home Records, 1850–1931 [database on-line]. Provo, UT, USA: Ancestry.com Operations, Inc., 2014.

64. *TheSan Francisco Call*, San Francisco, California, Sunday, February 16, 1896; pg. 13, California Digital Newspaper Collection, Center for Bibliographic Studies and Research, University of California, Riverside, http://cdnc.ucr.edu.

65. http://www.fold3.com/image/10400212/, NARA M324. Compiled service records of Confederate soldiers from Virginia units.

66. http://www.fold3.com/image/9085735/, NARA M324. Compiled service records of Confederate soldiers from Virginia units.

67. *TheSan Francisco Call*, San Francisco, California, Sunday, February 16, 1896; pg. 13, California Digital Newspaper Collection, Center for Bibliographic Studies and Research, University of California, Riverside, http://cdnc.ucr.edu.

68. http://www.fold3.com/image/10158130/, NARA M323. Compiled service records of Confederate soldiers from Texas units.

69. http://www.fold3.com/image/248518262/, NARA M347. "Unfiled Papers and Slips Belonging in Confederate Compiled Service Records.

70. *TheSan Francisco Call*, San Francisco, California, February 16, 1896, California Digital Newspaper Collection, Center for Bibliographic Studies and Research, University of California, Riverside, http://cdnc.ucr.edu.

71. *TheSan Francisco Call*, San Francisco, California, February 18, 1896, California Digital Newspaper Collection, Center for Bibliographic Studies and Research, University of California, Riverside, http://cdnc.ucr.edu.

72. *News-Democrat* (Paducah, KY) October 14, 1903 pg. 1 retrieved from https://www.newspapers.com, Newspapers made available courtesy of Chronicling America & University of Tennessee.

73. https://www.fold3.com/image/67126232, NARA M320. Compiled service records of Confederate soldiers from Louisiana units.

74. https://www.fold3.com/image/64833621, NARA M320. Compiled service records of Confederate soldiers from Louisiana units.

75. https://www.fold3.com/image/20/84588296, NARA M320. Compiled service records of Confederate soldiers from Louisiana units.

76. *News-Democrat* (Paducah, KY) October 14, 1903 pg. 1 retrieved from https://www.newspapers.com, Newspapers made available courtesy of Chronicling America & University of Tennessee.

77. *News-Democrat* (Paducah, KY) October 14, 1903 pg. 1 retrieved from https://www.newspapers.com, Newspapers made available courtesy of Chronicling America & University of Tennessee.

78. *San Francisco Call*, Vol. 94, No. 135, 13 October 1903, California Digital Newspaper Collection, Center for Bibliographic Studies and Research, University of California, Riverside, http://cdnc.ucr.edu.

79. California, County Birth, Marriage, and Death Records, 1849–1980 [database on-line]. Lehi, UT, USA: Ancestry.com.

80. http://www.fold3.com/image/280468720/, NARA M1091. Records from the Confederate Navy during the Civil War, organized by subjects ranging from ships to prisoners of war.

81. https://www.fold3.com/image/9085844, NARA M324. Compiled service records of Confederate soldiers from Virginia units.

82. R.A. Brock,, ed., "Plan to Rescue the Johnson Island Prisoners in Feb. 1863, by Capt. R. D. Minor, C. S. Navy," *Southern Historical Society Papers*, Vol. 23 (W.M. Ellis Printer, Richmond, VA) 1895 pgs. 283–290.

83. https://www.fold3.com/image/280468720,

NARA M1091. Records from the Confederate Navy during the Civil War, organized by subjects ranging from ships to prisoners of war.

84. United States War Dept., *Official Records of the Union and Confederate Navies in the War of the Rebellion*, Series 1, Vol. 10, "Report of Lieutenant Bradford, C. S. Navy, Regarding Suspicious Movements of the Enemy in James River." (Washington, DC: Government Printing Office) 1900 pgs. 683–684.

85. United States War Dept., *Official Records of the Union and Confederate Navies in the War of the Rebellion*, Series 1, Vol. 10, "Report of Lieutenant Bradford, C. S. Navy, Regarding Exchange of Fire with the Enemy." (Washington, DC: Government Printing Office) 1900 pg. 686.

86. *San Francisco Chronicle* (San Francisco, CA) February 25, 1919, pg. 11, retrieved from https://www.newspapers.com, Newspapers made available courtesy of Chronicling America & University of Tennessee.

87. Find A Grave, database and images (https://www.findagrave.com: accessed 15 April 2019), memorial page for James Otey Bradford (5 Nov 1841–Feb 1919), Find A Grave Memorial no. 110074532, citing Holy Cross Catholic Cemetery, Colma, San Mateo County, California, USA; Maintained by Athanatos (contributor 46907585).

88. Brett J. Derbes, "Brooks, Samuel Houston," Handbook of Texas Online (http://www.tshaonline.org/handbook/online/articles/fbreg), accessed February 02, 2014. Published by the Texas State Historical Association.

89. http://www.fold3.com/image/88699747/, NARA M331. Compiled service records of Confederate officers and enlisted men who did not belong to any particular regiment, separate company or comparable unit, or special corps.

90. http://www.fold3.com/image/88699733/, NARA M331. Compiled service records of Confederate officers and enlisted men who did not belong to any particular regiment, separate company or comparable unit, or special corps.

91. Brett J. Derbes, "Brooks, Samuel Houston," Handbook of Texas Online (http://www.tshaonline.org/handbook/online/articles/fbreg), accessed February 02, 2014. Published by the Texas State Historical Association.

92. *Grass Valley Daily*, May 7, 1885, California Digital Newspaper Collection, Center for Bibliographic Studies and Research, University of California, Riverside, http://cdnc.ucr.edu.

93. Brett J. Derbes, "Brooks, Samuel Houston," Handbook of Texas Online (http://www.tshaonline.org/handbook/online/articles/fbreg), accessed February 02, 2014. Published by the Texas State Historical Association.

94. Find A Grave, database and images (https://www.findagrave.com: accessed 16 June 2019), memorial page for Elbridge Brown (26 Oct 1845–15 Mar 1922), Find A Grave Memorial no. 31119863, citing Giddings City Cemetery, Giddings, Lee County, Texas, USA; Maintained by Jan Wukasch Pelosi (contributor 47041603).

95. https://www.fold3.com/image/20/66362607, NARA M268. Compiled service records of Confederate soldiers from Tennessee units.

96. https://www.fold3.com/image/20/67237562, NARA M269. Compiled service records of Confederate soldiers from Mississippi units.

97. https://www.fold3.com/image/20/67237562, NARA M269. Compiled service records of Confederate soldiers from Mississippi units.

98. https://www.fold3.com/image/20/67237547, NARA M269. Compiled service records of Confederate soldiers from Mississippi units.

99. https://www.fold3.com/image/20/67237547, NARA M269. Compiled service records of Confederate soldiers from Mississippi units.

100. Find A Grave, database and images (https://www.findagrave.com: accessed 16 June 2019), memorial page for Telamachus Cambridge Brown (1824–9 Apr 1910), Find A Grave Memorial no. 54759278, citing Modesto Citizens Cemetery, Modesto, Stanislaus County, California, USA; Maintained by Bette Locke (contributor 46821513).

101. Herrmann Schuricht, *History of the German Element in Virginia*, Vol. 2 (Theo. Kroh Publishers, Baltimore, MD) 1900 pg. 86.

102. Andrea Mehrländer, The Germans of Charleston, Richmond and New Orleans during the Civil War Period, 1850–1870 (Walter De Gruyter & Co., Berlin/New York) 2011 pg. 99.

103. Andrea Mehrländer, The Germans of Charleston, Richmond and New Orleans during the Civil War Period, 1850–1870 (Walter De Gruyter & Co., Berlin/New York) 2011 pg. 104.

104. Herrmann Schuricht, History of the German Element in Virginia, Vol. 2 (Theo. Kroh Publishers, Baltimore, MD) 1900 pg. 86.

105. https://www.fold3.com/image/20/64964560, NARA M331. Compiled service records of Confederate officers and enlisted men who did not belong to any particular regiment, separate company or comparable unit, or special corps.

106. https://www.fold3.com/image/20/64963783, NARA M331. Compiled service records of Confederate officers and enlisted men who did not belong to any particular regiment, separate company or comparable unit, or special corps.

107. Governor's Message and Annual Reports of the Public Officers of the State, and of the Boards of Directors, Visitors, Superintendents, and Other Agents of Public Institutions Or Interests of Virginia., Document 10 (Samuel Shepherd, public printer, Richmond, VA) 1861 pg. 11.

108. https://www.fold3.com/image/20/64963783, NARA M331. Compiled service records of Confederate officers and enlisted men who did not belong to any particular regiment, separate company or comparable unit, or special corps.

109. Herrmann Schuricht, *History of the German*

*Element in Virginia*, Vol. 2 (Theo. Kroh Publishers, Baltimore, MD) 1900 pg. 86.

110. Find A Grave, database and images (https://www.findagrave.com: accessed 15 April 2019), memorial page for Louis von Buchholtz (unknown–9 Jan 1889), Find A Grave Memorial no. 147563060, citing Holy Cross Catholic Cemetery, Colma, San Mateo County, California, USA; Maintained by TD Miller (contributor 46799665).

111. Texas, Muster Roll Index Cards, 1838–1900 [database on-line]. Provo, UT, USA: Ancestry.com.

112. http://www.fold3.com/image/10132356/, NARA M323. Compiled service records of Confederate soldiers from Texas units.

113. https://www.fold3.com/image/10132362, NARA M323. Compiled service records of Confederate soldiers from Texas units.

114. https://www.fold3.com/image/10132361, NARA M323. Compiled service records of Confederate soldiers from Texas units.

115. http://www.fold3.com/image/10936199/, NARA M323. Compiled service records of Confederate soldiers from Texas units.

116. Find A Grave, database and images (https://www.findagrave.com: accessed 15 April 2019), memorial page for John Wesley Clanton (18 Jul 1841–19 Apr 1916), Find A Grave Memorial no. 21768256, citing Santa Rosa Rural Cemetery, Santa Rosa, Sonoma County, California, USA; Maintained by Jack W. Davis (contributor 46900076).

117. http://www.fold3.com/image/65638275/, NARA M268. Compiled service records of Confederate soldiers from Tennessee units.

118. John Preston Young, *The Seventh Tennessee Cavalry (Confederate): A History* (Publishing House of the M.E. Church, South Nashville, TN) 1890 pg. 30–31.

119. John Preston Young, *The Seventh Tennessee Cavalry (Confederate): A History* (Publishing House of the M.E. Church, South Nashville, TN) 1890 pg. 45–46.

120. John Preston Young, *The Seventh Tennessee Cavalry (Confederate): A History* (Publishing House of the M.E. Church, South Nashville, TN) 1890 pg. 73.

121. John Preston Young, *The Seventh Tennessee Cavalry (Confederate): A History* (Publishing House of the M.E. Church, South Nashville, TN) 1890 pg. 78–79.

122. John Preston Young, *The Seventh Tennessee Cavalry (Confederate): A History* (Publishing House of the M.E. Church, South Nashville, TN) 1890 pg. 85.

123. John Preston Young, *The Seventh Tennessee Cavalry (Confederate): A History* (Publishing House of the M.E. Church, South Nashville, TN) 1890 pg. 86.

124. John Preston Young, *The Seventh Tennessee Cavalry (Confederate): A History* (Publishing House of the M.E. Church, South Nashville, TN) 1890 pg. 97.

125. John Preston Young, *The Seventh Tennessee Cavalry (Confederate): A History* (Publishing House of the M.E. Church, South Nashville, TN) 1890 pg. 120–121.

126. John Preston Young, *The Seventh Tennessee Cavalry (Confederate): A History* (Publishing House of the M.E. Church, South Nashville, TN) 1890 pg. 138.

127. *San Francisco Call*, Vol. 98, No. 68, 7 August 1905, California Digital Newspaper Collection, Center for Bibliographic Studies and Research, University of California, Riverside, http://cdnc.ucr.edu.

128. Find A Grave, database and images (https://www.findagrave.com: accessed 30 November 2019), memorial page for Clement C Clay (1836–1905), Find A Grave Memorial no. 128183621, citing Mountain View Cemetery, Oakland, Alameda County, California, USA; Maintained by Squeak (contributor 47437442).

129. Winfield J. Davis, *An Illustrated History of Sacramento County, CA: Containing a History of Sacramento County from the Earliest Period of Its Occupancy to the Present Time, Together with Glimpses of Its Prospective Future ... Portraits of Some of Its Most Eminent Men, and Biographical Mention of Many of Its Pioneers and Also Prominent Citizens of Today* (Lewis Publishing Co., Chicago, IL) 1890 pg. 769.

130. Winfield J. Davis, *An Illustrated History of Sacramento County, CA: Containing a History of Sacramento County from the Earliest Period of Its Occupancy to the Present Time, Together with Glimpses of Its Prospective Future ... Portraits of Some of Its Most Eminent Men, and Biographical Mention of Many of Its Pioneers and Also Prominent Citizens of Today* (Lewis Publishing Co., Chicago, IL) 1890 pg. 769.

131. *San Francisco Call*, Vol. 106, No. 30, 30 June 1909, pg. 4, California Digital Newspaper Collection, Center for Bibliographic Studies and Research, University of California, Riverside, http://cdnc.ucr.edu.

132. Winfield J. Davis, *An Illustrated History of Sacramento County, CA: Containing a History of Sacramento County from the Earliest Period of Its Occupancy to the Present Time, Together with Glimpses of Its Prospective Future ... Portraits of Some of Its Most Eminent Men, and Biographical Mention of Many of Its Pioneers and Also Prominent Citizens of Today* (Lewis Publishing Co., Chicago, IL) 1890 pg. 769.

133. *San Francisco Call*, Vol. 106, No. 30, 30 June 1909, pg. 4, California Digital Newspaper Collection, Center for Bibliographic Studies and Research, University of California, Riverside, http://cdnc.ucr.edu.

134. Find A Grave, database and images (https://www.findagrave.com: accessed 18 June 2019), memorial page for George Blake Cosby (19 Jan 1830–29 Jun 1909), Find A Grave Memorial no. 4522, citing Sacramento City Cemetery, Sacramento, Sacramento County, California, USA; Maintained by Find A Grave.

135. Lyman L. Palmer, W.F. Wallace, Harry Laurenz Wells, Tillie Kanaga, *History of Napa and Lake Counties, California: Omprising Their Geography, Geology, Topography, Climatography, Springs and Timber, Together with a Full and Particular Record of the Mexican Grants, Also Separate Histories of All the Townships and Biographical Sketches* (Slocum, Bowen) 1881 pg. 223.

136. http://www.fold3.com/image/20/77926989/, NARA M269. Compiled service records of Confederate soldiers from Mississippi units.

137. https://www.fold3.com/image/20/77927028, NARA M269. Compiled service records of Confederate soldiers from Mississippi units.

138. *Memphis Daily Appeal*, December 21, 1861, p. 1, c. 4 retrieved from https://www.newspapers.com, Newspapers made available courtesy of Chronicling America & University of Tennessee.

139. Dunbar Rowland, *The Official and Statistical Register of the State of Mississippi*, Vol. 2 (Brandon Printing Co., Nashville, TN) 1908 pg. 447.

140. Dunbar Rowland, *The Official and Statistical Register of the State of Mississippi*, Vol. 2 (Brandon Printing Co., Nashville, TN) 1908 pg. 448.

141. Dunbar Rowland, *The Official and Statistical Register of the State of Mississippi*, Vol. 2 (Brandon Printing Co., Nashville, TN) 1908 pg. 448.

142. Dunbar Rowland, *The Official and Statistical Register of the State of Mississippi*, Vol. 2 (Brandon Printing Co., Nashville, TN) 1908 pg. 449.

143. Dunbar Rowland, *The Official and Statistical Register of the State of Mississippi*, Vol. 2 (Brandon Printing Co., Nashville, TN) 1908 pg. 449.

144. Dunbar Rowland, *The Official and Statistical Register of the State of Mississippi*, Vol. 2 (Brandon Printing Co., Nashville, TN) 1908 pg. 449.

145. Dunbar Rowland, *The Official and Statistical Register of the State of Mississippi*, Vol. 2 (Brandon Printing Co., Nashville, TN) 1908 pg. 450.

146. Lyman L. Palmer, W.F. Wallace, Harry Laurenz Wells, Tillie Kanaga, *History of Napa and Lake Counties, California: Comprising Their Geography, Geology, Topography, Climatography, Springs and Timber, Together with a Full and Particular Record of the Mexican Grants, Also Separate Histories of All the Townships and Biographical Sketches* (Slocum, Bowen) 1881 pg. 223.

147. Find A Grave, database and images (https://www.findagrave.com: accessed 18 June 2019), memorial page for Richard William Crump (25 Sep 1828–23 Jul 1903), Find A Grave Memorial no. 124278127, citing Hartley Cemetery, Lakeport, Lake County, California, USA; Maintained by Kaimom (contributor 47983071).

148. *Mountain Democrat*, Vol. 8, No. 11, 16 March 1861 pg. 2, California Digital Newspaper Collection, Center for Bibliographic Studies and Research, University of California, Riverside, http://cdnc.ucr.edu.

149. *Army and Navy Journal*, Vol. 23 November 21, 1885 (New York) pg. 327.

150. Lieut. S.V. Seyburne, U.S.A., Adjutant Tenth Infantry, Tenth Regiment of Infantry in The Journal of the Military Service Institution of the United States, Vol, 13 (Military Service Institution, Governor's Island) 1892 pg. 420.

151. https://www.fold3.com/image/66423583, NARA M331. Compiled service records of Confederate officers and enlisted men who did not belong to any particular regiment, separate company or comparable unit, or special corps.

152. https://www.fold3.com/image/66423583, NARA M331. Compiled service records of Confederate officers and enlisted men who did not belong to any particular regiment, separate company or comparable unit, or special corps.

153. https://www.fold3.com/image/66423873, NARA M331. Compiled service records of Confederate officers and enlisted men who did not belong to any particular regiment, separate company or comparable unit, or special corps.

154. https://www.fold3.com/image/66423583, NARA M331. Compiled service records of Confederate officers and enlisted men who did not belong to any particular regiment, separate company or comparable unit, or special corps.

155. https://www.fold3.com/image/20/9723395, NARA M324. Compiled service records of Confederate soldiers from Virginia units.

156. https://www.fold3.com/image/66423883, NARA M331. Compiled service records of Confederate officers and enlisted men who did not belong to any particular regiment, separate company or comparable unit, or special corps.

157. https://www.fold3.com/image/66423583, NARA M331. Compiled service records of Confederate officers and enlisted men who did not belong to any particular regiment, separate company or comparable unit, or special corps.

158. https://www.fold3.com/image/66423891, NARA M331. Compiled service records of Confederate officers and enlisted men who did not belong to any particular regiment, separate company or comparable unit, or special corps.

159. https://www.fold3.com/image/66423583, NARA M331. Compiled service records of Confederate officers and enlisted men who did not belong to any particular regiment, separate company or comparable unit, or special corps.

160. https://www.fold3.com/image/66423583, NARA M331. Compiled service records of Confederate officers and enlisted men who did not belong to any particular regiment, separate company or comparable unit, or special corps.

161. *Army and Navy Journal*, Vol. 23 November 21, 1885 (New York) pg. 327.

162. Find A Grave, database and images (https://www.findagrave.com: accessed 15 April 2019), memorial page for Col Arthur Sinclair Cunningham (unknown–26 Jul 1885), Find A Grave Memorial no. 80521901, citing Myrtle Grove Memorial Cemetery, Eureka, Humboldt County, California, USA; Maintained by Athanatos (contributor 46907585).

163. Clement Anselm Evans, *Confederate Military History: A Library of Confederate States History*, Vol. 8 (Confederate Publishing Co., Atlanta, GA) 1899 pg. 304.

164. Joseph Wheeler, *Campaigns of Wheeler and His Cavalry, 1862–1865: From Material Furnished by Gen. Joseph Wheeler*, Parts 1–2 (Hudgins-Publishing Company) 1899.

165. Clement Anselm Evans, *Confederate Military History: A Library of Confederate States History*, Vol. 8 (Confederate Publishing Co., Atlanta, GA) 1899 pg. 305.

166. Find A Grave, database and images (https://www.findagrave.com: accessed 03 July 2019), memorial page for Henry Brevard Davidson (28 Jan 1831–4 Mar 1899), Find A Grave Memorial no. 4521, citing Mountain View Cemetery, Oakland, Alameda County, California, USA; Maintained by Find A Grave.

167. Charles James Fox Binney, *The History and Genealogy of the Prentice or Prentiss Family, in New England, Etc.* (Alfred Mudge & Son, Printers, Boston, MA) 1883 pg. 155.

168. George W. Cullum, *Register of Officers and Graduates of the United States Military Academy Class of 1852*, Supplement, Vol. 5 (Seeman & Peters, Printers, Saginaw, MI) 1910 pg. 76.

169. https://www.fold3.com/image/67292718, NARA M331. Compiled service records of Confederate officers and enlisted men who did not belong to any particular regiment, separate company or comparable unit, or special corps.

170. https://www.fold3.com/image/67292272, NARA M331. Compiled service records of Confederate officers and enlisted men who did not belong to any particular regiment, separate company or comparable unit, or special corps.

171. United States War Dept., *The War of the Rebellion: A Compilation of the Official Records of the Union & Confederate Armies*, Series 1, Vol. XXIV, part 3, Correspondence etc. (Government Printing Office, Washington, D.C.) 1889 pg. 847.

172. https://www.fold3.com/image/67292568, NARA M331. Compiled service records of Confederate officers and enlisted men who did not belong to any particular regiment, separate company or comparable unit, or special corps.

173. United States War Dept., *The War of the Rebellion: A Compilation of the Official Records of the Union & Confederate Armies*, Series 2, Vol. VII (Government Printing Office, Washington, D.C.) 1899 pg. 402.

174. https://www.fold3.com/image/67292710, NARA M331. Compiled service records of Confederate officers and enlisted men who did not belong to any particular regiment, separate company or comparable unit, or special corps.

175. Charles James Fox Binney, The History of the Prentice or Prentiss Family in New England etc.(Alfred Mudge & Son Printers, Boston, MA) pg. 155.

176. Find A Grave, database and images (https://www.findagrave.com: accessed 15 April 2019), memorial page for Col Henry De Veuve, Sr (26 Aug 1831–unknown), Find A Grave Memorial no. 84187911, citing Cypress Lawn Memorial Park, Colma, San Mateo County, California, USA; Maintained by Larry White (contributor 46875221).

177. The Lewis Publishing Co., *A Memorial and Biographical History of Northern California, Illustrated. Containing a History of This Important Section of the Pacific Coast from the Earliest Period of Its Occupancy … And Biographical Mention of Many of Its Most Eminent Pioneers and Also of Prominent Citizens of Today* (The Lewis Publishing Co., Chicago, IL) 1891 pg. 513.

178. http://www.fold3.com/image/88539098/, NARA M322. Compiled service records of Confederate soldiers from Missouri units.

179. James E. McGhee,, ed., *Guide to Missouri Confederate Units, 1861–1865* (The University of Arkansas Press, Fayetteville, AR) 2008 pg. 63.

180. http://www.fold3.com/image/88539098/, NARA M322. Compiled service records of Confederate soldiers from Missouri units.

181. http://www.fold3.com/image/88539098/, NARA M322. Compiled service records of Confederate soldiers from Missouri units.

182. http://www.fold3.com/image/88539098/, NARA M322. Compiled service records of Confederate soldiers from Missouri units.

183. The Lewis Publishing Co., *A Memorial and Biographical History of Northern California, Illustrated. Containing a History of This Important Section of the Pacific Coast from the Earliest Period of Its Occupancy … And Biographical Mention of Many of Its Most Eminent Pioneers and Also of Prominent Citizens of Today* (The Lewis Publishing Co., Chicago, IL) 1891 pg. 514.

184. The Lewis Publishing Co., *A Memorial and Biographical History of Northern California, Illustrated. Containing a History of This Important Section of the Pacific Coast from the Earliest Period of Its Occupancy … And Biographical Mention of Many of Its Most Eminent Pioneers and Also of Prominent Citizens of Today* (The Lewis Publishing Co., Chicago, IL) 1891 pg. 514.

185. The Lewis Publishing Co., *A Memorial and Biographical History of Northern California, Illustrated. Containing a History of This Important Section of the Pacific Coast from the Earliest Period of Its Occupancy … And Biographical Mention of Many of Its Most Eminent Pioneers and Also of Prominent Citizens of Today* (The Lewis Publishing Co., Chicago, IL) 1891 pg. 514–515.

186. Find A Grave, database and images (https://www.findagrave.com: accessed 03 July 2019), memorial page for John Andrew Devilbiss (19 Nov 1841–7 Jan 1937), Find A Grave Memorial no. 20553629, citing Winters Cemetery, Winters, Yolo County, California, USA; Maintained by Delores Sorenson (contributor 47015522).

187. Donald J. Hagerty, *The Life of Maynard Dixon* (Gibbs Smith, Layton UT) 2010 pg. 20.

188. Harry St. John Dixon, "Recollections of a Rebel Private" *The Sigma Chi Quarterly* 1885-86 pg. 303, https://history.sigmachi.org/files_resources/constantine-chapter_recollections.pdf.

189. Harry St. John Dixon, "Recollections of a Rebel Private" *The Sigma Chi Quarterly* 1885-86 pg. 304, https://history.sigmachi.org/files_resources/constantine-chapter_recollections.pdf.

190. Harry St. John Dixon, "Recollections of a Rebel Private" *The Sigma Chi Quarterly* 1885-86 pg. 318, https://history.sigmachi.org/files_resources/constantine-chapter_recollections.pdf.

191. https://www.fold3.com/image/20/66944423, NARA M269. Compiled service records of Confederate soldiers from Mississippi units.

192. Harry St. John Dixon, "Recollections of a Rebel Private" *The Sigma Chi Quarterly* 1885-86 pg. 306, https://history.sigmachi.org/files_resources/constantine-chapter_recollections.pdf.

193. Harry St. John Dixon, "Recollections of a Rebel Private" *The Sigma Chi Quarterly* 1885-86 pg. 309, https://history.sigmachi.org/files_resources/constantine-chapter_recollections.pdf.

194. Dunbar Rowland, *The Official and Statistical Register of the State of Mississippi*, Vol. 2 (Brandon Printing Co. Nashville, TN) 1908 pg. 833.

195. Harry St. John Dixon, "Recollections of a Rebel Private" *The Sigma Chi Quarterly* 1885-86 pg. 314, https://history.sigmachi.org/files_resources/constantine-chapter_recollections.pdf.

196. https://www.fold3.com/image/20/66944451, NARA M269. Compiled service records of Confederate soldiers from Mississippi units.

197. https://www.fold3.com/image/20/66944427, NARA M269. Compiled service records of Confederate soldiers from Mississippi units.

198. L.R. Garrett, "Harry St. John Dixon" *the Sigma Chi Quarterly*, Vol. XVI, No. 2 (Chicago, IL) 1896-1897 pg. 89.

199. L.R. Garrett, "Harry St. John Dixon" *the Sigma Chi Quarterly*, Vol. XVI, No. 2 (Chicago, IL) 1896-1897 pg. 90.

200. Find A Grave, database and images (https://www.findagrave.com: accessed 18 June 2019), memorial page for Harry St. John Dixon (2 Aug 1848–27 Aug 1898), Find A Grave Memorial no. 7281165, citing Mountain View Cemetery, Fresno, Fresno County, California, USA; Maintained by David M. Habben (contributor 835).

201. Find A Grave, database and images (https://www.findagrave.com: accessed 01 December 2019), memorial page for COL Caleb Dorsey (7 Sep 1833–21 Apr 1896), Find A Grave Memorial no. 113647371, citing Stockton Rural Cemetery, Stockton, San Joaquin County, California, USA; Maintained by Paul Schuler (contributor 47161101).

202. http://www.fold3.com/image/20/193266499/, NARA M322. Compiled service records of Confederate soldiers from Missouri units.

203. Helen P. Trimpi, *Crimson Confederates: Harvard Men Who Fought for the South* (University of Tennessee Press, Knoxville, TN) 2010 pg. 58.

204. Western Historical Co., *History of Boone County, Missouri. Written and Comp. from the Most Authentic Official and Private Sources; Including a History of Its Townships, Towns, and Villages. Together with a Condensed History of Missouri; the City of St. Louis ... Biographical Sketches and Portraits of Prominent Citizens* (Press of Nixon Jones, St. Louis, MO) 1882 pg. 415.

205. https://www.fold3.com/image/20/193266503, NARA M322. Compiled service records of Confederate soldiers from Missouri units.

206. John N. Edwards, *Shelby and His Men or the War in the West* (Miami Printing and Publishing Co., Cincinnati, OH) 1867 pg. 487.

207. *San Francisco Call*, Vol. 79, No. 144, 22 April 1896, California Digital Newspaper Collection, Center for Bibliographic Studies and Research, University of California, Riverside, http://cdnc.ucr.edu.

208. Find A Grave, database and images (https://www.findagrave.com: accessed 19 June 2019), memorial page for COL Caleb Dorsey (7 Sep 1833–21 Apr 1896), Find A Grave Memorial no. 113647371, citing Stockton Rural Cemetery, Stockton, San Joaquin County, California, USA; Maintained by Paul Schuler (contributor 47161101).

209. James Miller Guinn, *History of the State of California and Biographical Record of the Sierras, an Historical Story of the State's Marvelous Growth from Its Earliest Settlement to the Present Time* (The Chapman co., Chicago, IL) 1906 pg. 690.

210. Ordinances and Constitution of the State of South Carolina, with the Constitution of the Provisional Government and of the Confederate States of America (Evans & Cogswell Printers, Charleston, SC) 1861 pg. 6.

211. https://www.fold3.com/image/310754683, Callahan's List of Navy and Marine Corps Officers is a register of officers who served in the United States Navy and Marine Corps between 1775 and 1900.

212. James Miller Guinn, *History of the State of California and Biographical Record of the Sierras, an Historical Story of the State's Marvelous Growth from Its Earliest Settlement to the Present Time* (The Chapman Co., Chicago, IL) 1906 pg. 690.

213. *Students of the University of Virginia: A Semi-Centennial Catalogue with Brief Biographical Sketches* (Charles Harvey & Co., Publishers, Baltimore, MD) 1878 pg. 39.

214. William Willis Boddie, *History of Williamsburg: Something About the People of Williamsburg County South Carolina from the First Settlement by Europeans About 1705 Until 1923* (The State Co., Columbia, SC) 1923 pg. 360.

215. William Willis Boddie, *History of Williamsburg: Something About the People of Williamsburg County South Carolina from the First Settlement by Europeans About 1705 Until 1923* (The State Co., Columbia, SC) 1923 pg. 360.

216. United States Naval War Records Office, *Officers in the Confederate States Navy, 1861–65* (Government Printing Office, Washington, D.C.) 1898 pg. 36.

217. https://www.fold3.com/image/20/68357805, NARA M267. Compiled service records of Confederate soldiers from South Carolina units.

218. https://www.fold3.com/image/68357801, NARA M267. Compiled service records of Confederate soldiers from South Carolina units.

219. https://www.fold3.com/image/20/68357946, NARA M267. Compiled service records of Confederate soldiers from South Carolina units.

220. James Miller Guinn, *History of the State of California and Biographical Record of the Sierras, an Historical Story of the State's Marvelous Growth from Its Earliest Settlement to the Present Time* (The Chapman co., Chicago, IL) 1906 pg. 690.

221. The Lewis Publishing Co., *A Memorial and Biographical History of Northern California, Illustrated. Containing a History of This Important Section of the Pacific Coast from the Earliest Period of Its Occupancy … And Biographical Mention of Many of Its Most Eminent Pioneers and Also of Prominent Citizens of Today* (The Lewis Publishing Co., Chicago, IL) 1891 pg. 364.

222. https://www.fold3.com/image/85284451, NARA M267. Compiled service records of Confederate soldiers from South Carolina units.

223. https://www.fold3.com/image/85284463, NARA M267. Compiled service records of Confederate soldiers from South Carolina units.

224. https://www.fold3.com/image/85284448, NARA M267. Compiled service records of Confederate soldiers from South Carolina units.

225. Find A Grave, database and images (https://www.findagrave.com: accessed 20 June 2019), memorial page for Pvt Anthony White Dozier, Jr. (23 Jan 1842–31 Oct 1874), Find A Grave Memorial no. 17980229, citing George C Yount Pioneer Cemetery, Yountville, Napa County, California, USA; Maintained by Denise Ratterman Jackson (contributor 47044891).

226. Find A Grave, database and images (https://www.findagrave.com: accessed 20 June 2019), memorial page for Dr Leonard Franklin Dozier, Sr (1836–1917), Find A Grave Memorial no. 17979148, citing Tulocay Cemetery, Napa, Napa County, California, USA; Maintained by Randy (contributor 46846747).

227. Find A Grave, database and images (https://www.findagrave.com: accessed 20 June 2019), memorial page for Peter Cuttino Dozier (12 Jan 1835–24 Nov 1877), Find A Grave Memorial no. 29009126, citing Ukiah Cemetery, Ukiah, Mendocino County, California, USA; Maintained by Ancestry Seeker (contributor 46913946).

228. Find A Grave, database and images (https://www.findagrave.com: accessed 20 June 2019), memorial page for William Gaillard Dozier (5 May 1833–9 Nov 1908), Find A Grave Memorial no. 70726728, citing Cypress Lawn Memorial Park, Colma, San Mateo County, California, USA; Maintained by Larry White (contributor 46875221).

229. Find A Grave, database and images (https://www.findagrave.com: accessed 16 June 2019), memorial page for SGT Edward Charles Dozier, Sr (14 Aug 1843–9 Oct 1919), Find A Grave Memorial no. 137735936, citing Rio Vista Odd Fellows and Masonic Cemetery, Rio Vista, Solano County, California, USA; Maintained by Find A Grave (contributor 8).

230. University of Virginia, *Students of the University of Virginia: A Semi-Centennial Catalogue with Brief Biographical Sketches* (Charles Harvey & Co., Publishers, Baltimore, MD) 1878 pg. 43.

231. https://www.fold3.com/image/9003522, NARA M324. Compiled service records of Confederate soldiers from Virginia units.

232. https://www.fold3.com/image/8385533, NARA M324. Compiled service records of Confederate soldiers from Virginia units.

233. https://www.fold3.com/image/66886778, NARA M331. Compiled service records of Confederate officers and enlisted men who did not belong to any particular regiment, separate company or comparable unit, or special corps.

234. https://www.fold3.com/image/8385555, NARA M324. Compiled service records of Confederate soldiers from Virginia units.

235. https://www.fold3.com/image/20/6805152, NARA M324. Compiled service records of Confederate soldiers from Virginia units.

236. https://www.fold3.com/image/6805051, NARA M324. Compiled service records of Confederate soldiers from Virginia units.

237. https://www.fold3.com/image/20/6795032, NARA M324. Compiled service records of Confederate soldiers from Virginia units.

238. https://www.fold3.com/image/20/6795038, NARA M324. Compiled service records of Confederate soldiers from Virginia units.

239. https://www.fold3.com/image/6805138, NARA M324. Compiled service records of Confederate soldiers from Virginia units.

240. https://www.fold3.com/image/6805138, NARA M324. Compiled service records of Confederate soldiers from Virginia units.

241. 1880 United States Federal Census [database on-line]. Lehi, UT, USA: Ancestry.com.

242. Find A Grave, database and images (https://www.findagrave.com: accessed 15 April 2019), memorial page for J. L. Estill (unknown–7 Sep 1905), Find A Grave Memorial no. 23087562, citing Academy Cemetery, Clovis, Fresno County, California, USA; Maintained by dot (contributor 46604592).

243. *Confederate Veteran* Magazine, Vol. 13 (Nashville TN)1905 pg. 588.

244. http://www.fold3.com/image/10506722/, NARA M324. Compiled service records of Confederate soldiers from Virginia units.

245. http://www.fold3.com/image/20/10506751/,

NARA M324. Compiled service records of Confederate soldiers from Virginia units.

246. Jennings C. Wise, *The Military History of the Virginia Military Institute from 1839 to 1865, with Appendix, Maps, and Illustrations* (J.P. Bell, Lynchburg VA.) 1915 pg. 322.

247. Jennings C. Wise, *The Military History of the Virginia Military Institute from 1839 to 1865, with Appendix, Maps, and Illustrations* (J.P. Bell, Lynchburg VA.) 1915 pg. 498.

248. *The Recorder* (San Francisco, CA) May 16, 1911 pg. 1, col. 4 retrieved from https://www.newspapers.com, Newspapers made available courtesy of Chronicling America & University of Tennessee.

249. Find A Grave, database and images (https://www.findagrave.com: accessed 15 April 2019), memorial page for Oliver Perry Evans (2 Jun 1842–15 May 1911), Find A Grave Memorial no. 21145282, citing Holy Cross Catholic Cemetery, Colma, San Mateo County, California, USA; Maintained by Sarah Reveley (contributor 46801284).

250. 1850 U.S. Federal Census—Slave Schedules [database on-line]. Provo, UT, USA: Ancestry.com.

251. U.S. Military and Naval Academies, Cadet Records and Applications, 1800–1908 [database on-line]. Lehi, UT, USA: Ancestry.com.

252. *The San Francisco Examiner* (San Francisco, CA) Nov. 25, 1883 pg. 8, col. 4 retrieved from https://www.newspapers.com, Newspapers made available courtesy of Chronicling America & University of Tennessee.

253. *The San Francisco Examiner* (San Francisco, CA) Nov. 25, 1883 pg. 8, col. 4 retrieved from https://www.newspapers.com, Newspapers made available courtesy of Chronicling America & University of Tennessee.

254. https://www.fold3.com/image/20/251673926, NARA M331. Compiled service records of Confederate officers and enlisted men who did not belong to any particular regiment, separate company or comparable unit, or special corps.

255. https://www.fold3.com/image/20/251673926, NARA M331. Compiled service records of Confederate officers and enlisted men who did not belong to any particular regiment, separate company or comparable unit, or special corps.

256. https://www.fold3.com/image/251673911, NARA M331. Compiled service records of Confederate officers and enlisted men who did not belong to any particular regiment, separate company or comparable unit, or special corps.

257. Eppa Hunton, *Autobiography of Eppa Hunton* (The William Byrd Press, Inc. Richmond, VA) 1933 pg. 118.

258. https://www.fold3.com/image/20/251673920, NARA M331. Compiled service records of Confederate officers and enlisted men who did not belong to any particular regiment, separate company or comparable unit, or special corps.

259. *Daily Alta California*, Vol. 35, No. 12277, 25 November 1883, California Digital Newspaper Collection, Center for Bibliographic Studies and Research, University of California, Riverside, http://cdnc.ucr.edu.

260. *Sacramento Daily Union*, Vol. 62, No. 25, 19 September 1889 pg. 2, California Digital Newspaper Collection, Center for Bibliographic Studies and Research, University of California, Riverside, http://cdnc.ucr.edu.

261. https://www.fold3.com/image/20/13599268, NARA M323. Compiled service records of Confederate soldiers from Texas units.

262. https://www.fold3.com/image/20/13599213, NARA M323. Compiled service records of Confederate soldiers from Texas units.

263. Joseph Palmer Blessington, *The Campaigns of Walker's Texas Division, by a Private Soldier* (Lange, Little & Co., Printers, New York) 1875 pg. 98.

264. Joseph Palmer Blessington, *The Campaigns of Walker's Texas Division, by a Private Soldier* (Lange, Little & Co., Printers, New York) 1875 pg. 98.

265. Bradley Folsom, "Sixteenth Texas Infantry," *Handbook of Texas Online* (http://www.tshaonline.org/handbook/online/articles/qks16), accessed February 10, 2014. Uploaded on April 9, 2011. Modified on November 5, 2012. Published by the Texas State Historical Association.

266. *Sacramento Daily Union*, Vol. 62, No. 25, 19 September 1889 pg. 2, California Digital Newspaper Collection, Center for Bibliographic Studies and Research, University of California, Riverside, http://cdnc.ucr.edu.

267. *Sacramento Daily Union*, Vol. 62, No. 25, 19 September 1889 pg. 2, California Digital Newspaper Collection, Center for Bibliographic Studies and Research, University of California, Riverside, http://cdnc.ucr.edu.

268. Find A Grave, database and images (https://www.findagrave.com: accessed 16 June 2019), memorial page for George M. Flournoy (30 Nov 1832–18 Sep 1889), Find A Grave Memorial no. 105532464, citing Holy Cross Catholic Cemetery, Colma, San Mateo County, California, USA; Maintained by Find A Grave (contributor 8).

269. *The Times Picayune* (New Orleans, LA) October 26, 1890 pg. 12 retrieved from https://www.newspapers.com, Newspapers made available courtesy of Chronicling America & University of Tennessee.

270. Park Benjamin, *The United States Naval Academy, Being the Yarn of the American Midshipman* (G.P. Putnam's Sons, New York and London) 1900 pg. 435.

271. http://www.fold3.com/image/280471989/, NARA M1091. Records from the Confederate Navy during the Civil War, organized by subjects ranging from ships to prisoners of war.

272. United States War Dept., *Official Records of the Union and Confederate Navies in the War of the Rebellion* Published under the direction of The Hon. H. A. Herbert, Secretary of the Navy, by Lieut. Commander Richard Rush. U.S. Navy, Superintendent

Naval War College, and Mr. Robert H. Woods. By Authority Of An Act Of Congress Approved July 31, 1894 (Washington, DC: Government Printing Office) 1880–1901 pg. 648.

273. United States War Dept., *Official Records of the Union and Confederate Navies in the War of the Rebellion* Published under the direction of The Hon. H. A. Herbert, Secretary of the Navy, by Lieut. Commander Richard Rush. U.S. Navy, Superintendent Naval War College, and Mr. Robert H. Woods. By Authority Of An Act Of Congress Approved July 31, 1894 (Washington, DC: Government Printing Office) 1880–1901 pg. 679.

274. Arthur Wyllie, *The Confederate States Navy* (lulu.com) 2013 pg. 139.

275. John Thomas Scharf, *History of the Confederate States Navy from Its Organization to the Surrender of Its Last Vessel* (Rogers & Sherwood, New York) 1887 pg. 793.

276. Benjamin Cummings Truman, *Tourists Illustrated Guide to the Celebrated Summer and Winter Resorts of California* (H.S. Crocker & Co., San Francisco, CA) 1883 pg. 113–114.

277. *San Francisco Call*, Vol. 68, No. 141, 19 October 1890 pg. 2, California Digital Newspaper Collection, Center for Bibliographic Studies and Research, University of California, Riverside, http://cdnc.ucr.edu.

278. Find A Grave, database and images (https://www.findagrave.com: accessed 21 June 2019), memorial page for Capt. Richard Samuel Floyd (8 Sep 1843–17 Oct 1890), Find A Grave Memorial no. 57988269, citing Cypress Lawn Memorial Park, Colma, San Mateo County, California, USA; Maintained by Athanatos (contributor 46907585).

279. *The National Cyclopaedia of American Biography*, Vol. VII (James T. White, Inc., New York) 1897 pg. 122.

280. http://www.fold3.com/image/280468781/, NARA M1091. Records from the Confederate Navy during the Civil War, organized by subjects ranging from ships to prisoners of war.

281. http://www.fold3.com/image/280468781/, NARA M1091. Records from the Confederate Navy during the Civil War, organized by subjects ranging from ships to prisoners of war.

282. R.C. Foute, "Echoes from Hampton Roads," R.A. Brock, ed., *Southern Historical Society Papers*, Vol. 19 (William Ellis Jones Printer, Richmond, VA) 1890 pg. 247.

283. R.C. Foute, "Echoes from Hampton Roads," R.A. Brock, ed., *Southern Historical Society Papers*, Vol. 19 (William Ellis Jones Printer, Richmond, VA) 1890 pg. 248.

284. http://www.fold3.com/image/280468781/, NARA M1091. Records from the Confederate Navy during the Civil War, organized by subjects ranging from ships to prisoners of war.

285. *The National Cyclopaedia of American Biography*, Vol. VII (James T. White Inc. New York) 1897 pg. 122.

286. *The National Cyclopaedia of American Biography*, Vol. VII (James T. White Inc. New York) 1897 pg. 123.

287. *The National Cyclopaedia of American Biography*, Vol. VII (James T. White Inc. New York) 1897 pg. 123.

288. *The National Cyclopaedia of American Biography*, Vol. VII (James T. White Inc. New York) 1897 pg. 123.

289. Find A Grave, database and images (https://www.findagrave.com: accessed 15 April 2019), memorial page for Robert Chester Foute (14 Apr 1841–28 Jul 1903), Find A Grave Memorial no. 12143481, citing Cypress Lawn Memorial Park, Colma, San Mateo County, California, USA; Maintained by Scott Hutchison (contributor 46635174).

290. Methodist Episcopal Church, South, Minutes of the annual conferences of the Methodist Episcopal Church, South (Publishing House of the Methodist Episcopal Church, South, Nashville, TN) 1894 pg. 147.

291. https://www.fold3.com/image/20/84719900, NARA M269. Compiled service records of Confederate soldiers from Mississippi units.

292. https://www.fold3.com/image/84642612, NARA M269. Compiled service records of Confederate soldiers from Mississippi units.

293. Dunbar Rowland, *The Official and Statistical Register of the State of Mississippi*, Vol. 2 (Press of the Brandon Printing Co., Nashville, TN) 1908 pg. 517.

294. https://www.fold3.com/image/20/84719918, NARA M269. Compiled service records of Confederate soldiers from Mississippi units.

295. Dunbar Rowland, *The Official and Statistical Register of the State of Mississippi*, Vol. 2 (Press of the Brandon Printing Co., Nashville, TN) 1908 pg. 518.

296. http://www.fold3.com/image/84719897/, NARA M269. Compiled service records of Confederate soldiers from Mississippi units.

297. https://www.fold3.com/image/84719924, NARA M269. Compiled service records of Confederate soldiers from Mississippi units.

298. Dunbar Rowland, *The Official and Statistical Register of the State of Mississippi*, Vol. 2 (Press of the Brandon Printing Co., Nashville, TN) 1908 pg. 512.

299. Methodist Episcopal Church, South, Minutes of the annual conferences of the Methodist Episcopal Church, South (Publishing House of the Methodist Episcopal Church, South, Nashville, TN) 1894 pg. 147.

300. Dunbar Rowland, *The Official and Statistical Register of the State of Mississippi*, Vol. 2 (Press of the Brandon Printing Co., Nashville, TN) 1908 pg. 512–513.

301. Dunbar Rowland, *The Official and Statistical Register of the State of Mississippi*, Vol. 2 (Press of the Brandon Printing Co., Nashville, TN) 1908 pg. 514.

302. https://www.fold3.com/image/84719960, NARA M269. Compiled service records of Confederate soldiers from Mississippi units.

303. Methodist Episcopal Church, South, Min-

utes of the annual conferences of the Methodist Episcopal Church, South (Publishing House of the
Methodist Episcopal Church, South, Nashville, TN)
1894 pg. 147.

304.  Find A Grave, database and images (https://
www.findagrave.com: accessed 15 April 2019), memorial page for Edwin Augustus Garrison (17 Feb
1841–18 Apr 1894), Find A Grave Memorial no.
67461364, citing Colusa Community Cemetery, Colusa, Colusa County, California, USA; Maintained
by David M. Peirce (contributor 47460027).

305.  United States Bureau of Naval Personnel,
United States Navy Dept, Register of Commissioned
and Warrant Officers of the United States Navy and
Marine Corps (C. Alexander, Printer, Washington,
D.C.) 1848 pg. 127.

306.  Morning Union, Vol. 28, No. 4357, 22 April
1881 California Digital Newspaper Collection, Center for Bibliographic Studies and Research, University of California, Riverside, http://cdnc.ucr.edu.

307.  *Sacramento Daily Union*, Vol. 13, No. 57, 28
April 1881 California Digital Newspaper Collection,
Center for Bibliographic Studies and Research, Uni-
versity of California, Riverside, http://cdnc.ucr.edu.

308.  *California Historical Society* quarterly (San
Francisco, California Historical Society) 1922 pg.
237.

309.  *California Historical Society* quarterly (San
Francisco, California Historical Society) 1922 pg. 248.

310.  https://www.fold3.com/image/22618113,
NARA M1003. Applications for pardon submitted to
President Andrew Johnson by former Confederates
excluded from earlier amnesty proclamations.

311.  George W. Gift, "The Story of the Arkansas,"
*Southern Historical Society Papers*, Vol. 12 (William
Ellis Jones Printer, Richmond, VA) 1884 pg. 51–52.

312.  George W. Gift, "The Story of the Arkansas,"
*Southern Historical Society Papers*, Vol. 12 (William
Ellis Jones Printer, Richmond, VA) 1884 pg. 53.

313.  *The San Francisco Examiner* (San Francisco,
CA) February 11, 1879, pg. 3 retrieved from https://
www.newspapers.com, Newspapers made available
courtesy of Chronicling America & University of
Tennessee.

314.  *Sacramento Daily Union*, Vol. 37, No. 5712,
19 July 1869 California Digital Newspaper Collection, Center for Bibliographic Studies and Research,
University of California, Riverside, http://cdnc.ucr.
edu.

315.  *The San Francisco Examiner* (San Francisco,
CA) February 11, 1879, pg. 3 retrieved from https://
www.newspapers.com, Newspapers made available
courtesy of Chronicling America & University of
Tennessee.

316.  Find A Grave, database and images (https://
www.findagrave.com: accessed 04 July 2019), memorial page for Lieut George Washington Gift (1 Mar
1833–1 Feb 1879), Find A Grave Memorial no.
17979602, citing Tulocay Cemetery, Napa, Napa
County, California, USA; Maintained by Rubbings
(contributor 47671529).

317.  *Daily Alta California*, Vol. 38, No. 12754, 15
March 1885 California Digital Newspaper Collection, Center for Bibliographic Studies and Research,
University of California, Riverside, http://cdnc.ucr.
edu.

318.  https://www.fold3.com/image/69342893,
NARA M320. Compiled service records of Confederate soldiers from Louisiana units.

319.  https://www.fold3.com/image/254898347?
terms=war,confederate,civil,greenwall, NARA M347.
"Unfiled Papers and Slips Belonging in Confederate
Compiled Service Records" may contain information
on soldiers not found in service records.

320.  https://www.fold3.com/image/74329323,
NARA M320. Compiled service records of Confederate soldiers from Louisiana units.

321.  https://www.fold3.com/image/74329353,
NARA M320. Compiled service records of Confederate soldiers from Louisiana units.

322.  https://www.fold3.com/image/185393879,
NARA M320. Compiled service records of Confederate soldiers from Louisiana units.

323.  United States. War Dept., *The War of the Rebellion: A Compilation of the Official Records of the
Union and Confederate Armies*, Series IV, Vol. II
(Washington, DC: Government Printing Office)
1880–1901 pg. 582–583.

324.  J. Marshall Hanna, "Castle Thunder in Bel-
lum Days," Southern Opinion (Richmond) 1867.

325.  https://www.fold3.com/image/185393872,
NARA M320. Compiled service records of Confederate soldiers from Louisiana units.

326.  Handbook of Texas Online, C. Richard King,
"Greenwall, Henry," accessed March 03, 2019, http://
www.tshaonline.org/handbook/online/articles/
fgr40. Uploaded on June 15, 2010. Modified on
March 6, 2018. Published by the Texas State Historical Association.

327.  *Sacramento Daily Union*, Vol. 18, No. 126, 19
January 1884, California Digital Newspaper Collection, Center for Bibliographic Studies and Research,
University of California, Riverside, http://cdnc.ucr.
edu.

328.  *Daily Alta California*, Vol. 38, No. 12754, 15
March 1885, California Digital Newspaper Collection, Center for Bibliographic Studies and Research,
University of California, Riverside, http://cdnc.ucr.
edu.

329.  William Couper, ed., The Corps Forward:
The Biographical Sketches of the VMI Cadets who
Fought in the Battle of New Market (Mariner Pub-
lishing) 2005 pg. 81.

330.  Colonel Jennings C. Wise, The Battle of New
Market, May 15, 1864 (Dulaney-Boatwright Co.,
Lynchburg Va.) 1914 pg. 24.

331.  Harry Gilmore, Four Years in the Saddle
(Harper & brothers, New York) 1866 pg. 157.

332.  http://www.fold3.com/image/9785455/,
NARA M324. Compiled service records of Confederate soldiers from Virginia units.

333.  https://www.fold3.com/image/22871235,

NARA M1003. Applications for pardon submitted to President Andrew Johnson by former Confederates excluded from earlier amnesty proclamations.

334. The Californian (Salinas, CA) January 25, 1919 pg. 8, col. 3 retrieved from https://www.newspapers.com, Newspapers made available courtesy of Chronicling America & University of Tennessee.

335. *Santa Cruz Sentinel* (Santa Cruz, CA) December 23, 1897, pg. 3, Col.4, retrieved from https://www.newspapers.com, Newspapers made available courtesy of Chronicling America & University of Tennessee.

336. Find A Grave, database and images (https://www.findagrave.com: accessed 22 June 2019), memorial page for George Washington Gretter (9 Jun 1845–23 Jan 1919), Find A Grave Memorial no. 120014091, citing Pioneer Cemetery, Watsonville, Santa Cruz County, California, USA; Maintained by Find A Grave (contributor 8).

337. *Daily Alta California*, Vol. XXVII, No. 9070, 1 February 1875, California Digital Newspaper Collection, Center for Bibliographic Studies and Research, University of California, Riverside, http://cdnc.ucr.edu.

338. https://www.fold3.com/image/64936029, NARA M320. Compiled service records of Confederate soldiers from Louisiana units.

339. https://www.fold3.com/image/64936027, NARA M320. Compiled service records of Confederate soldiers from Louisiana units.

340. https://www.fold3.com/image/64936030, NARA M320. Compiled service records of Confederate soldiers from Louisiana units.

341. https://www.fold3.com/image/20/81578318, NARA M320. Compiled service records of Confederate soldiers from Louisiana units.

342. https://www.fold3.com/image/20/81578341, NARA M320. Compiled service records of Confederate soldiers from Louisiana units.

343. https://www.fold3.com/image/70404193, NARA M331. Compiled service records of Confederate officers and enlisted men who did not belong to any particular regiment, separate company or comparable unit, or special corps.

344. United States. War Dept., *The War of the Rebellion: A Compilation of the Official Records of the Union and Confederate Armies* (Washington, DC: Government Printing Office) 1880–1901 pg. 337–338.

345. United States. War Dept., *The War of the Rebellion: A Compilation of the Official Records of the Union and Confederate Armies* (Washington, DC: Government Printing Office) 1880–1901 pg. 340.

346. https://www.fold3.com/image/20/81578341, NARA M320. Compiled service records of Confederate soldiers from Louisiana units.

347. https://www.fold3.com/image/70403737, NARA M331. Compiled service records of Confederate officers and enlisted men who did not belong to any particular regiment, separate company or comparable unit, or special corps.

348. http://www.fold3.com/image/22846176/,

NARA M1003. Applications for pardon submitted to President Andrew Johnson by former Confederates excluded from earlier amnesty proclamations.

349. *Daily Alta California*, Vol. XXVII, No. 9070, 1 February 1875, California Digital Newspaper Collection, Center for Bibliographic Studies and Research, University of California, Riverside, http://cdnc.ucr.edu.

350. Ezra J. Warner, *Generals in Gray: Lives of the Confederate Commanders* (LSU Press, Baton Rouge LA.) 2006 pg. 134.

351. Mary Coffin Johnson, *The Higleys and Their Ancestry: An Old Colonial Vamily* (D. Appleton & Co., New York) 1896 pgs. 677–78.

352. Mary Coffin Johnson, *The Higleys and Their Ancestry: An Old Colonial Vamily* (D. Appleton & Co., New York) 1896 pgs. 678.

353. http://www.fold3.com/image/12681305/, NARA M311. Compiled service records of Confederate soldiers from Alabama units.

354. https://www.fold3.com/image/70407346, NARA M331. Compiled service records of Confederate officers and enlisted men who did not belong to any particular regiment, separate company or comparable unit, or special corps.

355. https://www.fold3.com/image/70407289, NARA M331. Compiled service records of Confederate officers and enlisted men who did not belong to any particular regiment, separate company or comparable unit, or special corps.

356. Mary Coffin Johnson, *The Higleys and Their Ancestry: An Old Colonial Vamily* (D. Appleton & Co., New York) 1896 pgs. 678.

357. https://www.fold3.com/image/70407272, NARA M331. Compiled service records of Confederate officers and enlisted men who did not belong to any particular regiment, separate company or comparable unit, or special corps.

358. http://www.fold3.com/image/12681244/, NARA M311. Compiled service records of Confederate soldiers from Alabama units.

359. Mary Coffin Johnson, *The Higleys and Their Ancestry: An Old Colonial Vamily* (D. Appleton & Co., New York) 1896 pgs. 678.

360. Find A Grave, database and images (https://www.findagrave.com: accessed 15 April 2019), memorial page for Horace Antonio Higley (29 May 1828–24 Nov 1873), Find A Grave Memorial no. 105259297, citing Holy Cross Catholic Cemetery, Colma, San Mateo County, California, USA; Maintained by Find A Grave (contributor 8).

361. Paul E. Vandor, *History of Fresno County, California, with Biographical Sketches of the Leading Men and Women of the County Who Have Been Identified with Its Growth and Development from the Early Days to the Present*, Vol. 2 (Historic Record Company) 1919 pg. 2310.

362. Paul E. Vandor, *History of Fresno County, California, with Biographical Sketches of the Leading Men and Women of the County Who Have Been Identified with Its Growth and Development from the*

*Early Days to the Present*, Vol. 2 (Historic Record Company) 1919 pg. 2313.

363. Paul E. Vandor, *History of Fresno County, California, with Biographical Sketches of the Leading Men and Women of the County Who Have Been Identified with Its Growth and Development from the Early Days to the Present*, Vol. 2 (Historic Record Company) 1919 pg. 2313.

364. https://www.fold3.com/image/71854277, NARA M331. Compiled service records of Confederate officers and enlisted men who did not belong to any particular regiment, separate company or comparable unit, or special corps.

365. George Bergner, *The Legislative Record Containing the Debates and Proceedings of the Pennsylvania Legislature for the Session of 1862* (Telegraph Book and Job Office, Harrisburg, PA) 1862 pg. 650.

366. https://www.fold3.com/image/71854156, NARA M331. Compiled service records of Confederate officers and enlisted men who did not belong to any particular regiment, separate company or comparable unit, or special corps.

367. George Bergner, *The Legislative Record Containing the Debates and Proceedings of the Pennsylvania Legislature for the Session of 1862* (Telegraph Book and Job Office, Harrisburg, PA) 1862 pg. 650.

368. http://www.fold3.com/image/71853729/, NARA M331. Compiled service records of Confederate officers and enlisted men who did not belong to any particular regiment, separate company or comparable unit, or special corps.

369. United States. War Dept., *The War of the Rebellion: A Compilation of the Official Records of the Union and Confederate Armies*, Series 1, Vol. XI (Washington, DC: Government Printing Office) 1884 pg. 537.

370. United States. War Dept., *The War of the Rebellion: A Compilation of the Official Records of the Union and Confederate Armies*, Series 1, Vol. XI (Washington, DC: Government Printing Office) 1884 pg. 544.

371. https://www.fold3.com/image/71853770, NARA M331. Compiled service records of Confederate officers and enlisted men who did not belong to any particular regiment, separate company or comparable unit, or special corps.

372. https://www.fold3.com/image/71853827, Compiled service records of Confederate officers and enlisted men who did not belong to any particular regiment, separate company or comparable unit, or special corps.

373. https://www.fold3.com/image/71853836, NARA M331. Compiled service records of Confederate officers and enlisted men who did not belong to any particular regiment, separate company or comparable unit, or special corps.

374. https://www.fold3.com/image/71853849, NARA M331. Compiled service records of Confederate officers and enlisted men who did not belong to any particular regiment, separate company or comparable unit, or special corps.

375. https://www.fold3.com/image/71853869,

NARA M331. Compiled service records of Confederate officers and enlisted men who did not belong to any particular regiment, separate company or comparable unit, or special corps.

376. https://www.fold3.com/image/71853879, NARA M331. Compiled service records of Confederate officers and enlisted men who did not belong to any particular regiment, separate company or comparable unit, or special corps.

377. https://www.fold3.com/image/71854004, NARA M331. Compiled service records of Confederate officers and enlisted men who did not belong to any particular regiment, separate company or comparable unit, or special corps.

378. https://www.fold3.com/image/71854039, NARA M331. Compiled service records of Confederate officers and enlisted men who did not belong to any particular regiment, separate company or comparable unit, or special corps.

379. https://www.fold3.com/image/71854055, NARA M331. Compiled service records of Confederate officers and enlisted men who did not belong to any particular regiment, separate company or comparable unit, or special corps.

380. https://www.fold3.com/image/71854136, NARA M331. Compiled service records of Confederate officers and enlisted men who did not belong to any particular regiment, separate company or comparable unit, or special corps.

381. Paul E. Vandor, *History of Fresno County, California, with Biographical Sketches of the Leading Men and Women of the County Who Have Been Identified with Its Growth and Development from the Early Days to the Present*, Vol. 2 (Historic Record Company) 1919 pg. 2313.

382. Paul E. Vandor, *History of Fresno County, California, with Biographical Sketches of the Leading Men and Women of the County Who Have Been Identified with Its Growth and Development from the Early Days to the Present*, Vol. 2 (Historic Record Company) 1919 pg. 2313.

383. Find A Grave, database and images (https://www.findagrave.com: accessed 22 June 2019), memorial page for Dr Henry St. George Hopkins (21 Oct 1834–25 May 1914), Find A Grave Memorial no. 23529585, citing Mountain View Cemetery, Fresno, Fresno County, California, USA; Maintained by Lester Letson (contributor 46627920).

384. State Of Idaho, *An Illustrated History of North Idaho, Embracing Nez Perces, Idaho, Latah, Kootenai, Shoshone Counties* (Western Historical Publishing Co.) 1903 pg. 638.

385. http://www.fold3.com/image/10490085/, NARA M324. Compiled service records of Confederate soldiers from Virginia units.

386. https://www.fold3.com/image/10490099, NARA M324. Compiled service records of Confederate soldiers from Virginia units.

387. https://www.fold3.com/image/9099533, NARA M324. Compiled service records of Confederate soldiers from Virginia units.

388. http://www.fold3.com/image/20/9094725/, NARA M324. Compiled service records of Confederate soldiers from Virginia units.

389. Antietam Battlefield Historical Tablet No. 355 Reserve Artillery, Army of Northern Virginia from http://antietam.aotw.org/tablet.php?tablet_id=3550.

390. https://www.fold3.com/image/10490106, NARA M324. Compiled service records of Confederate soldiers from Virginia units.

391. marker for the Amherst Artillery east of Gettysburg on Benner's Hill from http://gettysburg.stonesentinels.com/confederate-batteries/amherst-virginia-artillery/.

392. *Confederate Veteran* Magazine, Vol. XXIII (S.A. Cunningham, Nashville, TN) 1915 pg. 391.

393. State Of Idaho, *An Illustrated History of North Idaho, Embracing Nez Perces, Idaho, Latah, Kootenai, Shoshone Counties* (Western Historical Publishing Co.) 1903 pg. 638.

394. Find A Grave, database and images (https://www.findagrave.com: accessed 15 April 2019), memorial page for Landon C Irvine (6 Feb 1842–17 Jan 1918), Find A Grave Memorial no. 33934257, citing Hartley Cemetery, Lakeport, Lake County, California, USA; Maintained by NWpioneer (contributor 46896368).

395. Find A Grave, database and images (https://www.findagrave.com: accessed 15 April 2019), memorial page for Robert Hugh Irvine (24 May 1840–1 May 1926), Find A Grave Memorial no. 73613862, citing Harmony Grove Cemetery, Lockeford, San Joaquin County, California, USA; Maintained by NWpioneer (contributor 46896368).

396. James T. White & Co., *The National Cyclopedia of American Biography*, Vol. V (James T. White & Co., New York) 1891 pg. 398.

397. https://www.fold3.com/image/109770957, NARA M321. Compiled service records of Confederate soldiers from Maryland units.

398. William Worthington Goldsborough, *The Maryland Line in the Confederate Army, 1861–1865* (Press of Guggenheimer, Weil & Co., Baltimore, MD) 1900 pg. 23.

399. William Worthington Goldsborough, *The Maryland Line in the Confederate Army, 1861–1865* (Press of Guggenheimer, Weil & Co., Baltimore, MD) 1900 pg. 45.

400. https://www.fold3.com/image/11691818, NARA M324. Compiled service records of Confederate soldiers from Virginia units.

401. Marker of Beckham's Battalion Breathed's Battery at Gettysburg from http://gettysburg.stonesentinels.com/Confederate-batteries/breatheds-battery/.

402. https://www.fold3.com/image/20/8001332, NARA M324. Compiled service records of Confederate soldiers from Virginia units.

403. https://www.fold3.com/image/20/8001359, NARA M324. Compiled service records of Confederate soldiers from Virginia units.

404. *San Francisco Call*, Vol. 108, No. 8, 8 June 1910, California Digital Newspaper Collection, Center for Bibliographic Studies and Research, University of California, Riverside, http://cdnc.ucr.edu.

405. Find A Grave, database and images (https://www.findagrave.com: accessed 15 April 2019), memorial page for James C Kane (1842–16 Nov 1916), Find A Grave Memorial no. 105291909, citing Holy Cross Catholic Cemetery, Colma, San Mateo County, California, USA; Maintained by Athanatos (contributor 46907585).

406. Find A Grave, database and images (https://www.findagrave.com: accessed 15 April 2019), memorial page for John Kolb Law (19 Jan 1841–14 Dec 1913), Find A Grave Memorial no. 6536103, citing Merced Cemetery, Merced, Merced County, California, USA; Maintained by Row Walker (contributor 46489843).

407. James Miller Guinn, *History of the State of California and Biographical Record of the San Joaquin Valley, California: An Historical Story of the State's Marvelous Growth from Its Earliest Settlement to the Present Time* (The Chapman Publishing Co., Chicago, IL) 1905 pg. 325.

408. Find A Grave, database and images (https://www.findagrave.com: accessed 15 April 2019), memorial page for John Kolb Law (19 Jan 1841–14 Dec 1913), Find A Grave Memorial no. 6536103, citing Merced Cemetery, Merced, Merced County, California, USA; Maintained by Row Walker (contributor 46489843).

409. J.C. Bates,, ed., History of the Bar and Bench of California (Bench and Bar Publishing Co. San Francisco, CA) 1912 pg. 390.

410. James Miller Guinn, *History of the State of California and Biographical Record of the San Joaquin Valley, California: An Historical Story of the State's Marvelous Growth from Its Earliest Settlement to the Present Time* (The Chapman Publishing Co., Chicago, IL) 1905 pg. 325.

411. https://www.fold3.com/image/71749810, NARA M331. Compiled service records of Confederate officers and enlisted men who did not belong to any particular regiment, separate company or comparable unit, or special corps.

412. United States War Dept., Official Records;, Series 1, Vol. 19, Part I (Antietam—Serial 27), Pages 937–938 (Washington, DC: Government Printing Office) 1880–1901.

413. James Miller Guinn, *History of the State of California and Biographical Record of the San Joaquin Valley, California: An Historical Story of the State's Marvelous Growth from Its Earliest Settlement to the Present Time* (The Chapman Publishing Co., Chicago, IL) 1905 pg. 326.

414. United States War Dept., Official Records;, Series 1, Vol. 19, Part I (Antietam—Serial 27), Pages 937–938 (Washington, DC: Government Printing Office) 1880–1901.

415. http://www.fold3.com/image/71749776/, NARA M331. Compiled service records of Confed-

erate officers and enlisted men who did not belong to any particular regiment, separate company or comparable unit, or special corps.

416. https://www.fold3.com/image/71749810, NARA M331. Compiled service records of Confederate officers and enlisted men who did not belong to any particular regiment, separate company or comparable unit, or special corps.

417. James Miller Guinn, *History of the State of California and Biographical Record of the San Joaquin Valley, California: An Historical Story of the State's Marvelous Growth from Its Earliest Settlement to the Present Time* (The Chapman Publishing Co., Chicago, IL) 1905 pg. 326.

418. James Miller Guinn, *History of the State of California and Biographical Record of the San Joaquin Valley, California: An Historical Story of the State's Marvelous Growth from Its Earliest Settlement to the Present Time* (The Chapman Publishing Co., Chicago, IL) 1905 pg. 326.

419. James Miller Guinn, *History of the State of California and Biographical Record of the San Joaquin Valley, California: An Historical Story of the State's Marvelous Growth from Its Earliest Settlement to the Present Time* (The Chapman Publishing Co., Chicago, IL) 1905 pg. 326.

420. Find A Grave, database and images (https://www.findagrave.com: accessed 15 April 2019), memorial page for John Kolb Law (19 Jan 1841–14 Dec 1913), Find A Grave Memorial no. 6536103, citing Merced Cemetery, Merced, Merced County, California, USA; Maintained by Row Walker (contributor 46489843).

421. Joseph LeConte, *Memoir of John LeConte, 1818–1891* (Read before the National Academy, April 1894) 1894.

422. *Pittsburg Daily Post* (Pittsburg, PA) July 7, 1901 pg. 7, col. 3, retrieved from https://www.newspapers.com, Newspapers made available courtesy of Chronicling America & University of Tennessee.

423. *Mariposa Gazette*, Vol. LXVI, No. 48, 21 May 1921, California Digital Newspaper Collection, Center for Bibliographic Studies and Research, University of California, Riverside, http://cdnc.ucr.edu.

424. *San Diego Union and Daily Bee*, 7 July 1901, California Digital Newspaper Collection, Center for Bibliographic Studies and Research, University of California, Riverside, http://cdnc.ucr.edu.

425. Joseph Le Conte, *Memoir of John LeConte, 1818–1891* (Read before the National Academy April 1894), pg. 374–75.

426. Joseph Le Conte, *Memoir of John LeConte, 1818–1891* (Read before the National Academy April 1894), pg. 375.

427. Joseph Le Conte, *Memoir of John LeConte, 1818–1891* (Read before the National Academy April 1894), pg. 376.

428. https://www.fold3.com/image/165858719, NARA M258. These are compiled service records of Confederate soldiers who served in organizations raised directly by the Confederate government.

429. https://www.fold3.com/image/165858719, NARA M258. Thse are compiled service records of Confederate soldiers who served in organizations raised directly by the Confederate government.

430. Joseph Le Conte, William Dallam Armes, ed., *The Autobiography of Joseph Le Conte*, Vol. 3 (D. Appleton & Co., New York) 1903 pg. 184.

431. Joseph Le Conte, William Dallam Armes, ed., *The Autobiography of Joseph Le Conte*, Vol. 3 (D. Appleton & Co., New York) 1903 pg. 184.

432. Joseph Le Conte, William Dallam Armes, ed., *The Autobiography of Joseph Le Conte*, Vol. 3 (D. Appleton & Co., New York) 1903 pg. 184.

433. Joseph Le Conte, William Dallam Armes, ed., *The Autobiography of Joseph Le Conte*, Vol. 3 (D. Appleton & Co., New York) 1903 pg. 206.

434. Joseph Le Conte, William Dallam Armes, ed., *The Autobiography of Joseph Le Conte*, Vol. 3 (D. Appleton & Co., New York) 1903 pg. 231–33.

435. *Mariposa Gazette*, Vol. LXVI, No. 48, 21 May 1921, California Digital Newspaper Collection, Center for Bibliographic Studies and Research, University of California, Riverside, http://cdnc.ucr.edu.

436. *San Diego Union and Daily Bee*, 7 July 1901, California Digital Newspaper Collection, Center for Bibliographic Studies and Research, University of California, Riverside, http://cdnc.ucr.edu.

437. Find A Grave, database and images (https://www.findagrave.com: accessed 08 July 2019), memorial page for Joseph Quarterman Le Conte (26 Feb 1823–6 Jul 1901), Find A Grave Memorial no. 8862234, citing Mountain View Cemetery, Oakland, Alameda County, California, USA; Maintained by Shiver (contributor 46539565).

438. Joseph Le Conte, *Memoir of John LeConte, 1818–1891* (Read before the National Academy April 1894), pg. 386.

439. Find A Grave, database and images (https://www.findagrave.com: accessed 08 July 2019), memorial page for John Eatton LeConte (4 Dec 1818–29 Apr 1891), Find A Grave Memorial no. 155130518, citing Mountain View Cemetery, Oakland, Alameda County, California, USA; Maintained by Peterborough K (contributor 46537737).

440. https://www.fold3.com/image/306349015, Alphabetical lists of officers who served in the United States Army from 1789 to 1903, with supporting charts, tables, and military history.

441. Elliott & Moore, *History of Monterey County, California: With Illustrations Descriptive of Its Scenery, Farms, Residences, Public Buildings, Factories, Hotels, Business Houses, Schools, Churches, and Mines: With Biographical Sketches of Prominent Citizens* (Elliott & Moore, Publishers, San Francisco) 1881 pg. 127.

442. Elliott & Moore, *History of Monterey County, California: With Illustrations Descriptive of Its Scenery, Farms, Residences, Public Buildings, Factories, Hotels, Business Houses, Schools, Churches, and Mines: With Biographical Sketches of Prominent Citizens* (Elliott & Moore, Publishers, San Francisco) 1881 pg. 127.

443. Elliott & Moore, *History of Monterey County,*

*California: With Illustrations Descriptive of Its Scenery, Farms, Residences, Public Buildings, Factories, Hotels, Business Houses, Schools, Churches, and Mines: With Biographical Sketches of Prominent Citizens* (Elliott & Moore, Publishers, San Francisco) 1881 pg. 127.

444.  Elliott & Moore, *History of Monterey County, California: With Illustrations Descriptive of Its Scenery, Farms, Residences, Public Buildings, Factories, Hotels, Business Houses, Schools, Churches, and Mines: With Biographical Sketches of Prominent Citizens* (Elliott & Moore, Publishers, San Francisco) 1881 pg. 127.

445.  https://www.fold3.com/image/14039004, NARA M324. Compiled service records of Confederate soldiers from Virginia units.

446.  https://www.fold3.com/image/14039052, NARA M324. Compiled service records of Confederate soldiers from Virginia units.

447.  https://www.fold3.com/image/14038979, NARA M324. Compiled service records of Confederate soldiers from Virginia units.

448.  Gustavus Woodson Smith, The Battle of Seven Pines (G. C. Crawford, printer, New York) 1891 pg. 53.

449.  http://www.fold3.com/image/14039004/, NARA M324. Compiled service records of Confederate soldiers from Virginia units.

450.  https://www.fold3.com/image/14038979, NARA M324. Compiled service records of Confederate soldiers from Virginia units.

451.  Find A Grave, database and images (https://www.findagrave.com: accessed 22 June 2019), memorial page for Maj Benjamin Watkins Leigh, Jr. (18 Jan 1831–3 Jul 1863), Find A Grave Memorial no. 62015629, citing Gettysburg National Cemetery, Gettysburg, Adams County, Pennsylvania, USA; Maintained by Find A Grave (contributor 8).

452.  Elliott & Moore, *History of Monterey County, California: With Illustrations Descriptive of Its Scenery, Farms, Residences, Public Buildings, Factories, Hotels, Business Houses, Schools, Churches, and Mines: With Biographical Sketches of Prominent Citizens* (Elliott & Moore, Publishers, San Francisco) 1881 pg. 127.

453.  Elliott & Moore, *History of Monterey County, California: With Illustrations Descriptive of Its Scenery, Farms, Residences, Public Buildings, Factories, Hotels, Business Houses, Schools, Churches, and Mines: With Biographical Sketches of Prominent Citizens* (Elliott & Moore, Publishers, San Francisco) 1881 pg. 127.

454.  The Californian (Salinas, CA) November 17, 1904 retrieved from https://www.newspapers.com, Newspapers made available courtesy of Chronicling America & University of Tennessee.

455.  Find A Grave, database and images (https://www.findagrave.com: accessed 22 June 2019), memorial page for MAJ John Wickham Leigh, Sr (Jul 1824–17 Nov 1904), Find A Grave Memorial no. 178181994, citing Garden of Memories, Salinas, Monterey County, California, USA; Maintained by Anonymous (contributor 48056117).

456.  Lewis Publishing Co., *The Bay of San Fran-*

cisco, Vol. 2 (Lewis Publishing Co., Chicago, IL) 1892 pg. 328.

457.  Lewis Publishing Co., *The Bay of San Francisco*, Vol. 2 (Lewis Publishing Co., Chicago, IL) 1892 pg. 328.

458.  Lewis Publishing Co., *The Bay of San Francisco*, Vol. 2 (Lewis Publishing Co., Chicago, IL) 1892 pg. 328.

459.  *San Francisco Call*, Vol. 105, No. 9, 9 December 1908, California Digital Newspaper Collection, Center for Bibliographic Studies and Research, University of California, Riverside, http://cdnc.ucr.edu.

460.  Francis Richard Lubbock, Cadwell Walton Raines, ed., Six decades in Texas; or, Memoirs of Francis Richard Lubbock, governor of Texas in war time, 1861–63. A personal experience in business, war, and politics (B. C. Jones & Co., printers, Austin Texas) 1900 pgs. 441–42.

461.  Clement Anselm Evans, *Confederate Military History: A Library of Confederate States History*, Vol. XI (Confederate Publishing Co., Atlanta Ga.) 1899 pg. 85.

462.  Lewis Publishing Co., *The Bay of San Francisco: the Metropolis of the Pacific Coast and Its Suburban Cities*, Vol 2 (Lewis Publishing Co., Chicago, IL) 1892 pg. 329.

463.  Find A Grave, database and images (https://www.findagrave.com: accessed 15 April 2019), memorial page for Henry S Lubbock (Apr 1823–8 Dec 1908), Find A Grave Memorial no. 108008697, citing San Francisco Columbarium, San Francisco, San Francisco County, California, USA; Maintained by Athanatos (contributor 46907585).

464.  *San Francisco Call*, Vol. 104, No. 10, pg. 4, 10 June 1908, California Digital Newspaper Collection, Center for Bibliographic Studies and Research, University of California, Riverside, http://cdnc.ucr.edu.

465.  https://www.fold3.com/image/72294625, NARA M331. Compiled service records of Confederate officers and enlisted men who did not belong to any particular regiment, separate company or comparable unit, or special corps.

466.  https://www.fold3.com/image/72294625, NARA M331. Compiled service records of Confederate officers and enlisted men who did not belong to any particular regiment, separate company or comparable unit, or special corps.

467.  United States War Dept., *The War of the Rebellion: A Compilation of the Official Records of the Union and Confederate Armies*, Vol. 27, Part 2 (Washington, DC: Government Printing Office) 1880–1901 pg. 505.

468.  https://www.fold3.com/image/20/71221557, NARA M331. Compiled service records of Confederate officers and enlisted men who did not belong to any particular regiment, separate company or comparable unit, or special corps.

469.  https://www.fold3.com/image/72294599, NARA M331. Compiled service records of Confederate officers and enlisted men who did not belong

to any particular regiment, separate company or comparable unit, or special corps.

470. https://www.fold3.com/image/72294600, NARA M331. Compiled service records of Confederate officers and enlisted men who did not belong to any particular regiment, separate company or comparable unit, or special corps.

471. https://www.fold3.com/image/20/71221502, NARA M331. Compiled service records of Confederate officers and enlisted men who did not belong to any particular regiment, separate company or comparable unit, or special corps.

472. https://www.fold3.com/image/72294613, NARA M331. Compiled service records of Confederate officers and enlisted men who did not belong to any particular regiment, separate company or comparable unit, or special corps.

473. The Rev. Gross Alexander, *Steve P. Holcombe, the Converted Gambler: His Life and Work* (Press of the *Courier Journal* Job Printing Co.) 1888 pg. 126.

474. *San Francisco Call*, Vol. 104, No. 10, pg. 4, 10 June 1908, California Digital Newspaper Collection, Center for Bibliographic Studies and Research, University of California, Riverside, http://cdnc.ucr.edu.

475. The Rev. Gross Alexander, *Steve P. Holcombe, the Converted Gambler: His Life and Work* (Press of the *Courier Journal* Job Printing Co.) 1888 pg. 126.

476. The Rev. Gross Alexander, *Steve P. Holcombe, the Converted Gambler: His Life and Work* (Press of the *Courier Journal* Job Printing Co.) 1888 pg. 127.

477. Harvard College Class of 1864, Secretary's Report No. 7, 1864–1904 (George Ellis, Harvard College (Cambridge, MA) 1904 pg. 160.

478. http://www.fold3.com/image/70084095/, NARA M268. Compiled service records of Confederate soldiers from Tennessee units.

479. https://www.fold3.com/image/70084091, NARA M268. Compiled service records of Confederate soldiers from Tennessee units.

480. Federal Publishing Co., *The Union Army: A History of Military Affairs in the Loyal States, 1861–65—Records of the Regiments in the Union Army—Cyclopedia of Battles—Memoirs of Commanders and Soldiers*, Vol. 6, Cyclopedia of Battles (Federal Publishing Co., Madison, Wis.) 1908 pg. 641.

481. https://www.fold3.com/image/20/67790688, NARA M268. Compiled service records of Confederate soldiers from Tennessee units.

482. United States War Dept., *The War of the Rebellion: A Compilation of the Official Records of the Union and Confederate Armies*, Series 1, Vol. 2 (Washington, DC: Government Printing Office) 1880 pg. 476.

483. Harvard College Class of 1864, Secretary's Report No. 7, 1864–1904 (George Ellis, Harvard College (Cambridge, MA) 1904 pg. 160–61.

484. United States War Dept., *The War of the Rebellion: A Compilation of the Official Records of the Union and Confederate Armies* (Washington, DC: Government Printing Office) 1880–1901.

485. Harvard College Class of 1864, Secretary's Report No. 7, 1864–1904 (George Ellis, Harvard College (Cambridge, MA) 1904 pg. 161.

486. Harvard College Class of 1864, Secretary's Report No. 7, 1864–1904 (George Ellis, Harvard College (Cambridge, MA) 1904 pg. 161.

487. Find A Grave, database and images (https://www.findagrave.com: accessed 22 June 2019), memorial page for John Edgar McElrath (2 Jan 1844–6 May 1907), Find A Grave Memorial no. 121657459, citing Mountain View Cemetery, Oakland, Alameda County, California, USA; Maintained by Rob Melton (contributor 47909854).

488. *Daily Alta California*, Vol. 37, No. 12601, pg. 1, 13 October 1884, California Digital Newspaper Collection, Center for Bibliographic Studies and Research, University of California, Riverside, http://cdnc.ucr.edu.

489. *Daily Alta California*, Vol. 37, No. 12601, pg. 1, 13 October 1884, California Digital Newspaper Collection, Center for Bibliographic Studies and Research, University of California, Riverside, http://cdnc.ucr.edu.

490. *Daily Alta California*, Vol. 37, No. 12601, pg. 1, 13 October 1884, California Digital Newspaper Collection, Center for Bibliographic Studies and Research, University of California, Riverside, http://cdnc.ucr.edu.

491. Thomas P. Ochiltree, "A Famous Fighter," *The Daily Examiner* of San. Francisco, 7 Oct. 1888: pg. 12.
California Digital Newspaper Collection, Center for Bibliographic Studies and Research, University of California, Riverside, http://cdnc.ucr.edu.

492. *Daily Alta California*, Vol. 37, No. 12601, pg. 1, 13 October 1884, California Digital Newspaper Collection, Center for Bibliographic Studies and Research, University of California, Riverside, http://cdnc.ucr.edu.

493. *Daily Alta California*, Vol. 37, No. 12601, pg. 1, 13 October 1884, California Digital Newspaper Collection, Center for Bibliographic Studies and Research, University of California, Riverside, http://cdnc.ucr.edu.

494. Find A Grave, database and images (https://www.findagrave.com: accessed 15 April 2019), memorial page for Edward McGowan (unknown–11 Dec 1893), Find A Grave Memorial no. 105061145, citing Holy Cross Catholic Cemetery, Colma, San Mateo County, California, USA; Maintained by Athanatos (contributor 46907585).

495. Lewis Publishing Co., *The Bay of San Francisco: the Metropolis of the Pacific Coast and Its Suburban Cities: a History*, Vol. 2 (Lewis Publishing Co.) 1892, Pages 371.

496. Lewis Publishing Co., *The Bay of San Francisco: the Metropolis of the Pacific Coast and Its Suburban Cities: a History*, Vol. 2 (Lewis Publishing Co.) 1892, Pages 371.

497. Lewis Publishing Co., *The Bay of San Francisco: the Metropolis of the Pacific Coast and Its Sub-*

*urban Cities*: a History, Vol. 2 (Lewis Publishing Co.) 1892, Pages 371.

498. John Hallum, *Diary of an Old Lawyer: Scenes Behind the Curtain* (Southwestern Publishing House, Nashville, TN) 1895 pg. 186.

499. *The Friend: A Religious and Literary Journal*, Vol. XXXV (William H. Pile, Philadelphia, PA) 1862 pg. 304.

500. Tennessee. Supreme Court, William Wilcox Cooke, Reports of Cases Argued and Determined in the Supreme Court of Tennessee During the War, Vol. 44 (Fetter Law Book Co., Louisville, KY) 1867 pg. 374.

501. Edward Howland, *Grant as a Soldier and Statesman: Being a Succinct History of His Military and Civil Career* (J.B. Burr & Co., Hartford, CT) 1868 pg. 100.

502. Lewis Publishing Co., *The Bay of San Francisco: the Metropolis of the Pacific Coast and Its Suburban Cities*: a History, Vol. 2 (Lewis Publishing Co.) 1892, Pages 371–72.

503. James Miller Guinn, *History of the State of California and Biographical Record of the San Joaquin Valley, California: An Historical Story of the State's Marvelous Growth from Its Earliest Settlement to the Present Time* (The Chapman Publishing Co., Chicago, IL) 1905 pg. 1178.

504. James Miller Guinn, *History of the State of California and Biographical Record of the San Joaquin Valley, California: An Historical Story of the State's Marvelous Growth from Its Earliest Settlement to the Present Time* (The Chapman Publishing Co., Chicago, IL) 1905 pg. 1178.

505. James Miller Guinn, *History of the State of California and Biographical Record of the San Joaquin Valley, California: An Historical Story of the State's Marvelous Growth from Its Earliest Settlement to the Present Time* (The Chapman Publishing Co., Chicago, IL) 1905 pg. 1178.

506. https://www.fold3.com/image/88585822, NARA M322. Compiled service records of Confederate soldiers from Missouri units.

507. https://www.fold3.com/image/88585829, NARA M322. Compiled service records of Confederate soldiers from Missouri units.

508. James E. McGhee,, ed., *Guide to Missouri Confederate Units, 1861–1865* (The University of Arkansas Press, Fayetteville, AR.) 2008 pg. 141.

509. James E. McGhee,, ed., *Guide to Missouri Confederate Units, 1861–1865* (The University of Arkansas Press, Fayetteville, AR.) 2008 pg. 142.

510. James Miller Guinn, *History of the State of California and Biographical Record of the San Joaquin Valley, California: An Historical Story of the State's Marvelous Growth from Its Earliest Settlement to the Present Time* (The Chapman Publishing Co., Chicago, IL) 1905 pg. 1179.

511. James Miller Guinn, *History of the State of California and Biographical Record of the San Joaquin Valley, California: An Historical Story of the State's Marvelous Growth from Its Earliest Settlement to the

*Present Time* (The Chapman Publishing Co., Chicago, IL) 1905 pg. 1179–1180.

512. Find A Grave, database and images (https://www.findagrave.com: accessed 22 June 2019), memorial page for Thomas Jefferson McQuiddy (6 Mar 1828–20 Feb 1915), Find A Grave Memorial no. 43655402, citing Hanford Cemetery, Hanford, Kings County, California, USA; Maintained by JC (contributor 46996543).

513. United States: Southern Historical Press, 1978. pg. 934.

514. *History of Tennessee: From the Earliest Time to the Present: Together with an Historical and a Biographical Sketch of Lauderdale, Tipton, Haywood and Crockett Counties: Besides a Valuable Fund of Notes, Original Observations, Reminiscences, Etc., Etc.* United States: Southern Historical Press, 1978. pg. 935.

515. http://www.fold3.com/image/74276480/, NARA M268. Compiled service records of Confederate soldiers from Tennessee units.

516. United States. War Dept., *The War of the Rebellion: A Compilation of the Official Records of the Union and Confederate Armies*, Series 1, Vol X (Washington, DC: Government Printing Office) 1884 pg. 439.

517. https://www.fold3.com/image/74276476, NARA M268. Compiled service records of Confederate soldiers from Tennessee units.

518. https://www.fold3.com/image/20/72866066, NARA M331. Compiled service records of Confederate officers and enlisted men who did not belong to any particular regiment, separate company or comparable unit, or special corps.

519. United States. War Dept., *The War of the Rebellion: A Compilation of the Official Reports of the Union and Confederate Armies*, Series II, Vol. V. Correspondence, orders, etc., relating to prisoners of war and state from December 1, 1862, to June 10, 1863 (Washington, DC: Government Printing Office) 1899 pg. 16.

520. United States. War Dept., *The War of the Rebellion: A Compilation of the Official Reports of the Union and Confederate Armies*, Series II, Vol. V. Correspondence, orders, etc., relating to prisoners of war and state from December 1, 1862, to June 10, 1863 (Washington, DC: Government Printing Office) 1899 pg. 16.

521. United States. War Dept., *The War of the Rebellion: A Compilation of the Official Reports of the Union and Confederate Armies*, Series II, Vol. V. Correspondence, orders, etc., relating to prisoners of war and state from December 1, 1862, to June 10, 1863 (Washington, DC: Government Printing Office) 1899 pg. 14.

522. Thomas Richard Meux, Memoir and Autobiography of Thomas Richard Meux, M.D. 1921 (Meux Home Museum).

523. https://www.fold3.com/image/20/74276489, NARA M268. Compiled service records of Confederate soldiers from Tennessee units.

524. *History of Tennessee: From the Earliest Time to the Present: Together with an Historical and a Biographical Sketch of Lauderdale, Tipton, Haywood and Crockett Counties: Besides a Valuable Fund of Notes, Original Observations, Reminiscences, Etc., Etc.* United States: Southern Historical Press, 1978. pg. 935.

525. Find A Grave, database and images (https://www.findagrave.com: accessed 15 June 2019), memorial page for Dr Thomas R Meux (6 Aug 1838–2 Dec 1929), Find A Grave Memorial no. 33250894, citing Mountain View Cemetery, Fresno, Fresno County, California, USA; Maintained by Lester Letson (contributor 46627920).

526. Colusa Herald, Vol. 41, No. 145, 23 November 1926, pg. 2 California Digital Newspaper Collection, Center for Bibliographic Studies and Research, University of California, Riverside, http://cdnc.ucr.edu.

527. http://www.fold3.com/image/20/70065097/, NARA M267. Compiled service records of Confederate soldiers from South Carolina units.

528. J. F. J. Caldwell, The history of a brigade of South Carolinians, known first as 'Gregg's', and subsequently as McGowan's Brigade (King & Baird Printers, Philadelphia, PA) 1866 pgs. 17–20.

529. United States War Dept., The War of the Rebellion, Vols. 1–53 [serial no. 1–111] Formal reports, both Union and Confederate (Washington, DC: Government Printing Office) 1880–1901.

530. United States War Dept., The War of the Rebellion, Series 1, Vol. XIIM, Formal Reports, Both Union and Confederate (Washington, DC: Government Printing Office) 1885 pg. 691.

531. Report of Capt. Joseph J. Norton, "First South Carolina Rifles, of Battle of Ox Hill," *The War of the Rebellion: Official Records of the Union and Confederate Armies by United States War Dept.*, Series 1, Vol. XII (Washington, DC: Government Printing Office) 1885 pg. 691–92.

532. J. F. J. Caldwell, *The History of a Brigade of South Carolinians, Known First as "Gregg's," and Subsequently as McGowan's Brigade* (King & Baird Printers, Philadelphia, PA) 1866 pgs. 59–60.

533. http://www.fold3.com/image/70065124/, NARA M267. Compiled service records of Confederate soldiers from South Carolina units.

534. *The Times and Democrat* (Orangeburg, SC) 17 Sep. 1885 pg. 2 retrieved from https://www.newspapers.com, Newspapers made available courtesy of Chronicling America & University of Tennessee.

535. The Watchman and Southron (Sumter, SC) 13 Oct. 1885 pg. 1 retrieved from https://www.newspapers.com, Newspapers made available courtesy of Chronicling America & University of Tennessee.

536. *Colusa Herald*, Vol. 41, No. 145, 23 November 1926, pg. 2, California Digital Newspaper Collection, Center for Bibliographic Studies and Research, University of California, Riverside, http://cdnc.ucr.edu.

537. Find A Grave, database and images (https://www.findagrave.com: accessed 28 June 2019), memorial page for Maj John Brown Moore (21 Mar 1835–22 Nov 1926), Find A Grave Memorial no. 104143069, citing Colusa Community Cemetery, Colusa, Colusa County, California, USA; Maintained by Tess (contributor 47773539).

538. James Miller Guinn, *History of the State of California and Biographical Record of the San Joaquin Valley, California: An Historical Story of the State's Marvelous Growth from Its Earliest Settlement to the Present Time* (The Chapman Publishing Co., Chicago, IL) 1905 pg. 1283.

539. https://www.fold3.com/image/7912342, NARA M324. Compiled service records of Confederate soldiers from Virginia units.

540. http://www.fold3.com/image/7912248/, NARA M324. Compiled service records of Confederate soldiers from Virginia units.

541. William S. White, *Contributions to a History of the Richmond Howitzer Battalion*, Vol. 2 (Carlton McCarthey & Co., Richmond, VA) 1883 pg. 93.

542. William S. White, *Contributions to a History of the Richmond Howitzer Battalion*, Vol. 2 (Carlton McCarthey & Co., Richmond, VA) 1883 pg. 97.

543. William S. White, *Contributions to a History of the Richmond Howitzer Battalion*, Vol. 2 (Carlton McCarthey & Co., Richmond, VA) 1883 pg. 99–100.

544. *Reports of the Operations of the Army of Northern Virginia: From June 1862 to and Including the Battle of Fredericksburg, Dec. 13, 1862, Vol. 1* by Confederate States of America. Richmond 1864 pgs. 576–577.

545. https://www.fold3.com/image/7912297, NARA M324. Compiled service records of Confederate soldiers from Virginia units.

546. William S. White, *Contributions to a History of the Richmond Howitzer Battalion*, Vol. 3 (Carlton McCarthey & Co., Richmond, VA) 1884 pg. 52.

547. James Miller Guinn, *History of the State of California and Biographical Record of the San Joaquin Valley, California: An Historical Story of the State's Marvelous Growth from Its Earliest Settlement to the Present Time* (The Chapman Publishing Co., Chicago, IL) 1905 pg. 1283.

548. Find A Grave, database and images (https://www.findagrave.com: accessed 15 April 2019), memorial page for George Washington Mordecai (18 Apr 1844–14 Jun 1920), Find A Grave Memorial no. 67809727, citing Mordecai Ranch Cemetery, Madera, Madera County, California, USA; Maintained by Lester Letson (contributor 46627920).

549. *The Fresno Morning Republican* (Fresno, CA) January 3, 1910 pg. 5, retrieved from https://www.newspapers.com, Newspapers made available courtesy of Chronicling America & University of Tennessee.

550. http://www.fold3.com/image/20/72093741/, NARA M269. Compiled service records of Confederate soldiers from Mississippi units.

551. https://www.fold3.com/image/20/72093808,

NARA M269. Compiled service records of Confederate soldiers from Mississippi units.

552. https://www.fold3.com/image/20/72093785, NARA M269. Compiled service records of Confederate soldiers from Mississippi units.

553. http://www.fold3.com/image/20/72093919/, NARA M269. Compiled service records of Confederate soldiers from Mississippi units.

554. https://www.fold3.com/image/20/72093829, NARA M269. Compiled service records of Confederate soldiers from Mississippi units.

555. https://www.fold3.com/image/20/72093848, NARA M269. Compiled service records of Confederate soldiers from Mississippi units.

556. *The Fresno Morning Republican* (Fresno, CA) January 3, 1910 pg. 5, retrieved from https://www.newspapers.com, Newspapers made available courtesy of Chronicling America & University of Tennessee.

557. *The Fresno Morning Republican* (Fresno, CA) January 3, 1910 pg. 5, retrieved from https://www.newspapers.com, Newspapers made available courtesy of Chronicling America & University of Tennessee.

558. S. A. Cunningham, ed., *Confederate Veteran* Magazine, Vol. 18 (Nashville, TN) 1910 pg. 240.

559. Lucius Manlius Boltwood, History and Genealogy of the Family of Thomas Noble, of Westfield, Massachusetts (Press of the Case, Lockwood & Brainard Co., Hartford, CT) 1878 pg. 738.

560. Phil Noble, Edward Noble and the "Featherbed Aristocracy," University South Caroliniana Society newsletter Spring 2014, pg. 25.

561. 1850 U.S. Federal Census—Slave Schedules [database on-line]. Provo, UT, USA: Ancestry.com.

562. 1860 U.S. Federal Census—Slave Schedules [database on-line]. Provo, UT, USA: Ancestry.com.

563. Phil Noble, Edward Noble and the "Featherbed Aristocracy," University South Caroliniana Society newsletter Spring 2014, pg. 26.

564. https://www.fold3.com/image/83223279, NARA M267. Compiled service records of Confederate soldiers from South Carolina units.

565. https://www.fold3.com/image/20/83223288, NARA M267. Compiled service records of Confederate soldiers from South Carolina units.

566. https://www.fold3.com/image/75165613, NARA M267. Compiled service records of Confederate soldiers from South Carolina units.

567. https://www.fold3.com/image/83223364, NARA M267. Compiled service records of Confederate soldiers from South Carolina units.

568. https://www.fold3.com/image/71848480, NARA M331. Compiled service records of Confederate officers and enlisted men who did not belong to any particular regiment, separate company or comparable unit, or special corps.

569. https://www.fold3.com/image/83223386, NARA M267. Compiled service records of Confederate soldiers from South Carolina units.

570. *San Francisco Chronicle* (San Francisco, CA) October 4, 1920, pg. 9, retrieved from https://www.newspapers.com, Newspapers made available courtesy of Chronicling America & University of Tennessee.

571. *The Iron Trade Review*, Vol. 67, Issue 2 (The Penton Publishing Co., Cleveland, OH) 1920 pg. 1225.

572. Find A Grave, database and images (https://www.findagrave.com: accessed 15 April 2019), memorial page for MAJ Edward Noble (9 Dec 1823–14 Apr 1889), Find A Grave Memorial no. 118305658, citing Cypress Lawn Memorial Park, Colma, San Mateo County, California, USA; Maintained by Cam Thompson (contributor 47145083).

573. Find A Grave, database and images (https://www.findagrave.com: accessed 15 April 2019), memorial page for Patrick Noble (14 Jan 1845–1920), Find A Grave Memorial no. 118305679, citing Cypress Lawn Memorial Park, Colma, San Mateo County, California, USA; Maintained by Cam Thompson (contributor 47145083).

574. Find A Grave, database and images (https://www.findagrave.com: accessed 07 December 2019), memorial page for Eliza Davis Pannill Otey (31 Mar 1800–4 Jun 1861), Find A Grave Memorial no. 9345214, citing Saint John's Church Cemetery, Ashwood, Maury County, Tennessee, USA; Maintained by Mary Bob McClain (contributor 46546099).

575. S. A. Cunningham, ed., *Confederate Veteran* Magazine, Vol. 7 (Nashville, TN) 1907 pg. 120.

576. S. A. Cunningham,, ed., *Confederate Veteran* Magazine, Vol. 7 (Nashville, TN) 1907 pg. 120.

577. S. A. Cunningham,, ed., *Confederate Veteran* Magazine, Vol. 7 (Nashville, TN) 1907 pg. 121.

578. https://www.fold3.com/image/20/71790760, NARA M331. Compiled service records of Confederate officers and enlisted men who did not belong to any particular regiment, separate company or comparable unit, or special corps.

579. https://www.fold3.com/image/20/8998502, NARA M324. Compiled service records of Confederate soldiers from Virginia units.

580. https://www.fold3.com/image/20/71790491, NARA M331. Compiled service records of Confederate officers and enlisted men who did not belong to any particular regiment, separate company or comparable unit, or special corps.

581. http://www.fold3.com/image/20/71790491/, NARA M331. Compiled service records of Confederate officers and enlisted men who did not belong to any particular regiment, separate company or comparable unit, or special corps.

582. http://www.fold3.com/image/20/71790491/, NARA M331. Compiled service records of Confederate officers and enlisted men who did not belong to any particular regiment, separate company or comparable unit, or special corps.

583. United States. War Dept., *The War of the Rebellion: A Compilation of the Official Records of the Union and Confederate Armies*, Series 1, Vol. XXXII (Washington, D.C.: Government Printing Office) 1891 pg. 710.

584. https://www.fold3.com/image/20/71790491, NARA M331. Compiled service records of Confederate officers and enlisted men who did not belong to any particular regiment, separate company or comparable unit, or special corps.

585. http://www.fold3.com/image/20/71790491/, NARA M331. Compiled service records of Confederate officers and enlisted men who did not belong to any particular regiment, separate company or comparable unit, or special corps.

586. Myron Angel, ed., *History of Nevada: With Illustrations and Biographical Sketches of Its Prominent Men and Pioneers* (Thompson & West, Oakland, CA) 1881 pg. 608.

587. *San Francisco Chronicle* (San Francisco, CA) December 17, 1898 pg. 10, retrieved from https://www.newspapers.com, Newspapers made available courtesy of Chronicling America & University of Tennessee.

588. Charles Lanman, *Biographical Annals of the Civil Government of the United States: From Original and Official Sources* (Joseph M. Morrison, New York) 1887 pg. 401.

589. *Sacramento Daily Union*, Vol. 21, No. 3193, 21 June 1861, pg. 2 California Digital Newspaper Collection, Center for Bibliographic Studies and Research, University of California, Riverside, http://cdnc.ucr.edu.

590. http://www.fold3.com/image/71787295/, NARA M331. Compiled service records of Confederate officers and enlisted men who did not belong to any particular regiment, separate company or comparable unit, or special corps.

591. https://www.fold3.com/image/20/71787389, NARA M331. Compiled service records of Confederate officers and enlisted men who did not belong to any particular regiment, separate company or comparable unit, or special corps.

592. https://www.fold3.com/image/20/71788776, NARA M331. Compiled service records of Confederate officers and enlisted men who did not belong to any particular regiment, separate company or comparable unit, or special corps.

593. http://www.fold3.com/image/71787295/, NARA M331. Compiled service records of Confederate officers and enlisted men who did not belong to any particular regiment, separate company or comparable unit, or special corps.

594. https://www.fold3.com/image/20/71787354, NARA M331. Compiled service records of Confederate officers and enlisted men who did not belong to any particular regiment, separate company or comparable unit, or special corps.

595. http://www.fold3.com/image/71787295/, NARA M331. Compiled service records of Confederate officers and enlisted men who did not belong to any particular regiment, separate company or comparable unit, or special corps.

596. http://www.fold3.com/image/71787295/, NARA M331. Compiled service records of Confederate officers and enlisted men who did not belong to any particular regiment, separate company or comparable unit, or special corps.

597. https://www.fold3.com/image/20/71787389, Compiled service records of Confederate officers and enlisted men who did not belong to any particular regiment, separate company or comparable unit, or special corps.

598. http://www.fold3.com/image/71787295/, NARA M331. Compiled service records of Confederate officers and enlisted men who did not belong to any particular regiment, separate company or comparable unit, or special corps.

599. *Santa Rosa Republican* (Santa Rosa, CA) January 18, 1907 pg. 8, retrieved from https://www.newspapers.com, Newspapers made available courtesy of Chronicling America & University of Tennessee.

600. Charles Lanman, *Biographical Annals of the Civil Government of the United States: From Original and Official Sources* (Joseph M. Morrison, New York) 1887 pg. 401.

601. Find A Grave, database and images (https://www.findagrave.com: accessed 15 April 2019), memorial page for Judge William Wood Porter (8 Sep 1826–17 Jan 1907), Find A Grave Memorial no. 29134891, citing Santa Rosa Rural Cemetery, Santa Rosa, Sonoma County, California, USA; Maintained by Jeanie Leete (contributor 47019987).

602. Lewis Publishing Co., *An Illustrated History of Sonoma County, California. Containing a History of the County of Sonoma from the Earliest Period of Its Occupancy to the Present Time* (Lewis Publishing Co., Chicago, IL) 1889 pg. 581.

603. Lewis Publishing Co., *An Illustrated History of Sonoma County, California. Containing a History of the County of Sonoma from the Earliest Period of Its Occupancy to the Present Time* (Lewis Publishing Co., Chicago, IL) 1889 pg. 582.

604. Lewis Publishing Co., *An Illustrated History of Sonoma County, California. Containing a History of the County of Sonoma from the Earliest Period of Its Occupancy to the Present Time* (Lewis Publishing Co., Chicago, IL) 1889 pg. 581.

605. https://www.fold3.com/image/83807693, NARA M267. Compiled service records of Confederate soldiers from South Carolina units.

606. http://www.fold3.com/image/69373898/, NARA M267. Compiled service records of Confederate soldiers from South Carolina units.

607. http://www.fold3.com/image/83807709/, NARA M267. Compiled service records of Confederate soldiers from South Carolina units.

608. https://www.fold3.com/image/83807710, NARA M267. Compiled service records of Confederate soldiers from South Carolina units.

609. http://www.fold3.com/image/86059425/, NARA M267. Compiled service records of Confederate soldiers from South Carolina units.

610. Cornelius Irvine Walker, Rolls and historical sketch of the Tenth Regiment, So. Ca. Volunteers, in the army of the Confederate States (Walker, Evans & Cogswell, printers, Charleston SC.) 1881 pg. 114.

611. E. D. Pope,, ed., *Confederate Veteran* Magazine, Vol. 38 (Nashville, TN) 1930 pg. 477.

612. E. D. Pope,, ed., *Confederate Veteran* Magazine, Vol. 38 (Nashville, TN) 1930 pg. 477.

613. E. D. Pope,, ed., *Confederate Veteran* Magazine, Vol. 38 (Nashville, TN) 1930 pg. 477.

614. Lewis Publishing Co., *An Illustrated History of Sonoma County, California. Containing a History of the County of Sonoma from the Earliest Period of Its Occupancy to the Present Time* (Lewis Publishing Co., Chicago, IL) 1889 pg. 582.

615. Find A Grave, database and images (https://www.findagrave.com: accessed 07 December 2019), memorial page for LTC John Gotea Pressley (24 May 1833–5 Jul 1895), Find A Grave Memorial no. 16777037, citing Santa Rosa Rural Cemetery, Santa Rosa, Sonoma County, California, USA; Maintained by Cousins by the Dozens (contributor 46904925).

616. Find A Grave, database and images (https://www.findagrave.com: accessed 29 June 2019), memorial page for Col James Fowler Pressley (30 Aug 1835–13 Feb 1878), Find A Grave Memorial no. 18668907, citing Suisun-Fairfield Cemetery, Fairfield, Solano County, California, USA; Maintained by Stonewall (contributor 46536634).

617. E. D. Pope,, ed., *Confederate Veteran* Magazine, Vol. 38 (Nashville, TN) 1930 pg. 477.

618. Find A Grave, database and images (https://www.findagrave.com: accessed 29 June 2019), memorial page for William Burrows Pressley (18 Oct 1847–17 Oct 1930), Find A Grave Memorial no. 139921717, citing Rio Vista Odd Fellows and Masonic Cemetery, Rio Vista, Solano County, California, USA; Maintained by Find A Grave (contributor 8).

619. Find A Grave, database and images (https://www.findagrave.com: accessed 29 June 2019), memorial page for Harvey Wilson Pressley, Sr (21 Feb 1850–1928), Find A Grave Memorial no. 68488016, citing Anderson District Cemetery, Anderson, Shasta County, California, USA; Maintained by Kathy O (contributor 47091900).

620. 1870 United States Federal Census [database on-line]. Provo, UT, USA: Ancestry.com.

621. *Confederate Veteran* Magazine Vol. 24 (Nashville, TN) 1916 pg. 9.

622. http://www.fold3.com/image/12422962/, NARA M324. Compiled service records of Confederate soldiers from Virginia units.

623. http://www.fold3.com/image/20/13202523/, NARA M324. Compiled service records of Confederate soldiers from Virginia units.

624. https://www.fold3.com/image/20/12422995, NARA M324. Compiled service records of Confederate soldiers from Virginia units.

625. S.A. Cunningham, ed.,*Confederate Veteran* Magazine, Vol. 20 (Nashville, TN) 1912 pg. 460.

626. https://www.fold3.com/image/20/12423004, NARA M324. Compiled service records of Confederate soldiers from Virginia units.

627. Robert Alonzo Brock, "Diary of Colonel George K. Griggs of the Thirty-Eight Virginia Infantry," *Southern Historical Society Papers* Vol. 14 (Virginia Historical Society, Richmond, VA) 1876 pg. 253.

628. Robert Alonzo Brock, "Diary of Colonel George K. Griggs of the Thirty-Eight Virginia Infantry," *Southern Historical Society Papers* Vol. 14 (Virginia Historical Society, Richmond, VA) 1876 pg. 254.

629. Robert Alonzo Brock, "Diary of Colonel George K. Griggs of the Thirty-Eight Virginia Infantry," *Southern Historical Society Papers* Vol. 14 (Virginia Historical Society, Richmond, VA) 1876 pg. 254.

630. Find A Grave, database and images (https://www.findagrave.com: accessed 29 June 2019), memorial page for William Bond Prichard (17 Feb 1842–16 Nov 1915), Find A Grave Memorial no. 86634637, citing Cypress Lawn Memorial Park, Colma, San Mateo County, California, USA; Maintained by Hal Eaton (contributor 47745260).

631. William S. Powell, *Dictionary of North Carolina Biography*, Vol. 5 (University of North Carolina Press, Chapel Hill) 2000 pg. 207.

632. Virginia Military Institute, *Virginia Military Institute Official Register, 1907–1908* (The Eddy Press Corporation, Winchester Va.) 1908 pg. 120.

633. Charles D. Walker, Memorial, *Virginia Military Institute: Biographical Sketches of the Graduates and Eleves of the Virginia Military Institute Who Fell During the War Between the States* (J.B. Lippincott & Co., Philadelphia, PA) 1875 pg. 437.

634. https://www.fold3.com/image/29476391, NARA M270. Compiled service records of Confederate soldiers from North Carolina units.

635. https://www.fold3.com/image/29476427, NARA M270. Compiled service records of Confederate soldiers from North Carolina units.

636. Walter Clark,, ed., *Histories of the Several Regiments and Battalions from North Carolina, in the Great War 1861–1865*, Vol. 3 (E.M. Uzzell, printer, Raleigh NC) pg. 532.

637. Charles D. Walker, Memorial, *Virginia Military Institute: Biographical Sketches of the Graduates and Eleves of the Virginia Military Institute Who Fell During the War Between the States* (J.B. Lippincott & Co., Philadelphia, PA) 1875 pg. 437–38.

638. Charles D. Walker, Memorial, *Virginia Military Institute: Biographical Sketches of the Graduates and Eleves of the Virginia Military Institute Who Fell During the War Between the States* (J.B. Lippincott & Co., Philadelphia, PA) 1875 pg. 437.

639. https://www.fold3.com/image/32822030, NARA M270. Compiled service records of Confederate soldiers from North Carolina units.

640. https://www.fold3.com/image/20/32822206, NARA M270. Compiled service records of Confederate soldiers from North Carolina units.

641. Samuel Houston Dixon, *The Poets and Poetry of Texas: Biographical Sketches of the Poets of Texas, with Selections from Their Writings, Containing Reviews Both Personal and Critical* (S. H. Dixon & Co., Austin Texas) 1885 pg. 255.

642. Walter Herron Taylor, R. Lockwood Tower, *Lee's Adjutant: The Wartime Letters of Colonel Walter Herron Taylor, 1862–1865* (Univ of South Carolina Press) 1995 pg. 244.

643. 1850 U.S. Federal Census—Slave Schedules [database on-line]. Provo, UT, USA: Ancestry.com.

644. 1860 United States Federal Census [database on-line]. Provo, UT, USA: Ancestry.com.

645. https://www.fold3.com/image/72869605, NARA M331. Compiled service records of Confederate officers and enlisted men who did not belong to any particular regiment, separate company or comparable unit, or special corps.

646. United States. War Dept., *The War of the Rebellion: A Compilation of the Official Records of the Union and Confederate Armies*, Series I, Vol. XXVII/2 June 3–August 1, 1863, The Gettysburg Campaign. No. 549, Reports of Maj. Gen. Henry Heth, C. S. Army, commanding division (Washington, D.C.: Government Printing Office) 1880–1901 pg. 639.

647. 1880 United States Federal Census [database on-line]. Lehi, UT, USA: Ancestry.com.

648. *San Francisco Call*, Vol. 86, No. 31, 1 July 1899, California Digital Newspaper Collection, Center for Bibliographic Studies and Research, University of California, Riverside, http://cdnc.ucr.edu.

649. https://www.fold3.com/image/20/85277581, NARA M266. Compiled service records of Confederate soldiers from Georgia units.

650. https://www.fold3.com/image/20/37034079, NARA M266. Compiled service records of Confederate soldiers from Georgia units.

651. "The Eighth Georgia Regiment in the Battle at Stone Bridge," *Richmond Dispatch*, July 29, 1861 Vol. Xx—no.24, pg. 3.

652. https://www.fold3.com/image/6807866, NARA M324. Compiled service records of Confederate soldiers from Virginia units.

653. https://www.fold3.com/image/6807877, NARA M324. Compiled service records of Confederate soldiers from Virginia units.

654. United States. War Dept., Report of Brig. Gen. Fitzhugh Lee, Battle of Kelly's Ford. *The War of the Rebellion: A Compilation of the Official...*, Vol. 25, Part 1 (Washington, D.C.: Government Printing Office) 1880–1901.

655. Red Bluff News, No. 23, 3 July 1903, California Digital Newspaper Collection, Center for Bibliographic Studies and Research, University of California, Riverside, http://cdnc.ucr.edu.

656. Oscar Tully Shuck,, ed., History of the Bench and Bar of California (The Commercial Printing House, Los Angeles, CA) 1901 pgs. 929–30.

657. https://www.fold3.com/image/20/68382609, NARA M269. Compiled service records of Confederate soldiers from Mississippi units.

658. Clement Anselm Evans, ed., Confederate military history: a library of Confederate States history, Vol. 7 (Confederate Publishing Co., Atlanta, GA) 1899 pg. 115–116.

659. https://www.fold3.com/image/20/68382630, NARA M269. Compiled service records of Confederate soldiers from Mississippi units.

660. https://www.fold3.com/image/20/66434434, NARA M269. Compiled service records of Confederate soldiers from Mississippi units.

661. Cavalry Scouts by Wade Hampton in The Land We Love, Vol. 3 (Hill, Irwin & Co., Charlotte, NC) 1867 pg. 348–349.

662. Franklin Harper, ed., *Who's Who on the Pacific Coast: A Biographical Compilation of Notable Living Contemporaries West of the Rocky Mountains* (Harper Publishing Co., Los Angeles, CA) 1913 pg. 508.

663. United States. War Dept., *The War of the Rebellion: A Compilation of the Official Records of the Union and Confederate Armies*, Series 1, Vol. XLII (Washington, D.C.: Government Printing Office) 1893 pg. 1235–1236.

664. Ulysses Robert Brooks, *Butler and His Cavalry in the War of Secession, 1861–1865* (The State Co., Columbia, SC) 1909 pg. 318–19.

665. United States. War Dept., *The War of the Rebellion: A Compilation of the Official Records of the Union and Confederate Armies*, Series 1, Vol. XLII (Washington, D.C.: Government Printing Office) 1880–1901 pg. 946–947.

666. United States. War Dept., *The War of the Rebellion: A Compilation of the Official Records of the Union and Confederate Armies*, Series 1, Vol. XLI (Washington, D.C.: Government Printing Office) 1894 pg. 543.

667. https://www.fold3.com/image/20/68382672, NARA M269. Compiled service records of Confederate soldiers from Mississippi units.

668. Oscar Tully Shuck,, ed., History of the Bench and Bar of California (The Commercial Printing House, Los Angeles, CA) 1901 pg. 930.

669. Franklin Harper, ed., *Who's Who on the Pacific Coast: A Biographical Compilation of Notable Living Contemporaries West of the Rocky Mountains* (Harper Publishing Co., Los Angeles, CA) 1913 pg. 508.

670. Find A Grave, database and images (https://www.findagrave.com: accessed 30 June 2019), memorial page for George David Shadburne (13 Jun 1842–28 Mar 1921), Find A Grave Memorial no. 107914528, citing Holy Cross Catholic Cemetery, Colma, San Mateo County, California, USA; Maintained by Athanatos (contributor 46907585).

671. https://www.fold3.com/image/257135866, NARA M347. "Unfiled Papers and Slips Belonging in Confederate Compiled Service Records."

672. https://www.fold3.com/image/20/257136353, NARA M347. "Unfiled Papers and Slips Belonging in Confederate Compiled Service Records."

673. https://www.fold3.com/image/257136383, NARA M347. "Unfiled Papers and Slips Belonging in Confederate Compiled Service Records."

674. https://www.fold3.com/image/20/257135866, NARA M347. "Unfiled Papers and Slips Belonging in Confederate Compiled Service Records."

675. *Sacramento Daily Union*, Vol. 29, No. 4508, 2 September 1865, pg. 2, California Digital Newspaper Collection, Center for Bibliographic Studies and Research, University of California, Riverside, http://cdnc.ucr.edu.

676. Find A Grave, database and images (https://www.findagrave.com: accessed 15 April 2019), memorial page for Mark Harvel Shearin, Jr. (17 Nov 1839–10 May 1919), Find A Grave Memorial no. 94905232, citing Maxwell Cemetery, Maxwell, Colusa County, California, USA; Maintained by Martha Shanahan (contributor 47224652).

677. Thomas Clendinen Catchings, Mary Clendinen Catchings Torrey, Charles Robert Churchill, *The Catchings and Holliday Families: And Various Related Families, in Virginia, Georgia, Mississippi and Other Southern States* (A.B. Caldwell Publishing Co., Atlanta, GA) 1921 pg. 151.

678. Edwin F. Bean, *Bean's History and Directory of Nevada County, California. Containing a Complete History of the County, with Sketches of the Various Towns and Mining Camps ... Also, Full Statistics of Mining and All Other Industrial Resources* (Daily Gazette Book and Job Office) 1867 pg. 200.

679. https://www.fold3.com/image/77855277, NARA M269. Compiled service records of Confederate soldiers from Mississippi units.

680. E. Howard McCaleb, "Featherstone-Posey-Harris Mississippi Brigade" in *Southern Historical Society Papers* by R.A. Brock (Virginia Historical Society, Richmond, VA) 1876 pg. 330.

681. https://www.fold3.com/image/77855288, NARA M269. Compiled service records of Confederate soldiers from Mississippi units.

682. E. Howard McCaleb, "Featherstone-Posey-Harris Mississippi Brigade" in *Southern Historical Society Papers* by R.A. Brock (Virginia Historical Society, Richmond, VA) 1876 pg. 331.

683. E. Howard McCaleb, "Featherstone-Posey-Harris Mississippi Brigade" in *Southern Historical Society Papers* by R.A. Brock (Virginia Historical Society, Richmond, VA) 1876 pg. 332.

684. E. Howard McCaleb, "Featherstone-Posey-Harris Mississippi Brigade" in *Southern Historical Society Papers* by R.A. Brock (Virginia Historical Society, Richmond, VA) 1876 pg. 333.

685. https://www.fold3.com/image/20/73621422, NARA M331. Compiled service records of Confederate officers and enlisted men who did not belong to any particular regiment, separate company or comparable unit, or special corps.

686. Emily Van Dorn Miller, *A Soldier's Honor with Reminiscences of Major-General Earl Van Dorn* (The Abbey press, New York & London) 1902 pg. 271.

687. https://www.fold3.com/image/73621420, NARA M331. Compiled service records of Confederate officers and enlisted men who did not belong to any particular regiment, separate company or comparable unit, or special corps.

688. Thomas Clendinen Catchings, Mary Clendinen Catchings Torrey, Charles Robert Churchill, *The Catchings and Holliday Families: And Various Related Families, in Virginia, Georgia, Mississippi and Other Southern States* (A.B. Caldwell Publishing Co., Atlanta, GA) 1919 pg. 151.

689. Find A Grave, database and images (https://www.findagrave.com: accessed 16 April 2019), memorial page for Rufus Shoemaker (1830–9 Mar 1893), Find A Grave Memorial no. 100820478, citing Greenwood Memorial Cemetery, Grass Valley, Nevada County, California, USA; Maintained by Kat B (contributor 47447776).

690. https://www.fold3.com/image/11293504, NARA M324. Compiled service records of Confederate soldiers from Virginia units.

691. https://www.fold3.com/image/20/11293591, NARA M324. Compiled service records of Confederate soldiers from Virginia units.

692. United States. War Dept., *The War of the Rebellion: A Compilation of the Official Records of the Union and Confederate Armies*, Series 1, Vol. XI (Washington, D.C.: Government Printing Office) 1885 pg. 575.

693. United States. War Dept., *The War of the Rebellion: A Compilation of the Official Records of the Union and Confederate Armies*, Series 1, Vol. XII (Washington, D.C.: Government Printing Office) 1885 pg. 645.

694. *Santa Cruz Sentinel*, Vol. 92, No. 130, 1 December 1935, pg. 6, California Digital Newspaper Collection, Center for Bibliographic Studies and Research, University of California, Riverside, http://cdnc.ucr.edu.

695. *Santa Cruz Sentinel* (Santa Cruz, CA) October 20, 1940 pg. 1 retrieved from https://www.newspapers.com, Newspapers made available courtesy of Chronicling America & University of Tennessee.

696. *Santa Cruz Sentinel*, Vol. 90, No. 129, 29 November 1934, California Digital Newspaper Collection, Center for Bibliographic Studies and Research, University of California, Riverside, http://cdnc.ucr.edu.

697. Luther Prentice Allen, *The Genealogy and History of the Shreve Family from 1641* (Privately Printed, Greenfield, IL) 1901 pg. 420.

698. Luther Prentice Allen, *The Genealogy and History of the Shreve Family from 1641* (Privately Printed, Greenfield, IL) 1901 pg. 421.

699. Find A Grave, database and images (https://www.findagrave.com: accessed 16 April 2019), memorial page for Sgt George William Shreve (9 May 1844–19 Oct 1940), Find A Grave Memorial no. 96925118, citing Mountain View Cemetery, Oakland, Alameda County, California, USA; Maintained by kellybean (contributor 47383012).

700. William C. Pendleton, *History of Tazewell County and Southwest Virginia, 1748–1920* (W. C. Hill Printing Co., Richmond, VA) 1920 pg. 630.

701. https://www.fold3.com/image/9854763, NARA M324. Compiled service records of Confederate soldiers from Virginia units.

702. William C. Pendleton, *History of Tazewell*

*County and Southwest Virginia, 1748–1920* (W. C. Hill Printing Co., Richmond, VA) 1920 pg. 630–31.

703. https://www.fold3.com/image/9854785, NARA M324. Compiled service records of Confederate soldiers from Virginia units.

704. https://www.fold3.com/image/9854768, NARA M324. Compiled service records of Confederate soldiers from Virginia units.

705. *Watsonville Pajaronian*, December 28, 1899, California Digital Newspaper Collection, Center for Bibliographic Studies and Research, University of California, Riverside, http://cdnc.ucr.edu.

706. Find A Grave, database and images (https://www.findagrave.com: accessed 16 April 2019), memorial page for Robert Smith (1 Mar 1819–23 Dec 1899), Find A Grave Memorial no. 120014326, citing Pioneer Cemetery, Watsonville, Santa Cruz County, California, USA; Maintained by Find A Grave (contributor 8).

707. *The Sonoma Democrat*, June 4, 1887, California Digital Newspaper Collection, Center for Bibliographic Studies and Research, University of California, Riverside, http://cdnc.ucr.edu.

708. Find A Grave, database and images (https://www.findagrave.com: accessed 08 December 2019), memorial page for Mary Mazyck Gaillard Smith (6 Mar 1820–3 Oct 1857), Find A Grave Memorial no. 19215297, citing Saint Stephens Episcopal Church Cemetery, Saint Stephen, Berkeley County, South Carolina, USA; Maintained by Anne Lewis Wheeler (contributor 47758260).

709. *The Sonoma Democrat*, June 4, 1887, California Digital Newspaper Collection, Center for Bibliographic Studies and Research, University of California, Riverside, http://cdnc.ucr.edu.

710. Alley, Bowen & Co., *History of Sonoma County, Cal., Including Its Geology, Topography, Mountains, Valleys and Streams* (Alley, Bowen & Co., Publishers, San Francisco) 1880 pg. 658.

711. https://www.fold3.com/image/20/74904747, NARA M267. Compiled service records of Confederate soldiers from South Carolina units.

712. https://www.fold3.com/image/20/67844502, NARA M267. Compiled service records of Confederate soldiers from South Carolina units.

713. https://www.fold3.com/image/20/67844506, NARA M267. Compiled service records of Confederate soldiers from South Carolina units.

714. http://www.fold3.com/image/68797591/, NARA M267. Compiled service records of Confederate soldiers from South Carolina units.

715. https://www.fold3.com/image/68797704, NARA M267. Compiled service records of Confederate soldiers from South Carolina units.

716. https://www.fold3.com/image/68797676, NARA M267. Compiled service records of Confederate soldiers from South Carolina units.

717. United States. War Dept., Report of Major Robert DeTreville Commanding Ft. Moultrie. *The War of the Rebellion: A Compilation of the Official Records of the Union and Confederate Armies*, Series 1, Vol. XXVIII (Washington, D.C.: Government Printing Office) 1890 pg. 718.

718. United States. War Dept., Report of Major Robert DeTreville Commanding Ft. Moultrie. *The War of the Rebellion: A Compilation of the Official Records of the Union and Confederate Armies*, Series 1, Vol. XXVIII (Washington, D.C.: Government Printing Office) 1890 pg. 744.

719. https://www.fold3.com/image/20/67845250, NARA M267. Compiled service records of Confederate soldiers from South Carolina units.

720. https://www.fold3.com/image/68797691, NARA M267. Compiled service records of Confederate soldiers from South Carolina units.

721. https://www.fold3.com/image/20/67845265, NARA M267. Compiled service records of Confederate soldiers from South Carolina units.

722. https://www.fold3.com/image/20/74905013, NARA M267. Compiled service records of Confederate soldiers from South Carolina units.

723. Alley, Bowen & Co., *History of Sonoma County, Cal., Including Its Geology, Topography, Mountains, Valleys and Streams* (Alley, Bowen & Co., Publishers, San Francisco) 1880 pg. 658.

724. *The Sonoma Democrat*, June 4, 1887, California Digital Newspaper Collection, Center for Bibliographic Studies and Research, University of California, Riverside, http://cdnc.ucr.edu.

725. Find A Grave, database and images (https://www.findagrave.com: accessed 30 June 2019), memorial page for Capt. Robert Press Smith, Sr (6 Jan 1814–29 May 1887), Find A Grave Memorial no. 10006797, citing Santa Rosa Rural Cemetery, Santa Rosa, Sonoma County, California, USA; Maintained by Anne Lewis Wheeler (contributor 47758260).

726. Find A Grave, database and images (https://www.findagrave.com: accessed 30 June 2019), memorial page for Capt. Robert Press Smith, Jr. (10 Oct 1839–19 Oct 1899), Find A Grave Memorial no. 10006773, citing Santa Rosa Rural Cemetery, Santa Rosa, Sonoma County, California, USA; Maintained by Anne Lewis Wheeler (contributor 47758260).

727. Aurelius O. Carpenter, Percy H. Millberry, *History of Mendocino and Lake Counties, California, with Biographical Sketches of the Leading, Men and Women of the Counties Who Have Been Identified with Their Growth and Development from the Early Days to the Present* (Historic record Co., Los Angeles, CA) 1914 pg. 756.

728. https://www.fold3.com/image/6820086, NARA M311. Compiled service records of Confederate soldiers from Alabama units.

729. George Little, James R. Maxwell, *A History of Lumsden's Battery, C.S.A.* (R.E. Rhodes Chapter, United Daughters of the Confederacy, Tuskaloosa Ala.) 1905 pg. 7.

730. George Little, James R. Maxwell, *A History of Lumsden's Battery, C.S.A.* (R.E. Rhodes Chapter, United Daughters of the Confederacy, Tuskaloosa Ala.) 1905 pg. 9.

731. George Little, James R. Maxwell, *A History*

of *Lumsden's Battery, C.S.A.* (R.E. Rhodes Chapter, United Daughters of the Confederacy, Tuscaloosa Ala.) 1905 pg. 12–13.

732. http://www.fold3.com/image/20/6868080/, NARA M311. Compiled service records of Confederate soldiers from Alabama units.

733. George Little, James R. Maxwell, *A History of Lumsden's Battery, C.S.A.* (R.E. Rhodes Chapter, United Daughters of the Confederacy, Tuscaloosa Ala.) 1905 pg. 18.

734. George Little, James R. Maxwell, *A History of Lumsden's Battery, C.S.A.* (R.E. Rhodes Chapter, United Daughters of the Confederacy, Tuscaloosa Ala.) 1905 pg. 56.

735. George Little, James R. Maxwell, *A History of Lumsden's Battery, C.S.A.* (R.E. Rhodes Chapter, United Daughters of the Confederacy, Tuscaloosa Ala.) 1905 pg. 66–67.

736. Aurelius O. Carpenter, Percy H. Millberry, *History of Mendocino and Lake Counties, California, with Biographical Sketches of the Leading, Men and Women of the Counties Who Have Been Identified with Their Growth and Development from the Early Days to the Present* (Historic record Co., Los Angeles, CA) 1914 pg. 756.

737. https://www.fold3.com/image/20/8415312, NARA M324. Compiled service records of Confederate soldiers from Virginia units.

738. https://www.fold3.com/image/20/8415324, NARA M324. Compiled service records of Confederate soldiers from Virginia units.

739. S.A. Cunningham, ed., *Confederate Veteran* Magazine Vol. 17 (S. A. Cunningham, Nashville, TN) 1893 pg. 242.

740. https://www.fold3.com/image/20/8071440, NARA M324. Compiled service records of Confederate soldiers from Virginia units.

741. https://www.fold3.com/image/20/8071444, NARA M324. Compiled service records of Confederate soldiers from Virginia units.

742. https://www.fold3.com/image/20/8071448, NARA M324. Compiled service records of Confederate soldiers from Virginia units.

743. https://www.fold3.com/image/20/8071451, NARA M324. Compiled service records of Confederate soldiers from Virginia units.

744. R. A. Brock, ed., "Black Eagle Company—A Typical Command of Confederate Soldiers by H.E. Wood, Ex-Color Sergeant, 18th Virginia Regiment," *Southern Historical Society Papers*, Vol. XXXVII (Southern Historical Society, Richmond, VA) 1909 pg. 57–58.

745. California, Voter Registrations, 1900–1968 [database on-line]. Provo, UT, USA: Ancestry.com.

746. *The Berkeley Gazette* (Berkeley, CA) February 8, 1909, pg. 1, retrieved from https://www.newspapers.com, Newspapers made available courtesy of Chronicling America & University of Tennessee.

747. *San Francisco Call*, Vol. 105, No. 70, 8 February 1909—Page 10, California Digital Newspaper Collection, Center for Bibliographic Studies and Research, University of California, Riverside, http://cdnc.ucr.edu.

748. Lewis Publishing Co., *A Memorial and Biographical History of Northern California: Containing a History of This Important Section of the Pacific Coast from the Earliest Period of Its Occupancy to the Present Time* (Lewis Publishing Co., Chicago, IL) 1891 pg. 635.

749. Lewis Publishing Co., *A Memorial and Biographical History of Northern California: Containing a History of This Important Section of the Pacific Coast from the Earliest Period of Its Occupancy to the Present Time* (Lewis Publishing Co., Chicago, IL) 1891 pg. 635.

750. http://www.fold3.com/image/85426596/, NARA M267. Compiled service records of Confederate soldiers from South Carolina units.

751. United States. War Dept., Reports of Brig. Gen. Wade Hampton, C. S. Army, Commanding Cavalry Brigade, of Operations September 2–20. September 3–20, 1862. The Maryland Campaign. O.R., Series I, Vol. XIX/1 (S# 27) (Washington, D.C.: Government Printing Office) 1887 pg. 823.

752. http://www.fold3.com/image/64761457/, NARA M267. Compiled service records of Confederate soldiers from South Carolina units.

753. https://www.fold3.com/image/64761500, NARA M267. Compiled service records of Confederate soldiers from South Carolina units.

754. Lewis Publishing Co., *A Memorial and Biographical History of Northern California: Containing a History of This Important Section of the Pacific Coast from the Earliest Period of Its Occupancy to the Present Time* (Lewis Publishing Co., Chicago, IL) 1891 pgs. 635–636.

755. Find A Grave, database and images (https://www.findagrave.com: accessed 16 June 2019), memorial page for Waverly Stairley (1845–10 Jun 1932), Find A Grave Memorial no. 132373530, citing Sunset View Cemetery, El Cerrito, Contra Costa County, California, USA; Maintained by Dusty Poss (contributor 47667196).

756. Henry D. Barrows, ed., Luther A. Ingersoll,, ed., *A Memorial and Biographical History of the Coast Counties of Central California* (The Lewis Publishing Co., Chicago, IL) 1893 pg. 393.

757. *The Daily Exchange* (Baltimore, MD) March 30, 1858 pg. 1, retrieved from https://www.newspapers.com, Newspapers made available courtesy of Chronicling America & University of Tennessee.

758. North Carolina Argus (Wadesboro, NC) January 6, 1859, pg. 4, retrieved from https://www.newspapers.com, Newspapers made available courtesy of Chronicling America & University of Tennessee.

759. 1860 United States Federal Census [database on-line]. Provo, UT, USA: Ancestry.com.

760. https://fold3.com/image/264501603/, NARA M251. Compiled service records of Confederate soldiers from Florida units.

761. United States. War Dept., Reports of General

Braxton Bragg, C. S. Army. *The War of the Rebellion: A Compilation of the Official Records of the Union and Confederate Armies*, Series 1, Vol. XIV (Washington, D.C.: Government Printing Office) 1902 pg. 1087.

762. https://www.fold3.com/image/264501610, NARA M251. Compiled service records of Confederate soldiers from Florida units.

763. Henry D. Barrows, ed., Luther A. Ingersoll, ed., *A Memorial and Biographical History of the Coast Counties of Central California* (The Lewis Publishing Co., Chicago, IL) 1893 pg. 393.

764. Find A Grave, database and images (https://www.findagrave.com: accessed 9 December 2019), memorial page for John Ernst Steinbeck, II (1862–1935), Find A Grave Memorial no. 11621205, citing Garden of Memories, Salinas, Monterey County, California, USA; Maintained by Debbie (contributor 46570228).

765. Find A Grave, database and images (https://www.findagrave.com: accessed 16 April 2019), memorial page for John Adolph Steinbeck (1828–10 Aug 1913), Find A Grave Memorial no. 26934917, citing Woodlawn Memorial Park, Colma, San Mateo County, California, USA; Maintained by Diane Reich (contributor 40197331).

766. Lewis Publishing Co., *The Bay of San Francisco: The Metropolis of the Pacific Coast and Its Suburban Cities: A History* (Lewis Publishing Co., Chicago, IL) 1892 pg. 518.

767. https://www.fold3.com/image/68472967, NARA M268. Compiled service records of Confederate soldiers from Tennessee units.

768. https://www.fold3.com/image/68472967, NARA M268. Compiled service records of Confederate soldiers from Tennessee units.

769. http://www.fold3.com/image/66373406/, NARA M268. Compiled service records of Confederate soldiers from Tennessee units.

770. https://www.fold3.com/image/66373434, NARA M268. Compiled service records of Confederate soldiers from Tennessee units.

771. *San Francisco Call*, Vol. 83, No. 66, 6 February 1898, pg. 10, California Digital Newspaper Collection, Center for Bibliographic Studies and Research, University of California, Riverside, http://cdnc.ucr.edu.

772. Lewis Publishing Co., *The Bay of San Francisco: The Metropolis of the Pacific Coast and Its Suburban Cities: A History* (Lewis Publishing Co., Chicago, IL) 1892 pg. 518.

773. Lewis Publishing Co., *The Bay of San Francisco: The Metropolis of the Pacific Coast and Its Suburban Cities: A History* (Lewis Publishing Co., Chicago, IL) 1892 pg. 518.

774. Lewis Publishing Co., *The Bay of San Francisco: The Metropolis of the Pacific Coast and Its Suburban Cities: A History* (Lewis Publishing Co., Chicago, IL) 1892 pg. 518.

775. *Langley's San Francisco Directory for the Year Commencing 1887* (Francis, Valentine & Co., San Francisco, CA) 1887 pg. 58.

776. Find A Grave, database and images (https://www.findagrave.com: accessed 16 April 2019), memorial page for Edward B Stonehill (1829–5 Feb 1898), Find A Grave Memorial no. 92103645, citing Cypress Lawn Memorial Park, Colma, San Mateo County, California, USA; Maintained by Larry White (contributor 46875221).

777. Bailey Lord, *History of the San Francisco Bay Region*, Vol. 3 (American Historical Society, Chicago, IL) 1924 pg. 95.

778. Bailey Lord, *History of the San Francisco Bay Region*, Vol. 3 (American Historical Society, Chicago, IL) 1924 pg. 96.

779. Lyman L. Palmer, W.F. Wallace, Harry Laurenz Wells, *Tillie Kanaga, History of Napa and Lake Counties, California: Comprising Their Geography, Geology, Topography, Climatography, Springs and Timber, Together with a Full and Particular Record of the Mexican Grants, Also Separate Histories of All the Townships and Biographical Sketches* (Slocum, Bowen, San Francisco, CA) 1881 pg. 562.

780. https://www.fold3.com/image/68916636, NARA M267. Compiled service records of Confederate soldiers from South Carolina units.

781. https://www.fold3.com/image/73620990, NARA M331. Compiled service records of Confederate officers and enlisted men who did not belong to any particular regiment, separate company or comparable unit, or special corps.

782. https://www.fold3.com/image/67826881, NARA M267. Compiled service records of Confederate soldiers from South Carolina units.

783. Lyman L. Palmer, W.F. Wallace, Harry Laurenz Wells, Tillie Kanaga, *History of Napa and Lake Counties, California: Comprising Their Geography, Geology, Topography, Climatography, Springs and Timber, Together with a Full and Particular Record of the Mexican Grants, Also Separate Histories of All the Townships and Biographical Sketches* (Slocum, Bowen, San Francisco, CA) 1881 pg. 562–63.

784. https://www.fold3.com/image/67826998, NARA M267. Compiled service records of Confederate soldiers from South Carolina units.

785. Lyman L. Palmer, W.F. Wallace, Harry Laurenz Wells, Tillie Kanaga, *History of Napa and Lake Counties, California: Comprising Their Geography, Geology, Topography, Climatography, Springs and Timber, Together with a Full and Particular Record of the Mexican Grants, Also Separate Histories of All the Townships and Biographical Sketches* (Slocum, Bowen, San Francisco, CA) 1881 pg. 562.

786. Bailey Millard, *History of the San Francisco Bay Region*, Vol. 3 (The American Historical Society, Inc., Chicago, IL) 1924 pg. 96.

787. Lyman L. Palmer, W.F. Wallace, Harry Laurenz Wells, Tillie Kanaga, *History of Napa and Lake Counties, California: Comprising Their Geography, Geology, Topography, Climatography, Springs and Timber, Together with a Full and Particular Record of the Mexican Grants, Also Separate Histories of All the Townships and Biographical Sketches* (Slocum, Bowen) 1881 pg. 564.

788. *Sacramento Daily Union*, Vol. 82, No. 104, 21 December 1891, pg. 1, California Digital Newspaper Collection, Center for Bibliographic Studies and Research, University of California, Riverside, http://cdnc.ucr.edu.

789. Find A Grave, database and images (https://www.findagrave.com: accessed 16 April 2019), memorial page for Thomas Porcher Stoney (25 Apr 1835–19 Dec 1891), Find A Grave Memorial no. 108792798, citing Cypress Lawn Memorial Park, Colma, San Mateo County, California, USA; Maintained by Debbie Baker (contributor 47212247).

790. Malcolm G. McGregor, *The Biographical Record of Jasper County, Missouri* (Lewis Publishing Co., Chicago, IL) 1901 pg. 427.

791. https://www.fold3.com/image/193835291, NARA M322. Compiled service records of Confederate soldiers from Missouri units.

792. https://www.fold3.com/image/20/193824264, NARA M322. Compiled service records of Confederate soldiers from Missouri units.

793. John McCorkle, *Three Years with Quantrell: A True Story* (Armstrong herald print, Armstrong, MO) 1914 pgs. 76–78.

794. Ora Merle Hawk Pease, *History of Caldwell and Livingston Counties, Missouri* (National Historical Co., St. Louis, MO) 1886 pgs. 195–210.

795. Ora Merle Hawk Pease, *History of Caldwell and Livingston Counties, Missouri* (National Historical Co., St. Louis, MO) 1886 pg. 209.

796. John N. Edwards, *Noted Guerrillas or the Warfare of the Border* (Bryan, Brand, St. Louis, MO) 1877 pg. 149.

797. *San Francisco Call*, Vol. 111, No. 146, 24 April 1912 pg. 10, California Digital Newspaper Collection, Center for Bibliographic Studies and Research, University of California, Riverside, http://cdnc.ucr.edu.

798. *San Francisco Call*, Vol. 111, No. 150, 28 April 1912 pg. 51, California Digital Newspaper Collection, Center for Bibliographic Studies and Research, University of California, Riverside, http://cdnc.ucr.edu.

799. Find A Grave, database and images (https://www.findagrave.com: accessed 30 June 2019), memorial page for Charles Fletcher Taylor (19 May 1842–22 Apr 1912), Find A Grave Memorial no. 101589596, citing Greenlawn Memorial Park, Colma, San Mateo County, California, USA; Maintained by Ron Mac (contributor 46931715).

800. *Daily Alta California*, Vol. 81, No. 46, 15 August 1889, pg. 1&4, California Digital Newspaper Collection, Center for Bibliographic Studies and Research, University of California, Riverside, http://cdnc.ucr.edu.

801. Alexander E. Wagstaff, *Life of David S. Terry: Presenting an Authentic, Impartial and Vivid and Impartial History of His Life and Tragic Death* (Continental Publishing Co. San Francisco, CA) 1892 pg. 218.

802. Alexander E. Wagstaff, *Life of David S. Terry: Presenting an Authentic, Impartial and Vivid and Impartial History of His Life and Tragic Death* (Conti-

nental Publishing Co. San Francisco, CA) 1892 pg. 219–220.

803. Alexander E. Wagstaff, *Life of David S. Terry: Presenting an Authentic, Impartial and Vivid and Impartial History of His Life and Tragic Death* (Continental Publishing Co. San Francisco, CA) 1892 pg. 226–28.

804. *Press Democrat*, Vol. XI, No. 159, 8 January 1886, pg. 2, California Digital Newspaper Collection, Center for Bibliographic Studies and Research, University of California, Riverside, http://cdnc.ucr.edu.

805. *Sonoma Democrat*, Vol. XXXII, No. 44, 17 August 1889, pg. 2, California Digital Newspaper Collection, Center for Bibliographic Studies and Research, University of California, Riverside, http://cdnc.ucr.edu.

806. Find A Grave, database and images (https://www.findagrave.com: accessed 16 April 2019), memorial page for David Smith Terry (8 Mar 1823–14 Aug 1889), Find A Grave Memorial no. 6823201, citing Stockton Rural Cemetery, Stockton, San Joaquin County, California, USA; Maintained by Find A Grave.

807. https://www.fold3.com/image/20/12236241, NARA M324. Compiled service records of Confederate soldiers from Virginia units.

808. https://www.fold3.com/image/20/12559350, NARA M324. Compiled service records of Confederate soldiers from Virginia units.

809. https://www.fold3.com/image/20/12236314, NARA M324. Compiled service records of Confederate soldiers from Virginia units.

810. United States War Dept., Official Records, Series I, Vol. 29, Part 1 (Washington, D.C.: Government Printing Office) 1891 pg. 54.

811. United States War Dept., Official Records, Series I, Vol. 29, Part 1 (Washington, D.C.: Government Printing Office) 1890 pg. 63.

812. United States War Dept., Official Records, Series I, Vol. XXXVII, Part 1 (Washington, D.C.: Government Printing Office) 1891 pg. 53.

813. https://www.fold3.com/image/20/12236452, NARA M324. Compiled service records of Confederate soldiers from Virginia units.

814. https://www.fold3.com/image/20/12236381, NARA M324. Compiled service records of Confederate soldiers from Virginia units.

815. https://www.fold3.com/image/20/12236398, NARA M324. Compiled service records of Confederate soldiers from Virginia units.

816. William C. Pendleton, *History of Tazewell County and Southwest Virginia, 1748–1920* (W. C. Hill Printing Co., Richmond, VA) 1920 pg. 649.

817. Find A Grave, database and images (https://www.findagrave.com: accessed 16 April 2019), memorial page for CPT John Thompson (8 Jul 1839–7 Feb 1882), Find A Grave Memorial no. 68448930, citing Woodbridge Masonic Cemetery, Woodbridge, San Joaquin County, California, USA; Maintained by Marilyn Diaz (contributor 47098929).

818. *Breeder and Sportsman*, Vol. XXVI No. 9,

"Death of Col. H.I. Thornton," March 2, 1895, pg. 193.

819. *Breeder and Sportsman*, Vol. XXVI No. 9, "Death of Col. H.I. Thornton," March 2, 1895, pg. 193.

820. https://www.fold3.com/image/20/75120567, NARA M331. Compiled service records of Confederate officers and enlisted men who did not belong to any particular regiment, separate company or comparable unit, or special corps.

821. United States War Dept. *The Official Records of the Union and Confederate Armies* (Washington, D.C.: Government Printing Office) 1882 pg. 109.

822. https://www.fold3.com/image/20/75120598, NARA M331. Compiled service records of Confederate officers and enlisted men who did not belong to any particular regiment, separate company or comparable unit, or special corps.

823. http://www.fold3.com/image/13577245/, NARA M311. Compiled service records of Confederate soldiers from Alabama units.

824. United States War Dept., *The War of the Rebellion: A Compilation of the Official Records of the Union and Confederate Armies* Armies, Series 1, Vol. XXXVIII (Washington, D.C.: Government Printing Office) 1880–1901 pg. 842.

825. C.C. Goodwin, *As I Remember Them* (Salt Lake City, UT) 1913 pg. 212.

826. *Breeder and Sportsman*, Vol. XXVI No. 9, "Death of Col. H.I. Thornton," March 2, 1895, pg. 193.

827. C.C. Goodwin, As I Remember Them (Salt Lake City, UT) 1913 pg. 209.

828. *Breeder and Sportsman*, Vol. XXVI No. 9, "Death of Col. H.I. Thornton," March 2, 1895, pg. 193.

829. *Breeder and Sportsman*, Vol. XXVI No. 9, "Death of Col. H.I. Thornton," March 2, 1895, pg. 193.

830. Find A Grave, database and images (https://www.findagrave.com: accessed 16 April 2019), memorial page for Harry Innes Thornton (1834–25 Feb 1895), Find A Grave Memorial no. 115779702, citing Cypress Lawn Memorial Park, Colma, San Mateo County, California, USA; Maintained by Larry White (contributor 46875221).

831. Find A Grave, database and images (https://www.findagrave.com: accessed 9 December 2019), memorial page for James Ellis Tucker (25 Oct 1844–24 Feb 1924), Find A Grave Memorial no. 48336138, citing Saint Helena Cemetery, Saint Helena, Napa County, California, USA; Maintained by Connie (contributor 47390019).

832. S.A. Cunningham, *Confederate Veteran* Magazine Vol. 37 (S.A.Cunningham, Nashville, TN) 1893 pg. 328.

833. S.A. Cunningham, *Confederate Veteran* Magazine Vol. 37 (S.A.Cunningham, Nashville, TN) 1893 pg. 328.

834. https://www.fold3.com/image/20/7250290, NARA M324. Compiled service records of Confederate soldiers from Virginia units.

835. United States War Dept., *The War of the Rebellion: A Compilation of the Official Records of the Union and Confederate Armies* Armies, Series 1, Vol. XXV (Washington, D.C.: Government Printing Office) 1889 pg. 61.

836. https://www.fold3.com/image/20/7250293, NARA M324. Compiled service records of Confederate soldiers from Virginia units.

837. https://www.fold3.com/image/20/7250303, NARA M324. Compiled service records of Confederate soldiers from Virginia units.

838. https://www.fold3.com/image/20/7250451, NARA M324. Compiled service records of Confederate soldiers from Virginia units.

839. http://www.fold3.com/image/20/7250366/, NARA M324. Compiled service records of Confederate soldiers from Virginia units.

840. *The San Francisco Examiner* (San Francisco, CA) February 26, 1924 pg. 5, retrieved from https://www.newspapers.com, Newspapers made available courtesy of Chronicling America & University of Tennessee.

841. *The Bee* (Danville, VA) February 27, 1924 pg. 1 retrieved from https://www.newspapers.com, Newspapers made available courtesy of Chronicling America & University of Tennessee.

842. *The San Francisco Examiner* (San Francisco, CA) February 26, 1924 pg. 5, retrieved from https://www.newspapers.com, Newspapers made available courtesy of Chronicling America & University of Tennessee.

843. Find A Grave, database and images (https://www.findagrave.com: accessed 9 December 2019), memorial page for Mary Champney "Maye" Bourn Tucker (11 Feb 1855–2 Nov 1947), Find A Grave Memorial no. 48336134, citing Saint Helena Cemetery, Saint Helena, Napa County, California, USA; Maintained by Connie (contributor 47390019).

844. Find A Grave, database and images (https://www.findagrave.com: accessed 16 April 2019), memorial page for James Ellis Tucker (25 Oct 1844–24 Feb 1924), Find A Grave Memorial no. 48336138, citing Saint Helena Cemetery, Saint Helena, Napa County, California, USA; Maintained by Connie (contributor 47390019).

845. Paul E. Vandor, *History of Fresno County, California, with Biographical Sketches of the Leading Men and Women of the County Who Have Been Identified with Its Growth and Development from the Early Days to the Present*, Vol. 1 (Historic Record Co., Los Angeles, CA) 1919 pg. 626.

846. https://www.fold3.com/image/81123140, NARA M269. Compiled service records of Confederate soldiers from Mississippi units.

847. Paul E. Vandor, *History of Fresno County, California, with Biographical Sketches of the Leading Men and Women of the County Who Have Been Identified with Its Growth and Development from the Early Days to the Present*, Vol. 1 (Historic Record Co., Los Angeles, CA) 1919 pg. 626.

848. Paul E. Vandor, *History of Fresno County, California, with Biographical Sketches of the Leading Men and Women of the County Who Have Been Iden-*

tified with *Its Growth and Development from the Early Days to the Present*, Vol. 1 (Historic Record Co., Los Angeles, CA) 1919 pg. 626.

849. http://www.fold3.com/image/76646556/, NARA M331. Compiled service records of Confederate officers and enlisted men who did not belong to any particular regiment, separate company or comparable unit, or special corps.

850. United States War Dept., *The War of the Rebellion: A Compilation of the Official Records of the Union and Confederate Armies*, Series 1, Vol. XXIV (Washington, D.C.: Government Printing Office) 1889 pgs. 127–128.

851. https://www.fold3.com/image/76646919/, NARA M331. Compiled service records of Confederate officers and enlisted men who did not belong to any particular regiment, separate company or comparable unit, or special corps.

852. https://www.fold3.com/image/76646940/, NARA M331. Compiled service records of Confederate officers and enlisted men who did not belong to any particular regiment, separate company or comparable unit, or special corps.

853. Paul E. Vandor, *History of Fresno County, California, with Biographical Sketches of the Leading Men and Women of the County Who Have Been Identified with Its Growth and Development from the Early Days to the Present*, Vol. 1 (Historic Record Co., Los Angeles, CA) 1919 pg. 626.

854. https://www.fold3.com/image/76646871/, NARA M331. Compiled service records of Confederate officers and enlisted men who did not belong to any particular regiment, separate company or comparable unit, or special corps.

855. https://www.fold3.com/image/76646959/, NARA M331. Compiled service records of Confederate officers and enlisted men who did not belong to any particular regiment, separate company or comparable unit, or special corps.

856. Paul E. Vandor, *History of Fresno County, California, with Biographical Sketches of the Leading Men and Women of the County Who Have Been Identified with Its Growth and Development from the Early Days to the Present*, Vol. 1 (Historic Record Co., Los Angeles, CA) 1919 pg. 626.

857. Find A Grave, database and images (https://www.findagrave.com: accessed 16 April 2019), memorial page for Henry Clay Tupper (29 Dec 1842–29 Feb 1928), Find A Grave Memorial no. 41697003, citing Mountain View Cemetery, Fresno, Fresno County, California, USA; Maintained by Lester Letson (contributor 46627920).

858. George M. Gould, ed., The Jefferson Medical College of Philadelphia Benefactors, Alumni, Hospital, Etc., Its Founders, Officers, Instructors, 1826–1904: A History ·, Vol. 2 (The Lewis Publishing Co., New York, Chicago) 1904 pg. 106.

859. http://www.fold3.com/image/10545708/, NARA M324. Compiled service records of Confederate soldiers from Virginia units.

860. Antietam Battlefield Board, Antietam Battlefield Board Papers, Washington, D.C.: National Archives and Records Administration, 1891–1898, Entry 707, Record Group 92 (Historical Tablet text by Generals E.A. Carman and H. Heth).

861. http://www.fold3.com/image/20/75588673/, NARA M267. Compiled service records of Confederate soldiers from South Carolina units.

862. http://www.fold3.com/image/20/35914134/, NARA M270. Compiled service records of Confederate soldiers from North Carolina units.

863. https://www.fold3.com/image/74877054, NARA M331. Compiled service records of Confederate officers and enlisted men who did not belong to any particular regiment, separate company or comparable unit, or special corps.

864. https://www.fold3.com/image/74877084, NARA M331. Compiled service records of Confederate officers and enlisted men who did not belong to any particular regiment, separate company or comparable unit, or special corps.

865. https://www.fold3.com/image/74877106, NARA M331. Compiled service records of Confederate officers and enlisted men who did not belong to any particular regiment, separate company or comparable unit, or special corps.

866. https://www.fold3.com/image/74877123, NARA M331. Compiled service records of Confederate officers and enlisted men who did not belong to any particular regiment, separate company or comparable unit, or special corps.

867. http://www.fold3.com/image/20/74877037/, NARA M331. Compiled service records of Confederate officers and enlisted men who did not belong to any particular regiment, separate company or comparable unit, or special corps.

868. *Alexandria Gazette* (Alexandria, VA) January 24, 1874 pg. 1, retrieved from https://www.newspapers.com, Newspapers made available courtesy of Chronicling America & University of Tennessee.

869. Find A Grave, database and images (https://www.findagrave.com: accessed 16 April 2019), memorial page for Dr Tazewell Tyler (6 Dec 1830–8 Jan 1874), Find A Grave Memorial no. 84008816, citing Olivet Memorial Park, Colma, San Mateo County, California, USA; Maintained by StoneMiller, a Real-McCloy (contributor 47636351).

870. *The San Francisco Examiner* (San Francisco, CA) January 16, 1874 pg. 3, retrieved from https://www.newspapers.com, Newspapers made available courtesy of Chronicling America & University of Tennessee.

871. Grace Goodyear Kirkman, *Geneology of the Goodyear Family* (Cubery & Co., San Francisco) 1899 pg. 203.

872. Pensacola Gazette (Pensacola, Florida) February 1, 1845, pg. 2, retrieved from https://www.newspapers.com, Newspapers made available courtesy of Chronicling America & University of Tennessee.

873. https://www.fold3.com/image/245/307339924, NARA M616. Card index to service records of

volunteer soldiers who served in the Mexican War, arranged alphabetically by state or territory.

874. https://www.fold3.com/image/121542863, NARA M322. Compiled service records of Confederate soldiers from Missouri units.

875. https://www.fold3.com/image/121542863, NARA M322. Compiled service records of Confederate soldiers from Missouri units.

876. United States War Dept., Official Records: Series 1, vol 8, Part 1 (Pea Ridge) Report of General Sterling Price (Washington, D.C.: Government Printing Office) 1883 pg. 320.

877. http://www.fold3.com/image/20/122414992/, NARA M322. Compiled service records of Confederate soldiers from Missouri units.

878. https://www.fold3.com/image/20/122415018/, NARA M322. Compiled service records of Confederate soldiers from Missouri units.

879. https://www.fold3.com/image/20/122415111/, NARA M322. Compiled service records of Confederate soldiers from Missouri units.

880. http://www.fold3.com/image/20/121542794/, NARA M322. Compiled service records of Confederate soldiers from Missouri units.

881. https://www.fold3.com/image/121542886, NARA M322. Compiled service records of Confederate soldiers from Missouri units.

882. https://www.fold3.com/image/121542957/, NARA M322. Compiled service records of Confederate soldiers from Missouri units.

883. Find A Grave, database and images (https://www.findagrave.com: accessed 01 July 2019), memorial page for Maj Joseph P Vaughn (Feb 1830–3 Oct 1862), Find A Grave Memorial no. 33745057, citing Benicia City Cemetery, Benicia, Solano County, California, USA; Maintained by Heidi Mueller (contributor 46914456).

884. John James Lafferty, Bp. David Seth Doggett, *Sketches and Portraits of the Virginia Conference, Methodist Episcopal* (Christian Advocate Office, Richmond, VA) 1890 pgs. 37–38.

885. http://www.fold3.com/image/75433448/, NARA M331. Compiled service records of Confederate officers and enlisted men who did not belong to any particular regiment, separate company or comparable unit, or special corps.

886. http://www.fold3.com/image/75433448/, NARA M331. Compiled service records of Confederate officers and enlisted men who did not belong to any particular regiment, separate company or comparable unit, or special corps.

887. John Lee Holt, Letter from Private John Lee Holt to his wife July 29, 1862 in "I Wrote You Word: The Poignant Letters of Private Holt," James A. Mumper, ed. (H.E. Howard) 1991 pg. 101.

888. https://www.fold3.com/image/75433457, NARA M331. Compiled service records of Confederate officers and enlisted men who did not belong to any particular regiment, separate company or comparable unit, or special corps.

889. Find A Grave, database and images (https://www.findagrave.com: accessed 16 April 2019), memorial page for James R. Waggener (1830–30 Dec 1900), Find A Grave Memorial no. 29415613, citing Santa Rosa Rural Cemetery, Santa Rosa, Sonoma County, California, USA; Maintained by Jeanie Leete (contributor 47019987).

890. *Press Democrat*, Vol. XXVII, No. 44, 3 January 1901, pg. 3, California Digital Newspaper Collection, Center for Bibliographic Studies and Research, University of California, Riverside, http://cdnc.ucr.edu.

891. Annual Report by United States Military Academy. Association of Graduates (Seemann & Peters, Printers & Binders, Saginaw, MI) 1901 pg. 102.

892. Annual Report by United States Military Academy. Association of Graduates (Seemann & Peters, Printers & Binders, Saginaw, MI) 1901 pg. 103.

893. Annual Report by United States Military Academy. Association of Graduates (Seemann & Peters, Printers & Binders, Saginaw, MI) 1901 pg. 104.

894. http://www.fold3.com/image/22642688/, NARA M1003. Applications for pardon submitted to President Andrew Johnson by former Confederates excluded from earlier amnesty proclamations.

895. Annual Report by United States Military Academy. Association of Graduates (Seemann & Peters, Printers & Binders, Saginaw, MI) 1901 pg. 105.

896. Annual Report by United States Military Academy. Association of Graduates (Seemann & Peters, Printers & Binders, Saginaw, MI) 1901 pg. 104.

897. Find A Grave, database and images (https://www.findagrave.com: accessed 16 April 2019), memorial page for William Thomas Welcker (24 Jun 1830–3 Nov 1900), Find A Grave Memorial no. 20274667, citing Mountain View Cemetery, Oakland, Alameda County, California, USA; Maintained by Chris Nelson (contributor 46617359).

898. Find A Grave, database and images (https://www.findagrave.com: accessed 10 December 2019), memorial page for James White (5 Aug 1801–22 Jun 1886), Find A Grave Memorial no. 46061786, citing McDaniel Cemetery, Lowell, Benton County, Arkansas, USA; Maintained by TS Lundberg (Sternburg) (contributor 46889000).

899. https://www.fold3.com/image/20/223567243, NARA M317. Compiled service records of Confederate soldiers from Arkansas units.

900. https://www.fold3.com/image/20/223567247, NARA M317. Compiled service records of Confederate soldiers from Arkansas units.

901. https://www.fold3.com/image/20/223555102, NARA M317. Compiled service records of Confederate soldiers from Arkansas units.

902. https://www.fold3.com/image/20/223567251, NARA M317. Compiled service records of Confederate soldiers from Arkansas units.

903. https://www.fold3.com/image/20/255031584, NARA M317. Compiled service records of Confederate soldiers from Arkansas units.

904. https://www.fold3.com/image/20/255031598, NARA M317. Compiled service records of Confederate soldiers from Arkansas units.

905. Find A Grave, database and images (https://www.findagrave.com: accessed 10 December 2019), memorial page for Eunice Melvina Harvey Noble (14 Apr 1847–17 Dec 1929), Find A Grave Memorial no. 154728999, citing Ione Public Cemetery, Ione, Amador County, California, USA; Maintained by Anne Shurtleff Stevens (contributor 46947920).

906. Find A Grave, database and images (https://www.findagrave.com: accessed 16 April 2019), memorial page for Milton Edward White (4 Sep 1834–9 Jan 1923), Find A Grave Memorial no. 103684247, citing Park View Cemetery, Manteca, San Joaquin County, California, USA; Maintained by Chloé (contributor 47159257).

907. Virginia Military Institute, Official Register 1904–1905 (J. P. Bell Co., Lynchburg, VA) 1905 pg. 86.

908. Joseph Van Holt Nash, *Students of the University of Virginia: A Semi-Centennial Catalogue with Brief Biographical Sketches* (Charles Harvey & Co., Publishers, Baltimore, MD) 1878 pg. 15.

909. Abraham Lincoln papers: Series 1. General Correspondence. 1833–1916: R. O. Whitehead to Abraham Lincoln, Sunday, January 06, 1861, Library of Congress online, https://www.loc.gov/item/mal0583500/.

910. http://www.fold3.com/image/10429386/, NARA M324. Compiled service records of Confederate soldiers from Virginia units.

911. https://www.fold3.com/image/20/10429408, NARA M324. Compiled service records of Confederate soldiers from Virginia units.

912. https://www.fold3.com/image/20/10429548, NARA M324. Compiled service records of Confederate soldiers from Virginia units.

913. https://www.fold3.com/image/20/10429544, NARA M324. Compiled service records of Confederate soldiers from Virginia units.

914. Lew Wallace, The story of American heroism; thrilling narratives of personal adventures during the great Civil war, as told by the medal winners and roll of honor men (J.W. Jones, Springfield, OH) 1897 pg. 469.

915. Lew Wallace, The story of American heroism; thrilling narratives of personal adventures during the great Civil war, as told by the medal winners and roll of honor men (J.W. Jones, Springfield, OH) 1897 pg. 470.

916. *San Francisco Call*, Vol. 109, No. 96, 6 March 1911, California Digital Newspaper Collection, Center for Bibliographic Studies and Research, University of California, Riverside, http://cdnc.ucr.edu.

917. https://www.fold3.com/image/20/10429620, NARA M324. Compiled service records of Confederate soldiers from Virginia units.

918. http://www.fold3.com/image/10429386/, NARA M324. Compiled service records of Confederate soldiers from Virginia units.

919. *San Francisco Call*, Vol. 109, No. 96, 6 March 1911, California Digital Newspaper Collection, Center for Bibliographic Studies and Research, University of California, Riverside, http://cdnc.ucr.edu.

920. *San Francisco Call*, Vol. 109, No. 96, 6 March 1911, California Digital Newspaper Collection, Center for Bibliographic Studies and Research, University of California, Riverside, http://cdnc.ucr.edu.

921. Lew Wallace, The story of American heroism; thrilling narratives of personal adventures during the great Civil war, as told by the medal winners and roll of honor men (J.W. Jones, Springfield, OH) 1897 pg. 472.

922. William Thomas Moore,, ed., The Living Pulpit of the Christian Church (R.W. Carroll & Co., Cincinnati, OH) 1868 pg. 145.

923. Charles Foster McElroy, Ministers of First Christian Church (Disciples of Christ) 1833–1962 (Bethany Press, Springfield, MO) 1962 pg. 93.

924. http://www.fold3.com/image/88595909/, NARA M322. Compiled service records of Confederate soldiers from Missouri units.

925. http://www.fold3.com/image/20/88579121/, NARA M322. Compiled service records of Confederate soldiers from Missouri units.

926. James E. McGhee,, ed., *Guide to Missouri Confederate Units, 1861–1865* (The University of Arkansas Press, Fayetteville, AR) 2008 pg. 65.

927. James E. McGhee,, ed., *Guide to Missouri Confederate Units, 1861–1865* (The University of Arkansas Press, Fayetteville, AR) 2008 pg. 66.

928. James E. McGhee,, ed., *Guide to Missouri Confederate Units, 1861–1865* (The University of Arkansas Press, Fayetteville, AR) 2008 pg. 66.

929. James E. McGhee,, ed., *Guide to Missouri Confederate Units, 1861–1865* (The University of Arkansas Press, Fayetteville, AR) 2008 pg. 67.

930. Ezra J. Warner, Jr., W. Buck Yearns, Biographical Register of the Confederate Congress (Louisiana State University Press, Baton Rouge) 1975 pg. 258.

931. *The Los Angeles Times* (Los Angeles, CA) January 3, 1900 pg. 3, retrieved from https://www.newspapers.com, Newspapers made available courtesy of Chronicling America & University of Tennessee.

932. Find A Grave, database and images (https://www.findagrave.com: accessed 16 April 2019), memorial page for Peter Singleton Wilkes (8 Mar 1827–2 Jan 1900), Find A Grave Memorial no. 7117660, citing Stockton Rural Cemetery, Stockton, San Joaquin County, California, USA; Maintained by Find A Grave.

933. Shirley Grose, Amherst County Virginia Heritage (Amherst County Heritage Book Committee)1999 pg. 260.

934. Shirley Grose, Amherst County Virginia Heritage (Amherst County Heritage Book Committee)1999 pg. 260.

935. https://www.fold3.com/image/9367703, NARA M324. Compiled service records of Confederate soldiers from Virginia units.

936. https://www.fold3.com/image/9367707, NARA M324. Compiled service records of Confederate soldiers from Virginia units.

937. https://www.fold3.com/image/9367709, NARA M324. Compiled service records of Confederate soldiers from Virginia units.

938. Henry Robinson Berkeley, William H. Runge, ed., Four years in the Confederate artillery: the diary of Private Henry Robinson Berkeley (University of North Carolina Press) 1961 pg. 46.

939. Gettysburg Battlefield Marker, Army of Northern Virginia, Ewell's Corps Artillery Reserve, Nelson's Battalion, Kirkpatrick's Battery, Amherst Virginia Artillery.

940. https://www.fold3.com/image/9367733, NARA M324. Compiled service records of Confederate soldiers from Virginia units.

941. https://www.fold3.com/image/9367735, NARA M324. Compiled service records of Confederate soldiers from Virginia units.

942. https://www.fold3.com/image/9367747, NARA M324. Compiled service records of Confederate soldiers from Virginia units.

943. *San Francisco Call*, Vol. 80, No. 131, 9 October 1896, California Digital Newspaper Collection, Center for Bibliographic Studies and Research, University of California, Riverside, http://cdnc.ucr.edu.

944. *Sacramento Daily Union*, Vol. 1, No. 146, 13 August 1875 pg. 2 California Digital Newspaper Collection, Center for Bibliographic Studies and Research, University of California, Riverside, http://cdnc.ucr.edu.

945. *San Francisco Call*, Vol. 80, No. 131, 9 October 1896, California Digital Newspaper Collection, Center for Bibliographic Studies and Research, University of California, Riverside, http://cdnc.ucr.edu.

946. Find A Grave, database and images (https://www.findagrave.com: accessed 16 April 2019), memorial page for John Miller (1835–8 Oct 1896), Find A Grave Memorial no. 81512101, citing Sacramento City Cemetery, Sacramento, Sacramento County, California, USA; Maintained by Mac in Sac (contributor 47514506).

947. Find A Grave, database and images (https://www.findagrave.com : accessed 01 March 2020), memorial page for Lizzie Miller (1835–7 Feb 1900), Find A Grave Memorial no. 81512774, citing Sacramento City Cemetery, Sacramento, Sacramento County, California, USA ; Maintained by Mac in Sac. (contributor 47514506).

948. 1850 United States Federal Census [database on-line]. Provo, UT, USA: Ancestry.com.

949. 1860 United States Federal Census [database on-line]. Provo, UT, USA: Ancestry.com.

950. Georgetown University, Will J. Maxwell, General Register of Georgetown University (Washington D. C.) 1916 pg. 409.

951. https://www.fold3.com/image/7263588, NARA M324. Compiled service records of Confederate soldiers from Virginia units.

952. William Naylor McDonald, Bushrod C. Washington, ed., A history of the Laurel brigade (Sun job printing office, Baltimore, MD) 1907 pg. 89.

953. Historical Tablet, Antietam Battlefield, Munford's Brigade, Stuart's Cavalry Division 12 PM 16 September to 8 PM 18 September.

954. https://www.fold3.com/image/7263617, NARA M324. Compiled service records of Confederate soldiers from Virginia units.

955. https://www.fold3.com/image/7263606, NARA M324. Compiled service records of Confederate soldiers from Virginia units.

956. https://www.fold3.com/image/7263642, NARA M324. Compiled service records of Confederate soldiers from Virginia units.

957. https://www.fold3.com/image/7263624, NARA M324. Compiled service records of Confederate soldiers from Virginia units.

958. https://www.fold3.com/image/16588732, NARA M324. Compiled service records of Confederate soldiers from Virginia units.

959. https://www.fold3.com/image/16588746, NARA M324. Compiled service records of Confederate soldiers from Virginia units.

960. 1870 United States Federal Census [database on-line]. Provo, UT, USA: Ancestry.com.

961. California, Voter Registers, 1866–1898 [database on-line]. Provo, UT, USA: Ancestry.com.

962. *San Francisco Call*, Vol. 73, No. 157, 6 May 1893, California Digital Newspaper Collection, Center for Bibliographic Studies and Research, University of California, Riverside, http://cdnc.ucr.edu.

963. Find A Grave, database and images (https://www.findagrave.com: accessed 16 April 2019), memorial page for Edmond P Zane (unknown–7 May 1893), Find A Grave Memorial no. 107420643, citing Holy Cross Catholic Cemetery, Colma, San Mateo County, California, USA; Maintained by Athanatos (contributor 46907585).

# Bibliography

## Manuscripts, Journals & Papers

*Almareane W. Baker to Abraham Lincoln 1865-01-15 Images from the National Archives and Library of Congress 1865-01-15.*

Antietam Battlefield Board, Antietam Battlefield Board Papers, Washington DC: National Archives and Records Administration, 1891–1898, Entry 707, Record Group 92 (Historical Tablet text by Generals E.A. Carman and H. Heth.).

*The Friend: A Religious and Literary Journal*, Vol. XXXV (William H. Pile, Philadelphia, PA) 1862.

George Washington Gift Papers Folder 2, #1152, Southern Historical Collection, The Wilson Library, University of North Carolina at Chapel Hill Guide to the William Bowers Bourn Family Papers, 1845–1985 at Online Archive of California http://www.oac.cdlib.org/findaid/ark:/13030/tf3n39n6hj/.

Harvard College Class of 1864, Secretary's Report No. 2, July 1864–July 1867 (Harvard College, Cambridge, MA).

Le Conte, Joseph. *Memoir of John Le Conte, 1818–1891* (Read before the National Academy April 1894).

Meux, Thomas Richard. *Memoir and Autobiography of Thomas Richard Meux*, M.D. 1921 (Meux Home Museum).

Mumper, James A. ed., John Lee Holt, Letter from Private John Lee Holt to his wife July 29, 1862 in "I Wrote You Word: The Poignant Letters of Private Holt," (H.E. Howard) 1991 *National Archives and Library of Congress, the Papers of Abraham Lincoln: Doc 283272.*

_____. Abraham Lincoln papers: Series 1. General Correspondence. 1833–1916: R. O. Whitehead to Abraham Lincoln, Sunday, January 06, 1861, Library of Congress online, https://www.loc.gov/item/mal0583500/.

Seyburne, S.V. Lieut. U.S.A., Adjutant Tenth Infantry. "Tenth Regiment of Infantry." *The Journal of the Military Service Institution of the United States*, Vol. 13 (Military Service Institution, Governor's Island) 1892.

Shreve, George W. "Reminiscences in the History of the Stuart Horse Artillery C.S.A." Roger Preston

Chew Papers, Jefferson County Museum Charles Town, WV.

## Newspapers

*Colusa Daily Sun*, February 18, 1896.
*Colusa Herald*, November 23, 1926.
*Daily Alta California*, November 25, 1883.
_____, October 13, 1884.
_____, March 15 1885.
_____, August 15, 1889.
*The Daily Evening Express* (Lancaster, PA) July 18, 1867.
*The Daily Examiner* (San. Francisco, CA) Oct. 7, 1888.
*The Evening Star* (Independence, KS) July 11, 1905.
*Grass Valley Daily*, May 7, 1885.
*Los Angeles Star*, July 9, 1859.
*Memphis Daily Appeal* (Memphis, TN) December 21, 1861.
*News-Democrat* (Paduch, KY) October 14, 1903.
*Press Democrat* (Santa Rosa, CA) January 8, 1886.
*Red Bluff News*, July 3, 1903.
*Richmond Dispatch* (Richmond, VA) July 29, 1861.
*Sacramento Daily Union*, June 21, 1861.
_____, August 13, 1875.
_____, January 19, 1884.
*The San Francisco Call* (San Francisco, CA) May 6, 1893.
_____, February 16, 1896.
_____, February 18, 1896.
_____, April 22, 1896.
_____, October 9, 1896.
_____, July 1, 1899.
_____, October 13, 1903.
_____, August 7, 1905.
_____, June 10, 1908.
_____, December 9, 1908.
_____, February 8, 1909.
_____, April 13, 1910.
_____, March 6, 1911.
_____, April 24, 1912.
_____, April 28, 1912.
*The Sonoma Democrat*, June 4, 1887.
_____, August 17, 1889.

*Southern Opinion* (Richmond, VA) November 23, 1867.

*The Times and Democrat* (Orangeburg, SC) September 17, 1885.

*The Watchman and Southron* (Sumter, SC) October 13, 1885.

*Watsonville Pajaronian*, December 28, 1899.

## Official Publications

Annual Report by United States Military Academy. Association of Graduates (Seemann & Peters, Printers & Binders, Saginaw, MI) 1901.

Bergner, George. *The Legislative Record Containing the Debates and Proceedings of the Pennsylvania Legislature for the Session of 1862* (Telegraph Book and Job Office, Harrisburg, PA) 1862.

Governor's Message and Annual Reports of the Public Officers of the State, and of the Boards of Directors, Visitors, Superintendents, and Other Agents of Public Institutions Or Interests of Virginia., Document 10 (Samuel Shepherd, public printer, Richmond, VA) 1861.

Journal of the Executive Proceedings of the Senate of the United States of America from December 6, 1858 to August 6, 1861 inclusive, Vol. XI (Government Printing Office, Washington, D.C.)1887.

Lanman, Charles. *Biographical Annals of the Civil Government of the United States: From Original and Official Sources* (Joseph M. Morrison, New York) 1887.

"Ordinances and Constitution of the State of South Carolina, with the Constitution of the Provisional Government and of the Confederate States of America" (Evans & Cogswell Printers, Charleston SC.)1861.

"Reports of the Operations of the Army of Northern Virginia: From June 1862 to and Including the Battle of Fredericksburg." Dec. 13, 1862, Vol. 1. By Confederate States of America. Richmond 1864.

Tennessee Supreme Court. William Wilcox Cooke. "Reports of Cases Argued and Determined in the Supreme Court of Tennessee During the War," Vol. 44 (Fetter Law Book Co., Louisville, KY) 1867.

United States. *Naval War Records Office, Officers in the Confederate States Navy, 1861–65* (Government Printing Office, Washington, D.C.) 1898.

United States War Dept. *The War of the Rebellion: A Compilation of the Official Records of the Union and Confederate Armies*, 128 Vols. (Government Printing Office, Washington, D.C.) 1880–1901.

Works Progress Administration (WPA) in conjunction with the office of the Adjutant General and the California State Library. "California Militia and National Guard Unit Histories: Benham Guard," 1940, http://www.militarymuseum.org/BenhamGuard.html.

## Periodicals

*Army and Navy Journal*, Vol. 23, November 21, 1885 (Pub. New York).

*Breeder and Sportsman*, Vol. XXVI, No. 9. "Death of Col. H.I. Thornton," March 2, 1895.

Brock, R. A., ed. "Black Eagle Company—A Typical Command of Confederate Soldiers by H.E. Wood, Ex-Color Sergeant, 18th Virginia Regiment," Vol. 37 (Southern Historical Society, Richmond, VA) 1909.

Brock, R.A. ed. "Diary of Colonel George K. Griggs of the Thirty-Eight Virginia Infantry," Volume. 14 (Virginia Historical Society, Richmond, Va) 1876.

Brock, R.A., Ed. "Plan to Rescue the Johnson Island Prisoners." Feb. 1863, by Capt. R. D. Minor, C.S. Navy, Vol. 23 (W.M. Ellis Printer, Richmond, VA) 1895.

Couper, William ed. "The Corps Forward: The Biographical Sketches of the Vmi Cadets Who Fought in the Battle of New Market" (Mariner Publishing) 2005.

Cunningham S.A., ed., and founder. *Confederate Veteran* Magazine (Nashville, TN) 1893–1932.

Foute, R.C. "Echoes from Hampton Roads." R.A. Brock, ed., Vol. 19 (William Ellis Jones Printer, Richmond, VA) 1890.

Garrett, L.R. "Harry St. John Dixon." *The Sigma Chi Quarterly*, Vol. XVI, No. 2 (Chicago, IL) 1896–1897.

Gift, George W. *The Story of the Arkansas*, Vol. 12 (William Ellis Jones Printer, Richmond, VA) 1884.

Hampton, Wade. "Cavalry Scouts." *The Land We Love*, Vol. 3 (Hill, Irwin & Co., Charlotte, NC) 1867.

Hope, Major W.B. "From the Evacuation of Hampton in 1861, to the Fall of Richmond in 1865." *The Southern Workman*, Vols. 21–23, July 1892.

*The Iron Trade Review*, Vol. 67, Issue 2 (The Penton Publishing Co., Cleveland, OH) 1920.

Langley's San Francisco Directory for the Year Commencing 1887 (Francis, Valentine & Co., San Francisco, CA) 1887.

McCaleb, E. Howard. "Featherstone-Posey-Harris Mississippi Brigade" in Southern Historical Society Papers R.A. Brock, ed (Virginia Historical Society, Richmond, VA) 1876.

Methodist Episcopal Church, South, Minutes of the annual conferences of the Methodist Episcopal Church, South (Publishing House of the Methodist Episcopal Church, South, Nashville, TN) 1894.

Noble, Phil Edward. "Noble and the 'Featherbed Aristocracy,'" University South Caroliniana Society newsletter Spring 2014 Southern Historical Society Papers.

University of Virginia, Session of 1854–55 (H.K. Ellyson's Steam Presses, Richmond, VA) 1855.

## Books

Alexander, The Rev. Gross, *Steve P. Holcombe, the Converted Gambler: His Life and Work* (Press of the Courier Journal Job Printing Company) 1888.

Allen, Luther Prentice. *The Genealogy and History of the Shreve Family from 1641* (Privately Printed, Greenfield Ill.) 1901.

Alley, Bowen & Co. *History of Sonoma County: Cal.*

*Including Its Geology, Topography, Mountains, Valleys and Streams* (Alley, Bowen & Co. Publishers, San Francisco) 1880.

Angel, Myron ed. *History of Nevada: With Illustrations and Biographical Sketches of Its Prominent Men and Pioneers* (Thompson & West, Oakland, CA) 1881.

Barrows, Henry D. ed., Luther A. Ingersoll ed. *A Memorial and Biographical History of the Coast Counties of Central California* (The Lewis Publishing Co., Chicago, IL) 1893.

Bates, J.C. ed. *History of the Bar and Bench of California* (Bench and Bar Publishing Co., San Francisco, CA) 1912.

Bean, Edwin F. *Bean's History and Directory of Nevada County, California. Containing a Complete History of the County, with Sketches of the Various Towns and Mining Camps ... Also, Full Statistics of Mining and All Other Industrial Resources* (Daily Gazette Book and Job Office) 1867.

Benjamin, Park. *The United States Naval Academy, Being the Yarn of the American Midshipman* (G.P. Putnam's Sons, New York and London) 1900.

Bergeron, Arthur W., Jr. *Guide to Louisiana Confederate Military Units, 1861–1865* (LSU Press, Baton Rouge & London) 1996.

Berkeley, Henry Robinson, William H. Runge, ed. *Four Years in the Confederate Artillery: The Diary of Private Henry Robinson Berkeley* (University of North Carolina Press) 1961.

Binney, Charles James Fox. *The History of the Prentice or Prentiss Family in New England, Etc., from 1631 to 1883* (Alfred Mudge & Son Printers, Boston, MA) 1883.

Blessington, Joseph Palmer. *The Campaigns of Walker's Texas Division by a Private Soldier* (Lange, Little & Co. Printers, New York) 1875.

Boddie, William Willis. *History of Williamsburg: Something About the People of Williamsburg County South Carolina from the First Settlement by Europeans About 1705 Until 1923* (The State Company, Columbia, SC) 1923.

Calarco, Tom, Cynthia Vogel, Kathryn Grover, Rae Hallstrom, Sharron Pope, Melissa Waddy-Thibodeaux. *Places of the Underground Railroad: A Geographical Guide* (ABC-CLIO, Santa Barbara, CA) 2010.

Caldwell, J.F.J. *The history of a brigade of South Carolinians, known first as "Gregg's," and Carpenter, Aurelius O. Percy H. Millberry, History of Mendocino and Lake counties, California, with biographical sketches of the leading, men and women of the counties who have been identified with their growth and development from the early days to the present* (Historic record company, Los Angeles, CA) 1914 subsequently as McGowans Brigade (King & Baird Printers, Philadelphia, PA) 1866.

Catchings, Thomas Clendinen, Mary Clendinen Catchings Torrey, Charles Robert Churchill. *The Catchings and Holliday Families: And Various Related Families, in Virginia, Georgia, Mississippi and Other Southern States* (A.B. Caldwell Publishing Co., Atlanta, GA) 1919.

Clark, Walter. *Histories of the Several Regiments and Battalions from North Carolina, in the Great War 1861–1865*, Vol. 3 (E. M. Uzzell, printer) 1901.

Cullum, George W. *Register of Officers and Graduates of the United States Military Academy Class of 1852*, Supplement Vol. 5 (Seeman & Peters, Printers, Saginaw Mich.) 1910.

Davis, Winfield J. *An Illustrated History of Sacramento County, California: Containing a History of Sacramento County from the Earliest Period of Its Occupancy to the Present Time, Together with Glimpses of Its Prospective Future ... Portraits of Some of Its Most Eminent Men, and Biographical Mention of Many of Its Pioneers and Also Prominent Citizens of Today* (Lewis Pub. Co. Chicago) 1890.

Dixon, Samuel Houston. *The Poets and Poetry of Texas: Biographical Sketches of the Poets of Texas, with Selections from Their Writings, Containing Reviews Both Personal and Critical* (S. H. Dixon & Co., Austin, Texas) 1885.

Driver, Jr., Robert J., *The Confederate Soldiers of Rockbridge County, VA: A Roster* (McFarland, Jefferson, NC) 2016.

Edwards, John N. *Noted Guerrillas or the Warfare of the Border* (Bryan, Brand, St. Louis, MO) 1877.

_____. *Shelby and His Men or the War in the West* (Miami Printing and Publishing Co., Cinncinati, OH) 1867.

Elliott & Moore. *History of Monterey County, California: With Illustrations Descriptive of Its Scenery, Farms, Residences, Public Buildings, Factories, Hotels, Business Houses, Schools, Churches, and Mines: With Biographical Sketches of Prominent Citizens* (Elliott & Moore, Publishers, San Francisco) 1881.

Evans, Clement Anselm. *Confederate Military History: A Library of Confederate States History*, Vol. 6 (Confederate Pub. Co., Atlanta, GA) 1899.

_____. *Confederate Military History: A Library of Confederate States History*, Vol. 7 (Confederate Publishing Co., Atlanta GA.)1899.

_____. *Confederate Military History: A Library of Confederate States History*, Vol. 8 (Confederate Pub. Co. Atlanta Georgia) 1899.

Federal Publishing Co. *The Union Army: A History of Military Affairs in the Loyal States, 1861–65—Records of the Regiments in the Union Army—Cyclopedia of Battles—Memoirs of Commanders and Soldiers*, Vol. 6, Cyclopedia of Battles (Federal Publishing Co., Madison, Wis.) 1908.

Georgetown University, Will J. Maxwell, *General Register of Georgetown University* (Washington D. C.) 1916.

Goodspeed Publishing Co. *History of Tennessee Illustrated: Lauderdale, Tipton, Haywood & Crockett Counties* (Goodspeed Publishing Co., Nashville, TN) 1886.

Goodwin, C.C. *As I Remember Them* (Salt Lake City, UT) 1913.

Grose, Shirley, Amherst County Virginia Heritage (Amherst County Heritage Book Committee) 1999.

Guinn, James Miller. *History of the State of California and Biographical Record of the San Joaquin Valley, California. an Historical Story of the State's Marvelous Growth from Its Earliest Settlement to the Present Time* (The Chapman Publishing Co., Chicago, IL) 1905.

_____. *History of the State of California and Biographical Record of the Sierras, an Historical Story of the State's Marvelous Growth from Its Earliest Settlement to the Present Time* (The Chapman Publishing Co., Chicago, IL) 1906.

Hallum, John. *Diary of an Old Lawyer: Scenes Behind the Curtain* (Southwestern Publishing House, Nashville, TN) 1895.

Harper, Franklin ed. *Who's Who on the Pacific Coast: A Biographical Compilation of Notable Living Contemporaries West of the Rocky Mountains* (Harper Publishing Co., Los Angeles, CA) 1913.

Haughton, Andrew R.B. *Training, Tactics and Leadership in the Confederate Army of Tennessee* (Routledge, Abingdon, Oxon, UK) 2007.

Howland, Edward. *Grant as a Soldier and Statesman: Being a Succinct History of His Military and Civil Career* (J.B. Burr & Co., Hartford, CT) 1868.

Hune, Marguerite. *History of Solano County, California* (S.J. Clarke Publishing Co., Chicago, IL) 1926.

Hunton, Eppa. *Autobiography of Eppa Hunton* (The William Byrd Press, Inc., Richmond, VA) 1933.

Kautz, Lawrence G. *August Valentine Kautz, USA: Biography of a Civil War General* (McFarland, Jefferson, NC) 2016.

Lafferty, John, James David, Seth Doggett. *Sketches and Portraits of the Virginia Conference, Methodist Episcopal* (Christian Advocate Office, Richmond, VA) 1890.

Le Conte, Joseph. *Ware Sherman: A Journal of Three Months' Personal Experience in the Last Days of the Confederacy* (LSU Press, Baton Rouge, LA) 1999.

Le Conte, Joseph. William Dallam Armes, ed. *The Autobiography of Joseph Le Conte*, Vol. 3 (D. Appleton & Co. New York) 1903.

The Lewis Publishing Co. *A Memorial and Biographical History of Northern California, Illustrated. Containing a History of This Important Section of the Pacific Coast from the Earliest Period of Its Occupancy ... And Biographical Mention of Many of Its Most Eminent Pioneers and Also of Prominent Citizens of Today* (The Lewis Publishing Co., Chicago, IL) 1891.

_____. *The Bay of San Francisco: The Metropolis of the Pacific Coast and Its Suburban Cities*, Vol. 2 (Lewis Publishing Co., Chicago, IL) 1892.

_____. *An Illustrated History of Sonoma County, California. Containing a History of the County of Sonoma from the Earliest Period of Its Occupancy to the Present Time* (Lewis Publishing Co., Chicago, IL) 1889.

Little, George, James R. Maxwell. *A History of Lumsden's Battery C.S.A.* (R.E. Rhodes Chapter, United Daughters of the Confederacy, Tuskaloosa, AL) 1905.

Louisiana Historical Association, Center for Louisiana Studies at the University of Louisiana at Lafayette, *A Dictionary of Louisiana Biography*, Vol. 2 (Louisiana Historical Association) 1988.

Marshall, John A. *American Bastille: A History of the Illegal Arrests and Imprisonment of American Citizens During the Late Civil War* (T.W. Hartley, Philadelphia, PA) 1871.

McCorkle, John. *Three Years with Quantrell: A True Story* (Armstrong Herald Print, Armstrong, MO) 1914.

McDonald, William Naylor. Bushrod C. Washington, ed. *A History of the Laurel Brigade* (Sun Job Printing Office, Baltimore, MD) 1907.

McElroy, Charles Foster. *Ministers of First Christian Church (Disciples of Christ) 1833–1962* (Bethany Press, Springfield, MOS) 1962.

McGhee, James E. ed. *Guide to Missouri Confederate Units, 1861–1865* (The University of Arkansas Press, Fayetteville) 2008.

McGregor, Malcolm G. *The Biographical Record of Jasper County, Missouri* (Lewis Publishing Co., Chicago, IL) 1901.

McGriff-Payne, Sharon. *John Grider's Century: African Americans in Solano, Napa, and Sonoma Counties from 1845 to 1925* (iUniverse Inc, New York, Bloomington, IN) 2009.

Mehrländer, Andrea. *The Germans of Charleston, Richmond and New Orleans During the Civil War Period, 1850–1870* (Walter De Gruyter & Co. Berlin/New York) 2011.

Millard, Bailey. *History of the San Francisco Bay Region*, Vol. 3 (The American Historical Society, Inc., Chicago, IL) 1924.

Miller, Emily Van Dorn. *A Soldier's Honor with Reminiscences of Major-General Earl Van Dorn* (The Abbey Press, New York & London) 1902.

Moore, William Thomas, ed. *The Living Pulpit of the Christian Church* (R.W. Carroll & Co., Cincinnati OH) 1868.

Murray, J. Ogden. *The Immortal Six Hundred: A Story of Cruelty to Confederate Prisoners of War* (Stone Printing and Manufacturing Co., Roanoke, VA) 1911.

*The National Cyclopedia of American Biography*, Vol. VII (James T. White, Inc., New York) 1897.

Oates, William Calvin. *The War Between the Union and the Confederacy: And Its Lost Opportunities: With a History of the 15th Alabama Regiment and the Forty-Eight Battles in Which It Was Engaged* (Neale Publishing Co., New York and Washington, D.C.) 1905.

O'Meara, James, *Broderick and Gwin: The Most Extraordinary Contest for a Seat in the Senate of the United States Ever Known* (Bacon & Co. Printers, San Francisco, CA) 1881.

Palmer, Lyman L., W.F. Wallace, Harry Laurenz

Wells, Tillie Kanaga, *History of Napa and Lake Counties, California: comprising their geography, geology, topography, climatography, springs and timber, together with a full and particular record of the Mexican Grants, also separate histories of all the townships and biographical sketches* (Slocum, Bowen) 1881.

Pease, Ora Merle Hawk. *History of Caldwell and Livingston Counties, Missouri* (National Historical Co., St. Louis, MO) 1886.

Pendleton, William C. *History of Tazewell County and Southwest Virginia, 1748-1920* (W. C. Hill Printing Co., Richmond, VA) 1920.

Powell, William S. *Dictionary of North Carolina Biography*, Vol. 5 (University of North Carolina Press, Chapel Hill) 2000.

Quinn, Sandra L. *America's Royalty: All the Presidents' Children* (Greenwood Press, Westport, Conn.) 1983.

Roth, Lottie Roeder. "Edmund C. Fitzhugh and the Sehome Mine," *History of Whatcom County*. (Pioneer Historical Publishing Co., Chicago, IL) 1926.

Rowland, Dunbar, *The Official and Statistical Register of the State of Mississippi*, Vol. 2 (Press of the Brandon Printing Company, Nashville TN) 1908.

Schuricht, Herrmann, *History of the German Element in Virginia*, Vol. 2 (Theo. Kroh Publishers, Baltimore MD.) 1900.

Segars, J. H., Charles Kelly Barrow, eds. *Black Southerners in Confederate Armies: A Collection of Historical Accounts* (Pelican Publishing, Gretna, LA) 2007.

Shuck, Oscar Tully, ed. *History of the Bench and Bar of California* (The Commercial Printing House, Los Angeles, CA) 1901.

Smith, Gustavus Woodson. *The Battle of Seven Pines* (G. C. Crawford, printer, New York) 1891.

State Of Idaho, *An Illustrated History of North Idaho Embracing Nez Perces, Idaho, Latah, Kootenai, Shoshone Counties* (Western Historical Publishing Co.) 1903.

Taylor, Walter Herron, R. Lockwood Tower. *Lee's Adjutant: The Wartime Letters of Colonel Walter Herron Taylor, 1862-1865* (University of South Carolina Press, Columbia, SC) 1995.

Thomas, John Peyre. *The History of the South Carolina Military Academy: With Appendices* (Walker, Evans & Cogswell Co., Charleston, SC) 1893.

Thompson, Edwin Porter. *History of the Orphan Brigade* (L.N. Thompson, Louisville, KY) 1898.

Trimpi, Helen P. *Crimson Confederates: Harvard Men Who Fought for the South* (University of Tennessee Press, Knoxville, TN) 2010.

Truman, Benjamin Cummings. *Tourists Illustrated Guide to the Celebrated Summer and Winter Resorts of California* (H.S. Crocker & Co., San Francisco, CA) 1883.

Tucker, Spencer C. ed. *American Civil War: The Definitive Encyclopedia and Document Collection* (ABC-CLIO, Santa Barbara, CA) 2013.

Vandor, Paul E. *History of Fresno County, California, with Biographical Sketches of the Leading Men and Women of the County Who Have Been Identified with Its Growth and Development from the Early Days to the Present*, Vol. 1 (Historic Record Company, Los Angeles, CA) 1919.

_____. *History of Fresno County, California, with Biographical Sketches of the Leading Men and Women of the County Who Have Been Identified with Its Growth and Development from the Early Days to the Present*, Vol. 2 (Historic Record Company) 1919.

Villard, Oswald Garrison. *John Brown, 1800-1859: A Biography Fifty Years After* (Houghton Mifflin Company, Boston, MA) 1910.

Wagstaff, Alexander E. *Life of David S. Terry: Presenting an Authentic, Impartial and Vivid History of His Life and Tragic Death* (Continental Publishing Co., San Francisco, CA) 1892.

Walker, Charles D. *Memorial, Virginia Military Institute: Biographical Sketches of the Graduates and Eleves of the Virginia Military Institute Who Fell During the War Between the States* (J.B. Lippincott & Co., Philadelphia, PA) 1875.

Walker, Cornelius Irvine. *Rolls and Historical Sketch of the Tenth Regiment, So. Ca. Volunteers, in the Army of the Confederate States* (Walker, Evans & Cogswell, printers, Charleston, SC) 1881.

Wallace, Lew. *The Story of American Heroism; Thrilling Narratives of Personal Adventures During the Great Civil War, as Told by the Medal Winners and Roll of Honor Men* (J.W. Jones, Springfield Ohio) 1897.

Warner, Ezra J. *Generals in Gray: Lives of the Confederate Commanders* (Louisiana State University Press, Baton Rouge.) 2006.

Warner, Ezra, J., W. Buck Yearns. *Biographical Register of the Confederate Congress* (Louisiana State University Press, Baton Rouge) 1975.

Western Historical Company. *History of Boone County, Missouri: Written and Comp. from the Most Authentic Official and Private Sources; Including a History of Its Townships, Towns, and Villages. Together with a Condensed History of Missouri; the City of St. Louis ... Biographical Sketches and Portraits of Prominent Citizens* (Press of Nixon Jones, St. Louis, MO) 1882.

Wheeler, Joseph. *Campaigns of Wheeler and His Cavalry 1862-1865: From Material Furnished by Gen. Joseph Wheeler*, Parts 1-2 (Hudgins-Publishing Co.) 1899.

White, William S. *Contributions to a History of the Richmond Howitzer Battalion*, Vol. 2 (Carlton McCarthey & Co., Richmond, VA) 1883.

_____. Vol. 3 (Carlton McCarthey & Co. Richmond, VA) 1884.

Wise, Colonel Jennings C. *The Battle of New Market May 14, 1864* (Dulaney Boatwright Co., Lynchburg, VA) 1914.

_____. *The Military History of the Virginia Military Institute from 1839 to 1865, with Appendix, Maps, and Illustrations* (J.P. Bell, Lynchburg, VA.) 1915.

Young, John Preston. *The Seventh Tennessee Cavalry (Confederate): A History* (Publishing House of the M.E. Church, South Nashville, TN) 1890.

## Websites

Administration, N. A. (n.d.). Retrieved from http://www.fold3.com/image/92872133.

Antietam Battlefield Historical Tablet No. 355 Reserve Artillery, Army of Northern Virginia from http://antietam.aotw.org/tablet.php?tablet_id=3550.

Armistead, Gene C. "California's Confederate Militia: The Los Angeles Mounted Rifles," California and the Civil War, California State Military Museum. http://www.militarymuseum.org/LosAngelesMountedRifles2.html, accessed March 16, 2011.

Autobiographical Entries in the Confederate Memorial Literary Society's "Roll of Honour." http://www.moc.org/sites/default/files/PDFs/roll_of_honour_biographical_entries_for_website_ii_octob.pdf.

Barr, Alwyn "Galveston, Battle Of." http://www.tshaonline.org/handbook/online/articles/qeg01), accessed March 21, 2014. Uploaded on June 15, 2010. Modified on March 4, 2011. Published by the Texas State Historical Association.

Bergeron Jr., A. W. "The Richmond Howitzers." (2011, January 21). *Encyclopedia Virginia.* Retrieved from http://www.EncyclopediaVirginia.org/Richmond_Howitzers.

"California, County Birth, Marriage, and Death Records, 1849–1980" [database on-line]. Lehi, UT, USA: Ancestry.com.

California, Voter Registers, 1866–1898 [database on-line]. Provo, UT, USA: Ancestry.com.

California, Voter Registrations, 1900–1968 [database on-line]. Provo, UT, USA: Ancestry.com.

Cutrer, Thomas W. "Flournoy, George M." http://www.tshaonline.org/handbook/online/articles/ffl19), accessed February 17, 2014. Uploaded on June 12, 2010. Published by the Texas State Historical Association.

Derbes, Brett J. "Brooks, Samuel Houston." http://www.tshaonline.org/handbook/online/articles/fbreg), accessed February 02, 2014. Published by the Texas State Historical Association. http://www.findagrave.com/.

Dixon, Harry St. John. "Recollections of a Rebel Private." *The Sigma Chi Quarterly* 1885–86. https://history.sigmachi.org/files_resources/constantine-chapter_recollections.pdf. Handbook of Texas Online.

1880 U.S. Federal Census [database on-line]. Lehi, UT, USA: Ancestry.com.

1850 U.S. Federal Census [database on-line]. Provo, UT, USA: Ancestry.com.

1850 U.S. Federal Census—Slave Schedules [database on-line]. Provo, UT, USA: Ancestry.com.

1870 U.S. Federal Census [database on-line]. Provo, UT, USA: Ancestry.com.

1860 U.S. Federal Census [database on-line]. Provo, UT, USA: Ancestry.com.

1860 U.S. Federal Census—Slave Schedules [database on-line]. Provo, UT, USA: Ancestry.com.

"1862 War Tax Wal," *Piedmont Virginia Digital History: The Land Between the Rivers.* http://www.piedmontvahistory.org/archives14/items/show/747, accessed July 1, 2019.

Folsom, Bradley. "Sixteenth Texas Infantry." http://www.tshaonline.org/handbook/online/articles/qks16), accessed February 10, 2014. Uploaded on April 9, 2011. Modified on November 5, 2012. Published by the Texas State Historical Association.

Hobbs, Kenneth W. "Terry, David Smith." http://www.tshaonline.org/handbook/online/articles/fte29), accessed August 19, 2014. Uploaded on June 15, 2010. Published by the Texas State Historical Association.

King, C. Richard. "Greenwall, Henry." http://www.tshaonline.org/handbook/online/articles/fgr40, accessed March 03, 2019. Uploaded on June 15, 2010. Modified on March 6, 2018. Published by the Texas State Historical Association.

Marker for the Amherst Artillery east of Gettysburg on Benner's Hill from http://gettysburg.stonesentinels.com/confederate-batteries/amherst-virginia-artillery/.

Marker of Beckham's Battalion Breathed's Battery at Gettysburg from http://gettysburg.stonesentinels.com/Confederate-batteries/breatheds-battery/.

National Archives & Records Administration, http://www.fold3.com.

San Francisco Area, California, Funeral Home Records, 1850–1931 [database on-line]. Provo, UT, USA: Ancestry.com Operations, Inc., 2014.

Texas, Muster Roll Index Cards, 1838–1900 [database on-line]. Provo, UT, USA: Ancestry.com.

U.S. Military and Naval Academies, Cadet Records and Applications, 1800–1908 [database on-line]. Lehi, UT, USA: Ancestry.com.

U.S., Newspaper Extractions from the Northeast, 1704–1930 [database on-line]. Provo, UT, USA: Ancestry.com.

Works Progress Administration (WPA) in conjunction with the office of the Adjutant General and the California State Library. "California Militia and National Guard Unit Histories: Benham Guard," 1940, http://www.militarymuseum.org/BenhamGuard.html.

# *Index*